FROM PRIVATE TO FIELD-MARSHAL

The Author
From a Snapshot taken by an American Soldier at Coblenz, 1919

FROM PRIVATE
TO FIELD-MARSHAL

BY FIELD-MARSHAL
Sir WILLIAM ROBERTSON Bart.

G.C.B., G.C.M.G., K.C.V.O., D.S.O.
Hon. LL.D. Cambridge, Hon. D.C.L. Oxford

ILLUSTRATED

University Press of the Pacific
Honolulu, Hawaii

From Private to Field-Marshall

by
Field-Marshall Sir William Robertson

ISBN: 1-4102-2395-7

Reprinted from the 1921 edition

University Press of the Pacific
Honolulu, Hawaii
http://www.universitypressofthepacific.com

In order to make original editions of historical works available to scholars at an economical price, this facsimile of the original edition of 1921 is reproduced from the best available copy and has been digitally enhanced to improve legibility, but the text remains unaltered to retain historical authenticity.

Dedicated

TO THE MEMORY OF MY MOTHER

TO WHOSE AFFECTIONATE AND INSPIRING TEACHINGS

IN EARLY LIFE IS ATTRIBUTABLE SUCH MERIT,

IF ANY, AS MAY ATTACH TO MY CAREER.

PREFACE

THE only justification for publishing this book is that it describes the climbing of a soldier from the bottom to the top of the military ladder, and even in this feat there is nothing remarkable beyond the fact that it happens to be the first of its kind in the annals of the British Army.

Energy and determination are usually essential to advancement in any vocation, and are at the disposal of every one possessing a good constitution. Given the exercise of these qualities and the same help from real friends as I enjoyed—friends who had nothing to gain and perhaps something to lose by showing friendship—any man can equal what I have accomplished.

Still, the story here given may not be wholly without interest, especially to those who have their lives in front of them, and in the hope that it will prove to be so I have decided to let it go forth. Doubtless it has many defects, both in substance and style, which would have been less apparent if its preparation had been in more practised hands, and for these imperfections I ask lenient treatment.

In writing the chapters dealing with my service in the ranks and as a Subaltern Officer I have had to depend chiefly upon memory, which has become blurred and unreliable owing to the lapse of time and the crowded events of the last few years. Consequently it has not been possible to make this part of the book as complete as, to my mind, it deserves to be, for the period in question was in some ways the most fascinating and happy of all. For instance, I derived greater satisfaction from being promoted Lance-Corporal in 1878—the first rung of the ladder —than I did from being created a Baronet forty years later ;

and, as Lieutenant, I felt prouder to be in command at the railhead of a Frontier Expeditionary Force in India of less than 10,000 men than, as General, to be Chief of the Imperial General Staff in the greatest conflict the world has ever known, when the number of our troops ran into several millions.

In building up the chapters referring to the Great War, I was embarrassed by having not too little but too much material. The difficulty here was to make a suitable selection, and to include just so much about my share of the war as seemed appropriately to fall within the scope of the book. In particular I tried to avoid enlarging upon old controversies connected with the supreme direction of the war, and which occur to a greater or less extent in all wars. I felt that a discussion of them would merely bore the ordinary reader, who is content to know that the war was in fact won ; while it would be of little use to any one unless the points in dispute were thoroughly examined in the light of complete evidence, and this would require a book for itself as well as access to official documents which are not at my disposal. I have therefore made, as a rule, no more reference to these matters than was required to enable me to illustrate the work of the Imperial General Staff, of which I was Chief for about half the period of the war—four other officers filling that post at different times during the remaining half—and to emphasise the achievements, though very inadequately, of the regimental officers and men of the Imperial Forces who won the war for us, and with whom I have had the honour to be associated for nearly forty-four years.

W. R. ROBERTSON,
Field-Marshal.

CONTENTS

CHAPTER I

CHAPTER II

CHAPTER III

CHAPTER IV

CHAPTER V

CHAPTER VI

CHAPTER VII

CHAPTER VIII

CHAPTER IX

CHAPTER X

CHAPTER XI

CHAPTER XV

CHAPTER XVI

CHAPTER XVII

CHAPTER XVIII

CHAPTER XIX

LIST OF ILLUSTRATIONS

CHAPTER I

RECRUIT AT ALDERSHOT

Enlistment in 16th Lancers—The " Old Soldier " in the 'Seventies—
Barrack-room life—Rations—Pay—Kit and equipment—Uniform
—Drills—Treatment of sick—Breaking out of barracks—Sundays
—First Christmas Day—Night guards—Military offences and
punishments—Guard-room—Articles of War—Muster parade—
Punishment drill—Musketry course—Dismissed drills—Day guards
—I allow a deserter to escape and so commit my first " crime "—
Imprisoned in guard-room—My second " crime "—Promoted Lance-
Corporal—Backward state of training—Field-days—Reasons for
defective training—Lord Wolseley, Sir Evelyn Wood, and other
rising Generals effect great reforms—Successes in competitions at
skill-at-arms.

I WAS seventeen and three-quarters years old when, having
decided to seek my fortune in the army, I took the " Queen's
Shilling " from a recruiting sergeant in the city of Worcester
on the 13th of November 1877. The minimum age for enlistment was eighteen, but as I was tall for my years the
sergeant said that the deficient three months would involve
no difficulty, and he promptly wrote me down as eighteen
years and two months—so as to be on the safe side—and
that has been the basis of my official age ever since. For
some reason that has now escaped my memory I was
detained at Worcester for four days, receiving in the meantime two shillings and a halfpenny per diem for board and
lodgings. The odd halfpenny strikes one as being a queer
item, but it had no doubt been arrived at by Her Majesty's
Treasury after careful calculation of the cost actually
incurred. The recruiting sergeant, a kindly disposed individual, took possession of the whole sum, giving me in
return excellent, if homely, accommodation and food at
his own house.

The regiment I selected to join, the 16th (Queen's)

Lancers, was stationed in the West Cavalry Barracks, Aldershot, and on arrival there, on a wet and dreary November evening, the first people I met were the " orderly officer " and the regimental sergeant-major, both of whom showed a sympathetic interest in me. I was at once posted as No. 1514 to " G " Troop, the officer saying to me as I went off, " Give your watch to the sergeant-major of your troop, my lad," and, as I wrote home a few days later, I did so, " for it is unsafe to leave it lying about, and there is nowhere you can carry it with safety."

The regiment was commanded at the time by Colonel Whigham, who had originally served in the infantry. The adjutant, Lieutenant " Jimmy " Babington, was a fine horseman, a strict disciplinarian, and universally regarded as an ideal cavalry officer. He was more than that, as is shown by his selection in 1914, when nearly 60 years of age, to command one of the Kitchener Divisions. This he took out to France the following year, and from then onwards was continuously in command of the division or an army corps, in France or in Italy, until the end of the war, a task which proved to be beyond the physical powers of many a younger man in the hard and incessant fighting on the West Front.

" G " Troop was commanded by Captain Henry Graham, one of the most kind-hearted men under whom it has been my lot to serve. His subaltern, Lieutenant " Freddy " Blair, was somewhat of a terror to all shirkers and wrong-doers in the troop, but I have no recollection of having been on his black list ; and I am sure that neither of us then thought that forty-one years later I would be Commander-in-Chief of the Eastern Command and he would be my military secretary. But so it turned out.

The life of a recruit in 1877 was a very different matter from what it is now. The system introduced in 1871–72 by Mr. Cardwell—one of the greatest War Ministers the country has ever had—under which men enlisted for twelve years' regular service, had not yet had time to get into full swing. Regiments were, therefore, still composed mainly of old soldiers who, although very admirable comrades in some respects and with a commendable code of honour of their own, were in many cases—not in all—addicted to rough behaviour, heavy drinking, and hard swearing. They could not well be blamed for this. Year in and year out they went through the same routine, were treated like machines —of an inferior kind—and having little prospect of finding decent employment on the expiration of their twenty-one years' engagement, they lived only for the present, the single bright spot in their existence being the receipt of a few shillings—perhaps not more than one—on the weekly pay-day. These rugged veterans exacted full deference from the recruit, who was assigned the worst bed in the room, given the smallest amount of food and the least palatable, had to " lend " them articles of kit which they had lost or sold, " fag " for them in a variety of ways, and, finally, was expected to share with them at the regimental canteen such cash as he might have in the purchase of beer sold at 3d. a quart.

It so happened that I joined the regiment on pay-day, and accordingly the greater number of my newly-found companions spent the evening at the canteen—then a mere drinking saloon—or at public-houses in the town. On return to quarters, if not before, old quarrels were revived or new ones were started, and some of them had to be settled by an appeal to fists. One of these encounters took place on and near the bed in which I was vainly trying to sleep, and which was itself of an unattractive and uncomfortable nature. Argument and turmoil continued far into the night, and I began to wonder whether I had made a wise decision after all. I continued to wonder for several nights afterwards, and would lie awake for hours meditating whether to see the matter through, or get out of bed, put on my plain clothes (which I still had), and " desert." Fortunately for me another occupant of the room removed the temptation these clothes afforded, for, having none of his own, he one night appropriated mine, went off in them, and never came back.

Shortly before the period of which I write it had been the custom for a married soldier and his wife, with such children as they possessed, to live in one corner of the barrack-room, screened off with blankets, and in return for this accommodation and a share of the rations the wife kept the room clean, washed and mended the men's under-clothing, and attended to the preparation of their meals. This custom was not without its good points, as the women exercised a steadying influence over the men, while the latter seldom if ever forgot that a woman was in the room, and any one who did forget was promptly brought to order by the others.   Still, it could not be wholly without its undesirable side, and the transfer of all women to " married quarters " was a distinct change for the better.

The barrack-room arrangements for sleeping and eating could not be classed as luxurious.   The brown bed-blankets were seldom or ever washed ; clean sheets were issued once a month ; and clean straw for the mattresses once every three months.   Besides the beds, the only other furniture consisted of four benches and two deal tables.   The men polished their boots on the former, and the latter were used for cleaning the remaining articles of kit as well as for dining-tables.   Tablecloths there were none, and plates and basins (paid for by the men) were the only crockery, the basin being used in turn as a coffee-cup, tea-cup, beer-mug, soup-plate, shaving-mug, and receptacle for pipe-clay with which to clean gloves and belts.

The food provided free consisted of one pound of bread and three-quarters of a pound of meat, and nothing more of any kind.   Groceries, vegetables, and all other require-ments were paid for by the men, who had a daily deduction of 3½d. made from their pay of 1s. 2d. for that purpose. The regulation meals were coffee and bread for breakfast ; meat and potatoes for dinner, with soup or pudding once or twice a week ; tea and bread for tea.   If a man wished to have supper or something besides dry bread for breakfast and tea he had to purchase it from the barrack hawkers or canteen.   Putting the cost of this at 4½d. a day, he thus had to expend a total of eightpence a day on his food, besides which he was subjected to a further daily charge of a penny for washing.   This left him fivepence a day or about three shillings a week, and even this was not all clear pocket-money, for after the first free issue he had to keep up the whole of his underclothing as well as many articles of uniform, and also supply himself with cleaning materials, such as polishing paste for brasses, oil for steel equipment, and soft-soap for saddlery.

A beneficent regulation, recognising these drains on the unfortunate man's pay, laid down that in no case should he receive less than a penny a day! In my regiment the custom was never to give less than a shilling a week, but even this sum did not go far to supplement the allowance of food, to say nothing of beer and tobacco. The Government now provides ample food, practically all clothing, and the amount of pay actually received is five or six times greater than it used to be.

The " kit " with which I was issued free of cost consisted of a valise, stable-bag, hold-all (containing knife, fork, spoon, razor and comb, shaving, hair, lace, button, clothes and boot brushes), three baggage straps, tin of oil, tin of blacking, tin of brass paste, cloak, cape, lance-cap and plume, two forage caps, tunic, jacket, overalls (trousers), pantaloons, canvas ducks, jack-boots and spurs, Wellington boots and spurs, ankle-boots, braces, three shirts, three pairs of socks, two pairs of pants, two towels, and a piece of soap. Finally, I was given a lance, sword, pistol, cartridge-case, cap-case, and numerous belts—an amount of armament that completely staggered me.

Uniform was of a very unpractical kind, especially the undress part of it. This comprised skin-tight overalls, an equally tight " shell-jacket " cut off short above the hips, and a forage cap of about the size of a breakfast saucer, and kept in its place immediately above the right ear by a narrow chin-strap worn under the lower lip (never under the chin in the cavalry, except on mounted parades). There were no " British-warms " or woollen " jumpers " as to-day, and cloaks were not allowed to be worn when off duty without a regimental order to that effect. This order was never given except when the weather was very inclement. Later on the forage cap became a " free issue," and was thoroughly disliked by everybody because of its ugly shape and abnormally large size as compared with the regimental pattern.

The first occasion on which it was worn by the regiment was at an inspection by the Duke of Cambridge at York in

1881, when an unofficial hint was sent round the barrack-rooms beforehand that it was to be put well on the top of the head, and generally made to appear as hideous as possible. Every one did his best, or rather his worst, to comply with the hint, and when the Duke—never in too good a temper early in the day—came on parade, the sight of the disfigured regiment nearly gave him a fit. It was alleged that he went back to the Horse Guards and wrote a furious letter to the War Office condemning the cap, but it remained the regulation article for some years afterwards, although the original pattern was still allowed to be worn off parade, and at the expense of the owner.

The cavalry recruit was kept hard at work, riding-drill, stables, foot-drill, gymnastics, and school following each other in bewildering fashion from six in the morning till six in the evening, without any appreciable interval for rest. Riding-school was the terror of most recruits, few of whom had ever before been across a horse. For some weeks no saddle was allowed, no stirrups for some months, and the chief aim of the instructor, or "rough-rider," was not to give his pupil confidence but as many falls as possible. The "rough-rider" deserved his name, for he was as rough with a young horse as with a young recruit. He seldom possessed a decent pair of hands, and his system of training a horse was of the break-down rather than the break-in type. These unintelligent methods have long since passed into oblivion.

Gymnastics, or physical exercises, were conducted on much the same lines. Every recruit was expected to do the same thing in an equally proficient way, no allowance being made for differences in age, build, or general physical capacity.

A robust constitution was required in winter to withstand the cold and draughty stables and the biting winds which swept across the barrack square during foot-drill, where the shivering recruit would struggle to grasp the explanations of drill gabbled out by his instructor, and painfully endeavour to master the mysteries of the "goosestep" and the art of drawing swords "by numbers." I succumbed twice during my first winter, once being in hospital for two months with rheumatic fever brought on by exposure.

When a man " reported sick " he was marched at about nine o'clock in the morning to the medical inspection room of his regiment, and after waiting about in all weathers for an indefinite time was seen by a medical officer. If considered a case for admission he was given an aperient, whether he wanted it or not, in the shape of half-a-pint of vile-tasting liquid known as " black-strap." He was next marched off to hospital, which might be anything up to a mile or more away, and there he was interviewed by another doctor before being " admitted " to hospital. Next he was told off to a ward, where he might hope to arrive about mid-day, after having been on the move for some three or four hours. In the afternoon he would put on his hospital clothing, give his own into store, and lie down to await the visit of the medical officer in charge of the ward on the following morning. He was then again examined, treatment was prescribed, and if all went well he received it during the afternoon, or some thirty hours after he first set out from his barrack-room.

Accidents and other special cases would be dealt with more or less immediately, but ordinary medical cases dawdled on in the manner I have described, greatly to the discomfort of the patient and sometimes at the risk of his life. There was no nursing service, at any rate in the hospitals I had the misfortune to visit. Nursing and dressing were the duty of the " orderly " of the ward, and this individual was apt to regulate the amount of attention he gave to his patients by the amount of tips they gave to him.

Permission to be out of barracks after " watch-setting " —half-past nine at night—was sparingly granted, and all-night passes were practically never given. The " roll " was called at watch-setting, when every man not on leave had to answer his name, and to make sure that none went out afterwards one and sometimes two " check " roll-calls were made by the orderly sergeant-major at uncertain hours during the night. Each orderly-sergeant handed in at watch-setting a statement showing the number of men sleeping in each of his troop rooms, and equipped with this the orderly sergeant-major, accompanied by the corporal of the guard, visited the rooms and counted the sleeping occupants. It was a favourite device of absentees, before going out, to fold up their bed as in day-time, so that the visiting sergeant-major might perhaps not notice their absence ; while others would try to deceive him by leaving a made-up dummy in their beds. " Breaking-out of barracks " was the crime, and twenty-eight days' confinement to barracks was usually the punishment, for this form of absence.

To " break out " of barracks was a simple matter at Aldershot, for although the gates at the end of them were kept locked after watch-setting, and had high walls on either side, an unenclosed public road ran along the front which was accessible to everybody. This was not the case with all barracks, most of them being surrounded by high walls, topped with broken glass. When we were at Brighton, where the walls were of this kind, an amusing incident occurred in connection with a man who was trying to get back again after successfully breaking out. Not being able to scale the walls, he hit on the idea of returning in an officer's brougham, which was being brought back to barracks by a friendly coachman after depositing the officer and his wife at their house in the town. Unfortunately the military police sergeant looked inside the brougham before allowing it to leave the barrack gate, and the offender accordingly found himself in a worse predicament at orderly room next morning than if he had walked into barracks and surrendered.

Of all days of the week Sunday was the most hated—a sad confession to make, but none the less true. After morning stables there was a general rush, often with little or no time for breakfast, to turn out in " full dress " for "divine service"—attendance at which was compulsory. On return to barracks there was another scramble preparatory to the commanding officer's inspection of stables, horses, saddlery, and barrack-rooms. From early morning till half-past one in the afternoon there was more work to be done, more grumbling and swearing, and more fault-finding

than on any other day, all of which could have been avoided
had the inspections been carried out on a week-day. The
reason they were made on Sunday was certainly not because
there was no time for them on other days. The real reason
probably was that Sunday was the most convenient day for
the officers, as it left them greater leisure to follow their
social and sporting pursuits during the week. It was only
natural that the men should resent being hustled about and
made to do unnecessary work on the one day of the week
observed by everybody else in the country as a day of
rest.

Divine service was not held for all denominations at
the same time, but at hours suitable to local facilities. It
might be at any time between eight o'clock and noon, and
therefore it was not uncommon for men, on moving to a
new station, to ask to change their religion if by so doing
they would attend church or chapel at such an hour as
would enable them to escape from the detested inspections.
Many amusing stories are told about these changes, one being
of a man who asked his sergeant-major to enter him in the
books as belonging to the " Plymouth Brethren." He was
promptly told that no such religion was officially recognised,
and that he would be put down as a Roman Catholic !

On Christmas Day, 1877, I was detailed for my first
military " duty," that of stable-guard or looking after the
troop-horses out of stable-hours. The custom was to employ
the most recently joined recruits on this particular day, so
that the old soldiers might be free to make the most of their
Christmas dinner, which was provided by the officer commanding the troop, and included a variety of eatables never
seen on any other day, as well as a liberal supply of beer.
The casks containing the beer were brought some time
before to the barrack-room where the dinner was to be held,
and were there placed under charge of a man who could be
depended upon to see that they were not broached before
the appointed hour. Had this happened—as it sometimes
did—rather awkward incidents might have occurred when
the officers visited the room just previous to the dinner to
wish the men a merry Christmas and to receive similar
wishes in return. If any individual did, by some means or

other, contrive to start his festivities too early, efforts were made to keep him in the background until the officers had left.

It was the practice to see that all members of the troop who were absent on duty should be specially well-cared for, and in my case the dinner brought to the stable consisted of a huge plateful of miscellaneous food —beef, goose, ham, vegetables, plum-pudding, blanc-mange—plus a basin of beer, a packet of tobacco, and a new clay pipe !

At night the horses were looked after by a " night guard," which paraded about five or six o'clock in the evening and came off duty at *réveille* on the following morning.   It was mainly composed of recruits and other men who were required to attend training or do other work during the day-time.   The chief duties of a " sentry " of the night guard were to perambulate outside the stables, tie up any horse that might get loose (some of the old troop-horses were extraordinarily clever at slipping their head collars and finding their way to the corn-bin), see that the doors were kept closed, and, in the phraseology of the " orders," " call the corporal of the guard in the event of fire or other unusual occurrence."   The sentry was armed with either a sword or a carbine (no ammunition), though what assistance he was supposed to derive therefrom in the performance of his duties no one ever understood.

The nights were sometimes intensely cold and always interminably long, although the two hours " on " sentry were followed by four hours " off," and to the tired recruit the bales of forage offered tempting resting-places.   That way lay danger if not disaster, for once he succumbed to the temptation to sit down it was a hundred to one that he would fall asleep, and if he did he might wake up to find himself confronted by an officer or non-commissioned officer going the " rounds," with the result that he would be made prisoner and tried by court-martial.   The punishment for this crime was invariably two months' imprisonment, and although young soldiers must be made to realise their responsibilities when on sentry, a little more consideration in dealing with tired lads not yet out of their teens

would not have been misplaced. I have known more than
one lad ruined for life because of undue severity of punishment for a first offence.

Forty years ago every offence, however trivial, was
classed as a " crime," and the " prisoner " was interned in
the " guard-room." The latter, in the case of the cavalry
barracks at Aldershot, was about fifteen feet square, indifferently ventilated, and with the most primitive arrangements for sanitation. No means of lighting it after dark
were either provided or permitted. Running along one of
its sides was a sloping wooden stage, measuring about six
feet from top to bottom, which served as a bed for all
the occupants, sometimes a dozen or more in number ;
at the top was a wooden shelf, slightly raised above the
level of the stage, which acted as pillow ; and no blankets
(except in very cold weather) or mattresses were allowed,
except for prisoners who had been interned for more than
seven days. Until then their only covering, besides their
ordinary clothes—which were never taken off—consisted of
their cloaks, and they had to endure as best they could the
sore hips and shoulders caused by lying on the hard boards.
I shall describe presently how I once came to be incarcerated
in this horrible place for a period of three weeks, and
will only say here that I was exceedingly glad when the
first seven days were completed.

A prisoner charged with committing an offence was kept
in the guard-room until he could be brought before the
commanding officer, no other officer in the regiment having
power to dispose of his case, and if he were remanded for a
court-martial, as he not infrequently was, he might be
interned for several days before his trial took place. In
the meantime he would have for company all classes of
prisoners thrust into the room at any hour of the day or
night, some for drunkenness, some for desertion, some for
insubordination, and some for no offence at all which
merited confinement. This was not a healthy atmosphere
in which to bring up young soldiers, to many of whom the
shady side of life was as yet unknown, and, as will be shown
later, a more sensible and humane system was eventually
adopted. It should not be forgotten that these harsh and

short-sighted methods were more or less common to the age, and were not confined to the army.

The " Articles of War," based on the " Mutiny Act," constituted the law which then governed the soldier. The Articles contained a list of all military offences, with their punishments, and were read out to the men once a month after " muster parade." Originally—they dated back a long time—they were of excessive severity, inflicting death or loss of limb for almost every crime. They were not much more lenient in my early days from what I can remember of them, the termination of most of them being to the effect that " any soldier committing this offence shall, on conviction by court-martial, be liable to suffer death or such less punishment as may be awarded." In 1879 the Articles of War and the Mutiny Act were consolidated in the " Army Discipline and Regulations Act." This was repealed in 1881 and re-enacted with some amendments in the present Army Act, which is brought into operation annually by another Act of Parliament.

" Muster parade," I may explain, was held on the last day of each month, and was the only parade at which every officer and man had to be present. The paymaster was the important person, as he had to satisfy himself that every one for whom he had issued pay was actually serving in the regiment. It appears to have been a relic of the days when commanding officers received a lump sum of money for a given number of men, and could not be trusted to have that number in the regiment.

A man sentenced to undergo imprisonment, even if for some such short period as forty-eight hours, had his hair closely cropped off, and was thus made to look like a convict for several weeks after his discharge. " Confinement to barracks " included " punishment drill " for four separate hours each day except Sunday, and this again seemed to have been designed to destroy any shred of self-respect the unfortunate defaulter might possess. The " drill " consisted in being turned and twisted about on the barrack square, in quick time and with only a few short pauses during the hour, the men carrying their full kit, strapped on their shoulders, besides the lance and sword—a total weight of some 40 or 50 lbs. The drill could be made, and frequently was, according to the fancy of the sergeant in charge, extremely exasperating and fatiguing, and in order to escape from such degrading drudgery men would sometimes deliberately commit a second and more serious offence so as to be sent to prison. In the cavalry it was not feasible, as in the infantry, to spare the men for four hours a day from their other duties, and as a rule the punishment took the form of one hour's drill and one or two of employment on " fatigue duties."

In August 1878—or about nine months after joining—I was " dismissed " recruit-drill, this being the length of time usually taken to become classified as a trained cavalry soldier. The recruit training included a " course " of musketry of about three weeks' duration, most of the time being devoted to the deadly dull exercise known as " bob and joe "—the bringing of the carbine from the " ready " to the " present " and *vice versa*. Forty rounds of ball ammunition, no more and no less, regardless of requirements, were allowed for each and every recruit to make himself a proficient shot. The result was that not one in twenty was proficient, or anything like it. I remember that I carried off the prize for the best shot of my batch, the prize being three shillings !

As a trained soldier I now became available for " day-guard," which furnished the full-dress sentry on the barrack gate and was responsible for the safe custody of the prisoners in the guard-room. It was composed of a corporal, a trumpeter, and five men, and was paraded for inspection by the regimental sergeant-major. The parade of this guard was one of the chief events of the day, for from amongst the five men the sergeant-major selected the two whom he thought to be the smartest and best turned out to act as " orderlies " to the commanding officer and adjutant. To be thus selected was the ambition of the whole five, for while the three had turn about to spend the next twenty-four hours on sentry on the barrack gate, the chosen two passed their night in bed and had little to do during the day. I was lucky enough to be selected at my first two attempts, though I was not equally fortunate on all other occasions.

Being considered, I suppose, to be a promising and trustworthy lad, I was detailed in the summer of 1878, in company with another man and a corporal, to form the "escort" for bringing back from London a notorious deserter who had been arrested there by the civil police. He had been a burglar by profession before becoming a soldier, and notwithstanding the size of the escort he managed, with the assistance of some of his friends who appeared on the scene, and favoured by darkness, to make his escape while we were passing through the purlieus adjacent to Waterloo station. Crestfallen, we returned to Aldershot minus our prisoner. The corporal was at once placed "in arrest," whilst I and my companion were consigned to the guard-room, there to await trial by court-martial, and in all probability to be sentenced to not less than six months' imprisonment. At the end of three weeks the General commanding the Cavalry Brigade exercised, as I thought and still think, a sensible discretion by releasing us. Had he brought us to trial, the chances are that I would have followed in the steps of many another soldier of those days and have become a hardened offender against military law, a disgrace to myself, and a burden to the country.

This was my first "crime," and the second followed a week or two later. It consisted in allowing a led horse to break loose at exercise, and for this I was duly "reprimanded" by the commanding officer (Whigham) and warned that stern punishment would be meted out the next time I misbehaved. My future prospects were therefore beginning to appear somewhat gloomy, but thanks to the good sense of Graham, my troop commander, neither of the two offences were allowed to count seriously against me. He realised that such neglect as there might have been was attributable to nothing worse than youthful inexperience, and early in 1879 he took advantage of the temporary absence of the colonel to recommend me to the acting commanding officer for promotion to lance-corporal, thus obtaining for me the first step towards the rank of Field-Marshal.

Military training lagged far behind, notwithstanding the many lessons furnished by the Franco-German War of 1870, and was still mainly based on the system inherited from the Peninsula and Crimean campaigns. Pipe-clay, antiquated and useless forms of drill, blind obedience to orders, ramrod-like rigidity on parade, and similar time-honoured practices were the chief qualifications by which a regiment was judged. Very few officers had any ambition beyond regimental promotion. " Squadron leader " was a name and not a reality, for beyond commanding it on parade this officer had no responsibility or duty of any kind connected with the squadron as such. In all other respects each of the two troops which then formed a squadron was a separate and independent unit, the troop commander being subordinate only to the regimental commanding officer. Once a week or so the latter held his " field-day," when the regiment as a whole attended parade and spent the greater part of two or three hours in carrying out a series of complicated drill-book movements : equally good results could have been secured in half the time, and with half the expenditure of horse-flesh and strong language. For the remainder of the week training, as understood in those days, was the preserve of the adjutant, whose parades were attended only by those officers who were junior to him in rank, and by a comparatively small proportion of the men. For the drill of recruits on foot the adjutant was also responsible, and in riding drill the ridingmaster was supreme. Troop officers had no responsibility for either one or the other.

As already mentioned, Lancer regiments carried sword, lance, and a muzzle-loading horse-pistol, and about half-a-dozen men in each troop, known as scouts or skirmishers, had a carbine as well. They had a very sketchy knowledge of the use of this weapon and, like every one else, but a hazy idea of either scouting or skirmishing. Later, carbines were issued to all men, and the horse-pistols were withdrawn ; but for some years musketry was universally hated and deemed to be a degradation and a bore. In no case could it have been made of much value, since the annual allowance of ammunition was fixed at forty rounds a man, and thirty rounds of these were fired at distances between 500 and 800 yards.

Manœuvres as practised in more recent years were practically unknown, though there was a legend amongst the old soldiers that they had taken place at Cannock Chase some years before I joined. The nearest approach to them was the " field-day " held, perhaps half-a-dozen times during the year, by the Generals in command of the larger stations, or by the Commander-in-Chief, the Duke of Cambridge. The first one I attended was held on the ground at the back of the Staff College, the whole of the Aldershot garrison—about a division—taking part in it. I remember that towards the end of the battle—a field-day always entailed a " battle "—my squadron was ordered to charge a battalion of the opposing infantry. Down came our lances to the " engage," the " charge " was sounded, and off we went at full speed, regardless of everything except the desire to make a brave show worthy of our regimental predecessors who had delivered the immortal charge at Aliwal some thirty odd years before. The enemy received us in square, with fixed bayonets, front rank kneeling and rear rank standing, the orthodox method of dealing with a cavalry charge. Finding our opponents too strong—or for some other reason—the order was given, " troops right-about wheel," and so near were we that, in wheeling, the outer flank was carried on to the infantry and one of the horses received a bayonet in his chest. Being too seriously injured to live he was shot, but in other respects we were congratulated on having accomplished a fine performance. No doubt it was magnificent, but it was not the way to fight against men armed with rifles.

These defective methods of training in general were due in a large measure to the system of voluntary enlistment, under which recruits were received in driblets throughout the year, and, more especially perhaps, to the fact that the four different arms were kept severely apart from each other. Cavalry training was the business of the Inspector-General of Cavalry at the Horse Guards, the local General having little or no say in the matter. Artillery were mainly stationed at Woolwich and engineer units at Chatham, each having, like the cavalry, its own special Generals and staffs and its special representatives at the Horse Guards. Combined training of the different arms, without which it is nonsense to expect intelligent co-operation in war, was therefore impossible.

There may have been, and probably were, other obstacles in the way of improvement, but one would think that most of them could have been surmounted, given more impetus from the top. It was not forthcoming, and for this the Duke of Cambridge, Commander-in-Chief from 1856 to 1895 (thirty-nine years), must be held accountable. He was a good friend of the soldier and extremely popular with all ranks in the army, but he was extraordinarily conservative in his ideas on the training and education of both officers and men. He seems to have believed, quite honestly, that the army as he had found it, created by such a master of war as the Duke of Wellington, must be the best for all time, and he had not realised the changes which had since taken place in the armies of Europe. I have been told that he once took the chair at a lecture given to officers of the Aldershot garrison on the subject of foreign cavalry, when he proved to be a veritable Balaam in commending the lecturer to the audience. " Why should we want to know anything about foreign cavalry ? " he asked. " We have better cavalry of our own. I fear, gentlemen, that the army is in danger of becoming a mere debating society."

Many of the younger generation of officers were fully alive to the fact that better organisation, education, and training were necessary, the most notable amongst them being Lord Wolseley, the best-read soldier of his time. From 1882 onwards he was the moving spirit in the path of progress, and thanks to his energy and initiative, and to the support he received from Sir Evelyn Wood and other keen-sighted soldiers, apathy and idleness began to go out of fashion, and hard work became the rule ; study was no longer considered to be " bad form," but a duty and an essential step to advancement ; hunting on six days of the week was no longer admitted to be the only training required by a cavalry leader ; and in general the professional qualifications of our regimental officers began to reach a much higher standard. I shall refer to this matter again,

c

when describing my experiences at Aldershot some thirty years later.

Before leaving the subject of training, I may mention that once a year the non-commissioned officers and men of each troop had to compete between themselves for classification in the use of the sword and lance, the troop-winners then fighting off for the regimental prize. When first introduced, rather crude notions prevailed as to how the competition should be carried out, and it was the custom to place the two adversaries at opposite ends of the riding-school, give the order to attack, and then leave them to charge down on each other at full speed much in the same way as the picture-books represent the tournaments of centuries ago. With the single-stick used as a sword not much damage could be done ; but with a stout ash pole nine feet in length representing the lance the case was different. For the rider and his horse to be ridden down or rolled over was a common occurrence, and it was seldom that one or more of the competitors was not carried off to hospital, especially if the competition happened to follow pay-day. This rough business had its value as it taught the men how to defend themselves ; and incidentally it afforded a certain class of individual an opportunity for paying off old scores against any non-commissioned officer against whom he had a grudge. To him it was a matter of indifference what the umpire's decision might be, provided he " got one in " against the object of his resentment. When I became sergeant, and subsequently troop sergeant-major, I had occasionally to deal with attacks of this kind, but being careful at all times to keep fit in wind and limb by constant practice with foils and single-sticks, and by taking regular running exercise, I was capable of giving back quite as good as I received. My most successful year was, I think, 1886, when I was lucky enough to secure all the first prizes in the troop—sword, lance, and shooting—but pride had its usual fall (literally) when, as troop-winner, I fought for the regimental prize and, with my horse, was bundled head over heels by a better man.

CHAPTER II

NON-COMMISSIONED OFFICER

Promoted Corporal—Stationed at Brighton—My third and last " crime "—
Special duty at Chatham—Rejoin regiment and go to York—
Promoted Lance-Sergeant—Special duties while at York—Musketry
course at Hythe—Promoted Sergeant—Signalling course at Alder-
shot—Regiment goes to Dundalk—State of Ireland—Appointed
Assistant Instructor of Signalling—Lieutenant Dugdale—Success of
signallers announced in regimental orders—Assistant Instructor
of Musketry and Military Reconnaissance—Escort prisoners to
Limerick Gaol—Regiment goes to Dublin—Promoted Troop
Sergeant-Major — Suicide of predecessor — Influence of Troop
Sergeant-Major—Consider possibility of obtaining commission—
Difficulties in the way of this—Regimental officer's expenses—
Decline Commanding Officer's offer of a commission—Accept the
same offer made by his successor—Vexatious delays retard com-
mission—Pass examination for commission—Regiment goes to
Aldershot—Gazetted Second Lieutenant in 3rd Dragoon Guards—
Leave the 16th Lancers.

IN April 1879, or about a year and a half after en-
listing, I was promoted full corporal. This was, for the
time, almost unprecedented rapidity of advancement in the
cavalry, and it entailed my transfer to another troop under
other superiors having other ways. Shortly afterwards the
regiment was ordered to Brighton—a four days' march—
and I was selected to go on ahead in charge of the billeting
party to arrange for the accommodation of the men and
horses of the troop at the various halting-places. It was
in this way that I gained my first experience in those duties
of Quartermaster-General which were to devolve upon me in
the Great War.

Whilst at Brighton I committed my third and last
" crime." I had been detailed with two men to act as
escort to Major-General Newdigate, under whose command
some Volunteer battalions were having a field-day, or

" sham-fight " as the phrase went, on Brighton Downs. The day was observed as a holiday in the neighbourhood, and the holiday-makers, with the best of intentions, insisted upon offering more free drinks to my two men than were good for them. As I failed to keep a sufficiently sharp eye on them one of the two yielded to the temptation, and on the way home parted company with his horse, which galloped riderless back to barracks where it was seen arriving by the regimental sergeant-major. The man himself was picked up in the street helplessly drunk, and I, the responsible party, was placed " in arrest." (I may remind the reader that I was still in my teens.)

I had a very unpleasant interview with the commanding officer, Whigham, next morning at orderly room. Looking at the record of my two previous crimes as given in the " defaulters' book," he fiercely remarked, " First you allow a man to escape ; then you allow a horse to escape ; now you allow both a man and a horse to break loose. You are ' severely reprimanded,' and if you ever come before me again I will reduce you to the ranks." I knew that his bark was sometimes worse than his bite, but I also felt that he might be as good as his word, and that it behoved me to be more strict in future in supervising the men under my control. This was well rubbed into me later by the sergeant-major, a non-commissioned officer of the best type and for whose advice I always had the greatest respect.

A few years later the troop defaulters' book containing a list of my offences was either lost or wilfully destroyed. No one was able to discover what had become of it. The offences, not being of a serious nature, had not been recorded in the regimental defaulters' book, or anywhere else except in the missing book, and therefore I was necessarily given, as were all other men similarly situated, a clean sheet in the new book. It remained without an entry throughout my future service in the ranks.

Apparently my latest dereliction of duty was not deemed to be very heinous, for a few months after it occurred I was one of two non-commissioned officers in the regiment recommended to go through a twelve months' course at the riding establishment at Canterbury, in order to qualify for the post of ridingmaster. The final decision rested, of course, with the commanding officer, and he selected the other man. I was not sorry, as I had neither the desire nor natural ability to become an expert in equitation.

A more congenial post was given me in the summer of 1879, when I was ordered one day, on return to barracks from a long morning's drill on the Downs, to parade in " marching order " by three o'clock to proceed to Chatham in charge of three men detailed as mounted orderlies at the headquarters of the Chatham district. It was already past noon, but by the appointed hour my detachment was on parade, and we pushed on as quickly as our tired horses would permit, passing through Lewes and Uckfield, and reaching our first halting-place, Maresfield, about half-past seven in the evening. The only available accommodation was a small farmstead occupied by an irascible old lady who flatly refused to have anything to do with us, and consequently I had to ride on for another two miles to a police station and obtain the requisite authority compelling her to take us in. This brought her to her senses, and by the time we had groomed our horses and made them comfortable for the night, about ten o'clock, she had prepared for us an excellent supper to which we did full justice, having had no food since our meagre breakfast at seven o'clock in the morning.

Next day we made Tonbridge, where we were fortunate in at once securing good billets, gooseberry pudding being a highly-appreciated feature of the menu. The local members of the Kent Yeomanry showed us welcome hospitality in the evening.

The following day we reached Chatham, wet to the skin, and were attached to a company of the army service corps for quarters and rations. It was at Chatham, while holding this, my first independent command, that I made the acquaintance of the late Sir Evelyn Wood.

The views I held about my mission are shown in a letter I wrote home :

Taking all things into consideration it is good to have been selected for this work, as I am in sole charge and no one will interfere with me so long as the men turn out clean and smart when on duty and keep steady. I need hardly say that we were all picked out as likely to be a credit to the regiment to which we belong. I hope we shall be, as my Captain told me when starting that he would keep up a correspondence with the General Commanding (Sir Evelyn Wood, now in Africa with the French Empress) and will hear how I get on, and that if all goes correct he will, on my return, do his best for me.

He was a sensible officer this captain—I forget his name —to impress upon me, a young lad, the importance of keeping up the good name of the regiment, and I may add that on completion of the duty, about eight months later, the commanding officer received from the Chatham headquarters an official letter which was highly complimentary to myself and my men.

The regiment had meantime moved from Brighton to Woolwich, and the circumstances in which I rejoined it from Chatham will best be described by quoting from another letter :

Cock Hotel, Ware, Hertfordshire,
Sunday, 20.2.'81.

Last Wednesday about six P.M. I was sent for by the Brigade Major, and told to have myself and men ready by nine A.M. next morning to rejoin the regiment. That was all I could get to know. Next morning we left Chatham and covered the twenty-six miles to Woolwich in about four hours, finding out on arrival there that next day we would commence our journey to York, there to remain until further orders. On the first day we passed through Greenwich, Blackheath and Lewisham, over London Bridge, through the city, Islington, Shoreditch and on to Edmonton, eighteen miles. Yesterday we arrived at Ware, sixteen miles, where we halted for Sunday. The following shows the route from here to York :

Monday	.	.	.	Royston.
Tuesday	.	.	.	Huntingdon.
Wednesday	.	.	.	Peterborough.
Thursday	.	.	.	Bourne.
Friday	.	.	.	Grantham.
Saturday ⎱ Sunday ⎰	.	.	.	Newark.
Monday	.	.	.	Retford.
Tuesday	.	.	.	Doncaster.
Wednesday	.	.	.	Pontefract.
Thursday	.	.	.	York.

I remember that the winter was exceptionally severe, and that we had to lead our horses for a great part of the way, owing to the frozen and slippery state of the snow-covered ground.

Soon after arrival at York I was promoted lance-sergeant (or provisional sergeant), thus becoming a member of the sergeants' mess and terminating my barrack-room life with the men.

As sergeant, my horse, saddlery, and accoutrements were cleaned by a batman, who received six shillings a month from government for the additional work, as well as certain indulgences granted by his master. This was a welcome change, for there was no harder animal in the world to groom than a troop horse in winter, when, no part of him being clipped, his hair would be inches in length, and in spite of rubbing would remain wet from mud or perspiration for hours, and until he was dry the rubbing had to be continued. In winter, too, many men would be absent on furlough, which meant that two and sometimes three horses fell to the lot of each man present at stables.

After being employed for some weeks on mounted duty at the headquarters of the York district, I was placed in charge of the regimental remounts—about forty in number—and so occupied another semi-independent position. My selection for these different posts was probably due to the credit earned at Chatham.

The following August I was sent to the school of musketry at Hythe to qualify as assistant instructor of musketry. The curriculum was then about as unpractical and wearisome as it could well be, the greater part of the time—two months—being devoted to acquiring efficiency in repeating, parrot-like, the instructions laid down in the drill book. Little or no attention was paid to the art of shooting in the field, and the total amount of ball ammunition expended was restricted to the orthodox forty rounds per man. It was not till some years later, under such commandants as Ian Hamilton and Monro, that a more intelligent system, better suited to modern requirements, was introduced, and Hythe began to be a really useful institution.

Both in going and returning I travelled between Hull

and London by boat, making the journey at each end by rail. This may not seem a very expeditious route, nor was it. For instance, when returning from Hythe I had to spend a day in London waiting for a boat ; another two days were taken by the sea passage ; and as I arrived at Hull late on a Sunday I had to stay the night there before being able to get a train for York. To the financial mind, however, the itinerary was correct, for the travelling expenditure incurred was some pence, and perhaps even some shillings, less than it would have been had I travelled all the way by rail.

January 1882 saw me promoted full sergeant, by far the youngest of that rank in the regiment, both in age and service, and this led to my transfer to another troop, " B," commanded by Major Garrett. He was a general favourite with his men, and I have pleasant recollections of my time under his command.

In June I was deputed to go through a course of instruction at the school of signalling at Aldershot. It was considerably more advanced in its methods than the Hythe establishment, but was nevertheless not as up-to-date as it should have been.

Whilst I was at Aldershot the regiment moved from York to Ireland, headquarters and three troops going to Dundalk, and the remaining five troops to four other stations, of which Belfast was one. On completion of the signalling course I was ordered to join at Dundalk.

Ireland was at this period, as at many other times in her history, suffering from the effects of being a political shuttlecock, and the military were frequently called out to assist the police in the suppression of disorder. Evictions for non-payment of rent were the most common source of trouble, and some of them would be attended by thousands of sympathisers from the countryside, necessitating, in the opinion of the authorities, the presence of a considerable military force. I have known as much as a brigade of all arms employed on this duty, the evicted tenant being an old woman occupying a dilapidated hovel, and the unpaid rent amounting to a few shillings !

Having passed the examination at the signalling school,

obtaining 282 marks out of a possible 300, I was made assistant instructor of the regimental signallers, whose standard was then very low. The annual inspection took place about two months later, and consequently there was not sufficient time to make much improvement. The regiment was reported as being only " fair," and it occupied 44th place in the army " order of merit." The inspecting officer was pleased, however, to classify the assistant instructor, myself, as " very good." The commanding officer, now Schwabe in place of Whigham, was bent on achieving much better results, and he gave Lieutenant Dugdale, the " instructor," and myself a free hand to do as we liked on the understanding that the necessary improvement should be made. In this we succeeded at the next annual inspection, when the regiment took 12th place in the army and 3rd place in Ireland. In 1884 we did still better, the regiment being first in Ireland and missing first in the army only by a decimal. I felt very proud of myself when the following appeared in regimental orders :

Sir Thomas Steele, General Commanding the Forces in Ireland, has been pleased to express his intention of bringing at the first opportunity to the notice of H.R.H. the Field-Marshal Commanding-in-Chief, that the 16th Lancers have turned out the best squad of signallers in Ireland. The Commanding Officer wishes to express his sincere thanks to Lieutenant Dugdale, Sergeant Robertson, and the signallers for their exertion which has brought so much credit to the regiment.

During our connection with signalling I formed a close friendship with Dugdale, which lasted until his death. I still have the case of pipes he gave me as a memento of our combined success ; the handful of cigars he gave me at the same time was consumed that evening in the sergeants' mess. He was a splendid athlete, handsome, generous to a fault, and beloved by all who knew him. His death from a virulent attack of influenza some years ago, with that of his wife from the same cause on the following day, came as a great shock to their numerous friends. He was married subsequent to our signalling days, and it so happened that one of his daughters was the wife of one of my pupils at the Staff College some twenty-five years later.

Besides the signalling duty I officiated as sergeant-instructor of musketry. This appointment, as well as that of instructor (always an officer), was abolished in 1883, the Adjutant-General of the day, Sir Garnet Wolseley, quite rightly holding troop officers responsible for the training of their men in this branch of their work as in all others, but as musketry was still to a great extent a sealed book to most cavalry officers I continued to exercise, under the adjutant, a general supervision over the musketry arrangements, to train the recruits, and to prepare the annual musketry returns.

A third duty, which fell to me in the winter months, was that of assistant-instructor in sketching, map-reading, and other things coming under the heading of reconnaissance. Like most non-commissioned officers of the time I knew practically nothing about these subjects, but by reading such few books as existed — nearly all of which made very intricate what was really quite simple — I learnt a certain amount which I passed on to the half-dozen members of the class. Eventually I picked up a good deal of useful knowledge which proved to be helpful later in life when employed on intelligence work in the field, but it was a slow and laborious business. Fortunately I was a fairly good draughtsman. For much of what I learnt I was indebted to Captain Lord St. Vincent, a keen and capable officer, who had recently come to us from the 7th Hussars. He met his death in Egypt during the fighting of the 'eighties.

Having these specialist duties to carry out I was " excused "—as the phrase went—the ordinary troop and regimental duties of a sergeant, and on the whole had an interesting and pleasant time, for, as I wrote, " I have nothing else to do such as stables, guards, etc., have all Sunday to myself, and get up and go to bed when I like ! "

Whilst at Dundalk I was given an opportunity of showing whether I had profited from my previous failures to look properly after men committed to my charge. I was ordered to conduct eleven men from the Belfast district to Limerick gaol, where they were to undergo varying terms of imprisonment, some being of considerable length. My friend the regimental sergeant-major warned me that some of the prisoners were hardened criminals who might try to get away, and he reminded me of the deserter who had made his escape in London. The eleven prisoners were taken over at different railway stations *en route* to Limerick, and as I received them I handcuffed them and the four men of the escort together in one long string. This was not by any means a comfortable manner in which to make a railway journey extending over twelve hours, and some of the men begged that the handcuffs might be taken off, if only for a few minutes, so that they might rest their cramped and aching arms. I remained obdurate both to their entreaties and threats, and in due course they were safely delivered over to the prison authorities. Ruthless as this treatment may seem, it was the only way in which I could make sure of carrying out my mission, and after having accomplished it I proceeded to a sergeants' mess in the Limerick barracks, and there took part in a dance until *réveille* sounded the following morning.

Having thus completed what I thought to be a very creditable trip, I returned to Dundalk and reported that the eleven prisoners had been duly lodged in gaol. The journey was not, however, an unqualified success, for I managed to lose the key of one pair of the handcuffs—a matter which entailed, to the annoyance of the commanding officer, a lengthy correspondence between the regiment and the ordnance office. It terminated by my being ordered to pay threepence to defray the loss of the key. How much money had meanwhile been expended on stamps and stationery I cannot say.

At the end of February 1885 the regiment was suddenly ordered to move to Dublin (Island Bridge barracks) in relief of the 5th Lancers despatched to the Sudan. No sooner had we arrived there than we were confined to barracks and all leave was cancelled, owing to the demonstrations which were being held in Phœnix Park in sympathy with Mr. O'Brien, M.P., who had just been suspended in the House of Commons.

A month later I was promoted troop sergeant-major of " E " troop. My predecessor had been a medical student before joining the army, and as he was well educated his prospects would have been good had he not been addicted to periodical spells of hard drinking. He had been promoted in the hope that his increased responsibilities might help to keep him straight, and he had promised to abstain from drink, but before many months had elapsed the troop accounts, for which he was answerable to his troop officer, were found to balance on the wrong side and he was accordingly ordered to revert to the rank of sergeant and to hand over his duties to me. I was directed to go to his quarters to discuss matters, and I there found him to be quite drunk and incapable of explaining anything. When his condition became known to higher authority he was placed " in arrest " pending investigation by the commanding officer.

Next day a troop sergeant-major went to escort him to the orderly room, and finding his door locked he came for me. We returned together, and on breaking open the door discovered that the poor fellow had shot himself a few minutes before. Apparently he had felt unable at the last moment to face the ruin and disgrace which confronted him, and a round of service ammunition and a carbine had done the rest. For several days I was kept busy in unravelling the tangle into which the accounts had been allowed to fall, but beyond neglect and carelessness there was nothing seriously wrong with them, the actual deficiency in money amounting only to thirty-five pounds. For this miserable sum drink had claimed its victim, whose life, but for the one weakness, might have been so different.

" Paddy " Malone, the commander of my new troop, was a splendid specimen of manhood both in build and character, standing a good six feet six inches in height and made in proportion. Wyndham Quinn and Dugdale were the two subalterns, and from all three I experienced nothing but kindness during the three years I was their troop sergeant-major.

A troop sergeant-major occupies a position which enables him to exert, for good or for evil, great influence over his men. It is said that the non-commissioned officer is the backbone of the army, but it is equally true that he can do much harm unless he is strictly impartial and identifies himself with the interests of his men. Although the " old soldier " as I knew him eight years before was rapidly disappearing, a certain number still remained who, with some of the younger ones, required firm and tactful handling. In not a few cases the worst characters were the best workmen—that is, the best grooms and best riders—when money was scarce ; when it was plentiful they would fall under the spell of drink, and this would lead to absence, insubordination, and other military offences. Try as one might these men proved very hard to reform, and while I gained many gratifying successes I also had some failures in my efforts to make them see the folly of their ways.

The fault lay not nearly so much with the men—who were good fellows at heart—as with the authorities who neglected to provide them with congenial means of recreation, to place greater trust in their self-respect, and generally to call forth the better part of their nature. With the introduction of comfortable regimental institutes ; the substitution, except when a really serious dereliction of duty had been committed, of "minor offences" for "crimes"; the abolition of the practice of imprisoning all offenders in the guard-room no matter how trivial the offence ; greater liberality in the granting of leave ; and the adoption all round of more intelligent and sympathetic methods, a marked improvement in the behaviour of the men quickly followed, and their outlook on life automatically became quite different.

For some years before going to Dublin I had cherished the hope of obtaining a commission, but at first there seemed no more chance of this hope being realised than of obtaining the moon. Apart from ridingmasters and quartermasters it was very seldom that any one was promoted from the ranks—not more than four or five a year on an average—and moreover the initial step lay with the commanding officer, a strong backing from whom was a *sine qua non*. Whigham was not friendly disposed towards me, and he happened to be, I think, one of those who held the view that promotion from the ranks was not to the benefit of either the man or the State. During his regime, therefore, nothing was or could be done.

The idea of trying for a commission had originated with Leslie Melville, the rector of my native village. Both he and his wife had taken a kindly interest in me from early boyhood, and the lady, who had several relatives in the army, was particularly keen that I should make a name for myself. Some officers of the regiment, Dugdale more than any, gave me similar encouragement, and when Whigham was succeeded by Schwabe, and I had come to the front a little as a result of the special duties I had been carrying out, my prospects seemed brighter.

Setting to work more systematically and with greater confidence, I commenced to study for a " first class certificate of education," this qualification being necessary before I could be recommended for a commission. The certificate was duly secured in the autumn of 1883, and I then turned to the professional side, reading all the books on tactics, strategy, and past campaigns that I could lay hands on. They were few in number, as the regimental library did not cater for this kind of study—or for any other for that matter—and I could not afford to purchase many books. The deficiency had to be made up by reading very carefully those that were available. The ordinary drill books I knew from A to Z.

But there was another and much greater obstacle to be considered, about which I could not make up my mind for a long time. I had no private means, and without some £300 a year in addition to army pay it was impossible to live as an officer in a cavalry regiment at home. The infantry was less expensive, but I could not entertain the idea of leaving my old arm, the cavalry.

The money difficulty did not arise in the case of the so-called " ranker " who sought a commission through the ranks because he could not, owing to lack of brains or industry, obtain one through Sandhurst or the militia. Such rankers as these usually possessed ample money, and, being backed by private influence, would be given their commission, if at all, a year or two after enlistment, and were then able to resume the social status which they had temporarily laid down. The true ranker, having no influence behind him, had to toil for several years before receiving a commission, and even then the chances were that he would, owing to the want of private means, be miserable in himself and a nuisance to his brother officers.

All officers were, quite rightly, expected to live up to the standard of their regimental mess, and to bear a due share of the expenses—at some stations a very heavy item—incurred by the entertainment of mess guests, balls, race-meetings, and so forth. Considerable contributions had also to be made towards the upkeep of the regimental band, which was maintained only to a very limited extent from public funds. An absurd amount of costly uniform had to be purchased and constantly renewed, while chargers had to be paid for out of the officers' pockets, and had to be of first-class quality. A subaltern's pay was about £120 per annum. Ten years or more might elapse before Captain's rank was attained, and then the pay was less than £200 per annum.

It had hitherto been possible, as well as convenient, to find room in each regiment for at least one ranker by appointing him adjutant, a post which he could hold for an indefinite time. This brought him useful pecuniary benefit, and by entrusting to him much of the elementary training of the men the other officers were able to enjoy increased facilities for leave. But this system was rapidly passing away. Troop and squadron officers were now being made really responsible for the training and administration of their commands ; a higher degree of efficiency was being demanded ; and the post of adjutant, now limited to five years, was no longer regarded as the perquisite of the ranker, but was being eagerly sought after by all young officers who aspired to rise in their profession.

It will be understood that in these circumstances the ranker was not as welcome to the officers of a regiment as before, and as the financial obstacle seemed insurmountable I decided that I must give up all idea of realising my ambition, and I did.

The matter did not rest there for long, as one day in 1884 Schwabe expressed the wish that I should take a commission as soon as possible. Not having previously mentioned the subject to me, his generous offer came as a complete surprise, and I again went over all the old ground, wondering whether I dare accept the offer or not. Eventually, and with a sad heart, I reluctantly declined it, and I believe that Schwabe was as sorry as myself. He told me I was acting foolishly, and probably he was right. Soon afterwards he was succeeded in the command of the regiment by Colonel Maillard.

Sticking to my studies in the hope that something might yet turn up to justify going back on the decision to which I had come, I became more and more devoted to a military life and the old ambition soon reasserted itself. When, therefore, in 1886, Maillard made the same proposal as his predecessor had done, and appeared equally desirous that I should not refuse it, I determined to put aside my fears and take the risk of failure owing to lack of funds. He allayed my anxiety in this respect by promising to get me posted to a regiment in India if possible, where the pay would be higher and the expenses much lower than in England. Thus the die was cast.

Before he could recommend me for a commission, however, I had the mortification of having to undergo a further educational examination, the standard of the first class certificate having been raised since I took it three years earlier. A few weeks' study overcame this stumbling-block, and in April 1887 the recommendation was at last sent on its way to the Horse Guards. The reply came back in August that the outfit allowance of £150 granted to rankers on promotion could not be given me during the current financial year, as the Treasury allotment for that purpose had already been promised. I was given the choice of taking a commission without the allowance, and as I could not afford to do that the only alternative was to wait for still another year.

These vexatious delays terminated early in February 1888 when I appeared before a board of officers of the 4th Dragoon Guards at the Royal Barracks, Dublin, to be examined in the subjects qualifying for promotion to Lieutenant. The examination was very simple and was passed almost as a matter of course, for it would have been an unforgivable breach of etiquette for officers of one regiment to plough a candidate sent up by another.

In March my squadron was ordered to the Curragh, and a few weeks later the whole regiment moved to Aldershot, where I had joined it as a recruit about ten and a half years before.   On the 27th of June I was gazetted 2nd Lieutenant in the 3rd Dragoon Guards, then serving in India.

It was with real regret, not unmixed with anxiety as to what the future had in store for me, that I parted company with my comrades of the sergeants' mess, where I had spent many pleasant hours.   Maillard, who had always shown the most kindly interest in my welfare, presented me with a sword ; Dugdale insisted upon fitting me out with saddlery ; the members of the sergeants' mess gave me a silver-mounted dressing-case ; and from many others in the regiment, officers and men, I received expressions of goodwill.   The 16th Lancers had become a home to me, and I am proud to think that I once had the honour of serving in so distinguished a regiment.

CHAPTER III

SUBALTERN IN INDIA

Join Cavalry Depot at Canterbury—Officers' course of musketry at Hythe
—Leave England for India—Life on board a troopship—Join 3rd
Dragoon Guards—Camp of exercise at Meerut—Pass Lower
Standard Examination in Hindustani—Life at Muttra—Acting
Adjutant and Station Staff Officer—Beer-tasting committees—
Regiment attends Muridki camp of exercise *en route* to Rawal
Pindi—Ludicrous spectacle presented by native followers—State
of training in India and reforms effected by General Luck—Visit of
Prince Albert Victor to Muridki—Pass Higher Standard Examination
in Hindustani—Successes at Rawal Pindi District Assault-at-Arms—
On detachment at Murree—Pass examination in Persian—In charge
of Government Grass Farm at Rawal Pindi—In charge of Regi-
mental Signallers—Acting Station Staff Officer and Secretary of
Assault-at-Arms Committee—Pass examinations in Punjabi and
Pushtu — Black Mountain Expedition — Miranzai Expedition —
Some amusing incidents in connection with the latter—Posted to
Army Headquarters, Simla.

BEING unable to join my new regiment in India until the
" trooping season " of the following autumn I was posted
to the depot at Canterbury, where the depots of all cavalry
regiments serving abroad were then located. These consisted
almost entirely of recruits, and as their training was mainly
in the hands of the depot staff the officers had little to do
except enjoy themselves. I therefore took advantage of the
opportunity to attend an officers' course of musketry at
Hythe in order to qualify as " Instructor," as my sergeant's
certificate qualified me as " assistant instructor " only.
The chief novelty of the course was the maxim gun, then
in its experimental stage. After completing the course I
went on two months' leave, and having bid good-bye to my
mother—which proved to be our final parting—I sailed from
Portsmouth in the Indian troopship " Euphrates " on the
21st November, and reached Bombay about a month later.

These troopships have long since been replaced by transports hired from the merchant service, and no one was sorry for their supersession. They had a speed of only eight or nine knots ; were manned by naval personnel who thoroughly disliked the work and made no secret of it in their dealings with the soldiers ; and the accommodation was indifferent and disagreeable. The men were closely packed together on the lower deck, with a small space on the upper deck for use during the day. The majority of the junior officers' cabins were on or below the water-line, and consequently were more or less in permanent darkness and without fresh air. The children of the officers were located in one large cabin, known as the dove-cot, any berths not occupied by them or their nurses being assigned to the wives of the most junior officers, whether they themselves owned any of the infants or not. The noise which sometimes prevailed in this amalgamated nursery, especially in rough weather, can be better imagined than described. The wives and children of the men had quarters in the fore-part of the ship, and twice each night after 11 P.M. these were visited by the military officer of the watch in order to ascertain that the sentry on the door was fulfilling his duty of permitting no man to enter. I suppose the visits had been found necessary, but the perambulation by subaltern officers through a maze of cots containing sleeping women and girls could hardly be commended from the standpoint of refinement, and this was particularly the case when the sea was rough or the weather hot.

In passing through the Suez Canal our vessel ran into one of the banks—not an uncommon proceeding on the part of a troopship — and there we remained for about twelve hours before we could be got off. On arrival at Bombay we were besieged by the usual crowd of natives who wished to be employed as personal servants, this being the first trap into which the new-comer is apt to fall, unless he has been duly warned of it beforehand. Not a few of these gentry, more especially those who can speak English, make a practice of meeting transports and inducing officers arriving in India for the first time to engage them ; and after a few days they disappear, having meanwhile fleeced their newly-found and innocent " Sahib " of as many rupees as his trustful nature and ignorance of the country will allow.

From Bombay I proceeded to Muttra, the permanent station of my regiment, and thence to Meerut, where the regiment itself was attending a camp of exercise, or training camp, under the command of General Sir George Greaves. I received a most friendly welcome from all members of the officers' mess, which at once dispelled the anxiety I had felt as to the nature of the reception that would be accorded me, and I quickly settled down to my new life and surroundings.

Returning to Muttra on conclusion of the training, I began my first experience of an Indian summer, which is there both long and hot, and the greater part of the day, from about ten in the morning till six in the evening, must necessarily be spent indoors. By retiring early to bed and leading an abstemious life I avoided the rather common and injurious habit of sleeping during the day, and utilised the time in learning Hindustani. My munshi, or teacher, a man of a stout and lethargic type, was quite content with whatever progress his pupils made, or did not make, provided he regularly received his monthly pay of ten rupees. To keep awake when teaching after his mid-day meal was entirely beyond his powers, and he could not understand why I should wish to work while other Sahibs either took their lessons in the evening or not at all. By degrees I caused him to see that this was not my method of doing business, and within three months the " lower standard " examination was successfully negotiated, and a commencement made in preparing for examination by the " higher standard."

There was excellent sport in the vicinity of Muttra, including an unlimited supply of pig, and as there were no other troops in the station we were able to arrange both shooting and pig-sticking so as to derive full advantage from the abundant facilities available.

Of work there was very little : the weather was too hot to admit of much being done, and, as at all cantonments in the Indian plains, a large proportion of the men were sent to a hill-station for six months or so during the summer. The adjutant falling ill, I was detailed to act for him, and for several weeks this kept me more fully employed than would otherwise have been the case, and incidentally it gave me a chance to show what I could do. The adjutant also officiated as station staff officer and cantonment magistrate, and from carrying out these duties I learned something of the native customs of the country. The troop and squadron officers with whom I was directly associated, and in fact all the officers, were particularly pleasant and helpful, and on the whole I felt, and still feel, that I was fortunate in having been posted to the regiment. Walter, an ex-infantry officer, was the captain of my troop. Some thirty years later I unveiled the memorial erected in his village after the Great War. On it, as in so many other cases, was the name of his only son and child.

The non-commissioned officers and men of the regiment were of a good class and well-behaved. Drunkenness was the principal cause of the little misconduct there was, and this not infrequently had its origin in the practice which then prevailed in India of " tasting " the beer supplied to the canteen. Once a week three or four non-commissioned officers and men were detailed, in accordance with the regulations, to taste each cask of beer received, before it was issued for consumption. Sometimes there were a good many casks to be tasted, and therefore it was an easy matter for the tasters to find by the time they had finished that they had tasted too often—more especially so as the weather was hot and the tasting took place, as a rule, before breakfast. This pernicious custom has, I believe, been discontinued.

In November 1889 the regiment left Muttra by road for Muridki, near Lahore, where it was to attend a camp of exercise with twelve other cavalry regiments and some batteries of horse artillery, and afterwards proceed to its new station at Rawal Pindi. The march to Muridki occupied over five weeks, and thence to Rawal Pindi nearly three weeks, and it thus afforded a good opportunity for seeing the country. Starting at about six o'clock in the morning, the day's march of ten to fifteen miles would be finished by ten o'clock at the latest ; breakfast and stables took another three hours or so, after which there was usually plenty of rough shooting to be obtained quite near the halting-place. All officers were accompanied, as was the custom in those days, not only by a dozen to a score servants each—bearers, khansamahs, syces, sweepers, dhobis, bhistis, grass-cutters—but also by two or three generations of their servants' families and *their* belongings. For the conveyance of these " followers " each officer provided at least one and more often two or three bullock wagons, on and around which were piled and hung every imaginable kind of household effects, while on the top of all were perched the women, children, and grand-parents. A more ludicrous spectacle or unwieldy crowd could not be seen.

At Kurnaul, on the way to Muridki, the students of the native college challenged us at cricket. They wore the customary Indian dress, and as they played with naked feet, and the ground was as hard as flint, they had rather a poor time against our fast bowling, and did well to make as many as thirty-five runs. At several places I noticed that the young Indians were very keen on this game, and they were not over particular about the conditions under which they played it. At Lahore, for instance, I watched a school match in which the ball used was made of wood, and the pitch lay across no fewer than three distinct furrows !

At Ludhiana we crossed the Sutlej by a ferry-train and then entered the Punjab, or country of " five rivers "—the Sutlej, Beas, Ravi, Chenab, and Jhelum—all being tributaries of the Indus. The passage of the Beas in flat-bottomed boats took two days, and the Ravi, just beyond Lahore, was crossed by a bridge of boats.

The camp at Muridki was under the command of Major-General Luck, who had recently been appointed Inspector-General of Cavalry. He was considered by some officers of the old school to be more of a drill-sergeant than a cavalry commander, in that he required regimental officers to know far more about their men and horses and the details of drill than was either reasonable or necessary. To my mind he only asked of officers what it was their duty to give : he expected them to know their work and be able to instruct their men, and this is what many officers in India and elsewhere did not then know and could not do. He imparted a much-needed impetus to cavalry training before he left India to become Inspector-General at home.

Much useful elementary training, of a character hitherto unknown in India, was carried out during the first three weeks at Muridki, and subsequently the troops were divided into two opposing forces, placed fifty miles apart, and exercised in the rôle of independent cavalry. The scheme was apparently designed to afford instruction in long-distance reconnaissance duties and then finish with a great cavalry fight, which in those days was considered to be the orthodox prelude to the clash of the main armies. The operations, in general, were conducted on practical lines : we bivouacked each night as and where we could, under active service conditions, and lived mainly on the country through which we passed. There were some exciting, though not very edifying, encounters between the opposing patrols, and these were the matters of chief interest to junior officers such as myself. In one case a hostile party consisting of an officer and six men rode right round the rear of the force to which my regiment belonged before being observed, or at any rate stopped. I was sent with half a troop in pursuit when the party was at last seen, and rather proudly returned with all the horses, five of the men, and the officer's sword. He and one of his men escaped by jumping into a river and swimming across to the other side, and thus he no doubt took back to his General the information he had been sent out to obtain. Possibly he might have been less successful had we been able to use ball-ammunition instead of blank while he was in the water. This reminds me that the rough ground and dense clouds of black dust, in which we were usually enveloped when working in compact bodies, led to three men being killed and several others injured before the manœuvres terminated.

On the concluding day of the operations the Commander-in-Chief, Lord Roberts, and a large number of staff officers and ladies from Simla and Calcutta were present at the spot where it was expected that the great fight would occur, but the opposing commanders either decided not to fight at that particular place or time, or they failed to locate each other's main body, with the result that the fight did not come off ! The big - wigs were exceedingly wroth, according to camp gossip, at what they classed as the manifest incompetency of the commanders, but the fault probably lay as much with the big-wigs themselves—the framers of the scheme—as with those who carried it out.

Exactly who was to blame I cannot say, because it was not yet the custom for junior regimental officers to be told what was supposed to be happening, or what the scheme of operations was. All I know for certain is that my regiment, and I think most of the others, walked straight into its camp, from where it had started a few days before, without having seen a sign of the enemy, and was very pleased to get there at an earlier hour than had been anticipated.

Prince Albert Victor, elder brother of His Majesty, was present during the final stages of the training, and the proceedings were brought to an end on the 28th January with a review of all the troops and a charge in line on a front of nearly two miles. We in the ranks could see practically nothing for dust, and I doubt if the spectators saw much more. Other events which figured on the programme during the Prince's stay were a " darbar," attended by numerous Indian chiefs in full war attire, a smoking concert, and various competitions in skill-at-arms. A feature of the concert was an exhibition of sword-play by some " sowars " (native cavalrymen), which looked particularly fine as seen by the light of the huge camp-fire around which we sat. The Prince presented a silver cup for the best score made at tent-pegging, and being in good form at the time I was a strong regimental favourite. I struck the first peg fair in the middle, but, as sometimes happens, it split, and as I failed to carry it away I became, according to the rules, ineligible to take any further part in the competition. There was some keen rivalry shown amongst the native regiments in the " lance-exercise " competition, and I must confess that, although one of the judges, I was hopeful that the prize would go to the 18th Bengal Lancers, whose scarlet tunics reminded me of my old regiment the 16th Lancers. Sentiment had, however, to be kept in check, and another fine regiment, I forget which, carried off the prize by the narrow margin of five points out of a possible two hundred.

Whilst at Muridki I passed the examination in the higher standard of Hindustani, the language used being known as Hindi and the character Sanskrit, while for the lower standard the language is known as Urdu and the character is Persian. I had been examined in the higher standard three months before at Meerut, and felt fairly certain that I had been successful, but it turned out that the President of the Examining Board was not qualified to act as such and the proceedings were therefore annulled. According to the Indian Army Regulations (there are, or were, some twenty or thirty volumes of them) candidates, if successful, received their travelling expenses, and as the appointment of the wrong President was no fault of mine I claimed these expenses. The financial reply was that I could not have them as I had not, in fact, " passed," and my answer to this was that not only had I incurred the expenses because some one else had blundered, but that, for the same reason, I was now compelled to go through a further course of preparation, with its attendant cost. The correspondence continued to see-saw in this manner for several weeks, and at last my commanding officer became so infuriated with the sight of it that I gave up the contest.

On the 30th January 1890 the regiment left Muridki for Rawal Pindi, amongst the notable places passed through being Gujrat, where was fought the final battle in the Sikh war. Here, in my walk round, I came across a batch of school-boys squatted on the ground and poring over a small-scale map of Europe, which was being explained to them by their master. Like many people before them, they were surprised and puzzled most of all at the very small space occupied by England.

The 500 miles' march from Muttra to the Jhelum had lain over a dead-flat plain, but after crossing this river we entered the foot-hills of the Himalayas, whose snowy summits had already been visible many marches earlier. One afternoon I went some distance into these hills so as to get a better view of the sunset, and, forgetting that there was practically no twilight, remained gazing too long, with the result that darkness caught me in a labyrinth of rocks and ravines through which I had to crawl and scramble in the direction where I hoped the camp might be. After some hours' anxiety lest I would have to wait for daylight I fortunately saw the camp-fires and so found my way back. Between Jhelum and Rawal Pindi—I forget exactly where —I visited the spot on which Alexander the Great is supposed to have erected, in 326 B.C., the monument to his favourite charger, Bucephalus.

We reached Rawal Pindi, the Aldershot of northern India, on the 17th February, and shortly afterwards the annual district assault-at-arms took place. At this meeting I was more fortunate than at Muridki, winning the tent-pegging quite easily. The following year I took the first prizes in swordsmanship and fencing, and fought in the final for the chief prize—that for the best officer-at-arms—but being fairly and squarely unhorsed by an officer of the 11th Bengal Lancers I failed to win it. Another officer of this regiment against whom I fought was Lieutenant (now General Sir William) Birdwood. The chief prize fell to me a year later, as did two other prizes. These achievements, such as they were, were mainly due to keeping myself physically fit—not an easy thing to do in the plains of India unless one is blessed with a strong constitution, and is careful to safeguard it by temperate habits and suitable exercise.

I claim no credit for pursuing these habits, because I had not the wherewithal to do otherwise. Water was the only drink I could afford, while for smoking I had to be content with a fixed amount of tobacco and cheroots at two shillings a hundred. It was not altogether agreeable to be seen drinking water at mess when others were drinking champagne, or to defer smoking till leaving the mess because pipes were not allowed, but it had to be done.

After being at Rawal Pindi for a few weeks I was sent with a detachment to spend the hot season at the hill-station of Murree, where we were joined by a similar detachment of the Queen's Bays, the combined strength being about 300 men. I was appointed acting-adjutant for the whole and was of course responsible for the training and discipline of my own men. These duties occupied the greater part of the day, but by avoiding most of the social engagements common to hill-stations in India, I was able to give some three or four hours daily to the study of a third language—Persian.

My teacher, a native of Persia, was an exasperating but none the less attractive person, who had evidently led a scapegrace kind of life and possibly for that reason had taken refuge in India. At one time he would be most regular in his attendance and very smartly dressed. At other times he was quite the reverse, and for days did not put in an appearance. I induced him to mend his ways, and as he was a well-educated and capable instructor, the higher standard was successfully passed before I returned to Rawal Pindi in the autumn.

Immediately afterwards I was appointed by the General in command, Sir William Elles, to supervise the government grass farm, of about eleven thousand acres, then being started for the purpose of supplying the horses of the station with hay in place of the " dhub " grass which, according to the Indian custom, had hitherto been brought in daily by an army of " grass-cutters." This appointment proved to be a tiresome affair, as the native contractors were continually advancing plausible reasons why I should excuse their breaches of agreement, and as they had complete control over practically all the available coolie labour I was sometimes in the predicament of having to choose between accepting inferior work and getting no work at all.

Besides looking after my farm I was placed in charge of the regimental signallers, the commanding officer telling me at the time that a very unsatisfactory report on them had been received from army headquarters, and that there must be a great improvement. He added that he would allow me a free hand as to their training, while I in my turn must undertake to make them more efficient. I promised to do this, subject to there being no mistake with respect to the free hand, and thanks to the loyal co-operation of my men the regiment gained first place in the order of merit at the next annual inspection. Some time afterwards I was offered the appointment of assistant inspector of signalling in India, but I declined it as something more promising was then in sight.

Another appointment which occasionally devolved upon me, in the absence of the permanent holder, was that of station staff officer, in which capacity I served under Sir Power Palmer and Sir George Luck, who respectively held temporary command of the Rawal Pindi district. For two years I was also secretary of the district assault-at-arms committee. My hands were therefore fairly full, but by a proper adjustment of work I was able to take a share of regimental duties, as well as find sufficient leisure to qualify in two more languages, Punjabi and Pushtu, thus making five in all.

Pushtu resembles Persian in many ways, but the colloquial is difficult. I failed in it at my first attempt, partly because I had the misfortune to miss the train which was to take me to Peshawar for the examination, and had to travel all night in the guard's van of a luggage train in order to present myself at the appointed hour ; and chiefly because the wild man, a Mohmand, whom the examiners produced to converse with me, launched out into a long dissertation about the Christian belief in the Trinity. Not understanding in the least what he was talking about I made all kinds of wild and incorrect guesses in the endeavour to keep up the conversation, with the result that I was hopelessly ploughed. Six months' further study, plus a new munshi, enabled me to pass with flying colours. In 1920 this munshi, Ziaud-Din by name, sent his son to call on me when the latter, a youth of about twenty years of age, came to London to study law.

The pecuniary rewards given by the Indian Government for passing examinations in these languages was little more than sufficient to pay expenses, but this little was not to be despised for it helped to keep my head, financially, above water. Having established some reputation as a linguist, I was able to make a contract with my munshis to pay a fixed sum on passing instead of the customary monthly wage irrespective of passing. When studying Punjabi my only spare time was before 8 A.M. and after 5 P.M., and in order that the munshi might be on the spot when required I lodged him in the compound with the other natives of my household, and told him that he might call me as early as he liked for our first lesson. Determined to earn his money in as short a time as possible he appeared every morning by my bedside with maddening regularity at a very early hour, quietly but persistently calling out, " Sahib, Sahib," until I awoke. He reaped his reward within a few weeks, for as Punjabi has much in common with Hindi it was easy to master for examination purposes. He has apparently not yet forgotten his old pupil, as three years ago I received the following from him :

Pandit Dhanpat Rai (of Rahon), Officers' Punjabi Munshi, sends his most respectful salaams for Christmas Day and his best wishes for a happy new year.
Present address : Sadar Bazar, Peshawar (India).

A knowledge of oriental languages did not at the time appear to be of much professional use as the regiment was shortly due to go to South Africa, and indeed very few officers in British regiments serving in India took the trouble to study them, with the exception of Hindustani. I had the impression, however, that they might prove useful, and so it turned out, for it was largely owing to my knowledge of them that I was later appointed to the staff.

Before this happened I gained my initial experience of active service. Early in 1891 a punitive expedition under Sir William Elles was sent against certain of the Black Mountain tribes, who had continued to give trouble ever since the fruitless expedition of 1888, and whilst this expedition was in progress some 16,000 Miranzai tribesmen raided the frontier near Kohat, doing considerable damage and getting within two or three miles of that place. To deal with them a mixed brigade of infantry and artillery was ordered to be withdrawn from the Black Mountain and despatched to Kohat as quickly as possible, Sir William Lockhart to be in command.

On the 7th April I was suddenly deputed to go to Hassan Abdal, the railhead of the Black Mountain force, and make the necessary arrangements for railing the Kohat force to Kushalgarh, which was the selected base of the new operations and, at the time, the railway terminus in that direction. The transport animals, mainly mules, and their native drivers gave me a good deal of trouble, especially those that had to be entrained during the night, but, to quote from a letter I wrote home, " a knowledge of the vernacular expedites matters considerably, more particularly when rubbed in with a stout stick, a weapon I always carry."

The wives of certain officers were also the cause of some trouble, and in their case neither the vernacular nor the stick could be employed. Not having seen their husbands for some weeks, and not knowing when they might have another opportunity of seeing them, they came up by rail from Rawal Pindi to meet them when passing through Hassan Abdal. There were no buildings suitable for Europeans except the small wayside station and a three-roomed dak bungalow, and therefore these ladies monopolised practically all the accommodation available. They might more appropriately have stayed at home, but soldiering in India thirty years ago was conducted in an easy-going fashion in more ways than one.

Amongst the officers who passed through Hassan Abdal was Prince Christian of Schleswig-Holstein, who was then serving with his regiment in India. I had not met him before, and when he came to ask me for a railway warrant I remarked that he was looking rather dirty and ragged after his Black Mountain experiences. His good-humoured reply greatly helped to dispel the confusion into which I fell when he gave me his name. The Prince was universally regarded as a good officer, and was very popular with all ranks.

The brigade was despatched sufficiently quickly to reach Kohat before further damage was done there, and I was gratified to receive a telegram from Sir William Lockhart expressing his satisfaction at the rapidity and smoothness with which the railway movement had been carried out.

Being eager to see active service I telegraphed to headquarters at Rawal Pindi saying that I proposed going to Kushalgarh with the last train-load of troops, so as to ensure that everything was in order at that place. This was approved, but just as the train was due to start a second message arrived cancelling the first and telling me to go back to Rawal Pindi. This I put into my pocket and, quite improperly, ignored, hoping that once I got to Kushalgarh I would be allowed to accompany the force to Kohat and thence into the Miranzai country. The plot did not work out successfully, for three days later I was again directed, and in more peremptory terms, to return.

On arrival at Rawal Pindi, however, I was met by a staff officer who told me that I was to go back to Kushalgarh at once by the train in which I had just travelled, and take up the duties of Base Commandant. As I had had little or nothing to eat for the last two or three days—nothing being obtainable at Kushalgarh—I replied that I must first lay in a stock of supplies and would then proceed by a later train. He was not inclined to consent but did so at last, and during the day my orders were again changed, and I was told that I need not go back. Two days afterwards it was discovered that matters at Kushalgarh had got into a muddle, and I was then bundled off at a few hours' notice with direct instructions from the General to put them right. I accordingly started, having but a very vague idea of what was required of me in my new capacity. The important thing seemed to be to hurry up to the front all men, animals, and material arriving at the base, and send back to Rawal Pindi with equal despatch everything arriving from the front. By adhering to this rough rule I managed to give satisfaction to the authorities both at the front and the rear.

" Kushalgarh " signifies the " happy mountain," but a more abominable place in which to live cannot be imagined. Situated on the banks of the Indus—which was crossed at the time by a bridge of boats—it is notoriously hot in summer, and is devoid of everything save rocks and sand. My only shelter was a small Indian tent, and at times the heat was almost unbearable. It would have been entirely so had I not always been able to procure a cool drink by anchoring a hamper of lemonade and soda water in the river, then in flood from the melting snows of the Himalayas and icy cold a few feet below the surface. Once, for a period of two days, we had a plague of locusts ; on the table, in the bed, in clothing, in cooking utensils, everywhere were the locusts. They were so thick on the ground that one morning they actually stopped a train. There was a slight ascent to the station, and the crushing of the locusts made the rails so slippery that the train had to be brought in by a section at a time, a party of men being detailed to throw sand on the line and sweep away the pests in front of the engine. A terrific storm of wind followed, and this effectively cleared them off, but it also levelled all our tents and carried away my only suit of pyjamas !

Wishing to escape from the heat and to establish more favourable conditions under which to work, I told the native station-master that I proposed to use the ladies' waiting-room as an office during the daytime, as no ladies ever came to the station at that season, and there were none within fifty miles of it, but he suggested that I should first obtain the permission of the superintendent of the line. I therefore sent a brief telegram to the latter, who was well-known to me, and he at once gave his consent. Some months later, when the accounts of the expedition were being audited, I received a letter from the Adjutant-General at Simla asking for an explanation as to why I had sent an official telegram on what was evidently a private matter, namely, an application to use a ladies' waiting-room ! I explained the circumstances, very clearly I thought, but failed to satisfy him, and was directed not to repeat the irregularity in future, and meanwhile to defray the cost of the telegram amounting to eight annas.

This was not the only financial trouble into which I fell in connection with this expedition. On the breaking-up of the base I returned the camp equipment and other stores to the government arsenal at Lahore, and on their arrival it was alleged that many articles were missing, the value of which amounted to twenty thousand rupees. I was so informed in the usual Babu phraseology, and requested " kindly to remit same." The sum was so far in excess of my ability to pay that it struck me as being exceedingly comic, and after a lengthy correspondence, in which I maintained that the missing articles had been returned, the charge was " written off " and I was exonerated.

I may add here that I did not receive the medal for either of the expeditions referred to above, as I had not crossed the line of demarcation which qualified for it.

Early in 1892 the Intelligence Branch at army headquarters was about to be strengthened by an increased number of officers. The intention was to take these officers partly from native and partly from British regiments, and after they had served a period of probation as " attachés " to select from amongst them for permanent employment such as it was considered desirable to retain. It was necessary, of course, that they should possess the linguistic attainments required by the nature of the work they had to do, and as I had five languages to my credit I was one of those chosen from British regiments, and was ordered to proceed to Simla forthwith.

E

CHAPTER IV

IN THE INTELLIGENCE BRANCH, SIMLA

Indian Intelligence Branch reorganised by General Sir H. Brackenbury—Curious division of duties at Army Headquarters—Comparison with system at home—Society favourites thought to have best chance of Staff employment—Colonels Elles and Mason—First permanent Staff appointment—Countries dealt with by North-West Frontier Section, in which I am employed—Situation in Afghanistan—Kafiristan—Intricate frontier questions to be settled—Proceed on leave to England—Death of my mother—Frontier matters still disturbed on return to India—Question of Russian advance on India via the Pamirs—Ordered to reconnoitre route leading to Pamirs—Srinagar—Bridges in Kashmir—Gilgit—Rakapushi Mountain—Hunza—Meet Townshend and Fowler—Yasin—Darkot Pass—The Pamirs—Return to India via the Indus, Chilas, and Abbottabad—Pass examination in Gurkhali.

THE decision to reorganise the Intelligence Branch was due to the initiative of General Sir Henry Brackenbury, the Military Member of the Viceroy's Council. This General had previously been Director of Military Intelligence at the War Office, and he was quick to perceive that the Simla Branch required much overhauling if it was to cope efficiently with the military situation then prevailing on the North-West Frontier and in Central Asia. At the time the Intelligence and Mobilisation Branches were both subdivisions of the department of the Quartermaster-General, who was responsible for dealing with military operations and questions of military policy in general. He was therefore charged, in addition to his usual duties of supply, transport, and barracks, with what we now know as the duties of the General Staff, except that the Adjutant-General was responsible for training, and from this it followed that he occupied the position of Chief Staff Officer of the Commander-in-Chief.

It is significant of the illogical manner in which we

then conducted our Imperial military affairs that quite another system obtained at home. There the Adjutant-General was the Chief Staff Officer of the Commander-in-Chief, and had under him the Intelligence and Mobilisation Branches as well as training, while the Quartermaster-General was concerned only with the duties which properly belonged to him. Again, when the War Office was reorganised in 1904 the Commander-in-Chief was abolished on the ground that no one man could carry out the duties which had hitherto devolved upon him, and these were accordingly divided up between a number of army councillors, each of whom was made responsible for his department to the Secretary of State for War. In India, on the other hand, and at about the same period, it was the Military Member—roughly the equivalent of the War Secretary at home — who was for all practical purposes abolished, since he was made the subordinate of the Commander-in-Chief, and the latter became the supreme head of all military business in the country. Conditions in India differ considerably from those at home, and a Commander-in-Chief is undoubtedly necessary there, but the difference is not so great as to justify having an entirely different military system in other respects, and it is satisfactory to know that within recent years the two headquarters have been brought more into line.

Apart from the faulty organisation of headquarters as a whole, the Intelligence Branch had suffered because of the inadequacy—and perhaps of the inferior quality—of its personnel. Although much had been done by the Commander-in-Chief, Lord Roberts, to ensure that priority for staff employment should be governed by professional capacity, favouritism and social influence were not yet deemed by the outsider to be extinct. It was alleged that staff officers were still too often selected from amongst those who were likely to be successful performers in amateur theatricals, or be useful in some other way at the various entertainments provided for the amusement of Simla society. I was frequently asked on first arrival at this smart hill-station what my special accomplishment was—acting, singing, or whistling—and what my contribution to the amenities of the season was to be. It was taken for granted that I could do something of this nature, and do it well, and my interrogators were surprised to learn that I could contribute nothing.

Fortunately, this missing element in my equipment was a recommendation in the eyes of my new chief, Colonel (now General Sir) Edmund Elles, half-brother of the General under whom I had served at Rawal Pindi. He expected his subordinates to keep themselves physically and mentally fit by taking a share in all outdoor games and recreations, but he also demanded a full day's work. To his sound and able guidance I attribute much of the success, such as it is, which attended my subsequent career, and from both him and his wife, a lady of gentle and kind disposition, I received many proofs of sincere friendship. Some twenty years later, when I was commandant of the Staff College, their son was one of the students, and in the Great War he won distinction as commander of the Tank Corps.

I was equally happy in my immediate chief, Lieutenant-Colonel Mason of the Royal Engineers, who was in charge of the North-West Frontier section to which I was posted. He was a man of sterling character, an acknowledged expert on all questions relating to the frontier, and quite fearless in the expression of the military opinions which he was called upon to lay before his superiors. Of a retiring nature, he was slow to confide in new acquaintances, but I gained his confidence fairly soon, and he taught me much about the life, customs, and attitude of the heterogeneous tribes of the North-West Frontier, which I could have learned so well from no one else. It was due to him and to Elles that, within a few weeks of my arrival at Simla, Lord Roberts approved of my temporary appointment being made permanent for the usual period of five years, and in this way I received my first employment on the staff. Mason's death from an attack of enteric fever two years later was a great loss to the army.

My section dealt with the whole of the independent and semi-independent territories, including Afghanistan, Kashmir, and Baluchistan, which extend for some 2000 miles along the North-West Frontier from Tibet on the right to the Arabian Sea on the left. Of Kashmir and Baluchistan, both within the border of Indian administration, there is nothing special to say, while as to the trans-frontier tribes all that need be said is that trouble with one or another was constantly breaking out or threatening to do so. We knew really very little about their territory, and could not well obtain much information as the border-line was closed to us except when opened by a punitive expedition.

Afghanistan was of importance as being a " buffer " between India and Russian territory. The agreement with the Amir, Abdul Rahman, was that in return for an annual subsidy and other advantages he would have no foreign relations with any Power except the Government of India. The agreement was modified later, and exactly what the arrangement now is I do not know. The country had been torn with war and dissensions before Abdul Rahman assumed the rulership in 1880, and in 1892, when I went to Simla, he had not yet everywhere established order, although he had, by drastic methods, gone far in that direction.

Afghanistan is one of the most difficult countries in the world to govern, for the inhabitants, about five millions in number, are not of the same stock and lineage, and do not possess the same political interests and tribal affinities. The only bond of union among them is that of religion, and even this is neither strong nor durable, owing to the division of the people into the two great hostile sects of the faith of Muhammad, Shiahs and Sunnis. The latter are now far more numerous than the former. The two principal Afghan tribes, properly so-called, are the Duranis and Ghilzais, the former being found chiefly in the Kandahar and Farah Provinces and the Ghilzais in the Kabul Province. The Ghilzais are said to be the descendants of " Ghalzoe," i.e. the "son of a thief," whose birth took place within three months of the marriage of his parents. In the northern provinces the inhabitants are for the most part alien to the Afghan, being Turkomans in Turkistan and of Persian origin in Herat. The army, of which the Amir was proud, was about 130,000 strong, of whom 100,000 were regulars and 30,000 militia. It comprised the three arms, cavalry, artillery, and infantry.

Considered as a theatre of war, Afghanistan is a waterless, treeless, foodless, roadless, mountainous country, and has been described as Spain once was—a country in which a large army will starve and a small one will be murdered. The chief mountain range, the Hindu Kush, has a general elevation of between 12,000 and 18,000 feet, and is everywhere precipitous and arid. A more desolate and inhospitable region cannot be imagined.

The routes leading through the country between the Russian and Indian frontiers we used to classify in three groups : Pamirs line, Kabul line, and Kandahar line. I will refer to the Pamirs line later, merely saying here that the distance from the Russian frontier to Peshawar is about 600 miles. By the Kabul line there are several alternative routes as far as the capital, the distance from the Oxus to Peshawar being about 450 miles. By Herat and Kandahar the distance to Quetta is 650 miles. These distances, coupled with what has been said about the country, will serve to show the enormous difficulties to be overcome in conducting military operations on any of the three lines.

The Amir's policy was to permit no kind of interference with his internal affairs, and although he received subsidies and supplies of arms from us he would make few or no concessions in return, and all projects, such as railways and telegraphs, proposed for the better defence of the country he viewed with distrust. He maintained the same attitude towards foreign visitors, and beyond the few employees he had at Kabul, no European was allowed to set foot in the country except in the rare event of a " mission," and the members of it would always be closely watched.

Lord Curzon was the only person during my four years at Simla who entered Afghanistan as a guest, under the auspices of the Amir. He once gave me an amusing description of the attire he wore when meeting the Amir for the first time. It included a military frock-coat, cocked hat, boots of the Household Cavalry type, fierce-looking brass spurs, and an elaborate presentation sword lent by Sir William Lockhart. Lord Curzon was quite right, for this kind of display counts for much in the eyes of the Eastern chief, who remains quite unmoved by the sight of a top-hat, morning coat, and white spats.

At the time I joined the Intelligence Branch many complicated problems were constantly coming up for examination. Umra Khan of Jandol, of whom more will be said in the next chapter, was aggressively active on the borders of Kafiristan and elsewhere ; other semi-independent tribes were fractious, and threatened to indulge in one of their periodical outbreaks ; the Afghan-Persian boundary was in dispute ; while Russia was systematically pushing forward her outposts on the Pamirs and disturbing the peace of mind of the Amir, who feared that he might be deprived of territory which he asserted belonged to him. Kafiristan, it may be explained, was the name given by the Muhammadans to the country lying between the province of Kabul and Chitral, the inhabitants of which were pagans and were therefore regarded by the Muhammadans as infidels, or " kafirs." These kafirs have no connection with the Kafir of South Africa. They were finally subdued by Abdul Rahman about 1895, and compelled to accept the religion of Islam.

Following the Afghan Boundary Commission of 1884-88, an agreement had been reached with Russia in respect of the Russo-Afghan boundary from Badakhshan to Persia, but that separating the two countries in the vicinity of the Pamirs remained unsettled for several years afterwards. The trouble arose partly from the fact that in an agreement of 1872 the Oxus had been laid down as the boundary, and however clear this definition may have appeared to those who drafted the agreement, it proved to be far from clear when an attempt was made to put it into practice. The reason of this was that not one of the various streams in the Pamir region which go to form the Oxus is locally known by that name, while more than one of them can, at a pinch, be claimed as the main river according to the aims of the parties interested. The incident furnishes, amongst others I could quote, rather a striking example of the danger which attaches to the drafting of frontier agreements when dependent, as in this case, upon old and imperfect small scale maps and in the absence of complete topographical data.

When I went to Simla there was no good information

available as regards much of the vast area for which the Frontier Section was responsible. We had to rely largely upon the reports of travellers, and these seldom gave the kind of intelligence that was needed, much of it was many years old, while some of the travellers were themselves more renowned for their powers of graphic description than for the accuracy of their statements. By initiating new and extended reconnaissances, and introducing a better method of recording and compiling the information received, our stock of intelligence gradually improved both in quantity and quality. One compilation, *The Gazetteer and Military Report on Afghanistan*, occupied the greater part of my time for more than a year, the five volumes of which it was comprised aggregating some three thousand pages. It was a stupendous task, and I was glad when it was finished, but the knowledge I gained of the country was some compensation for the drudgery involved.

In January 1893, having been over four years in India, I took six months' leave to England as I wished to qualify for promotion to Captain, which in those days entailed going through what was known as a " garrison class," or special course of military education. I was also anxious to see my mother, who I knew to be in failing health, but on arrival at Malta was met by a telegram conveying the news of her death. To that extent the trip to England was a bitter failure.

When I returned to Simla in July 1893 affairs in Afghanistan and on the North-West Frontier generally were still in a very unsettled state, and in particular the activities of Russia on the Pamirs were feared—quite needlessly—to constitute a threat on India, in the future if not at the present. It is incomprehensible why those who held this view never seemed to appreciate the tremendous topographical difficulties to be overcome.

Another question constantly to the fore was whether, assuming the Pamir line of advance to be feasible for anything worth calling a military force, we ought to prepare for it by adopting what was known as a forward policy—that is, to push out our outposts and establish good communications between India and the furthest limit possible—or whether we should deliberately refrain from doing these things, so as

to place on the potential enemy the disadvantage of sur-
mounting the defensive barrier provided by nature. There
was much to be said on both sides, and much was said,
and the compromise eventually arrived at was probably
the wisest solution.

In June 1894 I was deputed to reconnoitre various routes
in the vicinity of the Pamirs, in order to obtain certain
information of which we were specially in need. Leaving
the railway at Rawal Pindi I travelled for about 150 miles
in a " tonga," or covered two-wheeled vehicle, drawn by
two ponies changed at various distances en route, and not
infrequently suffering from abominably sore shoulders.
For the first forty miles the road climbed up the Murree
hills, whence it descended to the Jhelum valley and then
followed that river through gorges and defiles to Baramula
at the entrance of the main valley of Kashmir, and within
a few miles of the point where the Jhelum leaves the Wular
Lake. From here I crossed the lake and ascended the river
to Srinagar in a kind of miniature houseboat, which was
roofed in with matting and had a crew consisting of a man,
his wife, and a baby. The lake is liable to sudden and
dangerous storms, which have caused many a boat to be
swamped and wrecked, but my trip was free from any
such adventure. The only disagreeable feature of the
twenty-four hours' voyage was that the baby—only a few
feet away from me—continued to howl for the greater
part of the night.

The Kashmir valley, some 20 miles wide and nearly
100 miles in length, is justly renowned for its scenery. It
is enclosed by high, wooded, snow-covered mountains and
intersected by numerous streams and lakes, which with a
profusion of fruit-trees of every species and wild flowers
of every hue, constitute a picture which cannot well be
surpassed in natural beauty. Srinagar, the " city of the
sun," is closely cut up with canals, and is sometimes styled
the Venice of the east. The impression I formed was that
its delights are more imaginary than real. Its jumbled
medley of houses, mainly constructed of timber and built
out of the water, were mostly in a ramshackle and ruinous
condition, with broken doors or no doors at all, and

windows stopped up with boards, paper, or rags ; the lanes between them were narrow, dirty, and ill-paved ; and the smells encountered were not savoury.

On this fringe of civilisation I completed my transport and supply arrangements.   Besides the food and equipment required for the use of myself and followers, corn had to be carried for the riding and transport animals, little or none being procurable between the Kashmir valley and Gilgit, a distance of 228 miles.

The road connecting Srinagar with Gilgit was good as roads go in this part of the world, and on the third day's march I crossed the Tragbal Pass, 11,950 feet in height.   It was covered with a thick carpet of flowers, chiefly primulas and orchids, of every colour, and afforded a most magnificent view.   Behind, thousands of feet below, was the broad expanse of the Wular Lake and the Kashmir valley, backed by the snow-crested range of the Pir Panjal ; and in front, some 50 miles away, could be seen the snowy domes of Nanga Parbat, 26,620 feet in altitude, towering above the mountain ranges on either hand and forming a landmark visible for hundreds of miles.   From the Tragbal the road descended to and crossed the Kishan-ganga, and then a long and severe climb led to the Burzil Pass, 13,650 feet high.   This pass is easy in summer, but is practically closed for the remainder of the year, and possesses a bad reputation for severe snowstorms at seasons when they are not usually expected.   It forms the line of demarcation between the forest-clad mountains of the south and the bare and arid region of the Hindu Kush to the north.

Some 40 miles farther on I reached Astor, famous for its abundance of ibex, markhor, and orial, and claiming to be the birthplace of polo or at any rate the land of its earliest adoption.   The game is played in a rough-and-ready manner, and any number of players up to about a score a side take part in it.

From Astor the road followed the river of that name down a deep valley enclosed by high and precipitous mountains to Ramghat, a ghastly place surrounded on all sides by lofty rocks and crags, and in summer-time as hot as a furnace. As Knight says in his book *Where Three Empires Meet*, " A man might almost as well pass his life in a stoke-hole as in this infernal oven." The river rushes with terrific force and deafening noise through a deep gorge 150 feet wide, over which the road is carried by the fine suspension bridge which shortly before my visit had replaced the " jhula " or rope-bridge common to the country.

The " jhula " is made of three ropes of twisted twigs, and is stretched across the river in the form of a triangle, two parallel ropes acting as hand-rails and the central or lower one as a footway. The three sets of ropes are tied together by similar ropes at every few feet, and the whole is bound to baulks anchored to high rocks or cliffs on either side, and as far as possible on the same level. In order to keep the side ropes apart cross-sticks are inserted at varying distances, and over these one has to step—a performance which calls for a certain amount of acrobatic skill, as the side ropes are in places as much as 3 feet above the foot-rope. There is a tremendous sag in the middle, and when there is a strong wind and the span is large—some are as much as 300 feet in length—the bridge is apt to swing dizzily about in a manner decidedly trying to the nerves of any one not accustomed to this mode of traffic. Perhaps the worst feature of the " jhula " is that one never knows whether it may be trusted to carry the weight put upon it, as the twigs of which it is made quickly dry and perish, and the ropes may then any day suddenly break.

Where something more substantial than a " jhula " is required, a bridge on the cantilever principle is constructed. It consists of timbers projecting one over another from the opposite banks, their shore ends being weighted down with masonry or rocks. In the absence of a bridge of any kind the natives cross on a " shinaz," or inflated hide of the ox or goat. Striding across this and passing each leg through a loop hanging down like a stirrup leather, the rider lays his chest upon the hide and plunges into the current, paddling with arms and legs as in the act of swimming. Much skill and dexterity are required in the management of these little floats to prevent a capsize. The passage of rivers is also made on rafts of inflated skins supporting a framework of light sticks or bamboos. When the shore is left these rafts go dancing wildly down stream, while the boatmen, armed with long poles, frantically strive to propel them across to the opposite bank before being swept past the desired landing-place.

About a quarter of a mile below Ramghat the Astor joins the Indus. The road to Gilgit followed the left bank of the latter for about fourteen miles, then crossed to the right bank by another fine suspension bridge, and than along the muddy, boiling Gilgit river to the Gilgit Agency. Here I acquired from our officers, about half-a-dozen in number, much useful information respecting the countries to be traversed before reaching my destination, and while supplies were being replenished and other arrangements completed for the onward march to the Pamirs I made a trip to Hunza, some 60 miles up the valley of that name. I covered this distance in two days each way.

The road up the Hunza valley—since greatly improved —crossed several glacier torrents and bad " paris."   " Pari " means a cliff, but the word is used to signify a cliff road strutted or bracketed to the face of a precipice, seldom more than a foot or two wide, and often of very shaky and sketchy construction.

The country is noted for the number and size of its glaciers, the Nagar river having its source in one of the greatest known. A few miles east of the road is the giant Rakapushi mountain, which rises sheer 19,000 feet above the level of the valley, its height above sea-level being 25,550 feet. There are several other summits to be seen which exceed 24,000 feet. Fruit-trees abound, especially the apricot, mulberry, apple, and walnut, and so prolific are the crops that the people live to a great extent upon them, as also do the animals and fowls.

To cope with the discomforts which attend a journey through the hot valleys in this part of the world the traveller needs to be young, and able to sleep soundly after the day's work is finished. Flies, of the most tenacious kind, are a perfect pest to him ; usually he is afflicted by an insatiable thirst which continues well into the night ; the cockroach goes to bed with him and climbs up the inside of his pyjamas to make the acquaintance of the caterpillar just fallen on his nose from the roof of the tent ; the mosquito searches out the most palatable parts of his ankles ; the jungle dog enters the tent to ascertain whether anything edible has been left on the ground ; and at last the native servant appears to announce that morning is here and breakfast ready. Having done such justice to the meal as he can, got into riding kit, and donned his blue spectacles as a protection against the sun's rays reflected from the bare and burning rocks, the traveller mounts an animal called a pony, and the march is resumed. But the discomforts, such as they are, sit lightly on the young and strong ; there is much to see of enthralling interest in these wonderful outlying regions of the Empire ; and such is the influence of the British "raj" that one feels that one is not only a man, but, in the eyes of the natives, a sort of king.

The people of Hunza and Nagar, known as Kanjutis, were for centuries professional brigands and slave-dealers. So great was the terror inspired by them that whole districts, formerly well - cultivated and populated, were totally abandoned by their inhabitants. Secure in their mountain strongholds, and having ready access to the passes leading north to the Yarkand valley, the Kanjutis were able to waylay and pillage with impunity the rich caravans travelling by the great trade route between India and Turkestan, and to raid the territory of their neighbours as and when they wished. This wholesale brigandage and raiding, as well as the slave-dealing scourge, were effectively put a stop to by the introduction of British administrative control which followed Colonel Durand's brilliant little Hunza-Nagar campaign in the winter of 1891.

On leaving Gilgit for the Pamirs my party consisted of an orderly provided by the 5th Ghurkas, who had accompanied me from India, a Pathan and two servants, eight other " followers " of various nationalities, a native guide, a dozen mules and ponies, and about a score sheep to supply us with meat. The guide claimed to be the " Raja " of one of the districts through which we were to pass, but unluckily for him some one else not only claimed that title but exercised it. I was afraid that this difference of opinion might be the cause of trouble, but it was not, my guide probably being regarded by the man in possession as so weak a pretender as not to be worth removing.

From Gilgit to Gupis, 70 miles, the road continued up the right bank of the Gilgit river, the valley seldom being wider than to give room for the roaring torrent 70 to 100 yards across and in places running like a mill-race. The mountain-tops rise high and steep on both sides, and when there is heavy rain or the snow is melting it is necessary to maintain a sharp look-out for the huge avalanches which come tumbling down. I was often kept awake at night by the terrific noise, resembling the sound of heavy gun-fire, caused by these masses of rock, weighing many tons, plunging down from thousands of feet into the river below.

At Gupis I found a small detachment of Kashmir Imperial Service troops, one of the many posts then scattered along the route between Astor and Chitral, each commanded by a British subaltern or captain. The work done at this period by these young and enterprising officers in consolidating British influence was of great value, and has perhaps never been adequately appreciated. Amongst those whom I met, two—Captain Townshend and Lieutenant Fowler—were destined to play a prominent part the following year in the operations in Chitral, and again in the Great War. Townshend was in command during the siege of Chitral and also at Kut-el-Amara, and Fowler was treacherously made prisoner on his way to Chitral. He was lucky not to have been murdered by some fanatic or other before Umra Khan released him, a month after his capture, and sent him in to the headquarters of the Relief Force. In the Great War he was Director of the " signal service " on the West Front.

A little above Gupis I crossed the Gilgit river by a rickety wire suspension bridge and entered the valley of Yasin. It was here that the intrepid traveller Hayward was murdered in 1870. The object was apparently plunder, as he was believed to be in possession of a considerable amount of gold as well as many valuable presents. The story is that, finding himself threatened, he sat up in his tent all night with his loaded rifle on the table before him, and in the early morning, being overcome with fatigue, he dozed off and was immediately pounced upon by his crafty enemies who had been closely watching him throughout the night. He asked permission to go outside and ascend a low mound in order to take a last look at the rising sun, and after this had been granted he was brutally done to death.

For the benefit of those who have not travelled in this part of the world, I may explain that passes of 13,000 feet and over are closed by snow for some five months or more every year, according to their altitude ; when the snow begins to melt, and for some weeks afterwards, the streams running down from them, and which may have to be crossed many times, are roaring torrents, and, as a rule, unfordable ; this means, in practice, that the routes may be actually open only for two or three months in the year—that is, after the streams go down and before the passes again become blocked with snow ; and, finally, all passes of 15,000 feet and over have on them perpetual snow, and this must be crossed before the sun has risen sufficiently high to make it too soft to traverse.

Above Yasin, 7300 feet in altitude, the valley is for the most part hemmed in by precipitous mountains thousands of feet high ; the débris of many landslips had to be crossed ; and the ever-recurring ascents and descents made progress slow and laborious. At 20 miles from Yasin the climb up to the Darkot Pass began ; bare rock took the place of earth ; and at 14,000 feet the first glacier was reached. Having crossed this, the track struck the edge of the snow-field, which led up to and over the pass. It was then mid-day, and as the hot July sun had made the snow so soft and yielding as to be impassable for either men or animals, there was nothing to do but to halt for the night and resume the journey early next morning when the snow would again be frozen hard.

I spent most of the afternoon in gazing upon the stupendous mountains which rose before me on all sides, and in which culminate the three great water-partings of Central Asia—the Hindu Kush, the Himalayas, and the mountains of Chinese Turkestan. From this region the melting snows descend eastwards to the Yarkand river and Gobi desert ; westwards to the Oxus and the Aral Sea ; and southwards to the Indus and Indian Ocean. As far as the eye could reach, gigantic peaks, clothed in perpetual snow, soared proudly up into the blue heavens at heights of 25,000 feet and more above sea-level, and this incomparable array of mountain majesty was rendered the more impressive by the apparent total absence of life of any kind, and by the great stillness which everywhere prevailed. No house, tree, bird, animal, or man was visible, the overpowering solitude being broken only by the distant thunder of an occasional avalanche, when a grey smoke would ascend to the sky showing where the mass of fallen snow had subsided. I remained absorbed and appalled by the magnitude of Nature's works, feeling but a very small atom in the Universe, until a cold shiver told me that the sun had disappeared behind the mountain-tops overlooking my camp, and that the temperature, according to its nightly custom, was rapidly falling below freezing-point. Wrapped up in all the rugs and blankets I possessed, and fortified by a hot meal, I lay down for a few hours' rest, but it was some time before the sensations of the afternoon allowed me to fall asleep.

The march was resumed at 2 A.M., the going then being quite hard and the snow sparkling in the light of a perfectly clear moon like a vast field of diamonds. The top of the pass, 15,200 feet, was reached after four hours' stiff climbing. From this point the pass runs either northwest over a glacier to the Baroghil Pass, 12,460 feet, or north-east over the surface of another glacier to the Shawitakh Pass, 12,560 feet. I followed the former, reaching the farther edge of the snowfield just as the heat of the new sun was causing it again to become soft and impassable. I halted for the night on the left bank of the Yarkhun river, which has its source in the adjacent glaciers and eventually joins the Kabul river near Jalalabad under the name of the Kunar. The following day I forded this icy-cold stream on the back of a yak, my bare feet and legs receiving the coldest bath they have ever had.

I was now on the outskirts of the Pamirs—the Roof of the World. " Pamir " signifies a more or less level valley of considerable width, and as the lowest of them is 12,000 feet above sea-level, the climate is severe ; in a few favoured spots only is there much grass ; trees there are none, and even bushes are scarce ; strong, biting winds are common, and on the whole the Pamirs cannot be recommended as a cheerful or comfortable country in which to live.

On completion of my work I returned by the Shawitakh track, and early in August left Gilgit for India, my orders being to follow the Indus from Ramghat to Chilas, occupied by us the year before, and thence proceed by Khagan to Abbottabad. The Indus part of the road was then only in course of construction, and there were many difficult stone-shoots and swift, dangerous torrents to be negotiated in the 53 miles to Chilas. Thence to Khagan there was little that could be dignified by the name of a road, and the track which served as one was in places as bad as it could be. The greatest height crossed was at the Babusar Pass, 13,585 feet.

At Abbottabad the little party which had shared my wanderings broke up. All the members of it had consistently served me well since we left Srinagar three months before, and a word of gratitude is also due to my intelligent and sure-footed riding mules, who had carried me over many perilous mountain sides with far greater safety than if I had attempted to traverse them on foot.

The Gurkha, the only soldier of the party, and a good type of his sturdy race, was a well-educated man, and during our long marches it had been my custom to converse with him in Gurkhali, his native tongue. In this way I acquired a sufficient knowledge of it to enable me, before leaving Abbottabad, to pass the prescribed examination and so bring up the number of oriental languages in which I had qualified to a total of six.

F

CHAPTER V

ON THE INTELLIGENCE STAFF OF THE CHITRAL
RELIEF FORCE

Punitive expedition sent into Waziristan—In temporary charge of Frontier
Section—Events leading up to the siege of Chitral Fort—Umra
Khan of Jandol—Despatch of Chitral Relief Force from India and
a detachment from Gilgit—Appointed to Headquarters Staff of the
Relief Force—Sir Robert Low—Colonel Bindon Blood—Captain
Nixon—Nature of country to be traversed—capture of the Mala-
kand Pass — Action at Khar—Passage of Swat river—Effective
action of cavalry—Reconnaissances to Panjkora river and towards
Umra Khan's headquarters—Fine fighting of Guides Infantry—
Reconnaissance up the Panjkora—Meet Roddy Owen—Advance on
Miankilai and flight of Umra Khan—Siege of Chitral is raised—
Reconnaissance down the Panjkora—Treacherously attacked by
my two guides—Severely wounded—Sent back to India—Mentioned
in Despatches and awarded D.S.O.—Promoted Captain—Preparation for Staff College Entrance Examination—Nominated for
entrance—Leave for England—Some reflections on service in India.

TOWARDS the end of 1894 a brigade of all arms was despatched
to the borders of the Mahsud Waziri country, and, as had
happened more than once before in our dealings with this
truculent tribe, the camp of the brigade was attacked one
morning at dawn while the troops were still asleep in their
tents. We suffered a considerable number of casualties, as
well as loss of prestige, and it was therefore decided to
employ a larger force under the command of General Sir
William Lockhart. Mason joined his staff as head of the
Intelligence, and Lockhart afterwards applied for me to
join it also, but this was not sanctioned as I was required
to take charge of the North-West Frontier Section pending
Mason's absence. I was naturally disappointed at losing
this promising opportunity of seeing active service, but my
chance—and a better one—was to come shortly on another
part of the frontier, in Chitral.

Chitral, one of the mountainous states bordering India

66

on the north, is about the size of Wales and has a population of upwards of a hundred thousand. Both the state and the capital are called by the same name, the capital being some 60 miles on the Indian side of the main watershed of the Hindu Kush. For some years past we had aimed at exerting our influence in the state, more especially over its external relations, as it was important that we should watch the northern passes to which it gives access, and be informed of what was taking place there.

In 1892 the Mehtar, or chief, died, and, as is customary in these frontier states, a scramble at once began for the Mehtarship. The old Mehtar left behind him seventeen sons born of his four legitimate wives, and of these Afzul-ul-Mulk and Nizam-ul-Mulk were supposed to have the strongest claims to the succession. Afzul-ul-Mulk, happening to be at Chitral at the time, while Nizam-ul-Mulk was in Yasin, 150 miles off, at once seized all the arms and money in the fort, murdered such of his brothers as he could put his hands on who were likely to give him trouble, and then started off to deal with Nizam-ul-Mulk. The latter deemed discretion the better part of valour and fled for refuge to our Agency at Gilgit, leaving Afzul-ul-Mulk in possession.

But although the brothers had been disposed of, the new Mehtar had still to reckon with an uncle, Sher Afzul by name, who, in the years gone by, had unsuccessfully tried to oust the old Mehtar and had since been an exile in Afghanistan. This individual, thinking that his chances were now more promising, suddenly appeared in front of Chitral fort, accompanied by a body of horsemen picked up *en route*, and Afzul-ul-Mulk, on going to the gate to ascertain what all the noise was about, was shot down, and expired immediately afterwards.

Sher Afzul then became Mehtar, but his reign was of even more brief duration, for as soon as Nizam-ul-Mulk heard of these events he set out from Gilgit to wrest the throne from him. He was joined by many adherents on the way, and before he reached Chitral fort Sher Afzul threw up the sponge and fled back to Afghan territory as rapidly as he had appeared.

Nizam-ul-Mulk professed himself to be a faithful ally of the British Government, and by his request a British officer, Captain (now Sir) Frank Younghusband, the well-known explorer, was deputed to reside in the country as our Political Agent.   Affairs then settled down, and it was hoped that there would be no further trouble, but on the 1st January 1895 Nizam-ul-Mulk was shot dead while out hawking by a partisan of his brother Amir-ul-Mulk, who for the previous two years had been living with Umra Khan, the ruler of the neighbouring state of Jandol.

This restless and ambitious chief had recently extended his authority over the Khanate of Dir and a considerable part of Swat, both of which marched with his own territory ; and thinking that his opportunity had arrived for still further extending his dominions he invaded Chitral, ostensibly with the object of supporting his friend Amir-ul-Mulk, but with the real intention of annexing the country.   There was, in fact, reason to believe that he was not wholly disconnected with the murder of Nizam-ul-Mulk.   He soon obtained a footing in the southern districts, and was afterwards joined by the persevering Sher Afzul, who again turned up from Afghanistan.   The two chiefs apparently made an agreement to combine forces in expelling the British officers, and then decide who should be the ruler. Collecting some 10,000 men they advanced on Chitral itself, where, after some sharp skirmishing on the 3rd of March, the native troops forming the escort of Surgeon-Major (later Sir) G. Robertson were shut up within the walls of the fort, and nothing more was heard of them for several weeks.

Surgeon-Major Robertson was our Political Agent at Gilgit, and had gone to Chitral at the end of January to report on the situation.   The besieged garrison consisted of 100 men of the 14th Sikhs, 300 men of the Kashmir Infantry, and about 150 followers and others, the whole being under the command of Captain Townshend.   If every one were put on half rations there were sufficient supplies of food to last till about the end of April, and the ammunition amounted to 300 rounds per rifle.

A few days later a British post of about 50 men was

captured at Reshun, between Chitral and Mastuj, and before the end of March the garrison of Mastuj, consisting of 300 men, was besieged.

These stirring events kept me fairly busy in the Frontier Section, but having learned much about the country and its inhabitants during my visit to the neighbourhood in the previous year, I was able to deal with them far more easily than would have been the case had this local knowledge not been acquired. When it became known in India that British troops had been attacked by Umra Khan and Sher Afzul, and were besieged by them, there was nothing to be done but to take immediate steps for their relief. The Government of India therefore decided :

(a) The 1st Indian Division, about 15,000 strong, to mobilise at Peshawar, move from a southerly direction through Swat and Dir, and fall on the rear of Umra Khan. This force, designated the " Chitral Relief Force," to be based on Nowshera (near Peshawar), and be under the command of Major-General (afterwards Sir) Robert Low.

(b) A column of 400 men of the 32nd Pioneers (a regular Indian native battalion), and two guns of a Kashmir mountain battery, to move at the same time from the Gilgit vicinity, where they then were, and, passing through Mastuj, endeavour to reach Chitral from the north. Colonel Kelly to command.

From the southern frontier to Chitral the distance was 190 miles, and from Gilgit to Chitral 220 miles. The number of pack animals required to feed and maintain the " Chitral Relief Force " amounted to nearly 30,000.

As explained in the preceding chapter, the duties connected with the management of field operations, which in these days belong to the General Staff, were performed at the time of which I write by the Intelligence and Mobilisation Branches of the Quartermaster-General's department. Upon them, therefore, devolved the task of working out the plan of operations, and in the case of the Intelligence Branch this fell upon my section. When it was finished, Sir George White, who had succeeded Lord Roberts as Commander-in-Chief, appointed me to the Intelligence Staff of the Force, of which the head was Captain (now General

Sir) John Nixon, 18th Bengal Lancers. The Chief of the Staff was Brigadier-General (now Sir) Bindon Blood, and from both these officers I received much friendly help during the campaign which went far to improve my crude knowledge of staff duties in the field.

Topographical information of the line of advance was vague, and almost entirely derived from native sources. Before entering Swat, the first independent country to be traversed, a range of rugged hills varying between 3000 and 6000 feet in height had to be crossed, and although these had confronted us for years at only a few miles from our boundary no one knew what their difficulties really were, or what the country on the other side of them was like. It was known, however, that at least four mountain ranges— of which the altitude of one varied between 10,000 and 20,000 feet—and three large rivers, the Swat, Panjkora, and Kunar, as well as many smaller streams, had to be crossed ; that the route could nowhere be called a road ; that the intervening country was a hotbed of fanaticism ; and that the tribes would almost certainly oppose our advance, whatever their subsequent attitude might be.

While the force was concentrating at Mardan at the end of March the intelligence officers were directed to obtain as much information as possible regarding the three passes giving access to the Swat valley—the Mora, Shakot, and Malakand—so as to enable the Commander to make his plan. By skilful dispositions and the dissemination of false intelligence he endeavoured to mislead the enemy as to which of the three passes, about seven miles apart, would be selected for attack, and he communicated the true objective to only the more senior commanders and staff officers.

I was not let into the secret, and on the afternoon of the 2nd April the Brigadier of the 1st Brigade, which I had been ordered to accompany, instructed me to be prepared to show the way next morning for the attack on the Shakot, opposite to which the brigade had just arrived. I had a shrewd suspicion that I was being intentionally misinformed, and deemed it wise to be prepared not only for going direct to the Shakot but also for making a flank march across country to the Malakand, which I thought would be the real point of attack. I laid my plans accordingly, and next morning when the brigade was about to move off, and I was ordered to conduct it to the Malakand and not to the Shakot, I greatly enjoyed seeing the look of surprise on the Brigadier's face at the readiness with which his order was carried out.

The enemy's strength at the Malakand was about 12,000 men, but probably not more than half that number had firearms, and of these only a comparatively small proportion were rifles, the remainder being old muzzle-loaders which, in some cases, were almost as dangerous to the owner as to his adversary. The unarmed men were employed in carrying away the killed and wounded, and in hurling down boulders upon the assaulting columns. The position itself, running along the crest for nearly two miles, was exceptionally strong, and was defended on either flank and down the forward spurs by a number of " sangars," or stone breast-works.

The dispositions for the attack were : 2nd Brigade in advance, two battalions turning the right flank while the two others delivered a frontal attack ; 1st Brigade in support ; 3rd Brigade in reserve ; three mountain batteries of artillery to co-operate with the infantry. As the fight progressed the battalions of the 1st Brigade were pushed up level with those of the 2nd, and just before the crest was reached the whole line paused for a few minutes to take breath. All being ready, the bugles sounded the advance, and, with a great shout, Highlanders, Riflemen, Sikhs, Dogras, Guides, Bedfordshires, Scottish Borderers, leaped forward and carried the position at the point of the bayonet, pursuing the enemy down the further side of the hill as far as the village of the Khar. The enemy's total loss was estimated at about 1500 men, while ours amounted to seventy killed and wounded.

Some of the enemy displayed the most reckless bravery, individual swordsmen and standard-bearers charging madly forward, and seeming to bear a charmed life until at last a bullet found its mark. Sometimes a dozen or more would start off on their wild career simultaneously, the last man left alive, undaunted by the fate of his comrades, holding on till he also fell, perhaps within a few yards of our line. I remember one leader in particular who, sword in hand, urged on his men from the roof of a hut. Standing out very clearly against the sky-line he drew upon himself a tremendous fusillade, but although evidently hit several times it was long before he was struck down never to rise again.

The so-called road leading up the pass was abominably bad even for pack animals, and many of the troops did not receive their supplies till next morning. The Brigade Staff came off no better, and we lay down to sleep supperless. Unknown to me till daylight appeared, there were several of the enemy's dead within a few feet of the spot where I happened to lie—a proof of the haste with which he had fled, as his custom is to carry his dead away.

Next day the 1st Brigade took the lead, and after descending from the pass was assailed near Khar by several thousand tribesmen streaming past its right flank from the Shakot and Mora Passes. We had a stiff little fight, which was brought to a successful conclusion by the charge of a squadron of the Guides cavalry. Coming round the end of a spur, the squadron suddenly discovered between one and two thousand of the enemy in the open, and without a moment's hesitation it galloped into them, driving them back helter-skelter into the hills. Next morning there was no sign of an enemy anywhere.

Supplies again failed to arrive till late in the evening, although another road up the Malakand had been found. On this occasion the Brigadier thought that better arrangements for dinner ought to have been made by our cook— a native—and he was accordingly called to account for his neglect. The result was most unfortunate, for during the night he decamped across the frontier, and next morning we found ourselves without a cook of any kind. What happened afterwards I cannot say, as the same day I was transferred to the 2nd Brigade, which was now ordered to resume the lead.

Three days later the Swat river, half a mile or more in width, was forced. It was unbridged, but fordable in certain places. The enemy, reinforced by a contingent sent by

Umra Khan, had so disposed his 5000 men as effectively to command the ford where it was expected the passage would be attempted. Seeing this, the Brigadier—Waterfield —ordered the 11th Bengal Lancers, a regiment with a deservedly fine reputation, the equally fine regiment of Guides cavalry, and the 15th Sikhs to cross by a ford higher up. After what had happened at Khar, the prospect of the dreaded cavalry falling upon their flank and rear was too much for the defenders, who at once evacuated their position and their retirement quickly became a demoralised flight, the cavalry pursuing them for several miles. The terrifying effect produced by the cavalry in the actions at Khar and the Swat was quite extraordinary and the news of it spread through the country-side for many miles. Unaccustomed for the most part to horses, and having exaggerated notions as to the power of mounted troops, the enemy never really recovered his morale, and the stubborn resistance he offered at the Malakand was not again encountered.

After the passage of the Swat I was sent on with the Guides cavalry to reconnoitre the route leading over the Laram Range by the Katgola Pass, and thence to Sado on the Panjkora river. This was the greatest obstacle we had yet met, though it was fordable by all arms on the day of my arrival. Two days later, when the 2nd Brigade had come up, I was directed to proceed with the cavalry to reconnoitre the Jandol valley towards Umra Khan's headquarters near Miankilai. We were warmly sniped from the neighbouring hills, and as there was evidence to show that large numbers of the tribesmen were collecting near Miankilai, we returned to Sado after completing a reconnaissance of about eight miles and obtaining the required information regarding the enemy's movements and the practicability of the route. In the morning we had forded the Panjkora fairly easily, but when we returned in the evening it had risen considerably, the current had become very swift, and several horses were lost in recrossing.

Next morning it had become quite unfordable and equally impracticable for swimming, and no further progress was possible pending the construction of a bridge or the discovery of another ford. As the latter could not be found, the former had to be taken in hand. A rough footbridge was completed on the 12th, and the Guides infantry were sent across to hold the bridgehead, but during the night the river again rose, washing the bridge away and leaving the Guides cut off from the remainder of the force. A suspension bridge was then commenced, and took four days to complete.

Meanwhile, on the 13th, the Guides went beyond the bridgehead in order to burn certain villages which had been harbouring " snipers " engaged in firing on our working parties, and when about to return the battalion was attacked by some 5000 tribesmen who had collected together on hearing of its isolated position. For some time the situation appeared critical, the enemy coming on in the most determined way, but the Guides splendidly upheld their reputation, and, moving as steadily as if on parade, slowly fought their way back to their entrenchments and there came under the shelter of the guns and troops posted on the left bank of the river. Unfortunately the battalion lost its gallant commanding officer, Lieutenant-Colonel Battye. A small reinforcement was sent across on rafts, as it was expected that the enemy would renew the attack during the night. It later transpired that this was his intention, but the discharge of some star shells by a mountain battery so alarmed him that he drew off, and no further molestation was attempted.

While waiting for the bridge to be completed I was sent with a squadron of the 11th Bengal Lancers and half a battalion of the Buffs to reconnoitre the left bank of the Panjkora up to Robat, being accompanied by that fine soldier and splendid horseman Roddy Owen. When hostilities first broke out Roddy was stationed at Quetta, and like many other officers he at once applied for employment. As this was not given he asked for and obtained ten days' leave, and of this he took advantage to join the Relief Force as a newspaper correspondent. When his leave expired the Simla authorities issued instructions directing him to return to India, but Roddy contrived on one plea or another to stay where he was, and at last Simla gave up the contest. He remained with the Force till the conclusion of the campaign, and afterwards made a journey from Chitral to the Pamirs. This was not a bad performance on the basis of ten days' leave, and was typical of Roddy's methods of getting his own way.

On the 17th the cavalry and 3rd Brigade, now in front, crossed the Panjkora, dispersed a miscellaneous gathering of the enemy in the Jandol valley, and on arrival at Miankilai learnt that Umra Khan had thrown his hand in and fled to Afghanistan. A day or two later the unlucky Sher Afzul, with 1500 followers, was captured by our ally the Khan of Dir. He was subsequently sent to India.

Pushing on from Miankilai, the advanced troops crossed the Janbatai Pass (7400 feet high) on the 19th, and arrived at Dir on the 21st, where news was received that the siege of Chitral had been raised three days before. This was the natural corollary of the successful advance of the Relief Force, and the main object of the campaign had thus been achieved within about a month of the date on which the order for mobilisation was given. From the first the enemy had been out-matched by our superior armament and organisation, but we had, apart from him, many difficulties to contend against, and the commander and his troops well deserved the high praise officially bestowed upon them.

The Gilgit detachment, which reached Chitral on the 20th April, had also achieved a great triumph. Composed entirely of native troops, with the exception of a handful of British officers, it had marched 220 miles through the highest mountain system in the world, when the country was inflamed with news of the rebellion, and at a season when the weather was still severe and the passes deep in snow, one of those traversed being 12,400 high.

Finally, neither the efforts of the Relief Force, nor those of the Gilgit detachment, could have availed but for the gallantry and cheerful endurance displayed by the invested garrison in holding out for forty-seven days until help arrived. In this case, again, all the troops were natives except a few British officers, and the siege will always rank as one of the finest episodes in the annals of the Indian Army. As to its intrepid commander, Captain Townshend, I imagine that he learnt many things which proved useful to him twenty years later in the still more famous siege of Kut-el-Amara.

Chitral being relieved and the enemy having dispersed, nothing remained for the Relief Force to do except to send on from Dir sufficient troops to consolidate order in the country, and open up permanent means of communication with India. The route followed by them presented extraordinary difficulties, especially at the Lowarai Pass (10,450 feet high and covered with snow), and required extensive improvements before transport animals could use it.

While this final movement was taking place I was ordered to report on the practicability of the road leading from Dir down the Panjkora to Robat, the place to which I had already made a reconnaissance up the same river from Sado. A company of the 4th Gurkhas was given me as escort, and the Khan of Dir provided two guides, who were said to be specially trustworthy men, one of them being known as the " Kazi." For the first two marches they were everything that could be desired, and most helpful both as to their knowledge of the country and in obtaining local supplies of food, but later they were not so satisfactory.

I was suffering from dysentery at the time, and on the third day's march gave my sword to the " Kazi " to carry as I was unable to bear its weight round my waist. Being mounted, I gradually forged ahead of the escort, and was followed by the two guides only. Suddenly, and to my utter amazement, I was twice fired at from behind, and could not imagine what had happened. Looking round I saw the " Kazi " rising from his knee, and in the act of throwing aside the smoking 12-bore breech-loader which he had been carrying since we left Dir, preparatory to achieving with his sword—or rather *my* sword—what he had failed to accomplish with his gun, for although he could not have been more than ten yards away when he fired he had missed me with both barrels. He was yelling with the fury of a madman, and I realised that he had become " ghazi "—a religious fanatic—not an uncommon occurrence on the frontier. The goat-track on the steep hillside along which I was riding would not permit me to move to the right or left, or to turn the pony round so as to face my man, and the only alternative was to dismount. In doing this I stumbled and fell, the result being that I was in a half-sitting position when the " Kazi " arrived at close quarters and proceeded to slash wildly at me. As there was neither time nor opportunity to draw my revolver while this vigorous sword practice was taking place, I could only scramble to my feet and floor the fellow with my fist. Just as I did this I observed that the other so-called guide, kneeling on one knee a few yards away, was waiting his opportunity to fire the moment he could do so without hitting his companion. Whilst my attention was distracted in this way the " Kazi " jumped up and the pair of them made off. Pulling out the revolver at last, I brought down the " Kazi " as he was in the act of flying up the hillside, and then I remembered no more till the Gurkhas arrived, they having hastened to the spot on hearing the sound of firing. They picked up the " Kazi," who had been hard hit but not killed, and a native hospital orderly did his best temporarily to patch up my wounds, which were later officially classed as " severe " but were not really serious.

We then commenced the return march to Dir, where the " Kazi," who turned out to be an adherent of Umra Khan, in whose service he had previously been, was tried by court-martial and sentenced to be shot and his body burnt. The sentence was carried out by a sergeant and six men of a Highland battalion—I forget which. I thought at the time, and still think, that however indifferent a marksman the " Kazi " may have been, he could not possibly have missed me with both barrels at so short a range but for the direct intervention of Providence.

On becoming fit to travel I was sent back to India, and my connection with the Chitral Relief Force terminated. A " mention in despatches " and the award of the Distinguished Service Order, then a rather rare decoration, tended to alleviate, but did not entirely dispel, the mortification I felt at not having put up a more finished fight and accounted for both my assailants. I was chaffed a good deal at the time for having been cut about with my own sword, and for not acting up to the standard displayed at the Rawal Pindi assault-at-arms. I deserved to be chaffed.

While serving with the Relief Force I became Captain in the ordinary course of regimental promotion, and was unusually lucky in reaching that rank in less than seven years after being commissioned.

After resuming duty in the Intelligence Branch at the end of the summer of 1895 I began to realise, as a result of a talk with my friend Mason, the necessity of graduating at the Staff College, for without that qualification my future professional advancement was doubtful. About thirty officers were admitted to the college annually, three-fourths of this number by open competition and the remainder, conditional on qualifying at the entrance examination, by selection. The examination was not very difficult, but it embraced many subjects—mathematics, military engineering, military topography, tactics, military history, strategy, military geography, military administration, military law, and a knowledge of two foreign languages, of which one must be either French or German.

As a rule competition was very keen, and therefore prospective candidates usually spent several weeks and even months at one of the cramming establishments in London which specialised in this branch of military education. As there were no such establishments in India, officers stationed in that country invariably took leave to England so as to obtain the help they needed. I could not get leave, nor could I afford to throw up my staff appointment in order to return home, and consequently there was nothing for it but to do without expert assistance.

I decided to take Hindustani, which I knew fairly well, as one of the two languages ; knowing nothing of German I selected French as the second, and, knowing very little of it, I enlisted the aid of a Frenchwoman who happened to be employed at Simla. My wife also took a hand in this subject, and in addition showed exemplary patience in hearing me recite the propositions of Euclid. For mathematics in general I procured the help of a local schoolmaster ; and, lastly, I received many useful hints from Lieutenant (now Major-General) Holman, who was also on the headquarters staff and was himself working for the examination preparatory to going home to complete his studies. For the rest I had to rely on my own resources, and they were rather a broken reed, for such meagre knowledge as I then possessed about some of the subjects was entirely self-acquired. Ten months were available in which to prepare for the examination, and I was oppressed with the thought that I had but the one chance of getting into the college, because by the time the next examination came round I would be over the regulation age for admission.

It will be understood from all this that the period of preparation was neither easy nor devoid of anxiety, but by rising regularly every morning between four and five o'clock, in winter as in summer, I was able to get through a large amount of spade work, crude and ill-directed though it might be, before going to office for the day. Progress was naturally both slow and doubtful, for having no one to guide me I approached my tasks by the most roundabout way, and when completed there was often no certainty that the results were correct.

In due course the fateful examination, lasting ten days, arrived, and perseverance then had its reward. I qualified in all subjects, and as I just missed securing one of the competitive vacancies Sir George White came to the rescue and recommended me for one of the vacancies to be filled by selection. Lord Wolseley, the Commander-in-Chief at home, approved, and in December 1896 I started with my wife and five months' old child for England. The voyage was very unpleasant, rough weather prevailing almost continuously. The nurse was the worst sailor of the party, next to myself, and succumbed as soon as we started, and in our cabin ! Fortunately the man-servant of the officer occupying the adjoining cabin was an obliging person, and undertook to look after the child during my wife's absence at meals. He had once been a prize-fighter !

My eight years' experience in India prompts me to say that a certain amount of service in this great dependency is an essential part of the education of every young officer. It broadens his views ; brings him into contact with the native troops of the Indian army, by the side of whom he may sooner or later be called upon to fight ; and affords him opportunities for seeing training conducted under more practical conditions than usually prevail in England. On the other hand, if it is unduly prolonged physical energy may deteriorate, with a corresponding loss in military capacity, and there will also be a tendency to become antiquated and stereotyped in method, owing to the difficulty of keeping pace with the development of military ideas in Europe. Modern means of communication have helped to diminish these dangers, but they have not entirely removed them and never can, and everything possible should therefore be done by those in authority to ensure that the army in India maintains close touch with the army at home. In principle this is now generally recognised, but in practice the recognition is not so apparent, and not a few obstructive prejudices and old-fashioned notions must be uprooted before the two armies can be brought into that intimate relationship which Imperial efficiency demands.

MAP ILLUSTRATING JOURNEY TO PAMIRS 1894
AND CHITRAL EXPEDITION 1895.

Scale 1 Inch = 45 Miles.

50 40 30 20 10 0 50 100

Russian Sphere of Influence ....
British .....Do..........Do ....
Under direct administration of Government of India.................

CHAPTER VI

STUDENT AT THE STAFF COLLEGE

Colonel Hildyard—His views on the education of officers—Nature of the
Staff College course—Colonel Henderson—Lord Roberts' appreciation of him—First year's work at the college—Go to France to learn
the language—Second year's work—Visit to battlefields of 1870 war
—Visit the Meuse Valley and Belgian Ardennes—Umpire at army
manœuvres—Sir H. Brackenbury—Inspection of Staff College by
Lord Wolseley—Value of Staff College training.

I JOINED the Staff College in January 1897 and was, I
believe, the first officer promoted from the ranks to enter
it as a student, though others have done so since. The
Commandant was Colonel (afterwards Lieutenant-General
Sir) H. Hildyard, Colonel (now Lieutenant-General Sir)
H. Miles succeeding him in 1898. Up to 1893, when
Hildyard assumed command, too much importance seems
to have been attached to the mere accumulation of knowledge and to preparation for written examinations, and the
capacity of the students on leaving the college was estimated
mainly by the number of marks gained in these examinations.
Everybody knows that the best performer on paper is not
always—one might say is not usually—the most proficient
in the field, and as Hildyard held strong views on the
impossibility of producing or discovering the best officers
by means of written examinations alone he gave the
curriculum a more practical character. In order to test
their powers of application the students were constantly
employed in the study of concrete questions regarding
organisation and administration, and in solving strategical
and tactical problems both in quarters and out of doors.
Hildyard proposed the entire abolition of written examinations by outside examiners, and although this was not
sanctioned the examinations were restricted to the first

year. Since then the students have been classified at the end of the second year according to the quality of their work throughout the course, and to the opinion formed by the Instructional Staff as to the likelihood of their becoming capable leaders and staff officers.

There were five military instructors or " professors," as they were then called—one for strategy and tactics, one for artillery and fortifications, one for administrative duties, and two for topography, as well as two for languages— French and German. Topography was the subject which the students liked least, and undoubtedly a good deal of time and temper were expended in making intricate " scales " which would never be required on service, in learning to draw the conventional signs for trees, churches, public-houses, and other topographical features, according to scale, and in chasing five-feet contours round the undulations of ground near the college, none of which were more than a hundred feet above the general level.

This seeming waste of effort was not without excuse, for some officers had but a hazy notion of how to make or read a map, and were not much surer of themselves in regard to the working of the magnetic compass. All this has been changed by having a better system of military education from the beginning, and the cadets at Sandhurst and Woolwich are now as proficient as were many of the students at the Staff College twenty-five years ago.

The professor of strategy and tactics was Lieutenant-Colonel G. F. Henderson, the author of *Stonewall Jackson*, *Spicheren*, and other military books and essays. " Hender," as he was familiarly known to us, was a past-master in his work, and his lovable and unselfish companionship was of itself a moral and professional education of life-long benefit. He was devoted to his pupils and, as Hildyard wrote of him some years later, " There was no paper, however crude, wherein he did not notice points for encouragement towards renewed effort ; so there was no paper, however complete, to which his practical and well-thought-out remarks did not add value. To him it was a labour of love, and each memoir, good or indifferent, received the same measure of attention from him."

About the time I joined the college Henderson first became the intimate friend of Lord Roberts, who tells us that he " formed a very high opinion of his abilities " and, like many others, " succumbed to the spell of his fascinating personality." The characteristically warm-hearted memoir which the Field-Marshal wrote in after years as a foreword to the posthumous publication of Henderson's *Science of War*, is perhaps the best appreciation extant. It is much too long to reproduce here, but I may quote the following :

The affectionate tributes to Henderson's memory by his many friends are a testimony to his pure and stainless character. Blessed with a cheerful temperament, he brightened the lives of all with whom he was associated, and his letters display a spirit of playful tenderness towards those whom he loved, which is most attractive. Generous and thoughtful for others, he took no thought for himself, and only valued money for what it might have enabled him to do for those who needed his help.

The influence of such a man must bear good fruit, and the more widely his writings are read, and the more closely his teachings are followed, the more successful will be our would-be commanders, and the better it will be for England when again she is forced to go to war.

That the prophecy contained in the last sentence was well fulfilled, the reader will, I think, agree when I say that amongst the students who passed through Henderson's hands between 1892 and 1899 were Haig, Allenby, and scores of others whose names became household words in the Great War; and all these officers would, I am sure, readily admit that such successes as attended their leadership were largely due to the sound instruction and inspiring counsel which they received from their old tutor some twenty years or so before. Of the different causes which are alleged to have given us the victory over Germany, not one should be assigned a more prominent place than the influence and teaching of Henderson at the Staff College.

Having passed into the college without the help of a crammer I was anxious as to how my work there would compare with that of the other officers, and so I told the commandant at the first interview I had with him after joining. His encouraging reply was that the lack of this form of education need not necessarily be a handicap, as " We do not want any cramming here ; we want officers to absorb, not to cram " ; and except in a few insignificant details, which I soon made good, I never felt at a disadvantage because of being differently equipped at the start from my contemporaries.

The first year's work was mainly of an elementary nature, and for the most part—though not entirely—was interesting and practical, and it formed a useful foundation for the more advanced studies of the second year. It was compulsory to " pass " in either French or German, and on the advice of our excellent French professor, M. Deshumbert, whom we all adored, I spent the summer vacation of two months with a family in France, French being the language I had selected.

On crossing over to France I left Newhaven at midnight, intending to embark on the boat going to Caen, where it was due to arrive about eight o'clock next morning. To my surprise I woke at four o'clock to find that the boat had already reached port, and then discovered that I had carelessly gone aboard the boat for Dieppe, which left Newhaven at the same hour as the one for Caen, where my bicycle and luggage, having been registered in London, had of course gone.

It was a great tax on my limited knowledge of French to explain to the ticket-collector why, having a ticket for Caen, I had come to Dieppe. I afterwards spent some ten hours in travelling across country by a very indifferent railway route, changing trains no fewer than six times, to the port where my belongings had gone and which was quite near to my destination—the small provincial town of Vire. I learnt more French that day than at any time during my two months in the country, as the " Pasteur " with whom I stayed and studied did not put in an appearance until *déjeuner*, and even. then was apt to be drowsy except when roused by an objectionable habit of coughing. Another thing I remember about the visit is that there was no bath in the house, and it was only after diligent search in the town that one was at last procured from a shop which dealt in antiques !

At the end of the year I " passed " in French, missing the "interpretership" by six marks out of the six hundred and twenty required to qualify. For this I had to wait till the following year. All the other examinations were successfully negotiated, as indeed they ought to be, for they were not difficult. Of the examiners who came to the college on this occasion was an officer who had unsuccessfully competed at the entrance examination the previous year—an incident which caused us much amusement, seeing that we, who had succeeded in securing vacancies, were being examined by one who had failed to do so. He appreciated the humorous side of the matter as much as we did, and I should add that no one doubted his competence to examine us in the particular subject for which the War Office had appointed him.

Early the following summer the senior division—as the officers in their second year are called—made the customary visit to the principal battlefields of the 1870 war—Woerth, Spicheren, Vionville, and Gravelotte—under the guidance of Henderson. These visits enabled us to picture on the ground itself the operations which took place, and to grasp the lessons they taught far better than could be done by merely reading about them.

When visiting the battlefield of Woerth we stayed at Niederbronn, a small spa prettily situated in the Vosges. It was much frequented by the Germans in summer, and by German officers from Bitche and other neighbouring places. The hotel proprietor, now dead, was a French Alsatian. He told us much about the French retreat from Woerth, which passed through Niederbronn, and was far from being in love with his new masters, or they with him. It was perhaps deemed politic that his daughter should marry a German, but the arrangement has since been badly upset by the reversion of Niederbronn to the French, and madame gave me the impression that she was painfully aware of the fact when I went there two years ago.

In company with Captain (now Lieut.-General Sir) G. Barrow of the Indian Cavalry I left England some days in

advance, in order to see certain places of interest before joining the main party at Metz.   We first went to Waterloo and
Ligny, and afterwards spent a few days in the Belgian
Ardennes and Meuse valley, which was already recognised
as a probable line of operations in the event of war between
Germany and France.   The forts d'arrêt at Liége and
Namur—twelve at the former and nine at the latter—had
been constructed some years before with the object of
blocking, or at any rate of temporarily checking, an advance
by this line.

One night we stayed at Marche, a small Belgian town
south of Huy, where we experienced some difficulty in
finding accommodation, and the hotel where we eventually
found quarters could only produce one room.   What was
still more inconvenient, the room contained but one bed,
which the landlady wished Barrow and myself to share,
and she apparently thought we were making an unnecessary
fuss about a very small matter when we insisted upon having
a bed each.   To add to our troubles during this day, or
rather to Barrow's, he lost his only pipe, which in the
case of any one but him would have meant the loss of
temper also.

In September I was detailed with other officers of the
senior division for employment on the umpire staff at
the army manœuvres, which took place in the vicinity of
Salisbury Plain.   The opposing forces consisted of an army
corps each, respectively commanded by the Duke of
Connaught and Sir Redvers Buller, this being the first
time for twenty-six years that manœuvres had been held.
At the end of the first day I was sent for by Sir Henry
Brackenbury, who was chief umpire of one side, and with
whom I had become acquainted when at Simla.   He told me
that he was dissatisfied with the way in which the umpire
duties were being performed, as he was unable to obtain
from the cavalry the early and complete reports regarding the
operations which he required ; and he directed me to leave
the cavalry regiment to which I was then attached and undertake the duty of procuring for him the information he wanted.
How I got it he said he did not care, but that he " must
have it, and have it in time."   There was no reason why

he should not, for it was simply a question of organisation, and of putting more life and activity into certain individuals on the umpire staff, who were inclined to look upon the manœuvres as a kind of glorified picnic in which they could share as much or as little as they desired. I introduced the necessary organisation, took effective, albeit somewhat disagreeable, steps to " get a move on " amongst the individuals mentioned, and it then became quite easy to meet Brackenbury's wishes.

I thought no more of the matter until he sent for me on the night the manœuvres terminated, when, taking my arm, he walked me up and down between the rows of tents for about half an hour, making in the course of our conversation some complimentary remarks about the assistance I had given him, and finished by saying that if at any time I stood in need of help he would gladly give it. Some years later I did need it, and he was then as good as his word. Like most men in high positions he had his detractors, and was thought by some people to be harsh and overbearing. It is true, I think, that he did not suffer fools gladly, but he always struck me as being genuinely kind-hearted, and he was rightly regarded as one of the most capable and progressive soldiers of his time.

About the middle of December, Lord Wolseley made his usual annual inspection of the college, saying a few encouraging words to each officer in turn, and expressing his appreciation of their work as reported to him by the commandant. This was the last parade for those of us who belonged to the senior division, and we afterwards dispersed to the four quarters of the globe, pleased to feel, or rather hoping, that we had gained the coveted letters P.S.C. (passed Staff College)—a matter that would not be known to us for certain till a few weeks later. But we had also a feeling of regret, for we had invariably received the utmost consideration and assistance from the commandant and his staff, while the students with whom we had been associated were, as always, some of the best fellows in the service.

We had been worked hard, but plenty of time was allowed for recreation, and, like all Staff College graduates, had many happy as well as amusing recollections of cricket, hockey, and especially of the drag. In bidding good-bye to each other none of us imagined that in less than a year we would again be working together, and putting into practice on the South African veld the lessons we had learned from " Hender " and the other professors at Camberley. Rightly or wrongly, we felt ourselves capable of competing with whatever task the future might have in store for us ; and the same self-confidence would not have been lacking had we known that in less than sixteen years some of us would be among the chief actors in the greatest drama the world has ever seen—the Great War.

This good opinion of ourselves should not be classed as conceit, for no soldier possessing an atom of sense, or having the remotest conception of the difficulties and uncertainties which attend the conduct of war, will dare to boast, even to himself, of what he thinks he can do. It was merely an illustration of the saying that " knowledge is power," and showed that the training received by the Staff College officer gives him a measure of self-reliance which he probably did not possess before, and which, if appropriately used, should be of great value to him in the future.

The Staff College does not aspire to make wise men out of fools, or to achieve any other impossibilities, and, like other educational institutions, it has had its failures. It can, however, and does, make good men better, broaden their views, strengthen their powers of reasoning, improve their judgment, and in general lay the foundations of a useful military career. Further, the benefits of the course are by no means confined to the lectures the students are given, or to the instructional exercises in which they take part, for in addition there is a smartening friction with other brains, and officers are enabled to rub shoulders with others of their own standing with whom they may have to work later in life. Haig, Allenby, Murray, Milne, Capper, Haking, Barrow, Forestier-Walker, and others who filled important posts in the Great War were amongst my contemporaries, and this personal acquaintance was very useful to me, as no doubt it was to them, when I was Chief of the General Staff in France in 1915, and still more so when

Chief of the Imperial General Staff from the end of 1915 to the beginning of 1918.

Again, at the college are to be found representatives of practically every branch of the British and Indian armies and the forces of the Overseas Dominions. There are few parts of the Empire that have not been visited at one time or another by some member of the staff or by one of the students, and the interchange of the various experiences acquired is most valuable.

Another advantage of the course is that the students are taught the same basic principles of strategy and tactics, and are accustomed to employ the same methods of administration. It is necessary in any business that the men responsible for its administration should abide by the same rules, follow the same procedure, and be fully acquainted with the best means for ensuring smoothness and despatch; and nowhere is the necessity greater than in the business of war, where friction, delay, and misapprehension are fraught with so many possibilities of mischief. It is only by the establishment of a sound system with which all officers are thoroughly familiar that these rocks can be avoided. As an illustration of the benefit conferred by a common school of training, I may mention that from the time Maude took over the chief command in Mesopotamia to the day of his death, and although all communication between us was conducted by telegraph, the local situation being difficult, precarious, and changing, not a single misunderstanding occurred between him as Commander-in-Chief and myself as Chief of the Imperial General Staff, nor did we ever fear that one would occur.

The same good results were obtained in similar circumstances in my dealings with Milne in Macedonia, Allenby in Egypt, and Monro in India, and I believe these officers were as satisfied at their end of the wire as I was at mine. In the case of Haig the exchange of views and the transmission of the War Cabinet's instructions were comparatively easy, since we could meet at frequent intervals and discuss matters verbally; but here, also, the work of both of us was facilitated by our Staff College training, and, as with all the other commanders I have mentioned, there was never, so far as I know, any material difference of opinion between us in regard to the main principles to be observed in order to win the war. That the mutual agreement and excellent comradeship established between Staff College graduates during the twenty years previous to 1914 were of inestimable value to the Empire throughout the Great War is, in my humble belief, beyond contradiction.

Lest I should be misunderstood I hasten to add that no one more fully recognises than myself that there are many good and even brilliant soldiers who are not Staff College graduates. They deserve, indeed, the greater credit for what they have achieved, because of the drawbacks against which they have had to contend. I know that they have felt the weight of these drawbacks, for they have told me so, and regretted that they had not enjoyed the benefit of two years' study at the college, and the equally beneficial exchange of ideas with men who, like themselves, meant to rise in their profession. I would therefore warn all young officers who wish to make their mark and serve their country well, that they may one day incur a considerable handicap if they fail to take advantage of the assistance which is afforded by the Staff College course.

CHAPTER VII

ON THE INTELLIGENCE STAFF, WAR OFFICE

ON leaving the Staff College officers usually return to regimental duty for at least a year before being employed on the staff, so that they may again be brought into touch with troops, but occasionally the rule is not observed. It was not in my case, for in order to meet the temporary want of an officer with staff experience in India I was sent direct to the Intelligence Branch of the War Office, then located at 29 Queen Anne's Gate, and presided over by Major-General Sir John Ardagh.

When first formed in 1873 it was a branch of the Quartermaster-General's department ; later it was placed under the Adjutant-General ; and was, when I joined it, more or less under the Commander-in-Chief, Lord Wolseley. It had a staff of about sixteen officers and, with the " Mobilisation

Section " of three or four officers, was the only semblance of a General Staff then in existence. The Mobilisation Section had originally been under the Director of Military Intelligence, was afterwards absorbed by the Adjutant-General's department, and then, like the Intelligence Branch, came under the Commander-in-Chief. Thus it will be seen that the two branches had been constantly tossed over from one high official to another, apparently in accordance with the predominant view or personality of the moment.

The Intelligence Branch was responsible for the collection and collation of military information regarding foreign countries, but it was not the recognised duty of the branch, or of any other, scientifically to study the information so collected and make it the basis of our own requirements. This basis had been fixed in a memorandum by Mr. Stanhope of the 1st June 1888, and it still held the field. According to it our army requirements had for their object the support of the civil power in the United Kingdom, the provision of men for the garrison of India and our fortresses and coaling stations at home and abroad, and, in addition, the ability to mobilise for home defence two army corps of regular troops, one army corps of regulars and militia combined, and the auxiliary forces not allotted to these three corps. Subject to these considerations, and their financial obligations, a further aim was to be able to send abroad, in case of necessity, two complete army corps, but, said the memorandum, " It will be distinctly understood that the probability of the employment of an army corps in the field in any European war is sufficiently improbable to make it the primary duty of the military authorities to organise efficiently for the defence of this country." To Mr. Stanhope's instruction regarding the " improbable probability " of the employment of even one army corps in any European war may therefore fairly be attributed the fact that our mobilisation arrangements dealt principally with home defence, and that broad military plans essential for the defence of the Empire as a whole received no adequate treatment in the War Office of that period.

Two years after the date of Mr. Stanhope's memorandum, a majority of the Hartington Commission recommended the creation of a new War Office department under a " Chief of the Staff," who was to devote himself entirely to collecting information, to thinking out great military problems, and to advising the Secretary of State for War on matters of " general military policy." Sir Henry Campbell-Bannerman, one of the Commissioners and Secretary of State for War from 1892 to 1895, dissented from the recommendation, and expressed the view that the new department was " unnecessary," and that although it existed in continental countries " those countries differ fundamentally from Great Britain " in that they were " concerned in watching the military conditions of their neighbours, in detecting points of weakness and strength, and in planning possible operations in possible wars against them. But in this country there is in truth no room for a ' general military policy ' in this larger and more ambitious sense of the phrase. We have no designs against our European neighbours." It seems to have been overlooked, or was too inconvenient to be admitted, that these same neighbours might have designs against us, at any rate in the future even if they had none then, and that the security of the Empire demanded that the Government should be furnished with considered military opinions on which to frame their plans of defence.

Sir Henry Campbell-Bannerman was at a loss to know where the new department " could find an adequate field in the circumstances of this country," and was " afraid that while there would be no use for the proposed office there might be in it some danger to our best interests. All that is in fact required for our purposes can be amply obtained by an adequately-equipped Intelligence Branch which, under the direction of the Adjutant-General, could collect all necessary information, and place it at the disposal, not of one officer or department alone, but of all the military heads, whose duty it would be to advise the Minister."

The above references to the Hartington Commission are not made for the purpose of condemning Sir Henry Campbell-Bannerman, but rather to illustrate the views then held by prominent public men in regard to preparation for war. To do the Hartington Commissioners justice I should add that all of them, except Sir Henry Campbell-Bannerman, agreed with the recommendation mentioned, but, on the other hand, the opinions he expressed must have been shared by many persons in both political parties, for, although there was a change of Government in 1895, nothing was done to introduce the system recommended until the necessity for it was forced upon us by the costly experience of the South African war. The consequences of this delay were set forth in the " Report of the War Office (Reconstitution) Committee, 1904," where it was stated that " if the recommendations of the majority of the Hartington Commission had not been ignored, the country would have been saved the loss of many thousands of lives and of many millions of pounds subsequently sacrificed in the war."

There was, moreover, no superior authority specially charged with the co-ordination of the different State departments concerned in war preparations, and in this connection it was stated in the evidence given before the Hartington Commission that " no combined plan of operations for the defence of the Empire in any given contingency has ever been worked out or decided upon by the two departments " (*i.e.*, War Office and Admiralty). The nearest approach to a superior authority of the kind required were the Defence Committee of the Cabinet and the Colonial Defence Committee. But the former, to the best of my knowledge, seldom met except when an emergency had already arisen ; it had no permanent nucleus and therefore had little or no continuity of policy or action ; and for these and other reasons it could not, and did not, properly consider the many complex military problems calling for solution.

The Colonial Defence Committee, having a succession of very capable secretaries, including the present Lord Sydenham, performed an extraordinary amount of valuable work —of which we reaped the benefit in the Great War—but its activities were mainly confined to the colonies, and, being composed of subordinate officials, it had no power to *decide* the questions with which it dealt. It could only make " recommendations," which were afterwards submitted for the approval of the departmental ministers concerned, and, as might be expected, this was not always given, while at best it took days, weeks, or even months to obtain.

The danger incurred by all this appalling want of foresight was the more serious because the other Great Powers were busily engaged in improving their General Staff machinery, various parts of Africa and China were in process of annexation or exploitation, several international boundaries and treaties affecting our military interests were in dispute, and our foreign diplomatic relations were in more than one case the reverse of cordial. Hence, while we may wish that the South African war had never been fought, we cannot be too thankful that its exposure of our defects compelled the adoption in 1904 (see page 136) of those reforms in our military system which, if they had not been made when they were, would have greatly aggravated the disadvantages under which we entered upon the war with Germany in 1914. It is perhaps not too much to say that the Empire was saved from disaster by the small community of Boer farmers who, a few years before, had fought against us.

On joining the Intelligence Branch I was posted to the section dealing with Asia and Russia in Europe. My Simla experience made me feel at home with Asiatic affairs, but I was strange to European Russia and ignorant of its language, for although before leaving the Staff College I had passed the French interpretership examination and made fair progress in German, Russian was a sealed book to me and still is. Captain (now Brigadier-General) Waters, the head of the section, was an accomplished Russian linguist, and being personally acquainted with the country he took charge of it himself, consigning to me the care of the non-Russian part of Asia.

After being employed in this manner for three months my "temporary" appointment to the staff was made permanent, and I was posted as Staff Captain in the Colonial Section, my immediate chief in this case being Captain (now Lieutenant-General Sir) E. Altham. From him I learnt much about the resources, administration, and defence of the different parts of the Empire of which I knew little or nothing before and which was valuable to me in after years. In many respects I was his debtor, but his handwriting was amongst the worst ever seen, except my own, and I frequently had to summon his confidential clerk to decipher the hieroglyphics which in the course of business he inflicted upon me.

Our Colonial Empire comprised some forty distinct and independent governments, and in addition to these organised states there were a number of dependencies under the dominion of the Sovereign which had no formed administrations, as well as large territories controlled by certain British Companies, and the protectorates, such as Somaliland and British East Africa, under the supervision of the Foreign Office. All military questions concerning these possessions found their way into my section, their number being exceeded only by the variety of their character. They included the training, equipment, administration, organisation, and employment of the local forces so far as these matters were referred for the advice or decision of the Home Government, and as the forces were still in a rudimentary stage such references were far more common than they now are.

Complicated questions regarding the armament and garrisons of coaling stations cropped up almost daily, besides a host of others relating to what was then termed Colonial Defence and is now known as Imperial Defence. One of these was the control of submarine cables in time of war, practical measures for which were then being worked out and have since proved to be of great value. The protectorates, though few in number, absorbed a great deal of our time, as they were invariably the scene of disturbances of some kind or other. Between 1896 and 1899 there must have been a dozen or more small wars in these territories, such as the Uganda mutiny and Sierra Leone rebellion, and not being equipped with personnel to deal with them the Foreign Office had constantly to ask the Intelligence Branch, as representing the War Office, for advice or information. This was not always easy to give, because so little was known about either the countries themselves, the quality and characteristics of the troops we had raised in them, or the power for mischief possessed by the hostile tribes.

The heaviest part of the work lay in South Africa, where trouble with the Transvaal had been brewing for some two years past and was daily becoming more acute. Every

Saturday the Cape mail brought us a budget of correspondence, official and private, which had to be sifted, studied, and distributed ; it was known that war-like stores were gradually being accumulated both by the Transvaal and Free State, and it was our duty to watch these as closely as conditions would allow ; special reconnaissances of main routes and strategical localities had to be initiated ; handbooks and summaries of the information obtained had to be prepared with a view to active operations ; the Cabinet had to be supplied with memoranda bearing on the military situation ; and many other matters, far too numerous to specify, called for urgent attention. Fortunately, Altham had a good knowledge of the country and was a quick worker, and while I struggled with the remainder of the Empire for which we were responsible, he dealt with the important and pressing business of South Africa. Considering the amount to be got through he achieved marvels, and this was recognised by the Royal Commission on the South African war, who pronounced the information contained in the hand-books, as well as in a " valuable " series of memoranda, to be in many respects remarkably accurate.

As everybody knows, the war lasted much longer and required far more troops than had been expected. Of the reasons for this I may mention two : the first was Mr. Stanhope's dictum that the " primary " duty of the military authorities was home defence ; the second, largely the corollary of the first, was the weakness of our military position as compared with the Boers when hostilities commenced. Throughout the long negotiations with the two Republics this disadvantage was keenly felt both by the local authorities and the War Office, but it was difficult, if not impossible, to remedy it, since to send out reinforcements and to make other necessary preparations might have destroyed all hopes of obtaining that peaceful solution which the Government desired. The position was therefore still dangerously weak when hostilities broke out on the 11th October, and in consequence we were penalised with the greatest of all handicaps in war—a bad start.

I recall the disadvantages which prevailed at the beginning, because they, more than anything else, were

H

answerable for the prolonged duration of the war. I am aware that certain people claimed in later years to have appreciated the situation correctly, and to have forecast more or less accurately the number of troops that would be required ; but I am afraid that these claims must be regarded as instances of being wise after the event. At any rate all the estimates which came to my notice at the War Office before the war, and a great many came, proved to be, with one exception, very much on the wrong side.

I am reminded of another forecast which proved to be inaccurate. At one of the many Cabinet discussions of the South African question some one apparently suggested that it would be a wise precaution to work out the probable cost involved in the event of war, and it fell to me to make the arithmetical calculation. Being furnished with the figures representing the estimated number of troops required and the time they would take in carrying out their task, I had merely to apply these and other data to the cost of previous British campaigns in somewhat similar countries, making of course due allowance for any difference there might be in the conditions. The answer to my sum was recorded on half a sheet of foolscap, and if it found its way to the Cabinet, as I suppose it did, I am sure it received a cordial welcome. What it was I shall not say—though I remember the figure well—and I would wager that no one would guess it in a dozen attempts, though it was perhaps as accurate as the estimate of the cost of any other war has ever been.

When General Sir George White was deputed in September 1899 to assume command of the troops in Natal, then being reinforced by certain units from India, Altham went with him as head of the Intelligence and I was placed in charge of the Colonial section. Another officer was appointed to fill the post I vacated, but he had not been with me more than a fortnight before he was ordered to join his battalion, which was proceeding to South Africa, and no sooner had he been followed by a new man than a further change was made for the same reason. No fewer than five different officers were given to me in this way before the end of the year, and it was under these conditions that, over and above the normal work of the section, I had to grapple with a multitude of questions for the proper treatment of which at least half a dozen General Staff Officers were required. Consequently I could but try, with the help of my ever-changing assistant, to deal with the more important matters, so far as an average sixteen-hour day would permit, and leave the remainder to look after themselves.

The rapidity with which the Boers proceeded after the outbreak of war to besiege first one place and then another, and to carry their offensive into adjacent British possessions, gave rise to much consternation amongst those whose private or commercial interests were affected. This brought to the War Office a flood of proposals from all classes of people, according to which, it was claimed, the situation could be at once retrieved and the aims of the enemy completely frustrated. All found their way to my table for examination and report, and as many of them were produced or backed by influential persons, a great deal more labour had to be devoted to answering them than they deserved. Practically all of them suffered from the defect common to other amateur prescriptions, in that while they clearly and often quite cleverly showed what it was desirable to do—a comparatively easy task—they failed to be so convincing as to how this could be done—which is never easy, especially to those responsible for doing it. The burden of responsibility makes an important difference in war, as it does in all other business calling for important decisions, and for this reason advice unaccompanied by a proper share of responsibility for execution should always be accepted with caution. My task in dealing with these proposals was made the harder because Sir John Ardagh, owing to indisposition, was not always present to back up my replies, but on the other hand I was invariably well supported by both Lord Wolseley and the Secretary of State for War, Lord Lansdowne.

Inventions with which utterly to destroy the enemy without loss to ourselves, and false reports of various devices on his part for destroying us, also arrived in large numbers, and these again, being sometimes forwarded by prominent public men, or having in them some particle of good, had to be examined and answered to the satisfaction of the authorities to whose notice they had been brought.

Another task which occupied much of my time was the preparation of a daily summary of events for the Queen, the Cabinet, and various departmental heads, showing the dispositions of the troops and the reinforcements in course of transit. Information as to these dispositions was difficult to obtain, as it always is when the military situation is unfavourable, for the local authorities themselves may not have it, and such as they have may be doubtful or unpalatable, and therefore they sometimes hesitate to forward it until it has been confirmed. Again, when information reached the War Office from the front it had to pass through rigidly prescribed channels, as in time of peace, and was often hours and sometimes days before it arrived at my table in Queen Anne's Gate, on the opposite side of St. James's Park. The Intelligence Branch was treated as a separate, and not very important, part of the War Office organisation.

The consequence was that I had to rely for my data largely upon the reports of war correspondents, which would often appear in the Press before the same information reached me officially, and sometimes the newspapers alone supplied the particular intelligence I wanted. As might be expected, the reports were not always reliable, but they served to furnish useful indications regarding events at the front, and by carefully following them day by day, and exercising due discretion as to the credibility of individual correspondents—which I was soon able to appraise—the summary proved to be remarkably correct. As it was the only document of its kind produced, the demand for it soon rose from half a dozen copies to five times that number. The accuracy of the summary, prepared in the manner described, is an illustration of the useful intelligence which can be gleaned by an enemy from a close study of his adversary's press, and it shows that the censorship of military news has greater justification than some people imagine.

December 1899 found Mafeking, Kimberley, and Lady-smith still besieged and parts of Cape Colony in rebellion, and the climax was reached in the second week of the month, popularly known as " black week," in which occurred the three reverses of Stormberg, Magersfontein, and Colenso. Then followed the despatch of Sir Redvers Buller's historic telegram on the evening of the 15th December, in which he expressed the view that he " ought to let Ladysmith go, occupy good positions for the defence of South Natal, and let time help us."

The first I knew about this telegram was at three o'clock the following afternoon, Saturday, when a member of the Government brought it in his pocket to the Intelligence Branch intending to discuss it with Sir John Ardagh before the Defence Committee of the Cabinet met at five o'clock that evening to consider what should be done. As Sir John was ill in bed I was summoned, the telegram was read over to me, and I was asked to advise. What puzzled the minister was that there should be any such great obstacle to the relief of Ladysmith as that implied by Buller's proposal to abandon the attempt. In his view the advantages of position seemed to be with us, seeing that Buller's force outside and White's force inside were together numerically superior to the Boer force in the middle ; we were the nutcrackers and the Boers were the nut, and he could not understand why they should not be promptly and completely crushed. The " nutcrackers " theory offers tempting results and has always been attractive to the layman, as well as to not a few professionals, but it happens to be one of those many operations of war which in theory seem so simple and in practice are so hard. Its successful application demands not only considerable superiority, either in numbers or morale, but also perfect timing, good intercommunication, and great determination on the part of the exterior forces and their commanders, and these are the very essentials which, in the given circumstances, are the most difficult to ensure.

I did my best to explain to the minister why this was so, but I could see that he was not altogether convinced, and when I told him that as the besieged force had only sixty days' supplies when first shut up some six weeks earlier, it could not hold out long after the end of the year unless the ordinary scale of rations had meanwhile been reduced, he ruefully observed that the prospect of the country having a happy new year was not very bright. I could not deny this, nor could I help remarking that the principal cause of all the trouble was the bad start we had made. Buller felt this as much as any one, and on the 20th of November had written : " Ever since I have been here, we have been like the man who, with a long day's work before him, overslept himself and so was late for everything all day." We had, in fact, as Lord Wolseley had said in the preceding September, " committed one of the greatest blunders in war, namely, we have given the enemy the initiative." Having made this mistake, we were now compelled to dance to the enemy's tune, and, amongst other things, transfer to Natal a large part of the field force originally destined to advance into the Free State from Cape Colony.

As it could serve no useful purpose to dwell upon reflections of this kind, I proceeded to adopt a more encouraging tone by saying that, notwithstanding the unsatisfactory outlook, there was as yet no sufficient ground for accepting Buller's suggestion to " let Ladysmith go," for it would probably be found that the garrison could hold out for a considerably longer time than that estimated on the ration basis, while its surrender must clearly have a serious military and political effect. Turning to the general situation I pointed out that our troops were dispersed in small bodies over a vast area and were acting upon no coherent or comprehensive plan, and consequently there had been a great lack of unified effort between them. Obviously, the most pressing need was a change in the High Command, since it was impossible for Buller properly to direct operations on a front extending for some 600 miles from Natal to Kimberley, to say nothing of the operations, in progress or contemplated, on the west and north sides of the enemy countries, and in addition exercise personal command over the Ladysmith Relief Force. The remedy was either to direct Buller to hand over the Natal Command to another officer, so that he might give his undivided attention to the operations as a whole, or to limit his sphere to Natal and replace him by another officer in the supreme command. The minister seemed to appreciate this argument, and after further conversation he started off for the Cabinet meeting, with the determination—greatly to his credit—of seeing the South African business through at all costs. The minister was Mr. Balfour.

What took place at the meeting is unknown to me, but the decision of the Government was to reject the proposed abandonment of Ladysmith, to provide large reinforcements, and to appoint Lord Roberts Commander-in-Chief of all troops in South Africa, Lord Kitchener to be his Chief of the Staff. So ended a somewhat memorable day in the annals of the British Empire.

On the following Monday Henderson, my old tutor at the Staff College, came to tell me that he was joining the headquarters staff of Lord Roberts as Director of Intelligence. We spent some time together considering alternative plans of campaign, and he then rejoiced my heart by saying that he intended to ask for me to go out as his assistant. Hearing no more about the matter before Lord Roberts and his staff left England on the following Saturday I sorrowfully concluded that Henderson's proposal had not been sanctioned. I had not expected that it would be, for I was the only officer at the War Office who had the situation at his fingers' ends, and could not hope that Ardagh would allow me to go away. However, on the 27th of December I was telegraphed for by Lord Roberts from Gibraltar, where he had stopped to pick up Lord Kitchener coming from Egypt, and as the order had gone forth that he was to be given everything and everybody he asked for I was duly liberated. Three days later I embarked at Southampton on the transport *Aurania*, heartily glad to escape from the depressing and uncongenial atmosphere common to official life in London in time of war.

CHAPTER VIII

ON THE HEADQUARTERS STAFF IN THE SOUTH AFRICAN WAR

Situation on arrival at Cape Town—Formation of mounted infantry—
Lord Roberts' plan of operations and measures taken to preserve
secrecy — Composition of Intelligence Staff at Headquarters—
Arrival of Headquarters at Modder river—Lord Roberts' care for
his troops—Mystifying Cronje as to the proposed line of advance—
General situation at this time—Buller asks for reinforcements—
Lord Roberts adheres to his plan—Cavalry division crosses Free
State frontier and relieves Kimberley—Pursuit of Cronje—Battle
of Paardeberg—Confusion caused by bad system of command—
Investment of Cronje—Cronje surrenders and is brought into camp
—He is sent to St. Helena—Grierson joins Headquarters—His
efforts to improve defective methods of staff work—Lord Roberts'
instructions in regard to battle of Poplar Grove—Imperfect arrangements for the battle enable Boer forces to make good their retreat—
Advance continued to Bloemfontein—Summary of events to date—
Standard of staff work and tactics inferior to strategy—Strategy
never so good again—Some reasons for this—Henderson's health
breaks down and he returns to England—He commences to write
the Official History of the War—His death in Egypt in 1903—The
soldier's difficulties in writing official histories—The advance from
Bloemfontein to Kroonstad and thence to Pretoria—Boer guerilla
warfare—Lord Roberts' plan—Hardships of march and fine spirit
of the men—Action of Diamond Hill—The advance to Middelburg
—The De Wet hunts—Recalled to the War Office—Reach rank of
Major—Promoted Brevet Lieutenant-Colonel for services in the
war.

On arrival at Cape Town on the 20th of January I found
Lord Roberts and the headquarters staff engaged in making
systematic preparations for the advance into the Free
State, and for giving the troops greater mobility than they
had hitherto possessed. This entailed a drastic change in
the normal organisation of the transport service, as well
as the provision of additional bodies of mounted men.
The latter were obtained partly by raising or expanding
local corps, and partly by forming mounted infantry battalions composed of companies drawn from line battalions.

In this way eight additional mounted infantry battalions were made up, and as an example of the conditions under which some of them were formed I may mention that the infantry battalion on board the ship which conveyed me was met on reaching port by a staff officer with orders to despatch one company that evening to De Aar, where it would find horses and saddlery and thereupon would become a mounted infantry company.

Three weeks later this same company, with others equally untrained, was sent forward to meet the enemy, and as something went wrong with the orders the first day's march did not begin till seven o'clock in the evening. Many of the men crossed a horse that day for the first time in their lives, and in the darkness of the night the horses often stumbled, many of the riders fell, and when camp was reached at daylight next morning a considerable number were absent, having been left lying on the ground while their mounts went on with the column. Later in the war the mounted infantry performed excellent work, but at first they could not manœuvre under fire, and by their bad riding galled both their horses and themselves. The need for more mounted troops was obvious enough, but a mounted infantryman who can neither ride nor properly look after his horse is not of much fighting value, and he is decidedly expensive in the matter of horseflesh. No more unfortunate animal ever lived than the horse of the mounted infantryman during the early period of the march from the Modder to Pretoria.

Lord Roberts' plan was to concentrate as large a force as possible in the vicinity of Lord Methuen's camp on the Modder near Magersfontein, pass round Cronje's left flank, then wheel north and get astride his communications with Kimberley, and after the relief of that place operate in the direction of Bloemfontein, so as to render the Boer positions south of the Orange river untenable. Lord Roberts was convinced, moreover, that by threatening Bloemfontein he would oblige the enemy to relax his hold on Natal, and would thereby effect the relief of Ladysmith.

The success of the plan depended upon keeping the enemy in doubt as to the proposed line of advance, and this was furthered by making demonstrations as if the intention were to force a passage at Norval's Pont, some 150 miles by rail east of Magersfontein, and by various other devices calculated to mislead. As the Boers had recently captured in Natal certain intelligence papers disclosing the original plan of campaign, which contemplated an advance into the Free State by Norval's Pont, they were the more easily imposed upon and induced to believe that this route would be the one followed. The real plan was at first made known to no one, I believe, except to Lord Kitchener, Sir William Nicholson (the military secretary), Henderson, and a few officers charged with making the necessary railway arrangements. It was not disclosed either to Kelly-Kenny or French (who commanded the troops waiting to be transferred from the Norval's Pont locality to the Modder) until the 29th of January, the day on which the transfer began. Other troops were meanwhile pushed up the western line, but the Boers apparently thought that this merely indicated a renewed but local attack on Magersfontein.

Henderson, always an ardent advocate for mystifying and misleading the enemy, was especially active, and revelled in the deceits he practised. He sent out fictitious telegrams to commanders in clear, and then on one excuse or another countermanded them in cipher ; circulated false orders implying a concentration of troops at Colesberg, in the Norval's Pont direction ; gave " confidential " tips to people eager for news whom he knew would at once divulge them ; and in numerous ways fostered the belief that never again would our troops hurl themselves against the carefully prepared Boer entrenchments at Magersfontein, and that Kimberley could and must look after itself pending a direct advance on Bloemfontein by the Norval's Pont route. One of his tools was a London newspaper correspondent to whom he gave a particularly " confidential " piece of information, with strict injunctions to keep it to himself. As Henderson hoped, it quickly appeared in the London Press, and was brought to our notice by the War Office as a serious indiscretion on the part of some of the staff ! A few days later, when the advance was begun in a direction quite different from that which had been told him, the correspondent became so irate and was so lacking in a sense of humour that he formally complained to Lord Roberts of the " unfair and dishonest treatment " he had received. On the whole it is probable that no military plan was ever kept better concealed from either friend or foe, and certainly the Boers did not discover it until too late to rectify their error.

In addition to Henderson, the Intelligence staff at headquarters consisted of four officers, including myself, designated Deputy Assistant Adjutant-Generals, though we had nothing whatever to do with the Adjutant-General's department. We were a happy party, and, having all been pupils of Henderson at the Staff College, looked forward with keen interest to the application in practice of the lessons and principles he had taught us in theory a few years before. The discussions we had with him in the small mess we formed, and which he joined, regarding the problems to be solved were a valuable education for all of us, but he nevertheless kept from us almost as much as from the Boers the secret of the selected line of advance. By degrees, however, our suspicions were aroused, and when headquarters was suddenly ordered to entrain at Cape Town for the front we were not surprised to learn that our destination was Lord Methuen's camp on the Modder.

On reaching this camp on the 8th of February the Commander-in-Chief immediately proceeded to visit the troops, and by his cheery smile and friendly recognition did much to revive the spirits of those who were feeling disheartened owing to previous failures and disappointments. Lord Roberts possessed an attractive personality, took infinite pains to secure the confidence and esteem of his troops, and to show them that their interests were also his—as they undoubtedly were. It is to be regretted that his example is not more frequently followed by other leaders, since the neglect of it greatly reduces the fighting value of the troops and cannot be made good by any other qualities of leadership, with the sole exception, perhaps, of an unbroken string of victories, and this rarely falls to the lot of the commander of whom regimental officers and men know and see little, and for whom they consequently care less.

Good relations between commanders and the rank and file are like all other forms of friendship—if they are to be maintained and bear fruit they must be nourished. Soldiers are human beings—rather more human than other people—and they will never respond whole-heartedly to the commander who treats them as mere automata to be used for his own purpose according to order, and without any thought being given to them as ordinary men. On the other hand, they will always be ready to offer the last ounce of their strength in extricating from any difficulty into which he may have fallen the General in whom they have confidence as a personal friend. Our men are exceedingly accurate judges of an officer's worth and character, and whilst they intensely dislike the officer who does not enter into their feelings and treats them as if they had none, they have unbounded admiration for the one who treats them kindly as well as justly.

The matter is one which calls for special attention in these modern days, when armies are very large and spread over vast areas, and when senior commanders can no longer live in or near to the camps and bivouacs of their troops, but must usually have their headquarters many miles distant from them. For several other reasons a commander's opportunities of being seen by his men, and of becoming personally known to them, are much fewer than formerly, and therefore there is the more need that he should make additional efforts to meet these new conditions, for the human factor remains unchanged and the men are as sensitive as ever to the human touch.

The daily arrival of troops near Magersfontein ought to have shown to Cronje the extreme danger of his position, but he still clung fast to the belief that it signified no more than a direct attack, and that we could not operate except in the immediate proximity to a railway. It was desirable to confirm him in these false impressions if our object of passing round his left flank was to be achieved, and Intelligence officers and agents were therefore kept busy reconnoitring the country in front of his position ;

information regarding water, camping-places, etc., alongside the railway was sought from every one likely to acquaint him with our enquiries ; telegrams in cipher, easy to decipher, were allowed to fall into his hands ; and all the other usual means of deception were practised. Lastly, as it was important that we should be informed early and accurately of his movements when eventually he found his flank turned, we induced certain Dutch-speaking men to join his commandos, with a promise of substantial pecuniary reward if they brought us the information we required.

The situation at the time was one of great anxiety. The siege of Kimberley had hitherto been a kind of passive investment, but on the 7th of February the Boers opened fire with the " Long Tom " (six-inch gun) which they had brought round from Ladysmith, and this so alarmed the inhabitants that two days later Kekewich, the commander of the besieged force, felt obliged to report to Lord Roberts that the danger of surrender was imminent. Other disquieting news was received from Buller as to his inability to relieve Ladysmith, and on the 9th of February he reported that in his opinion " the fate of Ladysmith is only a question of days unless I am very considerably reinforced."

All this constituted a heavy load, and Lord Roberts carried it bravely and correctly. He could not possibly send reinforcements to Buller in Natal without abandoning the plan he had so carefully considered and elaborated for an advance into the Free State, and in which he believed to lie the greatest prospects of success. Moreover, its abandonment would entail endless confusion and delay. He therefore stuck to it ; gave orders for the troops to cross the Free State frontier on the 11th of February ; and instructed General French, commanding the cavalry division, which led the way, to relieve Kimberley " at all costs." By skilful manœuvre and the display of commendable audacity, French was able to report on the evening of the 15th that his mission had been accomplished in conformity with Lord Roberts' instructions.

Cronje having meanwhile obstinately refused to budge from his trenches, our next task was to reap the fruits of the opportunity created by the cavalry, which had not only relieved Kimberley but had interposed between the investing force now retreating north of that place and the commandos at Magersfontein to the south, and had thus severed Cronje's communications with the Transvaal, to which he, a Transvaaler, attached great importance.

Cronje has been much criticised for his inaction, and it is right that he should be held responsible for the consequences of it, but on the other hand it is only fair to take into account the circumstances as they appeared to him at the time. It was a fact that the British troops had not previously operated at any great distance from a railway, and Cronje probably thought, and quite correctly, that to do so on this occasion would be a very difficult undertaking. February is the hottest month of the South African summer ; water was alarmingly scarce ; no rain had fallen for weeks past and the sandy plains offered but little food for the country-bred animals and still less for the English horses ; the Modder and the Riet were formidable obstacles, passable only at widely separated drifts ; and finally, to march round the flank of a mobile enemy knowing every inch of the terrain, while we knew little or nothing about it, was to incur such risks as not a few commanders would hesitate to accept. These and similar considerations could not fail to have a great influence on Cronje's decision, and he does not deserve to be dismissed merely as a stupid and sullen old Boer in the summary and superior fashion adopted by some of his critics ; and to do this is to belittle what undoubtedly was a bold conception on the part of Lord Roberts, and an arduous performance on the part of his troops.

Hearing of the relief of Kimberley and of the movement of other British columns round his left flank, Cronje at last realised his perilous position, and about ten o'clock on the night of the 15th he commenced to retreat up the right bank of the Modder so as to regain his communications with Bloemfontein. When our headquarters reached Jacobsdal early the following morning reports and rumours indicating the direction of his retirement began to come in, but they were so vague and contradictory that it was difficult to draw any reliable inference from them. This

may seem strange in these more modern days, seeing that
Cronje was moving between French's cavalry at Kimberley
and Kelly-Kenny's Division at Klip Drift on the Modder,
the distance between these two detachments being only
about 15 miles ; but it should be remembered that communications in the field had not then reached their present
state of perfection, and that there were no aeroplanes to
spy out the country and rapidly bring back the information
which we now expect to get as a matter of routine.

It was my special business to collect and study the
intelligence received concerning the Boer movements, and
although I knew that Cronje had three courses open to him,
it was as yet impossible to say which of the three he would
choose. He might retreat either by the west or the east side
of Kimberley and unite with the force just driven back by
French, or he might try to escape to the eastward and make
for Bloemfontein. Strategically, either of the two first
would have been the safest, but, as so often happens in war,
the least likely route—the third—was selected. I think
it was Moltke who once warned his students that when an
enemy seems to have three courses open to him, the chances
are that he will find a fourth and adopt it.

By mid-day on the 16th all doubts were dispelled by the
arrival at headquarters of one of the men whom we had
previously introduced into the commandos at Magersfontein. His account of Cronje's movements was evidently
reliable, and being corroborated by the information we had
received from other sources, it became possible to form a
definite opinion upon which the Commander-in-Chief could
safely determine his future action. The informant received
the promised reward and something in addition.

French was immediately ordered back from Kimberley to
head off Cronje at Koodoos Drift ; the 6th and 9th Divisions
were told to retard and harass the retreating commandos ;
and other troops were hastened up from the rear. Owing
to defective communications French did not receive his instructions till ten o'clock that night, but his squadrons were
set in motion before dawn next morning, and at about
eleven o'clock, having covered 26 miles since leaving
Kimberley, his horse batteries came into action against the

main body of Cronje's convoy, hampered by women, children, and dismounted men, just as it was beginning to descend to Vendutie Drift in order to gain the Bloemfontein road on the left bank.   Throughout the day French effectively frustrated all the enemy's attempts to cross the river, and his retreat having thus been arrested, Cronje's surrender became a question of time.

Headquarters remained at Jacobsdal during the 17th and 18th, and on the 19th moved to Paardeberg Drift, the scene of the battle of Paardeberg of the previous day.   We found considerable disappointment prevailing because the battle had not ended in the defeat and capture of Cronje's force, and one of the reasons given for this was the faulty manner in which the chief command had been exercised. Kelly-Kenny was the senior officer present and therefore ought to have commanded, but Lord Roberts had thought fit to appoint Lord Kitchener to give orders in his name, which amounted to placing him over Kelly-Kenny's head. Lord Kitchener had no time to make arrangements with either Kelly-Kenny or Colville, respectively commanding the 6th and 9th Divisions, as to the way in which he would communicate his orders, and, except for his aides-de-camp and one other staff officer, he possessed no machinery for such communication.   The two divisional commanders were therefore frequently at a loss to know during the course of the battle what was required of them, and owing to lack of effective control over the force as a whole there was no adequate co-operation between the different parts of it.

Throughout the war it was rather a favourite custom of Lord Roberts to use Lord Kitchener as a sort of second-in-command rather than as a Chief of Staff, and to depute him to take command of operations at a distance which he himself could not superintend.   But an itinerant commander cannot have the same grasp of local conditions as the commander on the spot, and if the latter is not competent to command his troops in action he ought to be replaced by some one who is, and not be superseded just as the fighting begins.   Further, if the Chief of Staff is constantly away from headquarters for days or even weeks at a time—as Lord Kitchener was—it is farcical to call him by that name, or to imagine that the duties of the staff can be properly carried out.

During the investment of Cronje we were sometimes very short of food, for, in addition to the difficulties experienced in bringing up the supply columns, De Wet had a few days before swooped down upon one of our convoys at Waterval Drift and captured about 180 wagon loads of supplies as well as some 500 slaughter oxen. On the first night of our arrival at Paardeberg our mess was without food of any kind until Lord Roberts, hearing of our plight, and with his characteristic kindness, sent us the remains of a leg of mutton, which was apparently all that his own mess possessed. In the darkness I clumsily allowed my share of it to fall to the ground, but my hunger was much too keen to allow me to be " put off " by the sand and other disagreeable and unknown things with which, when I retrieved it, and resumed my meal, I found the bone to be covered. We had no bread, and for several days were on half rations of biscuits, while we were not much better off for water. The Modder was certainly close at hand, but as dead animals from the enemy's laager higher up stream were constantly to be seen, and smelt, floating down, or caught up by the branches overhanging its banks, this means of quenching one's thirst was not pleasant.

We found plenty to do while at Paardeberg, as numerous deserters drifted in from the laager and had to be examined ; we had to watch the commandos hovering about in the vicinity with the intention of lending Cronje a hand to break out ; and there were many reports to be investigated of Boer reinforcements being sent from Cape Colony and Ladysmith. An interesting occupation was to arrive at an estimate regarding the strength of the force Cronje had with him, the best calculation we could make being 5000 men and 8 guns. The number actually amounted, when the surrender took place, to 3919 fighting men and 5 guns, to which of course should be added the deserters who had meanwhile given themselves up or had escaped through our lines.

The Boers hoisted the white flag soon after sunrise on the 27th, and about seven o'clock Cronje was brought in to

I

headquarters, where he was met by Lord Roberts and congratulated on the gallant defence he had made. The rugged features of the old Boer leader showed signs of the anxious times through which he had passed, but he carried himself bravely and like a man. Whatever mistakes his indecision had caused him to commit earlier in the operations, he had at any rate displayed a fine determination in compelling his despondent followers to hold out against superior forces for ten days in an impossible position, and he was entitled to receive, and did receive, the respectful sympathy of us all. Early in the afternoon he left with his wife for Cape Town *en route* to St. Helena.

We had a welcome addition to the headquarters staff about this time in the person of Lieutenant-Colonel Grierson, who arrived hot-footed from Berlin, where he had been employed as military attaché. He had his first meal at our frugal and impoverished mess, and like all newcomers to the country was suffering from an inordinate thirst which, quite unknown to him but fully realised by us, was slaked only at the expense of our last " sparklet " and small stock of whisky. It had been intended to place him in charge of the foreign military attachés accompanying headquarters, but this not being to his liking he so arranged matters as to become Assistant Adjutant-General, with the special duty of dealing with the movements and distribution of the troops—a duty which hitherto had been mainly performed by the Commander-in-Chief through the medium of his aides-de-camp and other officers of his personal staff.

Grierson, having for long made a close study of the methods of the German General Staff, was alive to the value of clear and definite orders, and at once set about introducing systematic arrangements for their issue. But his task was difficult and he made little headway, as many orders still continued to be sent out by the Commander-in-Chief direct or through his personal staff, and sometimes without the knowledge of the real staff and the administrative services. Grierson received more than one hint to go easy with his new-fangled ideas, and on one occasion at least he was told that he need issue no orders as the Commander-in-Chief would issue them himself. The battle of Paardeberg had already shown the disadvantages incurred by the absence of clearly expressed operation orders, and a further proof of this was furnished at the next action fought—Poplar Grove, on the 7th of March.

Following the surrender of Cronje, De Wet had collected several commandos astride the Modder facing our camp at Osfontein, their maximum strength being estimated at 14,000 men. We had more than twice that number and about five times as many guns. The situation of De Wet was in some respects not unlike that of Cronje on the day before the battle of Paardeberg, and the intention of Lord Roberts was to turn it to much the same account. The mounted troops under French were to make a détour of 17 miles round and out of reach of the enemy's left flank, and so cut off his retreat to Bloemfontein ; when these troops had been planted completely in rear of the enemy's line, Kelly-Kenny's division was to attack his left and drive him north towards the Modder ; the 7th Division was to threaten the centre, and the 9th Division the right. To make the plan a success it was necessary, first and foremost, to ensure that French should be sufficiently near to his destination before the Boers either knew of the turning movement or were alarmed by the advance of Kelly-Kenny against their left. In other words, accurate timing and perfect co-ordination were the predominant factors.

On the afternoon of the 6th Lord Roberts assembled the Commanding Generals at headquarters and gave to each a copy of the instructions he had himself prepared. These contained a very clear description of his general plan, but nothing about the time at which the different divisions were to start. This was verbally discussed afterwards, and apparently French left the conference under the impression that he was to start at 3 A.M., whereas Kelly-Kenny, who was to follow him for part of the way, understood that French would start at 2 A.M. In addition to this misunderstanding other difficulties arose owing to the absence of good staff arrangements, and, to cut a long story short, the movement of Kelly-Kenny's division next morning was entirely blocked for some time by the cavalry, and the cavalry itself was not able to move nearly so fast as had been expected. The result was that long before French had time to reach their rear the Boers perceived that an enveloping movement was in progress and promptly began to fall back eastward, thus escaping, with practically no loss, from the toils within which it had been hoped to entrap them.

The method adopted by Lord Roberts for conveying his intentions to his Generals is one that is often necessary, as it helps to preserve secrecy and enables a Commander-in-Chief to explain his plans in greater detail than is possible in the crystallised paragraphs of operation orders ; but it should never be made, as it was at Poplar Grove, a substitute for those orders. Had Lord Roberts' instructions been afterwards translated into concrete operation orders, and march-tables been worked out by the staff, definite hours of starting for each division would have been laid down in writing and all misunderstanding prevented or removed.

The failure at Poplar Grove was the more unfortunate because the Boers were then in a very despondent frame of mind. Cronje's force had been captured a few days before, Kimberley and Ladysmith had been set free, and if, as Lord Roberts intended, De Wet had been forced into the bed of the Modder, and there surrounded, the effect of this further disaster might have gone far to end the war. Whether better staff work and the issue of proper operation orders would have made success certain at Poplar Grove and so shortened the war by perhaps as much as two years, may be a debatable point, but there can be no question that success could not be expected unless these conditions were fulfilled.

After the action headquarters moved to Poplar Grove and remained there till the 10th. The army then again advanced, the left column, under French and including Kelly-Kenny's division, fighting a sharp engagement on the Driefontein ridge, of which we had a good view from Driefontein Farm. The severe punishment which the Boers received caused them to beat a hurried retreat, and they fell back that night in disorder towards Bloemfontein.

On the 11th we reached Assvogel Kop, Venter's Vallei

on the 12th, and next morning the Mayor of Bloemfontein
and three of the leading citizens came out and ceremoniously
surrendered the town.   Shortly afterwards it was entered
by the Commander-in-Chief and the headquarters staff,
and the Union Jack was hoisted on the President's house.
The troops bivouacked for the most part outside the town,
as Lord Roberts was anxious that the inhabitants, whom
it was hoped would soon become British subjects, should
be put to as little inconvenience and discomfort as possible.

Thanks to sound strategy and to the fortitude and
gallantry of the troops, the thirty days' operations which
terminated with the occupation of Bloemfontein had
changed the whole aspect of the war.   For the great results
achieved the principal credit must of course be accorded to
the Commander-in-Chief, since upon him rested the responsibility for the consequences of the strategical decision he
took, whether they proved to be good or bad, and moreover the success was largely due to the implicit confidence
which the troops placed in him.   To what extent, if any,
Henderson's counsels contributed to the strategy adopted
I am not in a position to say, and he was far too modest a
man to talk about it.   But one cannot help being struck by
the fact that, after he had left headquarters, the operations
were unproductive of similar marked successes, and that
there was a strong tendency to attach too much importance
to the occupation of towns and too little to the decisive
defeat of the enemy's forces, by which alone complete
victory could be secured.

If the standard of staff work and tactics in the march
from the Modder to Bloemfontein had equalled that of
strategy the results might have been even greater than they
were ; but the nature and value of staff duties were not yet
properly appreciated, while tactics suffered from a desire on
the part of the High Command to avoid casualties.   The
reluctance to fight what were termed costly battles tended to
hamper the subordinate commanders, who, not unnaturally,
felt that their capacity would be judged mainly by the number
of casualties incurred.   This feeling was apt to cause them
to hesitate when they should have displayed determination
and boldness, and in the long run the policy was liable to

defeat its own end, since half-hearted and indecisive fighting was likely to make the war-aggregate of casualties greater than if the struggle were relentlessly fought out from the first and without so much regard to immediate losses.

On the 17th, while headquarters was still at Jacobsdal, Henderson's health, which for some time past had been indifferent, completely broke down. He had been careless of himself, and so immersed in his work that he had neglected to fit himself out with the ordinary campaigning requirements, he carried no food for use in emergency, and as far as I remember he did not possess even a water-bottle. Added to this, the heat on the 17th was intense, the only water we had was particularly bad and had a most offensive smell, and the whole of the transport lagged far behind. We of the staff did our best out of our scanty store to provide for his needs, and I begged him to rest quietly on my camp-bed, but he was not to be persuaded. Most of the day he worked hard, dressed in pyjamas, studying the important events which were happening, discussing with the Commander-in-Chief the action to be taken, and generally doing the duty of a Chief of the General Staff, the real Chief of Staff, Lord Kitchener, being away at the front with Kelly-Kenny's division. The following day he became so ill that he had to be sent back to Cape Town. We parted from him with sorrow, and he of course was grievously disappointed to relinquish his work which had begun with such remarkable success. He was succeeded as Director of Intelligence by Lieutenant - Colonel (now Major - General Sir) Colin Mackenzie, a contemporary of mine at the Staff College.

From Cape Town Henderson was sent back to England, and owing to continued ill-health took no further part in the war. Later, he was appointed to write the official history of it, which he commenced with an account of the political events leading up to hostilities and a description of the military resources available on both sides. His idea was that without full knowledge of these conditions the reader would not be able properly to understand many of the earlier military decisions and dispositions which were to a great extent necessarily based upon them. At the end of 1902 his health again gave way and he was ordered to

Egypt, where he died in March of the following year, leaving behind him a gap in the British army which has not yet been filled, and a memory which is held in sincere affection by all who had the privilege to know him.

The Government subsequently decided that it was undesirable to publish in the history of the war any discussion of the questions which had been at issue between them and the two Republics before the outbreak of hostilities, or that had been the subject of controversy at home, and therefore that portion of it which Henderson had compiled was entirely recast.

In connection with this decision I may observe that for a soldier to write an official history of military operations, which shall be acceptable to the Government departments concerned, is invariably a ticklish task. On the one hand, it may be impossible for him to make clear the reasons for the military action taken unless he first describes the political conditions and instructions which, to a greater or less degree, governed that action ; while, on the other hand, a cold, comprehensive review of the proceedings which led up to those conditions and instructions does not, in the light of after events, always afford very pleasant reading to those who took part in them.

I remember one rather striking instance, amongst others within my experience, of an officer getting into trouble on this account. He was compiling, under my orders, the official report on certain military operations which had been preceded and were attended by particularly complicated questions of international policy, and knowing that undue reference to these questions would be resented, I gave him directions to leave them severely alone except in so far as it was absolutely essential to mention them, and even then he was to take his facts from the Blue books—already available to the public—and rigidly to exclude any political information of a secret or confidential nature that we might have in our archives. I trusted that by this means all objections would be obviated, and I know that the officer set about his work with the intention of creating none, and that he confined his political researches to the Blue books. But when his report was submitted to the departmental authorities in Whitehall for approval, before being printed off, some of its political paragraphs were considerably modified or expunged altogether, and a curt letter from the objecting department invited us to mind our own business in future.

Before continuing the advance beyond Bloemfontein it was necessary to refit and reorganise the army, and we had also to cope with a serious outbreak of typhoid—an epidemic which in those days was accepted as almost unpreventable in time of war. The medical services were not organised adequately to deal with the ever-increasing number of sick ; there was great difficulty in providing suitable accommodation for the patients ; eight wagon loads of medical comforts had been lost at Waterval Drift ; and the result of all this was that many of our fever-stricken men died whose lives might have been saved had better treatment and properly equipped accommodation been available. The efficiency of the medical arrangements for the care of the sick and wounded has since been improved a thousand-fold, as shown by the marvellous work done in the Great War, and in this respect as in many others the South African war was of inestimable benefit to us.

The system of guerilla warfare adopted by the Boers after the occupation of Bloemfontein, and continued throughout the war, made Intelligence duties much more difficult than before. The enemy's plan now was to act aggressively against different points on our line of communication, and to pick up elsewhere any helpless or unwary detachment which promised to be an easy prey, and as the bodies he employed were widely dispersed, moved swiftly, were subject to variable combinations, and were favoured by the nature of the country, it was impossible to place or number them for more than a few hours at a time. We derived much information from the mail-bags seized at various places, for the Boers wrote very freely to each other, but as a rule it came to hand too late to be of much use except for general purposes, and we had to rely mainly upon our Intelligence Scouts. These scouts, working under the direction of Captain (now General Sir) G. F. Milne, would track the commandos from place to place, and sometimes lie out watching them for several days and nights in succession, bringing or sending back most valuable intelligence. Most of them were recruited from South Africa, some being white and some coloured, while some of them came from other parts of the world. One of the latter was Mr. F. R. Burnham, the famous American scout. He was a great acquisition, and carried out many hazardous enterprises with skill and success.

The army being at last more or less reorganised and re-equipped, we set out for Pretoria on the 3rd May. The general plan was to advance on a front extending from Ladysmith to Kimberley, Buller on the right with about 45,000 men, Hunter and Methuen on the left with 10,000, the columns in the centre directly under Lord Roberts being about 43,000 strong. Brandfort was occupied the same day with the loss of about half a dozen men ; the passage of the Vet river was forced two days later ; the Zand river, the next obstacle, was crossed on the 10th, with the loss of about a hundred men ; and on the following day Kroonstad was abandoned and President Steyn went off to Lindley, proclaiming that place to be the new capital and seat of government of the Free State. From that time onwards organised co-operation between the two Republics ceased, the Free Staters apparently thinking that as they had borne the brunt of the British attack for nearly three months it was for the Transvaalers and not for them to defend the Transvaal. British headquarters entered Kroonstad on the 12th May and remained there for ten days, so as to allow the railway in rear to be repaired and the army to be pulled together once more.

I have already mentioned that Grierson held the appointment of Assistant Adjutant-General, but as a matter of fact he was charged with duties belonging to the department of the Quartermaster-General, a curious feature in the organisation of the headquarters staff being that it contained no officer designated by the name of that department. It was Grierson's business to allot accommodation for the troops, and in order to improve upon the defective arrangements made at Bloemfontein for the disposal of the sick he allocated the church and other public buildings in Kroonstad for the purpose, telling the Landrost to provide so many hundred mattresses by four o'clock in the afternoon. The Landrost raised many objections, and said that there was nothing like that number in the shops, upon which Grierson observed, in rather forcible language, that he was not thinking merely of what the shops could produce, that there must be a large number of mattresses in the town, and that the full number demanded must be forthcoming by the hour named. The Landrost went off to Lord Roberts to complain of having been harshly treated and threatened with punishment if he did not comply with the order, and Grierson was then sent for to give his side of the story. He admitted that in his conversation with the Landrost he had freely drawn upon all the languages with which he was acquainted, including Scotch and Hindustani, so as to ensure prompt compliance with his order, and that he had done so because he felt that the comfort of the sick should have priority over everything and everybody. He was quietly requested to treat the inhabitants with more sympathy and consideration in future, and, of course, he received the admonition with becoming respect. He gained his object, however, and in telling us of the incident that night at dinner he finished up by saying, " I got my beds, the men are now on them, and that, after all, is the only thing that matters."

Somebody present at dinner reminded us of the old story told of a similar incident that occurred in the Peninsula war, of which the sequel was rather different. General Craufurd, the commander of the famous Light Division, once directed the head man of a Spanish town to collect certain supplies for the troops, at a given time and place, otherwise he would be shot. The Spaniard complained to the Duke of Wellington of the General's high-handed conduct, and said that he could not possibly carry out the order. " Do you mean to tell me," the Duke asked, " that General Craufurd threatened to shoot you ? " " He did," replied the Spaniard, thinking the Duke was taking his part. The answer he got was : " Well, if I were in your place I would produce the supplies somehow, for, believe me, General Craufurd is a man of his word and will shoot you if you don't."

We left Kroonstad on the 22nd May, entered the Transvaal five days later, and Johannesburg fell on the 30th May. Next day it was formally handed over to us, our infantry marched through the main square, and the Dutch flags were hauled down from the government buildings and replaced by the Union Jack. A similar ceremony took place at Pretoria on the 5th June, and the Transvaal Government thus became vagabond like that of the sister Republic.

The three hundred miles march from Bloemfontein to Pretoria had been dull and irksome to a degree, and I suppose that no military operations were ever more lacking in interest and variety. Throughout the march the Boers, greatly inferior to us in numbers, would hold the river lines and other defensible positions, covering a wide front ; our mounted troops were then sent round one or other of their flanks with the object of enveloping them ; and when this movement had proceeded up to a certain point the Boers would withdraw out of harm's way to take up a similar position farther to the rear. But although no action worth calling a battle was fought, the march itself was attended by many hardships. Day after day our troops plodded silently on over the apparently endless prairies ; sometimes the sun was blazing hot, at others there was a bitterly cold wind against which no clothing seemed proof ; food was scanty, and shelterless bivouacs formed the only resting-places at night. In fact the march was unrelieved by any redeeming feature except hope, and our splendid infantry deserve the highest credit for the way in which they doggedly stuck to their monotonous daily toil until the fall of Pretoria, the second Boer capital, gave them their reward and brought the pacification of the country definitely within sight.

The Boers were now more than ever convinced that their one and only chance of salvation lay in striking the slender line of communications which trailed away for hundreds of miles in rear of our exhausted troops. De Wet became particularly active, capturing considerable numbers of prisoners, and burning and destroying large and invaluable quantities of food and stores. Refusing to be disturbed by these raids, vexatious and inconvenient though they were, the Commander-in-Chief set in motion all the troops he could collect to attack the enemy, some 6000 strong, who had taken up a position astride the railway about fifteen miles east of Pretoria. After some desultory fighting on the 11th and 12th of June the Boers disappeared during the night, part of them under De la Rey circling round to the western Transvaal, and the remainder under Botha retiring eastward. This engagement, known as the battle of Diamond Hill, cost us less than 180 casualties, of whom 20 were killed.

Before the advance could be resumed it was again necessary to refit the army, and make good the wear and tear amongst the men, animals, and material caused by the long march from Bloemfontein. This took about six weeks, and on the 23rd of July, when the troops again moved forward, the Boers at once evacuated Balmoral, which had been Botha's headquarters since the action at Diamond Hill, and two days later they retired through Middelburg, eighty miles east of Pretoria.

On the night of the 25th of July, the date of our occupation of Balmoral, there was a terrible storm of wind and rain—the worst of the many bad storms we had encountered. The troops suffered severely from exposure in their bivouacs, and next morning the adjacent hill-sides were covered with dead and dying transport animals. In many places whole teams of dead oxen and mules lay heaped together.

Much of this loss was due to neglect on somebody's part to order the transport columns to march earlier in the day. The order was not given till the afternoon, and consequently the columns were caught in the hills by the storm and darkness long before they had finished their march, the tracks became slippery and impassable, confusion reigned everywhere, a great part of the columns were out all night, and the animals perished by hundreds. It was pitiable to see these fine beasts in their death-throes being shot by the veterinary surgeons, who went about amongst them and mercifully put out of their agony those which had no chance of recovery.

After the occupation of Middelburg the forward movement was again suspended, and soon afterwards a great part of the troops in the Transvaal were turned on to pursue De Wet, who had crossed the Vaal from the Free State on the 6th of August.

Nine columns composed of about 30,000 men were engaged in this the first of the De Wet hunts, Lord Kitchener being in command of the combined operations. De Wet owed his escape on this occasion, as on many subsequent ones, to misunderstandings on the part of his pursuers, and in the circumstances it was practically impossible to prevent misunderstanding. Intercommunication between the different British columns was bad, and therefore they did not always know what each other had done or would do ; the enemy could always get the best possible information, whereas we could seldom depend upon what we obtained ; and such information as we got and sent to the columns often arrived too late to be of use. At headquarters we were usually able to trace De Wet's movements. The difficulty was to inform the columns within useful time.

Headquarters stayed at Pretoria throughout the remaining period of Lord Roberts' command, only a small portion of it accompanying him when the advance eastward was resumed on August the 26th. I was one of those left behind, and saw no more of the operations. Early in October I was ordered back for duty at the War Office, and a month later took up the same appointment of Staff Captain in the Colonial Section as I had held a year before. Meanwhile I had reached the rank of Major in the ordinary course of regimental promotion.

For my services in the war I was given a " mention in despatches," but only in the class then known as " also ran," and when the promotions and other rewards were published my name did not appear in the list. I had hoped that it would, but whatever chance of this there might have been was destroyed by my having incurred the displeasure of Lord Roberts, owing to a misunderstanding that arose in regard to certain instructions which I had issued to an officer just before I left South Africa. As this officer was on the spot when the mistake came to light and could give his version of it to headquarters, whilst I was in England and had no opportunity of giving mine either to Lord

Roberts or any one else, the blame for it rested with me. The matter was later put right by some of my friends, and in a Supplementary Gazette published in November 1901 I was promoted Brevet Lieutenant-Colonel. As the brevet took effect from the date of the first Gazette, November 1900, I lost nothing by the delay.

CHAPTER IX

HEAD OF THE FOREIGN INTELLIGENCE SECTION, WAR OFFICE

Resume work in Intelligence Division—Lord Roberts returns to England and becomes Commander-in-Chief—Visit defended ports—Intelligence and mobilisation combined under the charge of Sir W. Nicholson—Am made head of the Foreign Section of Intelligence—Promoted Colonel 1904—Selection of Military Attachés—Preparations for war hampered by lack of a policy—Our international position—Defence of India—Examination of it and Lord Kitchener's objections to our calculations—Esher Committee—Reorganisation of War Office and formation of General Staff—Post of Commander-in-Chief abolished—Sir N. Lyttelton becomes first Chief of the General Staff—Committee of Imperial Defence established—War preparations now become more feasible—Bogy of Russian attack on India disappears and contingency of war with Germany begins to take its place—Agreements made with France, Russia, and Japan—Expeditionary Force formed—Grierson and Huguet largely instrumental in this—Lord Roberts resigns from Committee of Imperial Defence—First attempt to give a military lecture—Visits between 1902-1906 to Northern Africa, Canada, America, the Balkans, Belgium, Portugal, Germany, and other European countries—Leave War Office on expiration of appointment—Placed on half-pay, 1907.

LORD ROBERTS returned to England at the end of 1900 and became Commander-in-Chief in place of Lord Wolseley, whose departure from the War Office was greatly regretted by all who had served under him. He had given many years of faithful service to the State, and the ungenerous criticisms levelled against him in Parliament, concerning his share of the defects exposed by the South African war, made a very unpleasant impression upon those who were aware of the numerous obstructions to military efficiency, in high as well as in low places, with which he had for so long to contend, not only when Commander-in-Chief but before he held that appointment. It is doubtful if, in face of these obstructions, any other man of the time could have done half as much for the education and training of the British Army as was achieved by this eminent soldier.

The war had shown the necessity for having a more efficient military organisation, both for foreign service and home defence, and following upon the appointment of Mr. Brodrick (now Earl of Midleton) as War Secretary various measures for improving the training, equipment, and organisation of the forces were carried out. The basis of them was, in addition to an adequate provision for home defence, the ability to send three army corps abroad. The unnecessarily large garrisons of defended ports were also brought under revision. These, consisting mainly of volunteers, had in many cases been recruited more in accordance with the local supply of men than with the needs of local defence, and they included an excessive number of garrison artillery, this branch being more popular than the infantry. It was therefore decided to bring the numbers into line with actual requirements, and for this purpose a War Office committee was appointed to visit the ports, twenty-six in number, and, in consultation with the local authorities, settle the garrison of each on the spot. I was made a member of the committee and so derived much useful knowledge of coast defence matters, which stood me in good stead in after years and more particularly when I was in command of the forces in Great Britain. The work of the committee extended over a period of about five months.

Several other useful reforms were made, both in the commands and at the War Office, but I shall mention only the one which directly concerned myself—the amalgamation of the Mobilisation and Intelligence Divisions under the control of Sir William Nicholson, whose title of Director of Military Intelligence was altered to Director-General of Mobilisation and Intelligence, and his functions were correspondingly enlarged.

The Intelligence Division was subdivided into three sections, of which the first, or Imperial, Section (practically the old Colonial Section under another name) was made responsible for the preparation of plans of operations for the military defence of the Empire, and for the collection of information relating to its military geography and resources, the United Kingdom and India being excluded in each case. The second, or Foreign, Section was made responsible for collecting information regarding the military resources, geography, and armed forces of all foreign countries, conducting correspondence with military attachés, and examining foreign journals and literature. The third, or Special, Section dealt with censorship, preparation of maps, maintenance of libraries, and office routine in general. Each of the three sections was placed under an Assistant Quartermaster-General, and divided into a number of sub-sections each headed by a Deputy Assistant Quartermaster-General. In this way the officers of the Intelligence Division once more took their designation from the Quartermaster-General's department, although they had no more connection with that department than they had had with the Adjutant-General's department, the designation by which they had been known for some years previously.

Altham was appointed head of the Imperial Section; Trotter, who had been Assistant Adjutant-General of the old Intelligence Division, remained with the Special Section; and to my surprise Nicholson selected me for the Foreign Section. Thus at one bound I went from Staff Captain to Assistant Quartermaster-General, and from being the junior of two officers in the Colonial Section I became the chief of a section having a staff of nine officers. This advancement came at a most opportune moment, for about the same time my promotion to Brevet Lieutenant-Colonel was announced, and according to the regulations of the period the appointment of Assistant Quartermaster-General automatically carried with it promotion to Colonel at the end of three years in the brevet rank just mentioned. As the brevet dated from the 29th November 1900, it followed that if I continued to hold the new post till the 29th November 1903, I would then become Colonel. This happened, and from being one of the oldest Lieutenants in the army in 1895 I became in less than nine years one of the youngest Colonels.

The new appointment had the further advantage of extending my studies to countries with which I had not

K

previously been officially connected. At Simla experience had
been gained in the affairs of India and the adjoining states ;
in the Colonial Section I had learnt something about the
remaining British possessions oversea ; the Foreign Section,
embracing all foreign countries, completed the circuit of the
globe, and gave me a valuable insight into international
questions of great importance.

On taking over · the new duties I found that, chiefly
owing to an inadequate staff, imperfect organisation, and
the lack of clear direction, there was not, with one exception,
which shall be nameless, a single up-to-date statement giving
a comprehensive and considered estimate of the military
resources of any foreign country. One reason for this was
that there was as yet no General Staff, and the Intelligence
Division, which strove to do the work of a General Staff,
had been starved. The few officers employed in it had
worked hard and done their best, but the system and circumstances were all against them.

There were in the Foreign Section some small non-
confidential hand-books, largely compiled from newspapers
and other unofficial publications, which related to the
strength and organisation of most of the foreign armies.
These, though good enough in their way as an elementary
basis to work upon, did not contain, and did not pretend
to contain, anything of much value in regard to strategical
questions, strong places, or the general military resources
of the countries to which they referred. There were also
various memoranda which dealt with certain operations
that we might have to undertake in the event of war, but
these, again, though useful for the specific purpose they
were intended to serve, did not give a complete survey of
the enemy's resources as a whole, or anything like it.

After ascertaining how matters stood I discussed them
with Nicholson and we agreed that we must make the best
tentative arrangements we could, and try to reach a higher
standard later on. The first essential was to obtain more
complete information than we then had, and to do this
more funds were required for intelligence work, as well as
a better method of appointing military attachés. More
funds were provided, thanks to the ready co-operation of

the Foreign Office ; more proficient military attachés were not, in all cases.

These officers were for the most part underpaid, and were all paid at the same rate, irrespective of the particular capital to which they were accredited. That Paris life was infinitely more expensive than life at Peking, and that the amount of information procurable by a military attaché was largely governed by the amount of money he could spend in entertaining those from whom he might hope to procure it, were facts which left the Treasury mind unmoved. The result was that these important posts were often given to officers who were rich, in preference to officers who were not, though the latter might be professionally much better qualified to fill them.

Other influences were brought to bear on the selection of military attachés (which did not rest solely or even mainly with the War Office), and it was not uncommon for an officer to be chosen because he was a society favourite, or had an attractive wife, or a friend in the Foreign Office, or for some equally insufficient reason. I have known officers to be selected who, besides being unsuitable on military grounds, had no knowledge of the language of the country to which they were sent, or of any other except their own.

I remember a military attaché at one of the European capitals who, regarded by the other attachés as a favourable target for their practical jokes, sent us a map, under every precaution of secrecy in the way of sealing-wax, red-tape, and extra envelopes, showing the peace distribution of the armed forces of a certain country, which he stated had been confidentially given to him by a friendly colleague. Incredible as it may seem, the price of the map and the name of its continental publisher were printed at the bottom, the sender either not having observed this or being too ignorant of European languages to be able to read it ! In the case of more than one military attaché the lack of a reasonable knowledge of the language of the country was responsible for many ludicrous as well as alarming reports being sent to us, and it was no doubt equally answerable for our not receiving much information that ought to have been sent. I tried to ensure that only properly qualified officers should be selected, but the exterior influences mentioned sometimes proved to be too strong for me.

Another improvement needed was to give my subordinates greater facilities for visiting the countries with which they had to deal, so that they might acquire a personal knowledge of them and not be entirely dependent, as some of them were, upon what they read or were told. The time and money expended upon these visits, which I sanctioned as frequently as possible, were more than justified. I was fortunate in having some very hard-working and capable assistants during the five years I was in charge of the Foreign Section. They included Lawrence of the 17th Lancers; Macbean, Forestier-Walker, Crowe, Fasson, Milne, and Thwaites of the artillery; Edmonds and Williams of the engineers; Romer, Malcolm, and Lynden Bell of the infantry; Holman and Black of the Indian army. Nearly all held high positions in the Great War. Milne commanded the British army in Macedonia from May 1916 onwards, and Lawrence became Chief of the General Staff on the West Front in January 1918.

Since it is not possible, and should never be necessary to try, to prepare at one and the same time for half-a-dozen different wars, soldiers charged with the duty of preparation aim at making ready for the greatest and the most probable war in which their army may become engaged. I set out with this purpose in view, and was immediately confronted with the difficulty of deciding what particular war ought to be regarded as the most probable, as this depended upon the policy of the Government, and upon that question I was not in possession of any definite pronouncement. I therefore took steps to obtain one, beginning with the examination of some old papers which dealt with our military obligations under various treaties and agreements, and I found that whilst the necessity for fulfilling some of these obligations was unlikely ever to arise, others were of great importance and in the near future might possibly make heavy demands upon us. I prepared a memorandum in which I reviewed the whole of them from a military standpoint, taking each one separately, and after discussing the responsibilities they involved I asked for instructions as to whether it was desired that the army should be prepared to carry them out. My object was twofold : first, to take steps for procuring the information required for those operations which, in pursuance of the policy of the Government, might one day have to be undertaken ; and, secondly, to avoid waste of time over those which in all probability would never be undertaken.

After being approved by my military superiors, the memorandum proceeded on its way to the ministers concerned, and I hoped to receive such a reply from them as would enable me to direct the work of my officers into the most profitable channels. One ministerial minute was, to the best of my memory, something like this : " I do not know what benefit you expect to derive from meditations of this kind. At any rate, I can contribute nothing useful. The policy to be adopted in the contingency you mention must necessarily be decided by the Government of the day, when the time comes, and it cannot be decided now." I quite realised that a *definite* decision could not then be reached in respect of a situation which might not arise for several years, if ever, since the attendant circumstances might change in the meantime ; but I had hoped, nevertheless, that my cherished memorandum would elicit somewhat better guidance than was furnished by the minute just quoted, and that I would not have to continue to rely entirely on my own judgment as to the preparations that should be made. I became wiser as I grew older.

Our international position was not altogether satisfactory at this period, and there were outstanding questions with more than one of the Great Powers which might any day give rise to trouble. For example, France was feeling sore over the Fashoda incident ; her colonial party were, we thought, unduly aggressive ; and, in general, it had become the fashion for the two nations to look upon each other as possible future enemies. There was never any good reason why they should have drifted into this regrettable frame of mind, but Germany may have been answerable for it to some extent. Russia, as for years past, was considered to be another country with whom we might come into conflict, and it was a common argument that her proceedings in the Middle East and Central Asia could best be countered by our forming an alliance with Germany.

I had not been a year in my new post, however, before I became convinced, and stated so officially, that instead of regarding Germany as a suitable ally we ought to look upon her as our most formidable rival, and that the contingency of war with her ought to set the standard of our military requirements. Either because of the disbelief that such a war would ever come, or because of the idea that if it came we would not fight it out on the Continent, this opinion was not yet shared by those responsible for laying down policy, and they decided that the defence of India as against Russia should be the first problem examined. The Commander-in-Chief, Lord Roberts, having passed most of his life in India, was also inclined to give that country priority of treatment, and for several months I was kept busy in preparing for the Defence Committee of the Cabinet a series of papers on the subject. Thanks to my four years' apprenticeship in the Intelligence Branch at Simla, and to the knowledge of the North-West Frontier which I had acquired on the spot, I was fairly well acquainted with the conditions which govern military operations in this part of the world, but some of the questions propounded were nevertheless beyond my power to answer.

I remember once being asked to prepare a statement showing the monthly progress likely to be made by the opposing forces, during the first six months of war, in the event of a Russian advance on India through Afghanistan. The situation in all wars is apt to develop in a totally unexpected manner, and this particular problem was beset with numerous uncertainties peculiarly its own : for instance, the attitude of the Afghans, who were constantly fighting amongst themselves and about whom the only sure thing was that they would pillage and murder both belligerents indiscriminately whenever occasion offered ; the feasibility of our collecting within given periods of time hundreds of thousands of camels for transport purposes, for which no reliable arrangements had been made or could be made, and which depended partly upon the season of the year ; and the rate at which roads and railways could be constructed across the 500 miles of mountainous country lying between the Russian and British frontiers.

These and similar calculations could be nothing more than mere guess-work, different people making different guesses, and this was especially so as regards railways, because no survey for them had ever been made except for the stretch between Quetta and Kandahar at the end of the last Afghan war, and even it had since been lost ! However, assisted by Holman, who was in charge of the Indian sub-section, I produced the required statement, with maps, showing what the dispositions of the British and Russian armies might be at the end of each month, and, in order that there should be no misapprehension about it, I added that it was practically worthless, and for the reasons once given by Moltke, who had said :

" It is a delusion to imagine that a plan of campaign can be laid down far ahead and fulfilled with exactitude. The collision with the enemy creates a new situation in accordance with its result. Some things intended will have become impracticable ; others, which originally seemed impossible, become feasible. All that the leader of an army can do is to form a correct estimate of the circumstances, decide for the best for the moment, and carry out his purpose unflinchingly."

When our calculations were communicated to India they did not at all meet with the approval of Lord Kitchener, the Commander-in-Chief, who was then pressing the home authorities to sanction certain reforms in the Indian army, including considerable additions to its strength. In order to show how utterly wrong the calculations were, he caused a " war game " to be played at Simla illustrating the danger to which India would be exposed if attacked by Russia, and he sent the " proceedings " of it to the India Office.

It is always wise when studying problems of this kind to take, within reason, the circumstances least favourable to oneself, and as there were many important matters connected with the Indian army which then urgently needed improvement Lord Kitchener may be excused for making his own case appear as bad as he possibly could. But he

" protested " a little too much in his war game. He
assumed, amongst other things, that Russia would be able
to transfer large numbers of troops from Europe to Central
Asia, and collect there hundreds of thousands of camels and
other transport animals, ready to jump across the Oxus—
a formidable river—and enter Afghanistan, almost if not
quite before we knew anything about what she was doing.
The result of this invaluable start and other exaggerations
was that, in the imaginary advance which followed, the
Russian troops bounded from one success to another with
the most astonishing rapidity, and to the complete overthrow of the existing arrangements for Indian defence.

The arrival of the " proceedings " created some excitement in Whitehall, where they were apparently regarded
as affording infallible proof of what Russia could actually
do, and undeniable evidence that we had been terribly out
in the calculations we had made. They found their way
to me for examination, and I had to explain that a war
game was by no means the same thing as war, and that
some of the assumptions made in the game were quite untenable. A lengthy correspondence with India ensued, and
officers were sent home to prove that the Indian calculations were right and ours were wrong. They failed to
carry their point, but the game probably went a long way
towards fulfilling Lord Kitchener's real purpose, which
was to obtain early sanction for the reforms he was
advocating.

In 1903 the Esher Committee, consisting of Lord Esher,
Sir John (afterwards Lord) Fisher, and Sir George Clarke
(now Lord Sydenham), was appointed to advise the Government as to the reorganisation of the War Office. It recommended that the old constitution should be replaced by an
Army Council on lines similar to the Board of Admiralty,
the post of Commander-in-Chief being abolished, and, most
important of all, that a General Staff should be created.
This system was introduced in February 1904. Lord Roberts
left the War Office, becoming a member of the new Committee of Imperial Defence, and the heads of the principal
departments were superseded by other officers, as the new
measures were held to require the services of new men.

That may have been so, but the scant courtesy with which the changes were made was the cause of much adverse comment, and not without reason, as it showed but little consideration for the feelings of the officers who were suddenly removed from their posts, after having served their country with distinction for a long period of years.

Nicholson was one of those to go, much to his surprise, for he had been frequently consulted by the committee with respect to the most suitable organisation to be established, and he apparently had hoped to become the first Chief of the newly-formed General Staff. He was quite stunned by his abrupt and unexpected dismissal, and although he became Quartermaster-General a year or two later, and subsequently Chief of the Imperial General Staff, he was never quite the same man again. He seemed to have been robbed of some of his old military zeal; and being hurt at the treatment he had received, his habit of appearing somewhat cynical in manner—though in reality a kind-hearted man—became rather more pronounced than before.

The General Staff was organised in three directorates— Military operations, Staff duties, and Military training— and the post of Chief of the General Staff was entrusted to Lieutenant-General Sir Neville Lyttelton. The Military operations directorate was practically the existing Intelligence Division under another name, the head of it being my old friend Grierson, and his three immediate subordinates were styled Assistant Directors. The Foreign Section of the directorate, of which I remained in charge, was expanded from four to eight subdivisions, the number of officers in it being increased from nine to twenty.

The Committee of Imperial Defence, also constituted on the recommendation of the Esher Committee, absorbed the functions of the Defence Committee of the Cabinet and of the Colonial Defence Committee. These measures, together with the long-overdue formation of a General Staff, went far to remedy the hopeless methods by which matters concerning the defence of the Empire had previously been conducted. For the first time naval and military questions now began to be seriously investigated, and the activities of the different State departments to be intelligently co-ordinated. Appreciable progress in the preparation for war became possible, and plans of operations for use in case of need were worked out between my section and the Imperial Section presided over by Altham, who was later succeeded by Callwell. Taking as a pattern the valuable report we had on one country—which I have previously mentioned as being the only one of its kind in our possession—the military resources of every country in the world in which our troops might conceivably be employed were surveyed, and by the end of 1906 reasoned conclusions thereon had been reached. In the nature of things this survey could only be provisional in the first instance, but it constituted a systematic beginning which could be and was subsequently developed and improved as facilities permitted.

We were also able, being at last organised as a General Staff, to furnish the Foreign Office and the Committee of Imperial Defence with considered military advice in regard to several international questions which had to be dealt with at this time. Amongst them our relations with France took a prominent place, for besides the Fashoda sore there were disputes connected with Morocco, Egypt, Siam, Madagascar, New Hebrides, various Colonial boundaries in West and Central Africa, and the fishing rights off Newfoundland, the latter wrangle dating back to the time of the old French ascendancy in North America. Owing to the clear vision of King Edward, who paid his first official visit to Paris in May 1903, to the efforts of the two Foreign Ministers, Lord Lansdowne and M. Delcassé, and to the goodwill shown by the two nations in general, these causes of friction were satisfactorily removed by the Anglo-French Agreement of 1904, and this, under stress of events, quickly developed into the " Entente " which was destined to prove so valuable to both countries ten years later.

The Entente with France led to a reconsideration of our long and dangerous rivalry with Russia, the chief bones of contention in this case being Afghanistan, Persia, and Tibet. The negotiations were very prolonged—India and the India Office as well as the Foreign Office taking part in them—and they were still going on when I left the War

Office at the beginning of 1907. In August of that year, however, an agreement was signed, for which Sir Edward (now Lord) Grey deserves great credit, and the triple entente, as confronting the triple alliance, was thus brought into being.

Another important question upon which the General Staff was asked to advise was the renewal and amendment of the Anglo-Japanese treaty signed in 1902. It had been concluded for a term of five years, but in 1905, while the Russo-Japanese war was still in progress, it was replaced by a new treaty of wider scope and covering a period of ten years.

A special advantage derived from these and similar investigations was that the bogy of a Russian attack on India, over which so much labour had been wasted in 1901 and 1902, was relegated to the background ; and more time and thought could be devoted to the real enemy, Germany, who, in the eyes of all but the wilfully blind, was pursuing a policy that was bound to bring her, sooner or later, into conflict with us. It is strange that so many people should have refused to accept this view. I remember that as late as 1912 a Cabinet Minister once said to me, in reply to my remark that war with Germany was inevitable : " No, General, I would not say inevitable, but conceivable." His way of stating the case may have been more technically correct than mine, for no war can, strictly speaking, be classed as inevitable till it has begun, but mine seemed to me the simpler and safer basis to work upon, and it did not prove to be inaccurate.

Grierson was as convinced as myself that the only policy consistent with the interests of the Empire was an active alliance with France and Belgium, and although no such alliance was made arrangements were unofficially put in train for ensuring mutual military assistance in case of war. I had some capital officers in my German and French sections whose business it was to work out the details, and as a matter of interest I may add that our prophecy at the time was that the Great War would come in 1915, the year in which, according to what has since transpired, the enemy apparently intended that it should come.

In combination with Colonel Huguet, the French military attaché in London, Grierson did more than any other officer of his time to establish good relations between the French and British armies, and it is true to say that the success which attended the despatch of the Expeditionary Force in 1914 was due first and foremost to his initiative and foresight when Director of Military Operations in 1904–1906.   During 1905 we visited in company portions of the Franco-Belgian frontier on which much of the fighting in 1914 took place, and the forecast he then made of the course of events proved to be in many respects singularly accurate, though I confess that neither of us foresaw the four years' struggle against entrenched positions extending from the North Sea to Switzerland.

Grierson was a great favourite with all officers in the directorate, and indeed was one of the most popular men in the army, particularly so with the rank and file.   He had an unrivalled knowledge of all foreign armies, more especially of the German army, and his sudden death from heart failure, when travelling by train through France on the 18th of August 1914 as Commander of the Second Army Corps, was one of the tragedies of the war.

The Expeditionary Force was formed after Mr. (now Lord) Haldane became Secretary of State for War in 1905. At the same time the militia was converted into the Special Reserve, with the duty of providing drafts for the regular battalions at the front ; and the volunteers became the Territorial Force of fourteen divisions for home defence. This organisation was a great improvement on the old one, but it nevertheless suffered from serious defects.   The Expeditionary Force was obviously not strong enough to intervene effectively in a Franco-German war—judging from the extensive preparations for war then being made by Germany ; the Special Reserve could not be kept up to strength and never was ; while, owing to inadequate training and other reasons, a considerable portion of the Territorial Force could not be made efficient, and by the terms of its engagement it was not available for service outside the United Kingdom.

The fact was, as so often before in our history, that the

strength and organisation of our army were not determined by the requirements of our liabilities, but by what our existing methods of recruiting could produce within the financial limits imposed by such annual estimates as it was politically expedient to lay before parliament. On the other hand, the measures taken to ensure the efficiency of the Expeditionary Force—such as it was—and to admit of its rapid despatch oversea were far in advance of anything previously attempted, while all the world knows that in the Great War the Territorial Force covered itself with glory in many a hard-fought battle, and provided an invaluable first reinforcement to the regular army in France and elsewhere. For these results—at the most critical period of the war—Lord Haldane is entitled to more gratitude than is usually accorded to him.

It will be remembered that in 1905 Lord Roberts resigned his seat on the Committee of Imperial Defence, as he was anxious to warn his countrymen of the danger in which they stood, and felt that he could not appropriately do this while a member of the committee. It so happened that I was present at the meeting at which he announced his decision and gave his reasons for it. In the discussion which ensued the veteran Field-Marshal was of course hopelessly outclassed by the professional debaters on the committee, his manner of expression being characterised rather by blunt honesty than dialectical skill, but he remained impervious to all arguments and in a plain and simple way stuck to his guns, being convinced that his first duty was to his country, which he believed—and rightly so—to be living in a fool's paradise. He has sometimes been taunted for not speaking out and getting more done when Commander-in-Chief, but I doubt if he himself fully realised the position until 1905. Having once realised it, nothing could turn him away from the object he had in view. England owes much to Lord Roberts, and the loss of many lives and much suffering might have been averted had his advice been accepted and acted upon by those responsible—soldiers as well as civilians—for the welfare of the Empire.

It was whilst serving as Assistant Director of Military

Operations that I acquired my initial experience as a military lecturer, the occasion being when I addressed the Royal Military Society at Dublin in 1905. At the time there was rather a mania for lectures on the part of the authorities, and those who had to make the local arrangements were often at a loss to find any one who had something useful to say, and was capable of saying it. This was perhaps the reason why Lord Grenfell, then commanding in Ireland, asked me to give a lecture on the North-West Frontier of India, and although I knew a good deal about that country I was terrified at the prospect of having to stand up and talk about it before an audience of some two or three hundred officers. I was even more scared when the moment arrived to begin, but by degrees my shaking limbs were brought under control and I managed to tell the story, previously committed to memory, without entirely losing my wits. In fact the performance was a mild success, judging from what Lord Grenfell was good enough to tell me, and afterwards I received several requests to speak at other military centres. I complied with as many as my duties would permit, as they gave me an opportunity of mixing with officers employed with troops, and incidentally the experience proved helpful when I later became Commandant of the Staff College.

As so often happens in the army, this form of imparting instruction was carried to excess, and officers and men became rather " fed up " with it both as regards quantity and quality. There is no more determined passive-resister in the world than Tommy, when compulsorily present at a lecture or a sermon which is not to his liking. He simply refuses to listen, and is invariably seized with an infectious cough which rapidly spreads throughout the audience or congregation, to the utter discomfiture of the speaker.

A similar craze for lectures broke out after the Great War—the idea, a perfectly good one, being to enlarge the scope of the soldier's education and so fit him for work when he left the army. Many lecturers, supposed to be experts in their particular line, were sent out for this purpose to the Rhine when I commanded there in 1919–20, and while some of them gave interesting and useful instruction, others did not, and in the aggregate they were too numerous. I had to ask the War Office to limit the number, and also to exercise more discretion in the selection of subjects. I explained that, for example, the proposed lectures on " Pond life " and " The anatomy of the rabbit " would scarcely appeal to those men who had already lived in the mud of Flanders for about four years, or to those who, hating rabbits at all times, had been consistently given them as rations on two or three days of the week while serving at home.

I utilised most of my annual leave between 1902 and 1906 in travelling abroad, making journeys to Northern Africa, Canada, the United States, and various countries in Europe, including France, Germany, Norway, Sweden, Denmark, Belgium, Holland, Luxemburg, Spain, Portugal, and the Balkan Peninsula.

On one occasion when visiting the environs of Metz I barely escaped being locked up as a spy. The German authorities were suspicious of all foreigners, and an order had been issued, of which I was ignorant, which forbade the latter being in the vicinity of the Metz forts without a special permit signed by the garrison commander. I was not at all desirous of obtaining information regarding the forts, as they were already sufficiently known to me. I was merely re-studying the battle of Gravelotte, and, when near St. Privat, a detective in plain clothes appeared on the scene and enquired in French whether I was a French officer. I gave him rather an abrupt reply in English, thinking he was one of the many so-called guides who frequent the battlefield, and he then, speaking in good English, told me who he was and demanded my passport. As I could not produce it, having left it at the hotel at Metz, he took me by the arm and said he must detain me in the village police station, pending investigation. I was careful to be civil to him, and when I expressed regret at having broken the rules, and informed him that I was an English colonel, he immediately apologised and we parted on good terms.

British officers travelling abroad sometimes make the mistake of being too off-hand in their dealings with foreign officials, with the result that they may be put to considerable inconvenience and even be kept under arrest, in unpleasant and unsanitary conditions, while a lengthy correspondence is conducted between the governments concerned before they are released. More than one such instance came to my knowledge when I was at the War Office.

After parting company with the detective, my wife, who was with me, and I cycled our hardest back to our hotel and, suspecting that further enquiries would be instituted, packed our boxes and started off for Niederbronn, whence I wished to visit the battlefield of Woerth. I was the more anxious to get away from Metz because my passport showed that I was Assistant Director of Military Operations, and had this become known there is little doubt after what had passed that I would have been detained.

One of the sights at Metz which attracts the attention of all visitors is a figure at the main entrance to the cathedral, which bears a striking likeness of the ex-Kaiser. Some years ago the figure of the prophet Daniel, draped in Eastern costume, was about to be placed there, and according to the local story the order went forth for the prophet to be given the ex-Kaiser's features. After the town was occupied by the French at the end of 1918 handcuffs were placed on the figure, and on them was hung a card inscribed in large letters, " Sic transit gloria mundi ! " They were still there when I visited Metz in June 1919.

I made several journeys to the Belgian Ardennes, Namur, Liége, and the Meuse valley between these two towns. They were of special interest because of the possibility of Germany violating Belgian neutrality in the event of her going to war with France, and it had become quite evident, from her railway extensions alone, that she meant to enter Belgium. Before her intentions became so obvious, opinions varied a good deal as to what she would do, as there was much to be said both for and against the operation ; but on balance it always seemed to me, and so I officially stated, that it would be attempted, notwithstanding the elaborate Liége and Namur defences which had been constructed at great cost in order to close this line of advance.

When visiting the Peninsula battlefields I first proceeded from Lisbon to the famous lines of Torres Vedras.

which proved to be a harder nut than Massena could crack
when he stumbled up against them in following Wellington
after the battle of Busaco. The passage of the Douro at
Oporto, the next place I visited, would in these days be
regarded as a minor operation, the French casualties being
estimated at five hundred killed and wounded, while the
British were only slightly over a hundred. But it was
nevertheless a fine performance. The river at Oporto is
some three hundred yards wide, the current is rapid and
the banks are precipitous and rocky, and to attempt
to cross such an obstacle in presence of the enemy, and
without a bridging train, was an extremely perilous and
daring undertaking. Had Soult and his staff taken reasonable precautions the attempt ought not to have succeeded.

There is a good club at Oporto, established many years
ago by the English colony engaged in the port wine trade,
and as the hotels are of a poor and unsanitary type I was
glad to accept the privilege of its hospitality. The club
was used by Soult and his staff before they were so suddenly
expelled from the town, and their signatures are to be seen
in the visitors' book. On the same page are the names of
Wellington and his staff, who it will be remembered ate
the dinner that had been prepared for Soult and his officers.

The plateau of Busaco affords a magnificent view of the
surrounding country, and on it now stands a large and
comfortable hotel, originally intended, I believe, as a palace
for the King of Portugal. Tennis, golf, and other games
are played on the ground where the battle was fought on
the 27th of September 1810. The battle ought to have
taken place on the 25th of the month, before the allies were
in position. Ney asked permission to attack on that day,
but Massena, like other French generals of his time, under-
rated Wellington, and after keeping Ney's messenger
waiting several hours he replied that all action should be
deferred until he arrived at the front. He leisurely appeared
about noon on the following day, and then fixed the battle
for the 27th of September. By that time the allies had
completed their arrangements for defence, and after inflicting some 4500 casualties on the French and losing
about 1500 men themselves they were able to withdraw

L

unmolested, " according to plan " as we would say in these days, to the lines of Torres Vedras.

For the journey to Canada and the United States I could not spare more than about two months, and therefore it was not possible to see much of these two wonderful countries. The voyage from Liverpool was made under most comfortable conditions, thanks to the kindness of the officials of the Allan Line.

From Quebec the steamer proceeded to Montreal, where I spent a few days, and then went on to Ottawa. From there I continued the journey to Sault Ste Marie, which was the farthest point west I had time to go. The amount of shipping which passes through the Sault Ste Marie, or " Soo," canals can be judged from the fact that although the passage is closed for some months in winter, the annual amount of tonnage fifteen years ago was more than twice that which passed through the Suez Canal. Since then the amount has become much greater. Wheat, timber, iron ore, and other minerals are the principal cargoes. From the Soo I descended Lake Huron to Detroit, and thence went to Toronto, the Niagara frontier, and Buffalo.

Although I saw but little of Canada, what I did see came to me as a great surprise. The large towns, with their fine thoroughfares and magnificent buildings, have an air of business and grandeur of which most people in England have little or no conception, and the rate and scale at which the Dominion has been developed must be seen to be correctly appreciated. I venture to say that a personal visit to our Overseas Dominions is an essential part of the education of all high officials at home whose duties are in any way connected with them, for without some such knowledge gained on the spot their work will probably be not only valueless but may be exceedingly mischievous.

From Buffalo I went to the Adirondacks, an interesting country with a delightful summer climate, and there, at Lake Placid, I struck my first " dry " town in the States. For some reason or other no one seemed to pay much attention to the embargo, and at the hotel where I stayed there was no difficulty in obtaining such wines as

I required. The following day, after a stage-coach drive of about forty miles, I arrived at another town where the sale of alcohol was prohibited, and there my experience was different. Remembering my good fortune of the day before, I asked the waitress at dinner to bring me a whisky and soda, and she reminded me that it was a " dry " town. Ignoring her answer I rather brusquely repeated the request, to which she replied that I could have nothing to drink there, and asked who I was " trying to get at." Having acquired a particularly bad thirst during the hot and dusty drive I interviewed the manager, but for a long time he, too, was obdurate. Finally he relented, took me to his wife's bedroom, and told me to wait there and see what happened. Shortly afterwards a waiter brought in a bottle of whisky, soda water, and a box of cigars, and told me that, by the orders of the " boss," I was to take what I wanted, be quick about it, and then clear out. I carried out all his instructions.

Every one has at different times discovered how small a place the world is, and a rather curious instance of this occurred during my drive through the Adirondacks. A fellow-passenger, an American, told me in the course of conversation that a few months before he had given to the British Consul at Batum an account of what he had seen of the Russian troops in Central Asia, through which he had recently travelled. I remembered having received this information at the War Office, for at the time we were in doubt regarding certain matters which the report very opportunely cleared up. I did not tell this to my companion as it was not desirable he should know where I was employed, but it struck me as being a remarkable coincidence that while travelling by stage-coach in America I should meet the unknown author of the information received from Central Asia.

The visit to the Balkans in the autumn of 1906 was perhaps the most instructive and interesting of all my journeys, for I had already made a close study of the literature regarding this complicated part of the world and required some local knowledge in order to complete it. The visit was rendered the more pleasant and useful by the assistance and hospitality I received from our official representatives at each place where I stayed—with one exception. Journeying from Calais I first went to Berlin and then to Vienna, staying a few days at each place, and afterwards continued the journey to Bucharest, or the " Paris of the East." Here I was the guest of the British Minister, Sir Conyngham Greene, who kindly arranged with the authorities for me to see some Rumanian troops, barracks, hospitals, and other military establishments.

From Bucharest I crossed the Danube at Rutschuk, and then proceeded via Plevna to Sofia, where different branches of the Bulgarian army were paraded for inspection. I was much impressed with the physique of the men and their smartness at drill, and came to the conclusion that the military education of both officers and men was of a higher standard than most people imagined. Less than forty years before the Bulgars were still in slavery to Turkey, and the progress the country had since made was phenomenal. Sofia, from being a collection of mud-hovels, had become a modern town with many fine and substantial buildings, education had advanced rapidly, public works had been instituted on a large scale, and the country in general had become one of the most efficient of all the Balkan States.

From Sofia I went via Adrianople to Constantinople, which from being amongst the most progressive, had become, under Turkish rule, the dirtiest and most retrograde capital in Europe. At the time of my visit the streets were still scavenged by tens of thousands of repulsive-looking dogs, who lived together in batches of a dozen or so, each batch on its own pitch, and if a strange dog ventured to intrude he was immediately attacked by the rightful owners. These unfortunate animals were subsequently deported wholesale to an island in the Sea of Marmora, and in true Turkish fashion were there left to die of hunger and thirst. The streets of Constantinople were mostly unpaved and badly lighted, the installation of electric light was forbidden except—for a consideration—in a few favoured cases, and the same remark applies to telephones, of which there were then but few. Indeed

everything possible seemed to be done to prevent the introduction of modern improvements, the object apparently
being to keep Europeans out of the town.

I attended, as most tourists do, the ceremony of the
Salamlik, and there noticed that I was being closely followed
by a detective—as all foreigners were on these occasions.
The Sultan was insane on the subject of espionage. He
insisted upon being kept fully informed of the movements
of strangers, and all classes, in order to curry favour with
him, played up to his idiosyncrasy. The result was that
over and above an army of professional spies there was a
host of unpaid amateurs who were constantly on the look-
out for some plot, real or imaginary, which they could
report. The only way in which one could move about, or
indeed do anything with reasonable convenience, was by
a liberal employment of bribes. At this period, too, all
power, civil and military, was centred in the hands of the
Sultan, and he was chief spiritual ruler as well. He was
therefore emperor and pope rolled into one.

I noticed that the German Embassy presented a particularly clean and prosperous appearance. The employées
were smartly dressed, the grounds and buildings were well
kept, and in general it was by far the most prosperous-
looking of all the embassies, not excluding our own.
Germany was then forging ahead in Turkey, and was
careful to impress the Eastern mind with her power and
prosperity, while we, who had once been predominant,
were fast falling behind and, like Gallio, cared for none of
these things.

After making a trip to the Black Sea through the Bos-
phorus, which somewhat resembles a winding river of
three-quarters of a mile or less in width, I was glad to get
away from Constantinople and its abominable smells, hideous
noises, dirty streets, and official obstructions. Salonika by
rail, via Dede Agach, was my next halting-place, and from
there I made several journeys into that ethnological museum
known as Macedonia. The mountainous nature of the
interior has always made the country difficult to conquer.
and the various invaders were never able to absorb the
people whom they found in it ; the large towns and sea-

ports attracted men of all races for purposes of business ; and in these and other ways it came about that for centuries the country was a sort of dumping-ground for many different nations.   Again, in addition to the Turks, there were four Christian sects in the country, Greeks, Bulgarians, Serbs, and Rumanians, each with its own special propaganda and aiming at making as many converts as possible.   No corner of the world presented such a conflict of ambitions and interests, and it is not to be wondered at that the Macedonian question seemed for so long to be insoluble.

From Salonika I went north through Uskub to Nish, and thence to Belgrade and Buda-Pesth, spending a few days at each place before returning to England.   A good deal has happened in the Balkans since 1906, and it is not unlikely that much more will happen before a definite settlement is made of that " Eastern question " which has been in existence ever since Turkish rule was established in Europe some 470 years ago.

According to the regulations of the time, the tenure of my appointment as head of the Foreign Section should have expired in October 1905, but for certain reasons it was extended to the end of January 1907.   My rapid promotion to the substantive rank of Colonel in November 1903, though fortunate in some respects, had the disadvantage of involving my removal from the regimental list, and therefore when I left the War Office I was placed on " half-pay."   This term might be supposed to have some connection with full-pay, but in fact it has none at all.   For example, the usual full-pay of a major-general was then £1500 a year, whereas the emoluments of an officer of that rank while on half-pay were only £500 a year.   A similar anomaly, not to say hardship, obtained in the case of officers of other ranks.   Another disadvantage of being on the half-pay list was that as there was no certainty whether or when fresh employment would be given, no settled plans for the future could be made.   In my case the prospect was brighter, as I was authoritatively informed before leaving the War Office that I would shortly be appointed Chief Staff Officer in one of the home commands.   This was the kind of appointment I most desired to have, and I accordingly entered upon my period of enforced idleness with comparatively little anxiety.

This system of half-pay, which renders an officer useless to his profession and country when in the prime of life, and at a time when his experience and accelerated promotion would seem to demand that his services should be fully utilised, is not one which strikes the ordinary man as being in the best interest of the State. I have always thought that there should be no insuperable difficulty in devising a more profitable system, given a less bureaucratic Treasury and more logical methods in the promotion of officers whose retention in the army is considered to be desirable.

CHAPTER X

BRIGADIER-GENERAL, GENERAL STAFF, ALDERSHOT

IN order to fill up the time and improve my knowledge of German I undertook while on half-pay to translate for the War Office certain German and Austrian military publications, and with the assistance of my wife—a good German linguist—the results were, I hope, fairly good, notwithstanding the many technical terms to be unravelled. Amongst these publications were the German official " Regulations for the employment of heavy artillery in the field," from which it was manifest that heavy artillery would play a prominent part in Germany's next war in Europe. This was not the only information of the kind which came to our notice, but we made no effort worth mentioning to provide ourselves with similar artillery, or with the means for producing either it or its ammunition when required, and there was the same indifference with regard to machine-guns. Years before 1914 Germany was known to be paying special attention to machine-gun organisation, and to have raised a considerable number of well-trained machine-gun units, whereas we began the war with no such units, and our battalions had but two machine-guns each.

As the date of my promised re-employment approached,

I was disappointed one day to receive a letter from the War
Office telling me that I would not be given the post which
I had been led to believe a few weeks before would fall to
me. Fortunately Sir William Nicholson, who was then
Quartermaster-General, offered me the post of Assistant
Quartermaster-General at Aldershot, and advised me not to
refuse it as something better might come along shortly. I
took his advice, although the post was no better than the
one I had already held for more than five years, while from
a financial standpoint it was inferior to it. On the other
hand, it afforded a means of learning the duties of a branch
of the staff in which I had hitherto not been employed, and
this experience later proved very useful, especially when I
was Quartermaster-General of the army sent to France in
1914. I took up my new duties in May 1907.

There were then about thirty thousand troops in the
Aldershot command, the principal formations being the 1st
and 2nd Divisions under Major-Generals Grierson and
Stephenson respectively, and the 1st Cavalry Brigade. Sir
John French was in chief command, Sir Archibald Murray
was his Chief of the General Staff, and the Major-General
in charge of Administration, my immediate chief, was at
first Major-General Heath and later Major-General (now
Sir) H. Lawson, both being helpful and considerate masters.

In December 1907 Sir John French was succeeded by
Sir Horace Smith-Dorrien, and at the same time Murray
went to the War Office as Director of Military Training.
Sir William Nicholson, who had recently become Chief of
the Imperial General Staff, gave me the vacancy left by
Murray—a far better post than the one I had expected to
receive earlier in the year, and in fact it was the best of its
kind. Once more, therefore, fortune had favoured me, and
the advancement was the more gratifying because it occurred
at Aldershot where, on a miserable November night thirty
years before, I had entered the cavalry barracks as a recruit
—a lonely and, for all practical purposes, a seemingly
friendless lad. I would often, when passing in that direction as Chief of the General Staff, gaze at the old barrack-
room where I first lived, and at its neighbour the guard-
room of evil memory, and wonder how it had come about

that I was now a General Officer and the right-hand man of the Commander-in-Chief.

Murray left everything connected with General Staff work in good order, and it was easy to take over from him the threads of peace training. My two assistants on the General Staff were Major Kerr of the Gordon Highlanders and Captain Nicholl of the Bedfordshire Regiment, both hard-working and capable officers. " Freddie " Kerr was a born soldier, possessed of sound military instinct, and popular with all who knew him. The army suffered a great loss when he was killed near Ypres in 1914. Colonel " Freddie " Wing, the staff officer for artillery duties, was a splendid horseman, keen and active, and in character as fine a type of man as could be met. He was killed at the battle of Loos in October 1915 when in command of a division. Brigadier-General " Peter " Buston was the Chief Engineer, and Major McMahon was in charge of the musketry. Colonel Kerr Montgomery and Colonel Alec Godley were respectively the senior General Staff Officers of the 1st and 2nd Divisions. Godley was later employed with the New Zealand Forces, being succeeded by Colonel De Lisle, and both of them commanded army corps during the Great War. The administrative services came under the charge of Major-General Robb when Lawson succeeded Stephenson in the command of the 2nd Division, while Kerr was succeeded on the General Staff by Lieut.-Col. (now Major-Gen. Sir) W. Campbell.

On the personal staff of the Commander-in-Chief were Major Clive Wigram, assistant military secretary, and now assistant personal secretary to His Majesty, and Captain Way, the aide-de-camp. Captain Arthur Wood, a son of Sir Evelyn, and Lieutenant Boscawen, a son of Lord Falmouth, were also aides-de-camp at different times. Boscawen, a charming boy and a most promising officer, won the D.S.O. and rose to the rank of Major in the Great War, meeting his death in the summer of 1918. This completes the list of staff officers with whom I was most frequently brought into contact. I always thought we were a happy family, and I hope the others were of the same opinion.

Having had the opportunity of seeing both sides of life in the army during the thirty years that had elapsed since I first went to Aldershot in 1877, it may be of interest to the reader if I compare some of the conditions under which a soldier then lived and worked with those which prevailed when I joined the Aldershot staff in 1907.

In my early days the soldier when off parade had the choice of three places in which to pass his time—the barrack-room, the library (a fusty, ill-kept place without a book or a newspaper worth reading), and the canteen, where besides bread and cheese little could be bought except beer. Inside the barracks these were the only facilities afforded for his recreation and self-improvement ; outside the barracks, in Aldershot, the "Soldier's Home," maintained by kind-hearted benefactors, was almost his only alternative to women and beer-shops, both of the lowest type ; and beyond an occasional cricket match he was not encouraged to play any outdoor game. In not a few regiments his officers saw little or nothing of him except when on parade or at stables ; they showed no interest in his personal concerns, and sometimes did not even know his name, although he might have been under their command for weeks. It was realised by some inspecting officers that this state of affairs was not what it should be, from the professional standpoint alone, and I have heard the most absurd replies given when troop officers have been asked to tell them a man's name, or what length of service he had. The great thing was to give an answer of some sort and give it quickly, whether it might be the right one or not.

By 1907 all this had been changed. Officers were now expected to know all about their men, to look after their minds as well as their bodies, and generally to identify themselves in peace with those upon whom they would have to depend in war. To this new demand they readily responded—as British officers always will once they know what is required of them—and much keenness and rivalry were displayed by regiments in making physical exercises more interesting, and in organising cross-country races and other useful forms of sport such as football, hockey, and boxing. By Smith-Dorrien's directions a number of first-class recreation grounds were later provided sufficient to meet all requirements.

A vast improvement was also noticeable in regard to the men's food, though it varied a good deal in different units. Formerly the rations had not only been inadequate and, for want of proper supervision, often of inferior quality, but there had been much waste and some corruption in their disposal, while the cooks were selected without reference to their culinary knowledge and were sometimes notoriously the dirtiest men in the regiment. Better rations were now supplied, economical use was made of them, and the cooks were taught their trade and made to understand that cleanliness is the first requisite of a good cook-house.

Again, in the old days the men dined in the same room where they lived and slept, and ate their meals off the same table on which they pipeclayed their accoutrements, the table itself being rarely cleaned more than once a day, and then perhaps only with the broom used for sweeping the floor. These objectionable customs had largely disappeared. Separate dining-rooms, wherever possible, were now allotted, the supply of crockery was improved, tablecloths were provided, and the meals were served up in a more palatable and decent form. With the establishment of what are called regimental institutes the soldier also had at his disposal various rooms — corporals' room, concert-room, writing-room, coffee-room, all reasonably furnished—where he could spend a comfortable hour when off duty, and with no temptation to get drunk.

The methods of giving instruction in riding, foot-drill, musketry, and other elementary forms of training had been improved out of all recognition since 1877, and the whole system of training in its more advanced stages had been changed for the better. Lord Wolseley, Sir Evelyn Wood, and other military reformers had insisted on going far beyond the antiquated instructions contained in the " drill books " of the period, and before the South African war the preparation of training manuals was taken in hand. That campaign delayed their completion, but on its termination the excellent book known as " Combined Training " was issued. It was followed, when the General Staff was formed in 1904, by the publication of "Field Service Regulations" and "Training Manuals" for each arm. These covered the entire field of individual and tactical training, and it is universally admitted that the principles they enunciated well stood the test to which they were put in the Great War.

To sum up, the soldier was no longer treated, as he used to be, as a being without intelligence and without the remotest chance of ever developing any, down whose throat it was the business of the non-commissioned officer to force as much parrot-like drill as possible but never to attempt to draw anything out. "Why did you do that?" the unfortunate man would be asked when accused of making a slip, and when he explained that he had done it because he thought it was the proper thing to do in the circumstances, the reply would be: "You have no right to think, do as you are told, and don't think again." This stupid attitude was going out of fashion. A man was taught to use his wits and act with initiative and responsibility, individual instruction was superseding squad drill, and a clear distinction was drawn between drill pure and simple and field training.

It must not be thought that perfection had been reached in any of these matters. Much remained to be done, and Smith-Dorrien was the man to do it. Full of energy himself, he expected every one in his command to be equally zealous and to take his profession seriously. He held strongly that the utmost should be done for the welfare of the men and their families, and that they should be trusted not to abuse the increased privileges granted to them. In carrying out these objects he was well supported by Grierson, Stephenson, Lawson, and his other immediate subordinates, and the aim of all was to try and bring out what was best in the men and not everlastingly be thinking of the worst.

We had learned many useful lessons in the South African war, both as to what to do and what not to do, more especially as to the use of ground, and we also had some surprises in the Russo-Japanese war. But there was still much difference of opinion as to the extent to which these lessons ought to modify previously-accepted methods. British officers, like other mortals, are not infallible, and their ideas are apt either to move too slowly and in strictly defined grooves, or to fly off to the opposite extreme. It was for the senior commanders and General Staff to steer a correct course between excessive regard for regularity and rule on the one hand, and the desire to throw all previous experience to the winds on the other—to see, in short, that methods of training kept pace with changing conditions but did not madly overrun them. Having shared in much fighting in past wars Smith-Dorrien was well qualified to judge of the probable characteristics of future wars, and the importance he attached, when commanding at Aldershot, to the right use of ground, the effect of rifle and machine-gun fire, and the necessity for carefully training section and other subordinate leaders proved, in the light of the Great War, that his appreciation was singularly accurate.

"Modern war," ran one of his training instructions, "demands that individual intelligence should be on a high plane. Battlefields now cover such extensive areas that control by officers is very difficult, consequently non-commissioned officers and even private soldiers very often find themselves left to their own resources : and it is only by being accustomed in peace training to use their common sense and intelligence that they are likely to be equal to their duties in war."

Another instruction laid down that "troops should be continually practised in improvising existing cover in every possible piece of ground gained which it is important to hold. Officers and non-commissioned officers should be trained to sight and trace trenches after dark as well as by day. Artillery, too, is very dependent on the hours of darkness in getting into position, and although it may as a rule be possible to select positions during the day, it must frequently happen that the actual digging of gun-pits and moving guns into them must take place at night."

Smith-Dorrien was particularly insistent during field training that individual officers and men should not unnecessarily expose themselves to view or fire, and would sometimes emphasise this in very downright terms. The admonition was not without good reason, and it was not forgotten by those to whom it was addressed.

Work was fairly strenuous all the year round, the normal stages of field training being squadron, battery, and company in March and April ; regimental and battalion in May and June ; brigade, divisional, and command from July to the middle of September ; individual training throughout the winter.

As at all other stations, training suffered from the two defects inherent to our army system—weakness of the battalions and inequality in the proficiency of the men under instruction, whose army service varied between one day and about twenty years. This complication was due to recruits dribbling in at all periods of the year—the result of voluntary enlistment as compared with universal service, which enables the whole of the recruits for one year to be received on the same day, and to be put through a systematic and progressive course of training.

These disadvantages were specially felt in regard to the training of the officers, for as battalions always contained a large percentage of recruits who had not completed their drill in barracks, and who therefore were not available for training in the field, the officers had no opportunity of commanding their units at full strength, and in some ways this destroyed the whole value of the training. To get over the difficulty two units would be put into one, but this brought in men who were strangers to the commander, and who regarded the work as a bore and of no benefit to themselves. Another expedient was to give the officers theoretical schemes to work out, the troops being imaginary ; but this again was a poor substitute for the real thing, for only few instructors are capable of making it useful to the instructed, and also it was unpopular.

Training was, in fact, largely a case of trying to make bricks without straw, and there was much truth in what a distinguished General once said to me : " Never forget, Robertson, that we have two armies—the War Office army and the Aldershot army. The first is always up to strength, and is organised, reorganised, and disorganised almost daily. The second is never up to strength, knows nothing whatever about the first, and remains unaffected by any of these organising activities.

It just cleans its rifle and falls in on parade." The army of no other European country laboured under the same disadvantages as we did, and it is to their undying credit that our officers stuck to their work in such discouraging circumstances, and in the Great War proved themselves to be such fine commanders.

Of the other training problems which engaged attention at Aldershot it may be added that the cavalry were issued with a new-pattern sword, the old custom of cutting and hacking at one's opponent giving place to the more lightning-like thrust. Definite efforts were made for the first time to provide the troops with travelling-kitchens (*i.e.* vehicles in which the food can be cooked whilst on the move and so be ready whenever wanted) ; and mechanical transport was worked out on a practical basis, thus solving some of the difficulties attaching to the supply of food and ammunition in the field. In the summer of 1909 the 1st Division was mobilised as an experiment, the necessary additional men, horses, vehicles, etc., being taken from other units at Aldershot and elsewhere. This was the first time any one had ever seen a British division at war strength, and it was the last till August 1914. The experience gained was valuable, and upon it were based many of the decisions for the movement and handling of large formations which were successfully practised in the Great War.

One of the most important innovations of all was the organisation of " communication companies." It can be understood that in the employment of large forces spread over wide areas a multitude of messages, orders, and instructions regarding fighting, feeding, moving, and many other matters have to be conveyed between commanders, staff, and troops, and that unless they are conveyed accurately and promptly serious consequences may ensue. Heretofore the arrangements for this service had been of the most sketchy and unsatisfactory kind. For use amongst themselves and with their brigade headquarters, the regiments, battalions, and batteries had each had their quota of " signallers," equipped with flags, lamps, heliographs, and other appliances for visual signalling, as well as a varying number of mounted orderlies and cyclists ; between brigades and divisions were telegraph companies working with cables conveyed on waggons, these units belonging to divisions ; and behind them were similar telegraph companies working with cable-waggons and the ordinary land lines of telegraph, these belonging to other formations or directly under army headquarters. This system was both unreliable and uneconomical, and was replaced first by " communication companies " and then by a " signal service " embracing all the different elements. A number of despatch riders and other necessary personnel and material were added to them, the whole being placed under one general control and without unduly interfering with details. The Russo-Japanese war had exemplified the importance of good means of communication, and before I went to Aldershot a temporary organisation for the purpose had been started. When Murray became Director of Military Training he placed it, with the approval of the Secretary of State for War, on a permanent basis, and its development rapidly followed. I shall show in a later chapter how exceedingly well it answered in the Great War.

The foregoing account of training must not be understood to imply that Aldershot alone was identified with laying the foundations of the original " Expeditionary Force." That was not the case. I have already referred to the training manuals published by the General Staff at the War Office, and upon these the training in general was based. We frequently received other forms of assistance from the Training Directorate and the individual officers serving in it. The object of both staffs was to work closely and helpfully together, and this I think was achieved. If it was not it was not the fault of the War Office staff.

Moreover, the Southern, Irish, and other commands played their part in training-duties, although it was on a much smaller scale, Aldershot being the largest military station in the United Kingdom, and the only one where a reasonable number of troops and a fair amount of suitable training-ground were available throughout the year. It also contained many military establishments not to be found elsewhere, such as the signalling school, army gymnastic school, school of cookery, aeroplane and balloon

M

factories and schools, and a large mechanical transport depot.

As the Aldershot area was much too restricted in size, as well as too familiar, for the advanced training of the higher formations, and as we had no legal powers by which ground elsewhere could be acquired, reliance had to be placed on the good-will of landowners and tenants. As a rule these met us in a most generous spirit, though there were some notable and tiresome exceptions. I remember one large landowner who declined to allow us the use of some " common " land which came under his control as lord of the manor, although he was a prominent member of the National Service League ! Another wealthy proprietor once refused, in spite of many entreaties, to grant the use of quite a small, though to us a very important, area which happened to be in the centre of a tract of country already conceded to us by other owners, and without which the contemplated operations would to a great extent become unreal.

A similar difficulty threatened on another occasion, but was overcome by the patriotism and good sense of the owner. Smith-Dorrien had decided that the operations should include the crossing of the Thames by a division during darkness, and there was only one locality available where an improvised bridge could be constructed and the passage made so as to fit suitably into the project as a whole. The ground on one side of the river had been obtained, but the owner of the fields on the opposite bank at first met our request with a blank refusal, and the position seemed hopeless. He had good reason for refusing, for he had recently received in connection with another matter very shabby and exasperating treatment at the hands of the superior military authorities. After a lengthy correspondence I succeeded in gaining a personal interview with him, when he proved to be quite amenable, and gave his full consent for us to do as we wished.

The system of obtaining ground for manœuvres only from those who were sufficiently patriotic to lend it was fundamentally bad and pleased nobody. Separate arrangements had to be made with all the owners, tenants, and sub-tenants concerned, and these would amount to some hundreds in number, and when, after months of correspondence and many personal interviews, consent had at last been obtained, it was always liable to be withdrawn or curtailed at the last moment. Further, some owners and tenants objected to being asked to do that which others were known to have refused to do, and they frequently told me that the only satisfactory system was for the Government to exercise legal powers, take what they wanted from all and sundry alike, and not trade upon the patriotism of those who did not like to refuse. It was really part and parcel of the old question of voluntary *versus* national service. In later years legal powers were taken, to the satisfaction of everybody worth counting.

The benefit troops derive from manœuvres depends almost entirely upon the way in which they are conducted. They are by no means the same thing as war, and cannot be made so because of the absence of bullets. Up to a point they can be rendered exceedingly valuable, but unless properly conducted they may be not only useless but highly mischievous because of the false teaching they give. At the period of which I write they were often accompanied by a considerable element of " eye-wash," and measures were not always taken to ensure that opposing commanders would be compelled to come to their decisions in an atmosphere resembling as far as possible the fog of war which prevails on the battlefield. For example, it was not uncommon for the supervising General to command one of the opposing sides himself, and, after issuing the orders to his own troops, cross over to the enemy's position and from there observe, and afterwards criticise, the action of both forces. Having himself set the problem, and knowing all that was happening on both sides during its solution, he obviously could not derive much instruction from it, or make an impartial criticism of the action of his opponent.

It was, in short, the custom for manœuvres to take the form of a series of " field-days " rather than of continuous operations in face of an enemy, and between the movements of each day there would be a close time when neither side need anticipate danger from the other. Conducted in this manner the so-called manœuvres did not give a true picture of what occurs in war, or anything like it, and might more appropriately have been called battle-drill; and as we were expected by our seniors to believe that they were a close approximation to the real thing, whereas they were nothing of the kind, they belonged to that class which, as I have explained, is more dangerous than useful. Thorough elementary instruction must of course be given before troops proceed to training of an advanced nature, and military commanders, like other people, must learn to walk before they attempt to run, but they will never become expert runners if their training is always restricted to walking.

Once when acting as director of some manœuvres, a year or two after leaving Aldershot, I was asked by a senior officer of the umpire staff at what time the troops might have their dinners. It was then about 2 P.M. on a Thursday. I replied that they could have them whenever they chose. "But," said he, "won't you sound 'stand-fast' or something, so that both sides can dine at the same time and without the risk of being interfered with by each other?" He gave me up as a hopeless lunatic, I think, when I answered: "'Stand-fast' will be sounded on Saturday afternoon when the operations are due to finish. Meanwhile everybody, umpires included, should make their own arrangements for eating, as on active service."

The chief reason why manœuvres were not more practical was that those who supervised them dare not give the opposing commanders a sufficiently free hand for fear the operations might get out of control. Granted the necessary imagination, there need have been no difficulty in preparing such schemes as would permit commanders to go all-out in their own way, and still compel them to keep within the limits imposed by conditions attaching to peace-training—such as time, money, and ground.

Smith-Dorrien determined that his manœuvres should, as far as possible, be carried out as in war; and as an example of this I may mention an incident which occurred in the first manœuvres he held in September 1908, on the Downs near Winchester. At the end of the first day's operations the cavalry brigade of one side went comfortably into bivouac, taking little or no precautions for security during the night, and being unaware that within a mile or two was the bivouac of one of the enemy's infantry brigades. Later on a battalion of this brigade discovered the presence of the cavalry, and at dawn next morning surrounded and took the whole of them prisoners. An umpire came to headquarters to ask for a decision as to what should be done, and was promptly told by the Commander-in-Chief that the cavalry must be placed out of action until the operations terminated. The lesson thus driven home was not likely to be forgotten, and outweighed the disadvantage of depriving the captured brigade of an additional day's training.

" Staff tours," which were much in favour with the War Office authorities when I was at Aldershot, are also fraught with danger unless properly managed. A " staff tour," I may explain for the benefit of the layman, is a form of training intended to give senior commanders and their staffs theoretical instruction in working out on the ground problems of strategy, tactics, marches, and the administration of an army in the field. No troops are employed, but the directing staff decide, according to the orders given and other measures taken by the officers under instruction, what the imaginary troops would accomplish.

One tour held whilst I was at Aldershot had rather a significant ending. Instructions had been issued shortly before by the War Office defining the action required in the event of invasion, and Smith-Dorrien decided to adopt them as the basis of his staff tour scheme, thinking that the officers would thereby derive useful practice in an operation which presumably they might one day be called upon to carry out in reality. During the tour certain defects were exposed which seemed to merit the attention of the authorities, and these were duly brought to notice when, according to custom, the proceedings were forwarded to the War Office. Smith-Dorrien received little thanks for his pains, and was told that his scheme had been based on conditions which were not likely to arise ; that if exercises of this particular kind became known diplomatic complications might ensue ; and that for the future they should be left alone. Whether invasion was a possible contingency or not was a matter upon which opinions had for long been divided, but as instructions for meeting it had been authoritatively issued, Smith-Dorrien was doing no more than his duty in giving his officers an opportunity of studying it.

King Edward paid his usual annual visit to Aldershot in May 1907, and also in 1908 and 1909. His custom was to arrive at 11.30 A.M. and leave about 4 o'clock the same day. As he did not ride, and as it was necessary that he should see as many of the troops as possible, the " scheme " had to be so arranged as to bring the troops near to places where his motor could be taken, and whence he could observe the operations. It was not an easy matter to achieve this and at the same time ensure that the various movements were properly connected and did not develop into unreal situations. One year the operations terminated with an infantry assault on the enemy's position, on the crest of which His Majesty had just arrived. Two battalions of the Guards made the assault at this point, and shortly afterwards, the " cease fire " having sounded, Grierson, the commander of the attacking side, arrived breathless near where the King stood. " Well, General," asked the King, " did you succeed in defeating the enemy ? " " Sir," said Grierson, with his usual diplomacy, " I threw into the assault all the troops at my disposal, including Your Majesty's Guards, and if they could not take the position no troops in Europe could ! " " Very good, very good," answered the King, with a broad smile on his face.

The last time King Edward saw the Aldershot troops at work was in 1909 at Emperor's Hill on the Chobham Ridges. In May the following year preparations were well advanced for another visit, but his death occurred a few days before the date on which he was due to arrive.

King George visited Aldershot several times when Prince of Wales, and has since regularly paid visits lasting for a

AT THE ARMY MANŒUVRES, 1913.

H.R.H. PRINCE ARTHUR OF CONNAUGHT. H.M. THE KING. THE AUTHOR.
H.R.H. THE DUKE OF CONNAUGHT.
BRIG-GEN. BULFIN.

week or ten days. In his practical way His Majesty made it quite clear to everybody that he wished to see the troops at their ordinary everyday work, and would have no change made in the normal training programme. He abhorred everything of the nature of a "set-piece," was quick to detect the intention to foist one upon him as the genuine article, and would roundly condemn any attempt to do, or to allow to be done, anything that would be impracticable in war. His visits were the more valuable to us because on return to London he would be instrumental in compelling the War Office to settle tiresome questions regarding which we had perhaps carried on a fruitless correspondence for months past.

With the same object in view His Majesty usually asked the Chief of the Imperial General Staff to be present during at least a part of his visit. Once when Sir William Nicholson was attending in this capacity the King led us a long morning ride in the hot sun, and as Nicholson neither liked nor was accustomed to horse-exercise he returned to the Royal Pavilion feeling rather stiff and sore, both in mind and body. During luncheon he had to submit to a certain amount of chaff on the subject, the King humorously condoling with him on the sufferings of the morning. Nicholson, who was fond of quoting scripture, replied, " Thank you, Sir, but I trust that I bear my trials with appropriate patience, for I know that whom the Lord loveth He chasteneth."

His Majesty was invariably accompanied by the Queen, and both of them would be employed for the greater part of the day in seeing the troops at work, visiting the various military establishments, enquiring into matters concerning the welfare of the soldiers and their families, and in informing themselves generally of the conditions of Aldershot life. Their Majesties always gave us the impression that they thoroughly enjoyed being amongst the troops, while we were delighted to welcome them and to render their visits pleasant.

The aeroplane, still in its infancy, was a feature of special interest at Aldershot during this period, the renowned Cody being amongst the bravest and most persevering of the pioneers engaged on this perilous work, as it then was.

Under every disadvantage as regards money and material, he laboured for months and even years on Laffan's Plain, assisted by his son, to construct a machine that would consent to leave the ground, remain a reasonable time in the air, and then return to earth without smashing itself to pieces. Eventually he succeeded in accomplishing, for the times in which he lived, some remarkable flights, but later he met the same fate as many other aviators of those early days. The country owes much to Cody.

Kites and dirigible balloons were also still in the elementary stage, and like all other aeronautical duties were under the supervision of Colonel (now Major-General Sir) J. Capper.

The tank was not yet in being, but its prototype, the " caterpillar," was, and was thought to have a great future as a tractor for dragging heavy guns and vehicles across broken ground. Universal sympathy was extended to the drivers, who, in consequence of the caterpillar's violent up-and-down motions, experienced all the sensations of acute sea-sickness, and looked it.

In June 1910, while engaged on a staff tour in Leicestershire, I received a letter from Sir William Nicholson offering me the post of Commandant of the Staff College. This unexpected offer, though flattering to me personally and possessing many attractive possibilities, had the drawback common to other army appointments in that the post was greatly underpaid. However, I determined not to be baulked of a promising opening on that account, but to have a try at filling what was one of the most important positions which an officer of my standing could in peace time be called upon to hold. At the end of July I bade farewell to Aldershot, where I had made many friends and had learned much of the practical side of my profession from the officers with whom I had been associated.

CHAPTER XI

COMMANDANT OF THE STAFF COLLEGE

WHILE at Aldershot I had been nominated to act as Chief of the General Staff to Sir Herbert Plumer, who was to command one of the opposing sides at the army manœuvres to be held in September, but my transfer to Camberley necessarily entailed the appointment of another officer, and as the Staff College was closed during August and September for the summer vacation I utilised these two months in thinking over my new duties and deciding how best to carry them out. This was not a matter to be settled without careful consideration, for there is no position in the army where greater influence for good or for evil can be exerted over the rising generation of officers than that of Commandant of the Staff College.

The history of the college dates back to 1799, when an institution for educating officers for staff employment was established at High Wycombe, the superintendent being, for some reason unknown to me, a retired French officer, by name General Jarry. In 1802 this institution was given the designation of " Senior Department of the Royal Military College," and a Junior Department for educating cadets was added to it. Eleven years later the Senior

Department was moved to Farnham and in 1821 to Sandhurst, and there the two branches continued to be known as the " Royal Military College." In 1862 the present Staff College was built, but both colleges remained under the same Governor until 1870, when the Staff College was separated from the Royal Military College for purposes of instruction, though it continued to be under it for administration. This system was most inconvenient, and while I was Commandant I induced the War Office to separate the two colleges for all purposes and so allow each to look after itself. The number of students in the early days was very small and, as I have said in a previous chapter, amounted in 1897 to about sixty. Shortly before I became Commandant this number had grown to a hundred and twenty, and the instructional staff to fifteen.

There was no adjutant or other administrative officer at the college, and many petty and tiresome details had therefore to be dealt with by me, whereas my whole time ought to have been devoted to instruction. Up to about thirty years before there had been an adjutant, and the story was that he had been abolished on the recommendation of the Commandant, who, having a large family, was desirous of appropriating the adjoining quarters occupied by the adjutant, also a married man. The War Office approved my proposal to revert to the appointment of an adjutant, and I avoided the difficulty as to quarters by asking for a bachelor so that he might live in the college with the other officers. I was fortunate in securing for the post a very excellent officer—Captain Brewis of the Warwickshire Regiment—who was invaluable to me and a great favourite with staff and students alike. To the deep regret of all who knew him, " Bobbie " Brewis was killed in the Great War.

The object of the Staff College being to train officers not only for staff work but also for the duties of command, the name is rather a misnomer, and I have always thought that " War School " would be more appropriate. I tried to get this designation adopted, but without effect. I tried, too, to get the pay of the Commandant increased, but for a long time failed in this also. I set to work rather subtly, so I thought, a few weeks after I had been promoted Major-General in 1912. I pointed out to the authorities that I was still being shown in the Army List as a Brigadier-General of the General Staff, whereas I was in fact a Major-General, and that I could not understand why I should be given a title inferior to that conferred upon me by the King. They were at first puzzled to know what to do, as Major-General of the General Staff was not a recognised appointment, but eventually the higher title was accorded me, and having extracted this concession I then claimed to be paid at a rate consistent with the title. This was refused, no good reasons being given, but when Sir John French became Chief of the Imperial General Staff he saw the justice of the case and a higher scale of pay was sanctioned—the same day that I ceased to be Commandant !

I have already referred to the improvement made in the curriculum after Hildyard became Commandant in 1893, and when he left in 1897 the course was more exclusively practical than at any other college in Europe. Before and after the South African war his system was continued by Miles, and other useful reforms were later introduced by the present Lord Rawlinson, especially in the substitution of work on the ground for the less practical form of work on paper. Summarised, the main subjects were as follows :

Military history and geography, strategy, and tactics, with special reference to modern campaigns, though older ones were also studied.

Principles of Imperial Defence, defence of frontiers, plans of concentration, naval strategy and bases, defended ports, food-supplies of United Kingdom, British and foreign submarine cables, staff duties at home and in the field, organisation of the British and principal foreign armies, landings on an enemy's coast, oversea expeditions in general.

System of transport and supply, economic geography, commercial law.

Medical and ordnance services as affecting commanders and staff officers.

Staff tours, as time and funds permitted.

There were many other subjects, but the above will suffice to show the variety of the work done.

Speaking generally, the first year was devoted to the acquisition of knowledge, and the second to its application. The solving of problems dealing with tactical situations, billeting, camping, and other duties which lend themselves to this method of treatment, was a special feature of the second year's work, as also was the guiding of troops (imaginary) across roadless and unknown country by night.

Staff tours, whose nature has already been explained, usually lasted three or four days, and I tried to conduct them in such a way as would test the students' tempers and physical powers as well as their knowledge. Information about the (imaginary) enemy would be given out at all hours of the day and night and emanate from all sources— newspapers, secret agents, prisoners, inhabitants, and aeroplanes—some of the news being reliable, some doubtful, some contradictory, and it was for the students to sift and piece together the different items, thus obtaining approximately the same amount of information as they might be expected to get in war before they could regulate the action of their troops. This meant that they occasionally had no opportunity of going to bed at night, or only for a short time, notwithstanding that they had been hard at work during the day, and had another similar day in prospect. They took it all in good part, and it served to bring home to them that staff employment in war is not, as some people think, all beer and skittles.

One staff tour was held annually in the Welsh mountains, so as to represent Indian frontier warfare, and on it the inexperienced students discovered what it means to make long mountain climbs on foot, and learnt how to protect camps at night in savage countries, capture passes crowned with *sangars*, arrange for the movement of long strings of pack animals following narrow tracks, and finally how to withdraw a force, sniped by hostile tribesmen from the adjacent hillsides, down the *nalas* to the frontier—at Bangor or Criccieth.

The benefit students derive from the Staff College course naturally depends upon the quality of the instruction, and good instructors, or directing staff as they are called, are not too easily come by. As a rule they are well up in the subjects with which they have to deal, or soon become so after joining the college, and there is no question as to their keenness to do their best for those under their charge. Not all, however, possess the gift of imparting in an interesting and intelligible manner the knowledge they have been at such pains to acquire ; some have a tendency to ride a particular theory to death ; and others to attach so much importance to regulations as to convey the idea that a knowledge of them is in itself a proof of military proficiency.

In order to keep myself acquainted with the kind of instruction given, and to correct what I thought to be wrong, I used to visit the lecture rooms at uncertain hours, and once caused some anxiety to the lecturer as well as amusement to the students, though I did not know this at the time. The lecturer had apparently intended to restrict the lecture to about twenty minutes, the orthodox duration being about fifty, and as I arrived on the scene just as he was coming to an end he proceeded to repeat the whole story again, so I discovered afterwards, the students loyally playing up to him by showing rapt attention in listening to what they had already heard only a few minutes before.

I had, as all Commandants have had, some good instructors and some who were not so good, but on the whole I was very well served and especially by the two senior assistants—Perceval of the Gunners and Johnny Gough of the Rifle Brigade—who were respectively in charge of the two divisions into which the students were formed. Gough had a high reputation as a brilliant and accomplished soldier, and it was a heavy loss to the army when, as Chief of the General Staff of the 1st Army, he was mortally wounded by a stray bullet in Flanders in February 1915, when going to visit his battalion in the trenches. He came of a renowned fighting family, and was the brother of Hubert Gough, who rose in the Great War from Brigadier to the command of the 5th Army, which fought so gallantly against overwhelming odds when the Germans made their great, but unsuccessful, bid for victory in March 1918.

Amongst the other officers employed on the directing staff were Furse, Barrow, Ross and Ballard (contemporaries of mine when a student), Howell (a rising soldier, killed in the Great War), Foster and Hull (since dead), Stewart (who had distinguished himself in Kelly's march from Gilgit to Chitral), Harper, Hoskins, Davidson, and Percival.

At the end of each term—there were three terms in the year—the directing staff of each of the two divisions met in conference to discuss the work done by the students and to classify them according to the ability they had shown. This classification underwent considerable alteration during the first year of the course, as the progress made by some of the officers was much greater than that made by others ; but in the second year it remained fairly constant, and by the end of that year it was perhaps as good an estimate of the students' capacity as could be made. There was no danger of favouritism, for if any one of the staff showed an undue leaning towards a student the others could be relied upon to see that impartiality was maintained. As previously mentioned, this method of deciding upon the students' qualifications was adopted while Hildyard was Commandant, in preference to the system hitherto in vogue by which they were placed in order of merit mainly according to the number of marks gained in paper examinations at the end of the course. It answered well, and this I think is proved by the fact that of the 180 officers who graduated during my régime very few failed in the Great War to come up to the expectation formed of them, and fewer still exceeded it.

The students are liable to be sent away from the college for misconduct, or if they show themselves unlikely to become proficient staff officers or commanders. It fell to my lot to dismiss two only. One was a young man from the Overseas Dominions who, both by ordinary education and natural ability, ought not to have been sent to the college, for he could never hope to be equal to a position of responsibility.

The other was a clever and gallant officer who foolishly persisted in refusing to grow a moustache, thus contravening the King's Regulations of the time, which directed that the upper lip should not be shaved. Many of the young men of the period were in the habit of shaving, and as strict orders had been issued by the War Office forbidding the practice, and telling General Officers to put a stop to it, the offender was duly warned by the directing staff of his division. As this had no effect he was brought before me, and when I asked him why he continued to break the regulations he replied that they merely forbade shaving, and that he did not shave, but only made use of the scissors to cut off such few hairs as would grow, and which looked very ugly when allowed to grow. No one would be so idiotic as to think that an officer is any better for wearing a moustache than he is for shaving or clipping it off, and the regulation has since been abolished, but staff officers are expected to set an example of obeying the King's Regulations, and I had no alternative but to report the matter. The officer was ordered to leave the college, and I am sorry to add that he was killed in the Great War.

On taking over command of the college the flaw in instruction which struck me most was one which is not uncommonly seen in other educational establishments—that is, the aptitude to dwell too much upon the theoretical aspect of a problem and the neglect to realise the difficulties which beset its solution in practice. Details, so-called, were thought to be petty and beneath the notice of the big-minded man, and yet they are the very things which nine hundred and ninety times out of a thousand make just the difference in war between success and failure. Whatever may be the case in peace time there are few or no small things in war, though some are of greater importance than others, and those who, like myself, attended the meetings of the War Cabinet for more than two years during the Great War will bear out this statement.

Another objectionable habit I noticed was the craving to employ high-sounding phrases such as "pivot of manœuvre," "interior lines," "offensive-defensive," and so on, all of which were right enough in their way, on paper, but in actual war do not greatly assist the ordinary commander in the thing that really matters, the defeat of the enemy. There is only one road to victory, given a capable opponent, and that is the road of hard fighting, of which there is usually a great deal. I was very insistent on this point, and in the solution of problems, whether on paper or on the ground,

I would always lead the student up to it and from it judge whether his solution was or was not sound. War, I would impress upon him, is largely a contest between the brains and grit of the opposing commanders, in which each endeavours to outwit, outlast, and beat the other.

In the course of my final address to the students who left the college at the end of 1912 I said :

It will further assist you to keep on the right lines if at all times you remember to study with the definite aim of obtaining guidance for future use in war, and not merely for the sake of amassing a store of information. Not one of us could compare perhaps with certain military historians who might be mentioned, as far as mere knowledge of past wars is concerned, and yet we do not admit that they would prove to be our best commanders. Why ? Simply because they do not study military history, we think, in the way that we do or ought to do, namely with the object of making actual use in war of the knowledge acquired. If we conduct our investigations from this standpoint we shall not be likely to waste time in fascinating, but valueless, hair-splitting dialectics ; we will not make too frequent use of stereotyped phrases which may mean one of several things or even nothing at all ; we shall not burden our minds with too many historical parallels ; and will not be so apt to form conclusions which, however attractive they may appear on paper, have little or no connection with the rough and bloody work of masses of men trying to kill each other.

The question of giving more instruction in duties connected with a retreat also called for attention. The training regulations dwelt with great persistence on the importance of the offensive, and the idea of fighting on the defensive was thought to be so obnoxious to the minds of the authorities that, for some time past, it had been deemed politic to leave defensive training severely alone. There was the greater inclination to leave it alone because of the impossibility of reproducing in peace some of the conditions —and the most important of them—which attach to a retreat in war. Still it was necessary to do all that could be done, for however valuable offensive action may be, and undoubtedly is, there could be no certainty that a defensive policy would not one day be imposed upon us, and for that contingency we ought to be prepared. I therefore made it

LORD ROBERTS, LADY ROBERTSON, AND THE AUTHOR AT A[STAFF COLLEGE GARDEN PARTY.

an almost invariable practice at all staff tours and other
exercises on the ground to create a situation that entailed
taking measures for retreat, and the following extract from
the final address referred to above bears on the same
subject :

Of all forms of making war the one that demands most
careful study is that of fighting a superior and well-trained force.
Every soldier feels, and ought to feel, a great aversion from retiring
from before the enemy without a trial of strength, and yet if the
enemy is found to be superior (I do not refer merely to numbers),
and is concentrated, there may be nothing for it but to fall back
and await a better opportunity, as many a good general has had
to do in the past.   For example, Moore to Corunna ; Wellington
in 1810 and again in 1812 ; Napoleon to Leipzig in 1813 and to
Paris in 1814 ; and Jackson and Lee in the American Civil War.
The great difficulty attaching to operations of this nature is to
reconcile two conflicting aims—the husbanding of one's own
forces and the infliction of loss upon the enemy—and it can only
be overcome if the commander possesses sound judgment and a
powerful iron will ; if the staff are accurate in their calculations
and untiring in their efforts ; and if the troops possess great
mobility, high morale, confidence in their leaders, and good
fighting capacity in general.   Remember, too, that the larger the
force the more difficult does the operation become.   Our regulations justly lay stress on the value of the offensive ; but if this
teaching alone is given, think what may be the effect on the troops
when they are ordered to retire instead of to go forward—that
is, to abandon that method of making war by which alone,
according to the training they have previously received, decisive
victory can be achieved.   Think, too, of the disintegration and
demoralisation which nearly always accompany retrograde movements, even when an army has not been previously defeated.   It
seems to me that there is practically no chance of successfully
carrying out this operation in war unless we thoroughly study and
practice it beforehand during peace.   If we have this practice,
the operation will then not come as a surprise to the troops in
war ; they will understand better what they are expected to do ;
and they will recognise it as being a form of war which may have
to be adopted by any army, and can be adopted, not only without
failure, but with a certain measure, ultimately, of success.   You
will do well to study the methods of Wellington in the Peninsula,
and the teaching furnished by the American Civil war on this
important subject.

I have reason to believe that this advice, published in

N

the *Army Review* by the order of the Secretary of State for War, Lord Haldane, caused other and more senior officers to give increased attention to defensive fighting, and thereby was indirectly of some help to them in the historic retreat from Mons.

Emphasis was also laid, day in and day out, on the importance of the staff cultivating close and friendly relations with the regimental officers, and of preventing the erection of the barrier which at one period separated the two with such pernicious effect. This advice, too, I believe, bore fruit in the Great War, as did also the injunction not to be content with merely giving orders, but, by watching and helping before matters had time to go wrong, ensure that they were carried out as the commander desired.

Another warning persistently rubbed in was the probability of war with Germany, and the responsibilities it would cast upon Staff College officers in particular. In this connection, and at the risk of being accused of unduly blowing my own trumpet, I shall quote from the final address I made to the students who left at the end of 1911 :

So far as one can judge from the present state of the world, you may any day find yourselves taking part in a war than which there has been no greater for the last hundred years or so, and it may be upon *you* to whom I am now speaking that to a great extent will depend how we emerge from that war. We are too apt to go on day by day discussing the probability and consequences of certain wars, without ever really recognising our own individual responsibility, and remember that officers who have been through the Staff College have the greater responsibility. You do not come here for the sake of passing examinations at the end of the first year, and of obtaining a P.S.C. at the end of the second. You come here in order that you may leave the college better and more efficient members of the military community. You should endeavour to increase the knowledge you have acquired, disseminate it amongst others, and, as I have often told you, *direct your studies and peace preparations in general to a special and definite end—that of fighting the most probable and most formidable adversary for the time being.*

Finally, remember that when the day for fighting comes, the qualifications demanded of you, whether on the staff or in command, will include, in addition to a good theoretical knowledge of your professional duties, the possession of a quick eye, a good digestion, an untiring activity, a determination to close with your enemy, and a firm resolution not to take counsel of your fears.

It was well understood between me and the students who " the most probable and most formidable adversary " was. We had often discussed him, and there was no need to mention him by name. That was seldom done, as the hint had long since been received from London that we were not in any way to meddle with questions which might, if they became known, give offence to a friendly (!) Power, and possibly lead to " diplomatic complications." " Mum " was the word, therefore, in regard to all work—and there was a great deal—which was designed to assist the students in studying the conflict which threatened us, and which we had in fact to meet within less than three years of the time when the above words were spoken.

Shortly before I became Commandant the Admiralty had established a War College at Portsmouth, with the object of giving instruction to naval officers somewhat similar to that given at the Staff College. The course was, however, much shorter, and in other respects was not regarded as being of quite the same importance, but I should imagine that it did a great deal of good, and it undoubtedly helped to bring the two services closer together. Two or three naval officers attended the Staff College for a few months as students, and military officers were sent to the Naval College ; the students of both colleges, with their instructors, occasionally took part in combined naval and military exercises, in which there was a useful exchange of ideas ; and in many ways the officers of the two colleges were able to learn much from and about each other. Amongst the naval friends I had the good fortune to make in this way was Sir Henry Jackson, then Commandant of the Naval College. He very kindly arranged for me to spend a week at sea with the 1st Battle Squadron, commanded by Admiral Sir Stanley Colville. The work of the squadron was full of interest for me, especially the " battle practice," and I was most hospitably treated by the Admiral and the officers of his fine flagship the *Collingwood*.

Besides making the usual trips to the more classical battlefields of 1870–71—Spicheren, Woerth, and Gravelotte —I revived the custom which had lapsed in recent years of taking the students to the battlefields near Amiens, Orleans, and Le Mans. I did so because these battles had a special value of their own, as they were fought by partially-trained and hastily-raised French troops, and I always felt that one day we ourselves might have to fight with the same kind of troops, as indeed we had to do in the Great War. I think I am justified in saying that the discussions which ensued and the knowledge that was acquired during these visits were of benefit to the students when employed with the troops of which our New Armies were composed.

During one of the visits to Orleans, the headquarters of a French army corps, I had an interesting conversation with the corps commander, who, as a young man, had fought in the French cavalry during the war. He had been present at the famous cavalry charge at Morsbronn, and then went with the remains of MacMahon's army to Sedan, where he took part in the cavalry charge which preceded the investment of that place, his regiment being one of the few to break through the German lines before the French forces were entirely surrounded. He was then sent south to the Loire, being present at the various battles near Orleans, and he was therefore able to give much information in regard to them.

One day he invited me to bring my fifty odd students after dinner to meet some of his officers at the military club. We were given a most cordial reception, and after the national anthem had been played by a large band outside the club, which was brilliantly illuminated, we were conducted inside. We entered a room profusely decorated with flowers and flags, and sat down to enjoy dessert, wine, coffee, and smokes. To my surprise our host got on his feet towards the end of the evening, and made a very eulogistic speech respecting the British army, and its past and present relations with the French army. One of his staff then read the English translation of the speech, which had evidently been prepared with much care, and it then remained for me to reply.

Having been taken unawares, and being at all times incapable of making a public speech on the spur of the moment, I felt that the only thing to do was to put on a bold front and try to score by replying in French. I knew that my vocabulary was very limited, and that my French pronunciation was execrably bad, but there seemed nothing for it but to do or die. After talking for the space of some ten minutes, and having tried the effect of a few jokes— which apparently were not understood and certainly did not amuse—the proceedings became distinctly flat, and as a total collapse seemed to be imminent I made a last despairing effort not to be beaten. I apologised for my ignorance of the French language, regretted I could not say half what I wished to say, and added that, being unable to speak further, I would call on my officers to sing a ditty commonly heard at similar reunions in England. I then proposed the health of the corps commander and asked the officers to sing " For he's a jolly good fellow." They responded with even more than the usual amount of noise and discord, and all that the French officers could grasp of the performance was a repetition of the same words. Next morning I bought the local newspaper in order to see what kind of account was given of the entertainment. The corps commander's speech, a very good one, was reported verbatim. Mine was not. I did not expect that it would be. But the reporter credited me with a far better speech than the one I had actually delivered, and added that, at the end of it, I called upon my officers to sing the well-known English song of which the chorus was, " For thou art a very good man ! "

On another occasion, in 1913, we were invited by General Picquart to meet the officers of the army corps at Amiens. Not to be again caught napping I took the precaution to ask Maurice—one of my staff and an excellent French scholar—to prepare a speech for me beforehand. It was well that I did so, for I had to reply to a most flattering welcome, and can claim (thanks to Maurice) to have come out of the ordeal with flying colours. I had a long talk with the General before we parted. He was a native of Strasburg, and as a boy of about ten years of age was in the city when the Germans besieged it in 1870. He described to me, with some emotion, how his family had lost all their property and treasures, and he evidently looked forward to the day of reckoning, and hoped that when it arrived we would be on his side. A few months afterwards he was thrown from his horse and killed.

So as not to lose all touch with the practical side of soldiering I used to attend the annual divisional and brigade trainings as far as college duties would allow. One year I was asked to prepare a scheme for the inter-divisional manœuvres of two of the commands in England, and to draft it in such a way as to test the leadership of two brigadiers who were shortly to be considered by the Selection Board for promotion to Major-General. I therefore so arranged matters that at the commencement of the operations the two officers found themselves opposing each other, each being in command of a detachment which was unlikely to be reinforced for a period of at least twelve hours, and I left them as free a hand as possible in dealing with the situation thus created, so that they might show what they could do. How they emerged from the test it was no part of my business as chief umpire to say, and I do not pretend to know what opinion was formed of them by the two General Officers under whom they were serving, and who exercised chief supervision over the operations; but I do know that they were not promoted when their turn came, and yet both of them rose to positions of high command in the Great War. Manœuvres afford the best means in time of peace for testing the capacity of an officer to command troops in war, but they are not always a reliable guide of a commander's merit; they are very different from the real thing.

In 1912 I was ordered to accompany the King during the army manœuvres in Cambridgeshire, and wishing to make myself acquainted with the country over which they were to take place, I motored through it a few days previous to the commencement of operations, being accompanied by Colonel Oxley, who was then on the directing staff of the college. One morning a powerful car suddenly emerged at full speed from a blind corner at some cross-roads we were passing, striking our lighter car—an open one—full broadside and turning it completely round and upside down. Oxley, I, and the chauffeur were shot clean out of it, fortunately landing on a patch of grass, for a distance, as we afterwards ascertained, of twelve yards. On picking ourselves up we were surprised to find that we were quite unhurt beyond a few bruises, and I still held in my hands the map and magnifying glass I had been using at the moment the collision occurred. The car was practically a wreck.

Oxley was wont to be a Jonah in his motor drives. Two or three days later his car was again struck by one coming from a side road, though he once more escaped with a shaking ; and one day, when motoring with me along the foot of the South Downs, there was further trouble. We met a ramshackle country cart being driven by a boy, in which were two large casks probably containing pigwash or some such mixture. As the road was narrow we slowed down almost to a halt, the boy directing his cart off the road and up the rather steep hill-side so as to pass us. This brought the full load of the cart to bear on the wheel next to us, and just as we were passing the axle gave way and the boy and the contents of his casks were flung into our car. Oxley was fairly well drenched, but, to his intense relief, it transpired that the casks held nothing worse than drinking water, and the total damage done, over and above the broken axle, was limited to barking the boy's shins. We gave him 2s. 6d. as compensation, and then proceeded on our journey.

During the manœuvres the King and his suite were accommodated in Trinity College, everything possible being done by the college officials to render the visit pleasant to all of us. At the end of the manœuvres the usual conference, or " pow-wow," was held in the hall of the college, some of the Fellows attending to hear how the soldiers acquitted themselves in the talking line. The time of day, immediately after luncheon, was not conducive to alert attention, and for the first hour or so the proceedings dragged on in a dull and dreary manner, with little or no prospect of ever coming to an end. This depressing circumstance, plus the lunch, was too much for some of the audience, and the Master in particular had to struggle very hard to prevent his nodding head from coming into contact with the table at which he sat at the top of the hall.

The following year the manœuvres were held in Northamptonshire. I was again attached to the King's suite, all of whom were the guests of Lord Spencer at Althorp. The party numbered about twenty, and included the Queen, the Duke of Connaught, and Prince Arthur of Connaught. Lord Spencer was a delightful host, surpassed in kindness, if at all, only by his daughter Lady Delia, who acted as hostess. By his invitation I went to Althorp a few days before the manœuvres commenced so as to talk over and arrange certain matters with him previous to Their Majesties' arrival, and I have the most pleasant recollection of the hospitality received.

On the day the manœuvres terminated I was informed by Clive Wigram, one of the equerries, that the King wished to see me. I found His Majesty with the Queen, Lord Spencer, and a few members of the suite in the famous picture gallery, and was then told by the King that in return for the services I had rendered during the last few years he proposed to make me a Knight Commander of the Victorian Order. I was more than surprised, somewhat nervous, and quite ignorant as to what I was expected to do, but Wigram came to the rescue, drew the sword he was wearing, handed it to the King, and told me to kneel down. Having duly knighted me the King put out his hand, and not knowing what else to do I shook it, rising to my feet at the same time. I ought to have kissed it, of course, as a sign of homage, but the King was probably quite as pleased to see me shake it. The incident brought a broad smile over the faces of the onlookers, and I beat as hasty a retreat as I respectfully could. I have always felt far more gratified with the honour thus simply and spontaneously conferred upon me as a mark of His Majesty's personal esteem, than with any of the rewards since received on the recommendation of ministers or my military superiors.

In the summer of 1913 I was told by Sir John French that he wished me to go to the War Office as Director of Military Training. This was much against my inclination,

as I have always disliked life in London, more especially
official life, and I was anxious to be given active command
of troops. However, the Field-Marshal was good enough to
make his request more palatable by promising me the
command of the 1st Division at Aldershot when it became
vacant in the summer of the following year.

The night before leaving the Staff College, in October
1913, I was entertained by the staff and students at dinner,
and I am not ashamed to say that in the short farewell
speech I made to them my heart was fairly in my mouth.
Black sheep are to be found in nearly every flock, but there
are an unusual small proportion of them at the Staff College.
Both staff and students are of the most attractive character,
hard workers, lovable companions whether at work or play,
and really good fellows in every sense of the word. I grieve
to think that over one hundred and fifty of the officers
who had graduated at Camberley met their death in the
Great War.

The next time I dined with a party of Staff College
officers was at Cologne in 1919, when in command of the
Army of the Rhine. Dillon, my private secretary, collected
all the P.S.C. officers then serving under my orders (I am
afraid one was unintentionally left out), and we spent a
pleasant evening together at my house overlooking the
river, discussing the old Camberley days and the great
events which had since taken place.

CHAPTER XII

DIRECTOR OF MILITARY TRAINING

Duties—Unsatisfactory responsibility for training—Arrangements for
command at home in time of war—"Staff" cannot "command"—
Question of invasion—Invasion ruled out as impracticable and
replaced by theory of raids—Reversion to invasion theory—
Question mainly one for the Admiralty—Constant discussions
finally settled in August 1914—Policy as to invasion during the
Great War—Economy exercised to the detriment of training—
"Curragh incident" and its effect on army officers—"Joe" Maude
—Collapse of the proposed coercion of Ulster and resignation of the
Secretary of State for War, the Chief of the Imperial General Staff,
and the Adjutant-General—Sir Charles Douglas—Army manœuvres
arranged for 1914—War with Germany declared—Am appointed
Quartermaster-General of the Expeditionary Force.

I JOINED the staff at the War Office for the third time on
the 9th October 1913. As Director of Military Training I
was responsible to the Chief of the Imperial General Staff
for the training of all troops at home, for the education of
officers (including the Cadets at Woolwich and Sandhurst
and the Officers Training Corps), and for questions connected
with home defence. The directorate was in good working
order, thanks to the efforts of Murray while in charge of
it from September 1907 to June 1912, excellent training
manuals had been prepared, and I had little to do except
ensure that the application of the principles they contained
kept pace with changing conditions.

There was, however, an objectionable flaw in the chain
of responsibility for training, in that all training instructions
were prepared under the orders of the Chief of the Imperial
General Staff, while the troops were inspected, not by him,
or his staff, but by a separate body of Inspectors located at
the Horse Guards under an Inspector-General, the latter
reporting the results of the inspections to the Army Council.

Gentlemen Cadets of the Royal Military Academy making a Cask-bridge.

The position therefore was that while the General Staff drafted the training instructions they had no opportunity —except by arranging occasionally to accompany the Inspector-General—of seeing and hearing for themselves how they worked in practice; and on the other hand the Inspector-General's Staff had this opportunity but were without the authority to change the instructions if found to be unsuitable.

The system had been introduced by the Esher Committee ten years before, the idea of having a separate inspecting branch having probably been taken from the large continental armies, in which it was necessary to have Inspectors constantly moving about between one command and another so as to ensure uniformity. With our comparatively small army there was not nearly the same necessity for them, as uniformity could have been safeguarded, and at far less expense, by inspections carried out by the Chief of the Imperial General Staff and his subordinates, and, moreover, the latter would have had the benefit of maintaining closer touch with the troops for whose training they were primarily responsible. Even if a separate inspecting staff were required it should have been placed under the orders of the Chief of the Imperial General Staff, as in foreign armies, and not made, as it was, independent of him.

This illogical system, which might have proved very mischievous had not the General Staff and Inspecting Staff been careful to work closely together, came to an end when a Commander-in-Chief of all troops in the United Kingdom was appointed in December 1915, as the Inspecting Staff was then made part of his headquarters and its independent status thus disappeared. Both he and the Inspecting Staff were abolished early in 1920.

The arrangements for the supreme command at home in time of war were also not as satisfactory as could be desired. The scheme for home defence contemplated the employment of a large number of troops; these were located in peace time in seven different commands, and thus served under the orders of seven different Commanders-in-Chief; and when required for home defence duties they would differ materially in composition and efficiency according to the conditions of the moment. In these circumstances, and on the accepted assumption that the greatest danger of an overseas attack would be in the earliest stage of the war, the exercise of supreme command was bound to be difficult and complicated, and therefore it was desirable that this duty should be definitely assigned to an officer selected during peace, so that he might, subject to the instructions of the Chief of the Imperial General Staff, draw up his plan and make himself acquainted beforehand with the many details which would affect its execution. No such officer was, however, in existence, nor was it intended to have one in war. As I have just said, the Director of Military Training was responsible in peace that suitable measures were taken for home defence, and although some additional senior commanders were to be appointed in war, the supreme control of all military operations in the United Kingdom was to be exercised by the War Office, that is, by the Chief of the Imperial General Staff.

This was not a sound arrangement, and it showed a strange forgetfulness of the elementary principles of military organisation. A *staff* officer cannot *command* troops and is not meant to do so ; while in any war which would render us liable to invasion it was practically certain that the Chief of the Imperial General Staff would have far too much to engage his attention in other parts of the world, and in the raising and training of additional troops, to admit of his being able to carry direct responsibility for the security of the home front, nor ought he to be troubled with every petty hostile raid by sea or air that might be attempted.

Had we been subjected in the Great War to any serious attack from oversea the truth of these remarks might have been established in a rather unpleasant manner. As it was, the system proved to be defective both as regards efficiency of defence and economy of personnel, and, like that of training, had to be remedied by the appointment of a Commander-in-Chief in 1915—the only way in which it could be remedied. Whatever may be said for or against the appointment of a Commander-in-Chief of the home forces in time of peace, there is no doubt that one is required when we have a great war on our hands. I shall refer to this question again in the chapter dealing with my experiences as Chief of the Imperial General Staff.

For years before I became Director of Military Training there had been a constant difference of official opinion as to the necessity of maintaining a home defence force. As mentioned in Chapter VII., it had been decided in 1888 that the provision of this force was the " primary duty " of the military authorities, and, notwithstanding the differences of opinion, this policy may be said to have held good till 1905, when it was replaced by one of an entirely opposite character, the Prime Minister, Mr. Balfour, then laying down that " the serious invasion of these islands is not a possibility that we need consider." A distinction was drawn at about the same time between invasion and raids, the feasibility of the latter being admitted, and the question then arose : When is a raid not a raid ? The answer eventually given was that an attack by a force not exceeding 10,000 men should be classed as a raid : if by more than that number the attack became invasion and therefore could be ruled out as impracticable.

Later it was discovered that two separate raids of 10,000 men each might be attempted simultaneously, so as to give one of them a better chance of succeeding; it was also admitted that raids on a smaller scale—from 500 to 2000 men each—against any one of several possible, though less important, objectives might be attempted ; and, finally, it was agreed that, as a raid would be a matter of, say, forty-eight hours only, and might be made without any warning, there would not be time to transfer troops from one vulnerable point in order to repel an attack on another. Provision had accordingly to be made to meet these conclusions, and the general result of accepting the policy as to raids and rejecting that of invasion was to add complications to a problem which was already loaded with complexity, and to make little if any reduction in the total number of troops required to give security.

The doctrine of no-invasion was replaced in 1909 by the original policy, Mr. Asquith, who was then Prime Minister, announcing in the House of Commons that it was " the business of the War Office to see that we have in all circumstances a properly organised and properly equipped force capable of dealing effectively with a possible invading force of seventy thousand men." This figure held the field when I became Director of Military Training, and I had not been long in the post before the eternal question was again brought forward for consideration.

In the many discussions which followed at the meetings of the Committee of Imperial Defence, the " blue-water school," or anti-invasionists, would at one time be on top, at another it was the " bolt from the blue " party, or pro-invasionists, who scored. Exactly which came out best depended chiefly upon the comparative debating skill of the representative spokesmen, and words continued to obscure and confuse the main issue until the question was definitely settled by the breaking out of war in August 1914.

This diversity of views was not conducive either to economy or to a good system of military organisation, and, as the responsible staff officer for home defence, I would often have been far more anxious than I was had there been no Territorial Force. Invasion or no invasion, this Force was, at any rate, a substantial military asset to have to fall back upon, and the services it rendered in many parts of the world during the Great War were a proof that there was more value in the volunteer movement than many people supposed.

To my mind, the possibility of invasion was essentially a question to be answered by the Admiralty, granted that the enemy, as in the case of Germany, had ample troops at his disposal, good communications between his garrison towns and ports of embarkation, and was prepared to risk losing his sea-communications in return for the prospective advantages to be gained once a landing was effected. More than a century had elapsed since our fleet had fought a really formidable enemy ; many new inventions had meanwhile been introduced ; naval operations are notoriously liable to the uncertainties of war ; and it was for the Admiralty to say whether, having regard to these considerations and to the strength of the enemy's fleet, they could undertake to prevent a landing. I always replied, therefore, to those who argued against the practicability of invasion that it was for the Admiralty to give a reasonable—not necessarily an absolute—guarantee, which would be acceptable to the Government, that they could in all circumstances prevent a hostile landing ; that if no such assurance could be given, we ought to be prepared to deal with a landing by military means ; and that, irrespective of the feasibility of the operation, it was conceivable that, owing to the mere threat of attack on our coast-towns, the Government might, in the event of war with Germany, be compelled by public opinion to retain at home a considerable number of troops urgently needed on the continent. It was, in fact, to meet this threat rather than to meet actual invasion or raids that suitable preparations for home defence were required.

During the time that I was Director of Military Training I do not remember that the Admiralty ever saw their way definitely to give the guarantee—and their hesitation was easy to understand—but there were those in high places who continued to argue that the navy alone afforded sufficient security, and who scoffed at the idea that Germany might seek to spring a surprise upon us by secretly preparing and despatching a raiding or invading force without a previous declaration of war. " Why," it was asked, " should it be contemplated for a moment that a civilised country like Germany will be guilty of such atrocious conduct as to make a deliberate attack upon a nation with whom she is still at peace ? No, a bolt from the blue, or invasion of any kind, is a preposterous theory, and even assuming it were attempted it could never succeed."

I have listened to the reiteration of these and similar arguments for hours at a time, but they do not seem to have been quite so much to the fore when war came along in 1914. Only four of our six regular divisions were at first allowed to proceed to France ; for a great part of the war the standard of 70,000 possible invaders was not only retained but increased ; and a considerable number of troops were for long kept back in this country. It was not until the war was nearly three years old that the reinforcement of the divisions abroad was allowed to take unquestioned precedence over the estimated requirements for the home front, and I have yet to learn that this policy was ever really opposed by those who, with great courage and still greater eloquence, had been so eager before the war to pour ridicule upon those who advocated the adoption of reasonable home defence measures. The truth is, that however bravely one may talk in time of peace, when brought up in war against the grim proposition of an enemy having at his disposal millions of soldiers, an undefeated fleet, and abundant transports, within a few hours steaming of our coast, no government dare rely, or would be allowed to do so by public opinion, solely upon the navy for the security of England—the nerve-centre of the whole Empire.

To revert to the question of training, I may recall the fact that reduction of expenditure on army services was constantly being pressed in the years immediately before the Great War; "estimates" had to be cut down to their lowest limit ; and there was, for practical purposes, but little additional preparation for the conflict so soon to burst upon us. I am reminded of one particular instance of this. It had been suggested to me that, in view of the experiences of the Russo-Japanese war, we ought to train the infantry in throwing hand-grenades, or bombs as we now call them. For this purpose I asked for the troops to be supplied with dummy-bombs, costing about twopence each, and also with a certain number of live grenades for purposes of demonstration. Sanction was obtained for a small number of the twopenny bombs, at a total cost of perhaps not more than thirty or forty pounds, while as regards the live grenades it was decided that they were too dangerous as well as too expensive to be issued. (They certainly did cost a great deal—I believe nearly £1 each.) The decision was toned down by giving permission for battalions to send a few selected men to see live grenades thrown by expert sappers ! I should think that some scores of millions were thrown by our men in the Great War, costing about sixpence apiece.

The War Minister of the day was not to be blamed for the scarcity of funds. His business was, as it always is, to show a saving on the estimates of the preceding year. Our policy was a policy of peace, and war on a great scale on the continent was hardly allowed in the picture at all so far as the army was concerned. The accepted plan was that, in certain eventualities, we should send oversea an Expeditionary Force of one cavalry and six infantry divisions, that the Territorial Force would be employed for home defence, and that the Special Reserve would supply the Expeditionary Force with drafts. Beyond these limits the German danger was disregarded, and the people as a whole cared little or nothing for the army so long as there was a strong navy, and, uninformed by their leaders, they were not encouraged to care anything for it. They were more concerned with internal politics, social reforms, and the enjoyment of agreeable week-ends.

In March 1914 occurred the unfortunate " Curragh incident," which arose, it will be remembered, in connection with the proposal to use troops for the coercion of Ulster, then busy arming and drilling with the intention of opposing the introduction of Home Rule. The members of the Government responsible for the proposal appear to have given no thought to its practical side as a military question, and were completely taken aback when certain officers at the Curragh, whose regiments were to be employed, sent in their resignations and declined to serve. Soldiers cannot be treated as if they had neither souls nor consciences, and to expect them to undertake a duty which may lead to shooting down those with whose ideals and religion they are in sympathy is to expect a great deal.

While the crisis lasted I was besieged by excited officers in the War Office and from elsewhere asking my advice as to what they should do, for they were determined, they said, to stand by their comrades who had declined to obey an order which they considered to be both unjust and illegal. I had no hesitation in telling them to go away, make their minds easy, and get on with their work, as I felt sure that in the long run any intention there might be of employing troops against the Ulster men would be abandoned.

One of the officers who came to see me was " Joe " Maude, the head of the training branch of my directorate, and afterwards the commander of the forces in Mesopotamia in the Great War. I had brought him only a short time before from the Curragh, where he had been on the General Staff and had made many friends amongst the officers

o

implicated. He told me that he felt it to be his duty to resign his commission, as they had done, and it was with some difficulty that I persuaded him to take my advice and sit tight.

I had no knowledge, nor had any other director in the General Staff I think, of the proposal to use troops in the manner mentioned until it had been more or less decided to use them, and when officially informed of it my first question was : " Which directorate will be responsible for making the necessary arrangements and issuing the orders ? " The responsibility for operations *outside* the United Kingdom rested with the Director of Military Operations ; that for operations *inside,* but only as against oversea attack, rested with me—the Director of Military Training ; and the Adjutant-General dealt with the use of troops in aid of the civil power. The case of Ulster did not fall within any one of these three spheres, and not wishing to have anything to do with it each of us argued that it was not his business. In the end it was settled that if troops had to be employed the duty would come under the heading of home defence, and the arrangements to be made would accordingly fall upon me.

I then asked a few further questions : " Are we supposed to be going to war with Ulster ; that is, will the troops be on ' active service ' ? If we are not going to war what are we going to do, as the case is obviously not one of suppressing civil disorder because there is no disorder at present ? If we are going to war, is mobilisation to be ordered, and what ammunition, supplies, and transport are the troops to take ? What instructions are to be given to the General in command regarding the nature and object of his mission ? "

Coupled with the Curragh resignations, these questions brought matters to a head, for there was no answer to some of them, and when the light had thus been turned on the affair became one of heated discussions, alleged misunderstandings, impatient explanations, and a general running to and fro between the different offices and departments in Whitehall. In the course of two or three days the whole proposal deservedly came to an inglorious end, and we were exceedingly glad to hear the last of it and be allowed to get on with more sensible work. The Secretary of State for War, the Chief of the Imperial General Staff, and the Adjutant-General resigned their appointments, and Mr. Asquith took charge of the War Office in addition to his duties of Prime Minister.

The new Chief of the Imperial General Staff was Sir Charles Douglas, a very conscientious officer who would insist upon working more hours a day than his state of health justified, and it was largely due to this habit that he died a few weeks after the Great War broke out. He had quite a unique knowledge of the details of all army matters, and although he had the reputation of being somewhat abrupt and overbearing in manner I always found him to be a very considerate chief as well as a good friend.

For the manœuvres of 1914 I had, subject to his approval, selected an area in the west of England, and together we spent several days going over the ground and considering how my suggested scheme of operations would work out. It involved the passage of the Severn by a force retiring before an enemy of superior strength, and Douglas was at first rather afraid that the operations might get out of control and end in a fiasco, but later he accepted the scheme. As I have already said, manœuvre schemes in the past had usually led up to and finished with a pitched battle, into which both sides threw themselves headlong and hoped for the best. Douglas agreed with me that a change was desirable, and that as our army might one day find itself being driven back in war by a superior force it would be well to give it some practice beforehand. The manœuvres were due to take place in September, but before then we were engaged in the real thing in France, and were being driven back by overwhelming masses of Germans. The study of the manœuvres we had planned was most helpful to me during the first few weeks of the war, when I was hard put to it to keep the troops supplied with what they needed.

As the Director of Military Training became, in war, Chief General Staff Officer of the home defence force, there seemed to be no chance when war broke out of my going to France. At the last moment, however, Grierson, who had been originally nominated Chief of the General

Staff of the Expeditionary Force, was given the command of the Second Army Corps, and Murray, originally intended to be Quartermaster-General of the Force, was selected to succeed him. The appointment of Quartermaster-General thus became vacant and Douglas was good enough to give it to me. Within forty-eight hours I once again left the War Office, and joined the headquarters of the Expeditionary Force then mobilising at the Metropole Hotel in Northumberland Avenue.

CHAPTER XIII

QUARTERMASTER-GENERAL, BRITISH EXPEDITIONARY FORCE

Organisation, and duties of G.H.Q.—System of supply and maintenance—
The I.G.C.—His duties are curtailed—The " Directors "—My Staff
—Arrive at Paris with the Commander-in-Chief—Stay at the Hôtel
Crillon—Visit Joffre at Vitry-le-François—Reach G.H.Q. at Le
Cateau—Concentration of the Force—Various situations to be
thought out—Discuss change of base with I.G.C.—Commander-in-
Chief's conference before battle of Mons—The retreat from Mons—
Replacement of clothing and equipment lost in the retreat—Con-
fusion caused by change of base—Control of railways in French
hands—Difficulty of knowing where troops were—Plight of refugees
—Willing spirit shown by all ranks to help each other—Despatch
riders—G.H.Q. move successively to St. Quentin, Noyon, Com-
piègne, Dammartin, Lagny, Melun—The move from Dammartin to
Lagny—Force becomes part of Paris garrison under Gallieni—
Battle of the Marne—Brutalities of German troops—G.H.Q. at
Coulommiers and Fère-en-Tardenois—Want of heavy artillery on
the Aisne—Move round to Flanders—First battle of Ypres—State
of trenches—Cross the Channel with Lord Roberts—His death at
St. Omer—Succeed Murray as Chief of the General Staff at G.H.Q.

THE staff of an army, according to the British system, is
composed of three branches—General Staff, Adjutant-
General's Staff, and Quartermaster-General's Staff. The
General Staff deals with training, operations, intelligence,
and general military policy ; the Adjutant-General with
recruiting, mobilisation, discipline, medical services, and
the chaplains' department ; the Quartermaster-General
with supplies and transport, and the issue of all military
stores. Stated in a simpler form, the Adjutant-General
recruits the men with which to fight, tends to their spiritual
needs, tries them by court-martial when accused of breaking
the regulations, takes care of them when sick or wounded,
and buries them when they die. The Quartermaster-General
clothes, arms, feeds, and houses them, and supplies them
with all they need with which to fight, viz. horses, motors,

lorries, bicycles, ammunition, guns, entrenching-tools, barbed wire, bombs, and a thousand other things. He also moves them, according to the direction of the General Staff, by rail and sea. The staffs of the Adjutant-General and Quarter-master-General thus put and maintain the army in the field ready for use by the General Staff, who arrange, according to the instructions of the Commander-in-Chief, all matters connected with the actual fighting.

The welfare of the army and the success attending the operations largely depend upon the way in which the three branches work together and upon the personality of the Chief of the General Staff, who is the recognised head of the whole staff and the principal confidant and adviser of the Commander-in-Chief. The staff of the Expeditionary Force were fortunate in this respect, for Murray was a help-ful colleague to do business with, and possessed a thorough knowledge of staff duties in general. The same may be said of the Adjutant-General, Sir Nevil Macready, with whom I worked from the commencement of the war until a few months before he became Commissioner of the Metro-politan Police in the summer of 1918.

The system by which the immense volume of food, ammunition, clothing and other war material is conveyed to the troops may now be explained, and for the information of the non-military reader I may first observe that an " army " consists of two or more army corps ; an " army corps " of two or more divisions ; a " division " of three or four infantry and artillery brigades respectively and certain other troops ; a " brigade " of infantry of three or four battalions, and a " brigade " of artillery of three or four batteries.

When an expeditionary force is sent abroad, " bases " are established at selected oversea ports, and there large depots of food, stores, men, animals, etc., are formed, and from these the supplies are sent up by rail to a " regulating station." From this place trains, each carrying the right proportion of each kind of article required, are despatched to " railheads," *i.e.* the stations nearest to the front-line troops to which it is feasible to work the railway. Each railhead may serve one or more army corps according to circumstances, and at it the supplies are loaded on convoys of motor lorries called "supply columns." Each column then conveys the supplies of its division or other formation to which it belongs to previously selected rendezvous called "refilling points," where they are met at an appointed hour by horsed wagons of the "regimental train." These, having been loaded with their proper quota of supplies, carry them to the units to which they belong. The distances traversed by the supply columns may be as much as forty miles between railhead and refilling point, and the horsed wagons may cover six or seven miles each way. Ammunition and other stores are distributed from railheads in much the same manner as food, the ammunition convoy being known as the "ammunition park." This explanation is very crude, but it will suffice to give a rough idea of the system in force at the commencement of the Great War.

It will be understood that, owing to the movement of the troops or to interference by the enemy, changes of railheads and refilling points may have to be made at very short notice. These changes, unless properly and promptly notified, may dislocate the entire proceedings, and, in the case of a retreat, cause roads to become blocked with transport and so jeopardise the safety of the whole army.

The arrangements for carrying out this delicate system were, according to the regulations, mainly vested in a General Officer known as the "Inspector-General of Communications," or I.G.C., who occupied a position second in importance only to that of the Commander-in-Chief himself. His headquarters were at the base, distant perhaps a hundred miles or more from the front line, or at some place between the two. By the nature of his duties he was something like the managing directors of Harrods' Stores and Carter Paterson rolled into one, it being his business to see that ample stocks of food and war material were maintained at the bases, and thence conveyed, in the manner just described, in sufficient quantity and to such places at the front as directed by the Quartermaster-General in furtherance of the Commander-in-Chief's plans. It will thus be seen that the Quartermaster-General was not responsible for the actual performance of the duties enumerated at the beginning of this chapter, and only in a limited degree for prescribing the method of their execution. He was answerable for seeing that they were not left undone rather than for doing them.

Before the war I was convinced that the system would not work in practice. Telegraphic communication between the front and the I.G.C., upon the efficiency of which everything hinged, was liable to be interrupted or blocked ; and in any case notification by him or to him regarding alteration of railheads or refilling points, consequent on a change in the tactical situation, was bound to be slow and uncertain. It followed from this that orders issued by the I.G.C. on these matters might well become impossible of execution hours before they left his office. They did so from the day fighting began, and with the approval of the Commander-in-Chief I swept away the regulations, and so far as the distribution of food and ammunition was concerned the responsibility of the I.G.C. was made to end at the railheads, to be selected by me, the onward transport then becoming a matter for my staff and not for his. Later, his duties at the front were further restricted, and it was recognised that, instead of retaining the almost complete freedom of action assigned to him by the regulations, he must be guided by the instructions of the Quartermaster-General. This officer is the mouthpiece of the Commander-in-Chief for purposes of supply, and is much better placed for knowing his wishes than an I.G.C. can possibly be. Major-General Robb, who first held the post, and his successor, Major-General Maxwell, at once fell in with these views, and the change of system worked quite smoothly.

As the army grew in strength, more decentralisation and elasticity had to be introduced, and it is not unlikely that the I.G.C. may disappear altogether from future regulations. If he does I shall think that we have gone too far in the opposite direction, and burdened General Headquarters, whose chief business is fighting, with work that can be done more suitably and economically by an organisation in rear.

To complete this account of the method of supplying an army in the field I should add that under the Adjutant-General, Quartermaster-General, and I.G.C., respectively, according to the duties to be performed, are the "Directors" of the different administrative services—*e.g.* medical, veterinary, remounts, supply, transport, ordnance—who with their assistant directors, deputy assistant directors, and other officers are responsible for actually issuing to the troops what they require. These officers are not uncommonly regarded by the general public as belonging to the staff, but this is not the case. Their duties and status are quite different. The staff, properly so-called, are the assistants of the Commander-in-Chief, they may take action in his name, and they are the medium through which he communicates his orders ; the administrative officers are responsible, each in his own sphere, for making such administrative arrangements as will enable these orders to be carried out.

The officers at first employed on the Quartermaster-General's staff were : Colonel Dawkins, Assistant Quartermaster-General, with Major Jebb of the Bedfordshire Regiment and Captain Percival of the army service corps as Deputy Assistant Quartermaster-Generals. Captain Woodroffe of the horse artillery was my aide-de-camp. I can never be too grateful to these four officers for the assistance they rendered, especially in the retreat from Mons, when the supply of the army was a matter of extraordinary difficulty. Day and night they toiled like slaves with never a thought for their own comfort or interest. I was also greatly assisted at this period, and in fact during the whole time I was Quartermaster-General, by Sir John Cowans, under whose direction the initial arrangements for the maintenance of the army were made by the Quartermaster-General's department of the War Office.

As soon as the troops began to cross the Channel I sent Dawkins off to France, with Jebb and Percival to help him, to arrange for the reception of the troops at the front and generally to get the department into working order. I remained behind in England with the Commander-in-Chief and the Chief of the General Staff, as it was necessary to keep in close touch with them and be ready to advise upon matters under my charge.

We left London on the afternoon of the 14th August, crossed the Channel from Dover on H.M.'s Cruiser *Sentinel,* and reached Boulogne about 5.30 P.M. The streets seemed to be full of British soldiers waiting to be sent to the front, and a very cordial welcome was extended to them by our French allies. After visiting some of the rest camps, where we found the troops cheery and full of enthusiasm, we left at 7.20 P.M. for Amiens, the headquarters of our line of communication, and there spent the night. Next morning we proceeded to Paris, which was reached shortly after noon. The Commander-in-Chief and some of the staff stayed at the British Embassy, whilst I and some others put up at the Hôtel Crillon, where the manager, M. Décquis, placed the best rooms at our disposal, and gave us what I have always thought to be the best dinner I ever had. He produced an equally good English breakfast at five o'clock next morning, and when I asked him on leaving for the bill he replied that he would send it to me at Berlin, and that for the present he would accept nothing, feeling only too pleased to have been of service to us. I went to Berlin after the war, but I have not yet received the bill. The incident was a standing joke between us on the many occasions I stayed at the Crillon when called to Paris on duty during the war, and I must add that M. Décquis never relaxed his efforts to make these visits as comfortable as the first one was.

We left Paris by motor early on Sunday morning, 16th August, to see General Joffre at his headquarters at Vitry-le-François. He was in excellent spirits and with much pride showed us a German standard which had been captured a day or two before in some small engagement on the southern flank. After we had taken lunch with him and his staff, and business had been concluded, we proceeded to Rheims, passed the night there, and next day joined our own headquarters at Le Cateau, the offices of which were located in a large school in the centre of the town.

I and the four officers of my staff were billeted in a small house close by, the owner being a kind-hearted old lady who occupied the adjoining house. Woodroffe quickly got our small mess into working order, and saw that nothing was lacking in the way of either food or drink. Our soldier-cook—still a dark horse—played up well, and was assisted by the woman cook of our landlady, though by what means they were able to understand each other's language was a mystery.

This difficulty once led to a rather noisy altercation, which called for the intervention of Woodroffe. Hearing heated arguments taking place in the kitchen, in the most extraordinary mixture of French and English, he proceeded there to enquire what was the matter, and found the two cooks engaged in a tug of war at opposite sides of a frying-pan of potatoes which were to be cooked for breakfast. It transpired that the kitchen fire had refused to burn properly, and that the French cook was trying to explain to ours that she had a good fire next door and would take the potatoes there to cook, while our man was under the impression that she wished to appropriate them for herself, and he was determined not to let them go at any price. Woodroffe restored peace, and we got our potatoes by the required time.

About a week later, when the German troops were nearing the town, I was able to repay the hospitality of our landlady by sending her off in a motor in the direction of Paris, as she had no other means of getting away. On passing through Le Cateau in 1919 I found that both her houses had been destroyed—like many others in the town.

The British Expeditionary Force, composed of six divisions and a cavalry division, had a total strength of, roughly, 160,000 men, 60,000 horses, 490 guns, and 7000 vehicles. That part of it sent out in the first instance numbered only about 100,000 men, and consisted of a cavalry division and two army corps each of two divisions. Of the remaining two divisions one did not begin to arrive till after the battle of Mons had been fought, and the other, for reasons unknown to me, did not reach us for several days later. Had there been less delay in our coming to a decision to join France more time would, of course, have been available for the whole six to arrive, and had they been present at the battle the course of the war might have been different.

The Force, as at first sent out, completed its concentration just south of Maubeuge on the 20th August, and on the following day commenced to move forward. On the 22nd it reached positions in the vicinity of Mons, its right being in touch with the left of the 5th French army near Thuin, south-west of Charleroi. It is interesting to recall that Mons was occupied by a detachment of Wellington's army at the beginning of Napoleon's last campaign about a hundred years earlier.

Whilst G.H.Q. remained at Le Cateau I devoted all my spare time to visiting the areas through which the troops were moving. Some fifty per cent of the infantry was composed of reservists just called up, and as most of them were not in hard condition the blazing August sun and long stretches of white dusty roads made marching and the carrying of some 60 lbs. of kit and equipment a heavy burden. All the more reason, therefore, why the Quarter-master-General's staff should be active, and personally see to it that there was no shortage of food or water, that the billets and bivouacs were as good as could be found, and that the transport conveying the requirements of the troops should reach its destination in good time. It was my purpose to ensure that this was done.

I had also to think out the different situations which my department might have to meet during the next few days. The strength and direction of the enemy's main advance had not yet been clearly disclosed, but the view held at French G.H.Q., as late as the 22nd August, was that the Germans were not sufficiently strong to secure themselves against a determined attack in the Ardennes—for which General Joffre had made preparations—and at the same time launch a great attack against the Allied left. On the contrary, it was deemed possible for the British army and 5th French army to envelop the German right, and it was in pursuance of this plan that the British army marched to Mons. But there was no certainty that the French view would prove to be right. The enemy was well known to have an intense craving for enveloping methods, and there were rumours that he had larger forces north of the Meuse than the French seemed to think, and if, instead of our enveloping his right, he should succeed in enveloping our left our line of communication would be seriously endangered, and we might in consequence be compelled to abandon our sea-bases at Havre and Boulogne and establish others further to the south. Moreover, I knew before leaving England that Lord Kitchener was of opinion that we were concentrating too far forward, and events since then tended to show that he was right.

Be these things as they might it was my business to be prepared for the worst that might happen as well as for the best. He is merely a fool who, holding a high position in war, refuses to contemplate anything but success. " J'ai l'habitude," said Napoleon, " de penser trois ou quatre mois d'avance à ce que je dois faire, et je calcule sur le pire." Confidence is an essential element in war, and in public should always be seen on the faces of all leaders and staff officers, while any who are not endowed with a reasonable sense of humour should make room for others who are.

But confidence and cheeriness do not mean that one should be cocksure of everything going as one would wish, especially at the beginning of a war when the unexpected is so apt to be the rule. It was necessary that the Quarter-master-General's staff should examine the situation from every point of view, and introduce such elasticity into the supply arrangements as would promptly afford the Com-mander-in-Chief the greatest possible choice of action. In short, it should be prepared to meet any and every reasonable contingency, for no matter how skilful the plans of the Commander-in-Chief might be, they would almost certainly fail in execution if the troops were not properly fed and quartered, and kept supplied with ammunition. Assuming that the Allies' plan of operations proved successful, these demands could be met with comparative ease ; but on the other hand it might be very difficult to meet them if, in spite of the confidence which prevailed, we were opposed by very superior numbers and compelled to fall back from the positions taken up.

I therefore decided to summon the I.G.C., Major-General Robb, to G.H.Q. and discuss possible developments with him, as it was essential that there should be a clear under-standing between us as to what it might become necessary to do. He arrived on the 22nd August—the day before the battle of Mons—and before he left we had settled the main principles upon which we would act in the event of the sea-bases having to be replaced by others. On return to his headquarters at Amiens he made such preliminary arrangements as he could for effecting the change.

There are not many other instances in military history I imagine, if any, of measures having been taken before the first battle of a campaign to change the base of an army which has been deliberately selected after long and careful consideration. It was fortunate that they were taken on this occasion, for within a week the German advance had progressed to such a point that the Commander-in-Chief gave me orders to change the bases to St. Nazaire, with an advanced base at Le Mans. Amiens, the advanced base, had then already been evacuated by us, and the Germans occupied it on the 31st August. This change of base to the Loire, at a very critical period, was a striking example of the value of sea-power, and of itself was a sufficient return for the money we had expended in maintaining our naval supremacy.

At 5 A.M. on Sunday the 23rd August the Commander-in-Chief, accompanied by the heads of his staff, met the commanders of the I. and II. Corps and Cavalry Division at Sars-la-Bruyère, a few miles south of Mons, to explain the situation. From information received from French G.H.Q. he understood that little more than one, or at the most two, of the enemy's army corps, with perhaps one cavalry division, were in front of our positions, and he was aware of no out-flanking movement by the enemy. There were, as a matter of fact, four army corps and three cavalry divisions, or about 160,000 combatants, within striking distance of the British army of less than half that fighting strength, and at 10.30 A.M. our first battle in the Great War opened in earnest.

The subsequent retreat from Mons, which terminated south of the Marne on the 3rd September, will for all time be regarded as one of the finest performances of the British army. Hopelessly outnumbered from the start, and fighting on a length of front far exceeding their powers to hold, there was no way by which our troops could avoid retreat, and by all the rules of war they ought to have suffered not only defeat but annihilation. They would admit neither, rules of war notwithstanding. Composed of the finest British personnel, well-trained, excellent shots, and led by that incomparable commander the British regimental officer, they time and again turned on the pursuing enemy and made him pay a heavy price for his boastful claim to invincibility. Bruised, battered, and sometimes beaten to their knees, they were never beaten in spirit, and even in the darkest hour it never seemed to cross their minds that they were or could be beaten. They knew they were being forced back by an enemy far stronger numerically than themselves ; they were sometimes hungry, often thirsty, and many were too tired to keep awake even when marching ; but they continued to fight grimly on with a determination which has never been surpassed and never will be. Officers and men of the regular army, as we knew them in those days, were seen at their best, and it is an unforgettable privilege to have been associated with them. By the time the vicinity of Le Cateau was reached the 4th Division (the fifth in number to be despatched from home) began to come up and supplied a welcome reinforcement, but it was far from being sufficient effectively to arrest the onward march of the enemy's masses.

Since the war ended we have been asked to believe that the Allies owe their victory to the foresight and energy of some political leader or other, to the employment of certain mechanical contrivances, to the enormous output of munitions, to unity of command, to the rottenness of autocratic government, and so on, according to the taste or interest of those who expressed or inspired these statements. Perhaps the statements were not meant to be taken literally, for no man of sense would attribute our victory to any one cause, especially as all classes combined so loyally to secure it. Still, they were rather frequently made, and therefore it is well to remind ourselves occasionally of the endurance and heroism displayed by the fighting men, notably in the retreat from Mons, in the three battles of Ypres, on the Somme, and in the desperate struggles of 1918. I sometimes think that the French set us an example in this respect, for they invariably award chief credit for success to their armies alone, and are careful not to detract from it by the advancement of other claims. It is significant of their point of view that at the official dinner at the Elysée on the day of the victory march through Paris in 1919, to which I had the honour of being invited, some ten or twelve non-commissioned officers and men were included among the hundred and twenty guests present.

In the retreat a large amount of clothing (caps, jackets, great-coats, etc.), and equipment (shovels, rifles, valises, wagons, guns, machine - guns, etc.), were either lost, captured, or thrown away because they could not be carried, and it was my duty to see that they were immediately replaced. The ordnance regulations were of the most stringent red-tape description, and before stores were allowed to be issued commanding officers had to render, sometimes in triplicate, elaborate " army forms " setting out their demands and giving full reasons for them. It was absurd to suppose that this procedure could be adhered to when the troops were constantly at close grips with a pursuing enemy ; when the wretched forms, with all other army stationery, had, perhaps, been left behind or thrown away ; and when the commanding officers, killed, wounded, taken prisoner, or for some other reason could not readily be found. There was no authority at all, to the best of my memory, for the free issue of clothing to officers. They were expected to get it, I imagine, as in peace, from Savile Row or other places inhabited by the military tailors of London.

The senior ordnance officer at G.H.Q. was at first terribly perplexed to know what to do, for, owing to the strict financial control exercised over the smallest details, and which had its origin in the Treasury, his professional capacity was mainly estimated by the way in which he kept his accounts, and produced innumerable " vouchers " for the action he took. He must often have thought me most irrational and unsympathetic, for I would listen to nothing about his regulations so long as officers and men were going about bareheaded for want of a cap, or had their backs exposed to drenching rain for lack of a coat. I insisted that the missing articles must be replaced at once, whatever the regulations might or might not be, and said that the entire responsibility would be mine if he got into trouble. The officer in question, Colonel (now Major-General Sir Charles) Mathew, played up well, and the army owed him much for the efforts he made to replenish it with the thousand and one things included in the term " ordnance stores " of which it was short.

The matter was further complicated because the sea-bases, from which the different articles had to be obtained, were, as already stated, in process of being moved from Havre and Boulogne to St. Nazaire. Even when the move had been completed, many days, and in some cases weeks, elapsed before the required articles became available. In the hurry and confusion attending evacuation of the original bases, the ships had been loaded on no system except that of getting out of the place as rapidly as possible, the Germans then being at Amiens and their advance parties pushed forward in the direction of Rouen. Different kinds of stores were inextricably mixed; machine-guns were on one ship and their tripods on another, while the articles wanted first were, as often as not, at the bottom of the ship, below sacks of oats and bales of hay, and therefore were the last that could be got out. Moreover, the establishment of a new base, even at a good port, is a matter which demands considerable time and previous preparation, and in many respects St. Nazaire happened to be particularly inconvenient and deficient of the facilities required.

Another factor which militated against the prompt supply of food and stores was that we did not control the railways we used, and could not expect to do so. Trains were allotted to us daily by the French authorities, they were necessarily restricted in number, and the time and place of their arrival were very uncertain, as in the circumstances they were bound to be. The trouble was aggravated when they could no longer pass through Amiens and had to proceed to the front *via* Paris, for besides the exodus of people from that city which was then taking place, Joffre was transferring masses of troops from his right to his left, and for these and other reasons there was a widespread

P

congestion and dislocation of all railway traffic. I found that the only sure way of getting trains up by the time they were wanted was to send the indefatigable Percival down to Paris by motor, and for him to board the train and compel the station-master to send it forward. Many a time he did this, and was instrumental in producing food for the troops which but for his efforts they would not have received.

The distribution of supplies after they reached railheads was another difficulty, as the ever-changing situation and frequent interruption of communication made it impossible to know where particular units might be at any given time. I could only guess as to the place where they might be, send their food to it, and a further supply to other probable places, in the hope that if the first consignment did not reach them the second would. The expedient was also adopted of dumping supplies—flitches of bacon, sides of beef, cheese, boxes of biscuits—alongside the roads so that the troops might help themselves as they passed. Much of the food thus deposited had to be left where it was put, either because it was not found in the darkness, or from want of time to use it or of means to carry it away, but on the whole the object of ensuring that plenty of food should be obtainable when and where wanted was fairly well achieved. Compliance with routine regulations, and the extra expense incurred by issuing double or treble the normal allowance of rations, were not considerations to be taken into account.

Distribution was further hampered by the endless stream of refugees fleeing before the advancing enemy, and it was not until steps had been taken to shepherd them into batches, under proper supervision, that either troops or transport could move along the roads with some semblance of regularity. The flight of these fugitives was a strange mixture of tragedy and comedy. All the men were old or very young; the children, some laughing, some crying, went by in droves; and tired mothers, carrying their infants on their backs, crawled along the hot and dusty roads with fear and despair depicted on their terror-stricken faces. Two, three, and even four generations of a family could sometimes be seen making their way together to the rear, some on foot, others riding in farm-carts, donkey-carts, ox-wagons, on bicycles, in perambulators, according to age and circumstances, whilst the household effects and farm stock with which they were accompanied were of the most varied description. Cows, sheep, goats, pigs, fowls, geese, ducks, cats, and dogs, carried or driven, were amongst the number, and vehicles of every kind, from a wagon to a wheelbarrow, were brought into use and laden with every imaginable article from beds to bird-cages. As if to intensify the distress and misery of the scene, the distant sky was black with smoke rising in dense clouds from the burning villages which had been set on fire either deliberately or by the enemy's shells, these same villages having been but a few hours before and for many years previously the homes of those who were now fleeing from them, knowing and caring not where, so long as they were safe from the Hun.

Having said so much about the difficulties to be overcome, I ought to add that my duties, like those of all other senior officers, were greatly lightened by the splendid manner in which all ranks, forgetful of self, were animated by the sole desire to help each other. In numberless ways the retreat brought out, and in quarters where least expected, the best qualities of man, and showed how much good there is even in what appear to be the most forbidding and unresponsive natures.

I have already mentioned the assistance rendered by the members of my staff, and I was equally indebted to the administrative officers who worked with me, especially to Colonels Gilpin, King, and Ford, and Major Crofton-Atkins of the army service corps, who superintended the transport and food arrangements. The despatch riders, too, performed invaluable service in carrying messages to and from the troops and the various supply and ammunition columns. The work of a despatch rider at the time was very different from what it was after trench warfare set in. Headquarters of brigades and divisions were constantly moving from one place to another, and the despatch rider had to find them —in a strange country and perhaps at night—as best he could. As often as not he would arrive near the place where he had hoped or guessed they would be, only to discover that it was occupied by the enemy. Most of our despatch riders were boys under twenty years of age who had joined on the outbreak of war, many of them from the universities, and the manner in which they carried out their duties in the face of great hardships and dangers confirmed me in the opinion that the English boy has no superior. I am prepared to go further and say that he has no equal.

During the retreat G.H.Q. moved successively to St. Quentin, Noyon, Compiègne, Dammartin, Lagny, and Melun. Dammartin is only fifteen miles from Paris, and on our arrival there the Force became for the time being a part of the Paris garrison commanded by General Gallieni. This was not a pleasant duty to contemplate—the defence of the French capital—and had an ominous look about it. Luckily it did not last long.

As can be imagined our personal feeding arrangements were rather sketchy and uncertain during the hurry of the retreat, but at Dammartin we hoped for better things and were looking forward to the enjoyment of a roast leg of mutton for dinner. Suddenly, however, the order was given to move to Lagny, and as it was then seven o'clock we had to go off without any dinner at all, the leg of mutton, just ready for eating, being packed up in a newspaper and taken away on the floor of a motor lorry. It was none the worse next day, except for being cold.

On this occasion Dawkins and I travelled together, and as we were inside the Paris perimeter and the night was dark, we had rather an exciting journey. German officers, disguised as English staff officers, were reported to be going about in motors within the lines, and the French Territorial troops on picquet, of whom we encountered several, were menacingly inquisitive as to who we were, addressing their enquiries over the sights of their rifles or at the point of the bayonet.

At last we reached Lagny, about midnight, and as it was impossible to secure a billet at that hour we tried to persuade the proprietor of a small café to make us an omelette by way of dinner, preparatory to passing the night in the car.

Whilst discussing the omelette, which there seemed little prospect of our getting, a woman entered the café and offered us the use of two rooms in her house close by, and afterwards gave us supper. Next morning she cooked us an excellent breakfast, and I later discovered that in order to accommodate us she and her husband had sat up all night. This is the sort of kindness that really counts, and on the first opportunity I intend to revisit Lagny and, if I can find them, once more thank my host and hostess for their hospitality. At Melun we were equally well treated, the owner of the house at which we stayed placing everything he had at our disposal.

The advance from the Marne to the Aisne, immediately after a retreat of 170 miles before a numerically superior enemy flushed with success, is no less a glorious page in the history of the British army than that of the retreat itself. The battle of the Marne, as it is called, or Joffre's great counter-stroke which changed the whole course of the campaign, commenced on the 6th of September and continued, so far as we were concerned, till the 10th of September. G.H.Q. meanwhile moved first to Coulommiers and then to Fère-en-Tardenois.

In passing through the country from which the Germans had just been expelled, it was interesting to compare the behaviour of their troops in retreat—the severest test which war can bring—with that of our own men in similar circumstances, and there is no doubt that our type of discipline, based chiefly upon good relations between officers and men, stood the test far better than the boasted iron discipline of the German army. Everywhere was wanton and wicked destruction—shops gutted, fields and streets littered with empty wine-bottles, household goods deliberately destroyed, and filthy deeds committed too abominable to mention. Some of the troops, perhaps many, had behaved well, according to what we heard, but others were accused of the most brutal acts.   How thankful England should be that she was spared from the unspeakable miseries and horrors of invasion !

Shortly after our arrival on the Aisne the enemy brought up more heavy artillery from Maubeuge, which had just fallen, and the period of trench warfare destined to last for

nearly four years set in. With it arose demands for heavy
artillery on our side, more gun ammunition, more machine-
guns, bombs, barbed wire, and other artillery and engineering stores, none of which could be even approximately met,
so defective had been our war preparations. When first
sent out, the Expeditionary Force had, as already mentioned,
only two machine-guns per battalion or about a hundred
and fifty in all, while of the 490 pieces of artillery twenty-
four only were of " medium " type, the remainder being the
ordinary " light " field-guns or field-howitzers. There was
no "heavy" artillery. These twenty-four medium guns were
supplemented on the Aisne by sixteen 6-inch howitzers of an
inferior kind, and some rather old guns of 4.7-inch calibre.
How utterly insufficient these numbers were, can be understood when I say that on Armistice Day we had in France
alone well over 40,000 machine-guns and close on 6500
guns and howitzers, of which over 2200 were of medium and
heavy calibre.

As regards artillery ammunition, no one, either before
the war or in the early part of it, dreamt that the demand
would reach the colossal figure it eventually did reach. At
any rate no adequate provision was made by the responsible
authorities to meet it, and to the best of my memory we
began the war with a reserve of considerably less than a
million rounds, whereas at one time during the war we
had in France alone a reserve of twenty million rounds, to
say nothing of other theatres and the enormous stocks in
England. It was the same story with respect to the special
requirements of trench warfare, although the Russo-Japanese
war had furnished much valuable guidance in the matter.
Hand grenades, for instance, or bombs, were practically non-
existent before the war, and at first had to be improvised
by filling jam-tins and similar receptacles with the necessary
explosives. The number of bombs expended during the
war must have run into scores of millions, and a reserve of
five or six millions at the front was quite an ordinary
number.

To cope with the ever-increasing duties of my department
sanction was given while we were on the Aisne for an additional Assistant Quartermaster-General and one Deputy

Assistant Quartermaster-General. The former appointment was filled by Colonel Lynden Bell, and the latter by my aide-de-camp, Woodroffe, his place being taken by Captain Lucas, another Horse Gunner.

On the 3rd of October the British army commenced to move round to Flanders so as to frustrate the enemy's attempt to reach the Channel ports. The cavalry went by road and the divisions by rail, the arrangements for the journey devolving on the staff of the Quartermaster-General. It was desired, as in all such cases, to detrain as near to the enemy as possible so as to avoid unnecessary marching, and sufficiently far away from him that the operation could be completed without interruption. His cavalry was apparently being pushed well forward in the direction of the ports, and as only vague information was forthcoming as to what was behind it, the detraining stations had to be decided upon, in consultation with the General Staff, whilst the transfer was taking place. For example, one division was at first sent to Boulogne, and afterwards ordered to detrain much farther east. It will be understood that this uncertainty not only caused inconvenience and discomfort to the troops, but rendered future arrangements for their supply difficult to make. As the war went on and experience was gained, the transfer of masses of men from one part of the line to another became a comparatively easy matter, but seeing that the transfer from the Aisne to Flanders was the first to be undertaken, and that the enemy was not stationary but on the move, the troops may be credited with having accomplished a fairly good performance.

G.H.Q. reached Abbeville on the 8th of October and shortly afterwards moved to St. Omer, where they remained for many months. About this time the 7th Division and some of the other troops which had been sent to assist the Belgians in saving Antwerp were absorbed in the Expeditionary Force, having previously been controlled by the authorities in London. It took us some days properly to get hold of these contingents, find out where they were, who they were, and what they had got with them. They had been hurriedly put together in the first instance, both

Admiralty and War Office taking a hand, and as they had had a trying time since disembarkation many confused matters connected with them had to be adjusted. For example, some of the mechanical transport drivers had been engaged by the Admiralty at a much higher rate of pay than that given to those engaged by the War Office, and obviously we could not pay different rates to different men for doing the same army work. I think we settled the question by giving the Admiralty men the choice between voluntarily joining the army and going home. On another occasion I was asked to sanction the payment of £1700 which had been expended by a naval officer in mounting certain guns on railway trucks. On asking for further details regarding the ownership of the trucks and the origin of the guns, I was told that the trucks had been " taken " and the guns " found."

Hard fighting commenced as soon as we arrived in Flanders, and it became a near thing which side would win ; but despite the shortage of artillery, machine-guns, ammunition, and reinforcements, and the overwhelming numerical superiority of the enemy, who poured in corps after corps at Ypres, hoping to finish off our attenuated army once and for all, the matchless pluck of the British soldier won the day.

As a theatre of war Flanders has always had an evil reputation, and it never deserved it more than in the winter of 1914–15. The desperate fighting of the first battle of Ypres had barely been concluded when the troops were called upon to face the most atrocious weather, long periods of continuous rain alternating with gales of wind, snow and frost, and although every measure that could be suggested was taken to compete with these conditions, it was impossible to keep the water-logged trenches either dry or in a reasonable state of repair. The men often had to stand waist-high in bitterly cold water ; the communications between the first-line trenches and the rear were as bad as they could be ; and the sufferings endured were almost, if not quite, without parallel. Life in the trenches came all the harder because the troops were new to the work, many being fresh from the tropics, and some twenty thousand men were invalided during the winter on account of " trench feet " alone.

To make matters worse, the Germans had the advantage of higher, drier, and generally much more favourable ground, from which they looked down into our miserable, muddy lines, and were able to bombard them, with their superior artillery, in a manner that would have broken the hearts of any ordinary troops. To this treatment we could give no adequate reply owing to the lack of heavy artillery and of ammunition for such guns as we had. I remember that at one time I had, with the Commander-in-Chief's approval, to issue orders restricting the expenditure to two rounds per gun a day, so depleted were our stocks and precarious our prospects of replenishing them. I claim to have as good a knowledge as any one of the British soldier, but to this day it is a marvel to me how he continued to hold on during that first terrible winter in Flanders.

By the end of 1914 the Expeditionary Force had reached a strength of five cavalry divisions and eleven infantry divisions, of which two in each case were Anglo-Indian. In addition a considerable number of Territorial battalions and Yeomanry regiments had been sent out from home. The New Armies were in course of formation and training, and were not yet ready to be put in the field.

Early in November the Commander-in-Chief sent me to England to represent to the War Office the urgency of the ammunition position, and to press for an increased supply. On return to France Lord Roberts crossed the Channel on the same boat as myself, and we had a long conversation on the war and our neglect to prepare for it. Notwithstanding his great age, his clear military instinct was as prominent as ever, but it occurred to me that for a man of his years he was trying himself too highly in attempting the journey, and this unfortunately proved to be the case. He arrived at St. Omer on the 11th November, was suddenly taken ill on the 13th, and died at 8 P.M. on the following day. Previous to the despatch of his body to England a short, simple service was held at the Mairie on the 17th, at which I had the mournful honour of being one of the pall-bearers. Contingents of British, Indian, and

French troops, and many foreign officers attended to do homage to the veteran Field-Marshal, and as the body left the Mairie on its homeward journey, the day being gloomy and dispiriting, the sun burst forth and threw a brilliant rainbow over the town, thus making a fitting termination to one of the most impressive ceremonies I have ever witnessed.

In January 1915 the Commander-in-Chief asked me to become Chief of the General Staff in place of Murray, who was about to return to England. The offer was a tempting one, as it meant an increase of pay as well as of position, but I did not wish to accept it. I had become interested in my work, I knew that the Commander-in-Chief had previously asked for another officer to succeed Murray, which was sufficient proof that I was not his first choice, and although he had appeared quite satisfied with me as Quartermaster-General, there was no certainty that either of us would be equally happy if I became his Chief of the General Staff. I therefore asked to be allowed to stay where I was, and after further discussion a final decision was, by my request, deferred for a day or two. In the end I realised that it was my duty to put personal considerations aside, and on the 25th of January I took up the new post, being succeeded as Quartermaster-General by Major-General Maxwell.

I was extremely sorry to separate from my old staff, who had served me so loyally during a time of stress and anxiety, and I would pay a special tribute to my friend Dawkins, now dead. He had a high sense of duty, not a crooked element in his character, great capacity for work, and was beloved by all of us. "The Deputy," as he was familiarly called, had a bad habit of sitting up late at night to work or read the newspapers, of which neither my reproof nor the chaff of the other officers could cure him. In honour of the season, and to the amusement of the mess, I gave him permission on Christmas night to sit up for an hour later than he usually did !

CHAPTER XIV

CHIEF OF THE GENERAL STAFF, BRITISH EXPEDITIONARY FORCE

IN my new capacity I became, according to official phraseology, the Commander-in-Chief's " responsible adviser on all
matters affecting military operations, through whom he
exercises his functions of command, and by whom all orders
issued by him will be signed." The regulations further laid
down that the General Staff duties comprised the study of
proposed operations ; framing, issue, and despatch of operation orders ; plans for movements to the points of concentration ; measures of security ; inter-communication ;
reconnaissances ; provision and distribution of maps ; and
the supply of information to the Adjutant-General and
Quartermaster-General regarding the situation and the
probable requirements of the troops.

There was much more than this to be done, and as a
first step I obtained the Commander-in-Chief's consent to
make certain changes in the personnel and organisation of
the General Staff itself. Of the two branches into which it

was divided, Operations and Intelligence, the former was inclined to regard the latter as its own particular hand-maid—which was wrong—and it also included a small sub-section known as " O (b)," which had been designed mainly to conduct telegraphic correspondence with formations at the front. In this way the whole of the work had a tendency to filter through the Operations branch to the sub-chief, from him to the Chief of the General Staff, and then to the Commander-in-Chief. Bottle-necks are notorious for making nothing and obstructing everything, and this one was the more objectionable because of the increasing amount of work to be done. The Expeditionary Force upon which the existing system had been based was already double its original strength, many more divisions would shortly arrive, and therefore it was necessary that greater decentralisation of staff work should be initiated.

Moreover, units, large and small, were coming out from home indifferently trained in their common military duties, and knowing next to nothing about the conditions attaching to trench warfare. The war of trenches had brought up new problems for which our accepted methods of instruction made little provision, and the New Armies, as well as the drafts, were still being trained on much the same lines as the old regular army had been. It was essential to set up machinery for giving these new arrivals the requisite addi-tional training before they went into the trenches, the machinery to include schools of instruction manned by officers and non-commissioned officers who were specialists in their business ; to make similar arrangements for the training of drafts at the bases ; bring formations at the front in closer relation with these drafts and cause them to take a greater interest in them ; and inaugurate systematic instruction for regimental officers and non-commissioned officers, whose professional standard had fallen to a low level owing to the number of casualties we had suffered.

Lastly, special means had to be provided for dealing with questions regarding new units such as mining com-panies, new inventions such as trench-mortars, and a host of others relating to new methods of making war in general and trench war in particular.

I decided to form three separate branches, Operations, Intelligence, and General Staff duties (*i.e.* training and all other duties not included in the two first-named branches). In the Operations branch was one officer charged solely with keeping the artillery ammunition account, and with advising me how we could best use the small amounts then being received. Every single round had to be jealously guarded, for consignments of ammunition did not then come out as later in the war by hundreds of tons at a time in special ships and barges, but in driblets of thirty or forty rounds, much in the same way as if despatched by parcel post.

The head of each branch was made responsible to me personally, all three being expected to keep in touch with each other and not to shut themselves up in water-tight compartments. Colonel (now Major-General) E. Perceval took charge, as sub-chief of the General Staff, of Staff duties, and acted for me in my temporary absence ; Colonel (now Major-General Sir) F. Maurice became head of the Operations branch, and Colonel (now Lieutenant-General Sir) G. Macdonogh remained as head of the Intelligence.

Perceval, as mentioned in a previous chapter, had served under me at the Staff College, and his professional.knowledge and untiring energy were as valuable to me in France as they had been at Camberley. He was given command of a division in July 1915, being succeeded as sub-chief by Colonel (now Major-General Sir) R. Whigham, another of my Staff College assistants. Maurice, who had also been with me at the Staff College, was, like his father the late Sir Frederick Maurice, possessed of quite exceptional talents. He was particularly well read in military history, had a thorough grasp of the principles of strategy and tactics, and, what was more to the point, held sound views regarding their practical application. He could express himself temperately and clearly both verbally and on paper, and he devoted every spare minute of the day and night to thinking out how best to beat the formidable enemy in front of us. There was, I may remind the reader, a great deal of thinking of this nature to be done at the time, for not much daylight was yet visible.

Most of the junior officers in the three branches had been trained under me at the Staff College, and were as capable and loyal a body of assistants as any man could wish to have. They included, at different times, Radcliffe, Bartholomew, Montgomery, and Tandy (artillery), Hutchison (cavalry), Elles and Cox (engineers), Deedes (infantry), and Wigram (Indian army).

Being a believer in having small messes on service, the only members of the one I formed were the sub-chief, Maurice, and my two aides-de-camp—Lucas and Montagu Stopford, the son of Lionel Stopford, one of my contemporaries when a student at the Staff College. My predecessor had lived with the Commander-in-Chief and had no separate mess of his own, and although this arrangement had its advantages it also had its drawbacks. The General Staff office and the principal General Staff officers were always liable to be located some distance away from the quarters of the Commander-in-Chief, and it seemed best that I should be near them. Moreover, it is just as well that the Commander-in-Chief and the Chief of his Staff should occasionally have a close time of their own, for, unless they possess more angelic tempers than ordinary mortals can hope to have, the constant mental strain to which they are subjected by the stress of war may cause them to get on each other's nerves. If that happens there will be trouble, and the effect of it may be felt by the whole army.

Outside the General Staff, and omitting my two helpful colleagues the Adjutant-General and Quartermaster-General, the senior officers upon whom I had chiefly to rely for assistance were Du Cane the Artillery Adviser, Fowke the Engineer-in-Chief, and Fowler the Director of the Signal Service. The nature and amount of guns and ammunition we required, the best use to make of such material as we had and hoped to have in the future, and the most suitable system of artillery organisation in general, were all questions regarding which much difference of opinion still existed at the beginning of 1915, and it was largely owing to Du Cane's judgment and foresight that the right course was steered and the foundations of our artillery supremacy were correctly laid. He was afterwards employed in the Ministry of Munitions for the greater part of 1916; he then commanded an army corps on the West Front for about one and a half years, and was the senior British military representative at the headquarters of the allied armies from April to November 1918.

Fowke had to deal with and advise on matters connected with trench warfare, the supply of engineering material, and new methods of solving the most difficult problems with which the Royal Engineers had ever been confronted. He became Adjutant-General in France in February 1916, and continued to hold that post until the end of the war.

Fowler was in charge of the Signal Service from the first day of the war until the last, and superintended its expansion from a strength of about 1600 in 1914 to one of over 70,000 in 1918. I had first met him twenty years before when travelling through Kashmir; he had served on my staff at the Staff College; and in pre-war days we had often taken part together in staff tours designed to afford instruction in the working of signal communications with an army in the field. During the retreat from Mons he had accomplished marvels in keeping up connection between G.H.Q. and the troops, and he was indispensable to me whilst I was Chief of the General Staff in 1915.

In Chapter X. I have described the original formation of " Communication Companies." These had later become the "Signal Service"; and for the benefit of those who are unacquainted with the duties of this service I may say that upon the efficiency with which they are performed the power of a commander to handle his troops greatly depends. Just as in a human body the nerves convey the information obtained by the senses to the brain, and the orders from the brain to the muscles, so the signal communications of an army convey the information obtained from all sources to the commander, and orders from the commander to his troops. Loss of efficiency or sluggishness of the nerves results in partial paralysis of the body, and a corresponding paralysis of the army results from the failure of its signal communications.

The maintenance of communication on the West Front, particularly in the forward area, was very difficult owing to the heavy shell-fire, mud, and exposure which were experienced, and as no one means could be relied on many alternative methods had to be provided. Telegraph and telephone by wire and cables, wireless telegraphy, telegraphy through the ground (power buzzer), visual signalling with electric lamps, helios and flags, carrier pigeons, messenger dogs, message-carrying rockets, firework signals, motor-cyclist despatch riders, mounted orderlies, cyclists, and finally runners were all employed in turn according to circumstances. The telephone cables, being too vulnerable overground, had sometimes to be buried to a depth of six or eight feet to protect them from shell fire, a task which entailed the digging of hundreds of miles of trenches. During 1917 some 80,000 miles of telephone wire were buried in this way. Further to the rear, out of range of the enemy's artillery, the telegraph and telephone were used much in the same way as we are accustomed to in civil life. The number of messages dealt with on the different systems was astonishing, and in the great battles of 1917 and 1918 they amounted to tens of thousands in a day.

The Royal Flying Corps, as the Royal Air Force was called in 1915, was under the command of Major-General (now Lieutenant-General Sir) David Henderson, who had been Director-General of Military Aeronautics before the war, and may be termed the father of the corps. The detachment on the West Front was commanded by Brigadier-General (now Air-Marshal Sir) Hugh Trenchard, of whose excellent work I had many proofs when serving with him. At the time the corps was still very much in its infancy and below the requisite strength, but it had considerably improved as compared with its condition in August 1914. The development and unrivalled efficiency it eventually attained are amongst the greatest achievements of the war. The country owes much to the Flying Corps, and especially to the men, or rather boys for the most part, who flew and fought the machines with such marvellous courage and skill. The pity of it is that so many of these gallant lads lost their lives. I always maintained that they were taken too young, and the answer given me was that the younger ones were always the most daring. No doubt this was so, but this same daring was sometimes little less than recklessness, and led to loss of life which would have been avoided by men a year or two older.

The Military Secretary, working directly under the Commander-in-Chief, and dealing with all appointments, promotions, and rewards, was another officer with whom I had much to do, as all nominations for employment on the General Staff throughout the Force were made by me before submission for the Chief's approval. Colonel " Billy " (now Major-General Sir William) Lambton held the post and filled it, so I thought, exceedingly well. He was a pleasant and practical officer to do business with, and his numerous friends were extremely sorry when, as a divisional commander later in the war, he had the misfortune to be seriously injured by his horse coming down with him.

I should like to correct the idea, prevalent at one time if not now, that life at G.H.Q. was one of ease and indolence. It was very strenuous, and as a general rule the staff were kept hard at work, either in their offices or at the front, from early morning till ten o'clock or later at night. It should be remembered, too, that they carried great responsibilities. Officers who have done splendidly with troops at the front, or have shown high ability in administration, may still fail, and have been known to fail, to bear the heavier burdens resting upon them when employed at G.H.Q. To be of any real use there a General Staff officer must not be content with carrying on according to established routine, he must initiate ; he has to decide tangled questions which come before him because they have proved to be too much for the commanders and staffs at the front ; being at the top of the military structure, there is no one upon whom he can lean ; and he is oppressed with the thought that a slip on his part may set going a series of actions involving perhaps the loss of thousands of lives.

Earlier in the war I had known staff officers to be so run down by constant work and worry as to faint away at their office tables, and this at a time when high spirits, confidence, and energy were especially needed. Good work calls for good physical and mental health, and I insisted upon my staff taking exercise at least once during the day, preferably on horseback, and going off to bed, whenever possible, by ten o'clock at night. In my own mess we seldom missed going for a ride at 6.30 A.M., returning for breakfast at 8 A.M., and with this invigorating recreation in hand we were able to commence the day's work on cheerful terms with ourselves and everybody else. I followed the same rule afterwards when at the War Office, as did the other principal members of my staff (with one exception), regularly joining the " Liver Brigade " in the Row for about an hour every morning, and sometimes taking a second ride in the afternoon.

Another matter upon which I laid stress was that staff officers at G.H.Q. should carefully maintain friendly relations with the troops and headquarters, small as well as large, at the front. By this means only is it possible to learn what the feeling of an army really is, where the shoe pinches, and how it can be eased. A sympathetic listening to the numerous worries that daily beset subordinate commanders, a friendly chat with them about their personal duties and interests, the passing on of news about affairs on other fronts and in other theatres, all help to establish that spirit of comradeship and mutual confidence without which the wheels of the military machine will never go round smoothly and efficiently. I used to visit some headquarters or troops practically every day, attending to office work in the evening, and the other officers of my staff were expected to do the same, as far as their other duties would permit. Being less important personages than myself, they were able to pick up information which was not vouchsafed to me, and it was for the common good that they should tell me, as they did, anything useful that came to their notice.

To supplement their rather restricted opportunities a certain number of " liaison officers " were employed as a more permanent link between G.H.Q. and the front. Each morning before leaving they would visit the staff offices and prime themselves with what the army or army corps with which they were connected should know, would bring back in the evening all the information gained that G.H.Q. should have, and at both ends would clear up, if they could, any points about which there might be misapprehension. Similar but more extensive arrangements were made for keeping up connection with the headquarters of the French and Belgian armies, each of the three Allies having a " military mission " permanently located at the headquarters of the other two. The French Mission at our G.H.Q. comprised a considerable number of officers, as there were daily many questions in regard to civil administration, the use of railways, etc., which had to be dealt with, quite apart from those affecting the fighting.

I shall not attempt to describe in detail the operations which took place on the British front in 1915. That has been done in the despatches of the Commander-in-Chief, and, moreover, this book is not meant to be a history of the war. My observations will be of a general nature, and as the operations have not escaped criticism I would in the first place remind the reader that they should be judged not merely by what we may have failed to achieve, but also by what we prevented the enemy from achieving.

The problem confronting the Commander - in - Chief throughout 1915 was one of extreme difficulty. The enemy was within a short distance of the Channel ports, the loss of which would be very serious to us, if not fatal, and at any moment he could close down his Russian operations sufficiently to allow of reinforcements being sent to the West Front while we were still weak in men, practically without heavy artillery, and woefully short of artillery ammunition of all kinds. The necessity for safeguarding the Channel ports, together with our lack of men and munitions, indicated that the policy most favourable to us would be to defer offensive operations until we possessed a well-trained and well-equipped army adequate to our needs. This, however, would be to take a narrow view of the situation, as it would leave out of account the effect a defensive attitude might have upon our Allies, to say nothing of its destructive influence upon the morale of our own troops.

It must also be remembered that the Commander-in-Chief was not in all respects master in his own house. Theoretically he was an independent commander and responsible only to his own Government, but his instructions laid down—quite rightly—that " the special motive of the Force under your command is to support, and co-operate with, the French army against our common enemies," and obviously he could not so co-operate and at the same time retain complete independence of action. The enemy was in possession of a large and valuable part of French territory ; Russia, suffering from a series of defeats, was crying out for pressure to be relieved by energetic action on the West Front; certain prospective allies were sitting on the fence, wondering on which side to descend or whether to come down at all ; and if General Joffre thought that this situation could best be met by an early offensive his British colleague could hardly do otherwise than support him to the best of his power. For these and a score of other reasons a defensive policy was not practicable, and yet it is true that our armies were not in a condition to fight with any good prospect of obtaining decisive results.

Having before her our experiences of 1915 and 1916, and not forgetting perhaps the lessons she herself had learned in the Civil War, America seems to have decided, when she joined the Allies in 1917, not to commit her troops to battle until they were fully ready and of sufficient strength to be more or less self-supporting : in the end, and in consequence of the enemy's action, she was obliged to forgo this decision and hurry to the assistance of the British and French armies as best she could. The inexorable fact is that, when opposed by a capable adversary, the unprepared nation is invariably compelled by force of circumstances to put its troops into battle piecemeal and before they have been properly trained to fight, with the result that losses are incurred out of all proportion to the progress made in winning the war, while the lives thus sacrificed are usually amongst the best which the nation possesses.

To what cause history will attribute our unreadiness I shall not attempt to prophesy, but when I think of the terrible events of 1914 and 1915 ; of the privations and mental strain suffered by the men of our attenuated battalions through being kept in the front line for weeks at a stretch owing to the lack of reinforcements ; of men being shot down

like rabbits when trying to pass through the enemy's wire
entanglements which had not previously been demolished
because of the shortage of artillery; and of the heavy loss
of life in the hastily-raised and inexperienced divisions of
the New Armies, I wonder what are the feelings of those
who, occupying high positions in the years before the war,
made no serious effort to provide such an army as the
inevitable struggle with Germany would demand, and
deliberately held up to scorn those who, putting patriotism
before self-interest, strove to warn the country of the peril
in which it stood.

As a corollary of our unreadiness the Commander-in-
Chief was further hampered by the uncertainty which
prevailed throughout the greater part of 1915 regarding the
reinforcements, guns, and ammunition which he might hope
to receive within a given period of time. No one could
possibly say long beforehand when particular divisions of
the New Armies would be ready to take the field, or whether
contracts for war material would or would not be fulfilled
by the agreed date, while both men and material, originally
ear-marked for France, were liable to be diverted at the last
moment, and were diverted, to other theatres of war. It is
not my purpose, for the moment, to question this dissemination of resources. I merely wish to point out how difficult it
was to utilise to the best advantage such resources as became
available for the West Front, owing to the absence of any
reliable basis upon which a definite and comprehensive plan
of campaign could be constructed.

Neuve Chapelle, the first battle in 1915, was fought on
the 10th, 11th, and 12th March. We lost some 2500 killed
and over 8000 wounded, while the enemy left thousands of
dead on the field and removed, according to our intelligence
reports, at least 12,000 wounded by train.

Judged by more recent standards this battle would be
classified as quite a minor engagement, but its importance
should not be estimated merely by the numbers engaged,
the duration of the fighting, or the results immediately
achieved. It helped to nourish the offensive spirit of the
troops, who had endured months of heart-breaking submission to the enemy's will under the most trying climatic

conditions ; it created a corresponding feeling of disquiet and disappointment in the German ranks ; it afforded many encouraging proofs that, given an adequate supply of guns and ammunition, the enemy's lines need not be regarded as impregnable ; and, finally, the elaborate arrangements made for the employment of artillery fire, which were introduced on this occasion for the first time, furnished useful guidance for both the British and French armies in the greater attacks undertaken at a later period of the war.

The second battle of Ypres, commencing at 5 P.M. on the 22nd of April and ending on the 24th of May, is prominent as being the first action in which asphyxiating gas was used. The brunt of the attack fell on a French division which was holding the line Steenstraat-Langemarck on the extreme left of our Second Army, where the 1st Canadian Division was posted. Within an hour the position had to be abandoned, the smoke and fumes of the gas hid everything from view, the ground was covered with men in a dying or comatose condition, and in the panic and confusion which prevailed it was impossible for any one to realise at first what had actually happened. Owing to the retirement of the French division—for which the division could not be blamed, as no troops would have held their ground against this unexpected form of attack—the left flank of the Canadian Division became completely exposed, and had it been driven in the whole of the British troops in the salient would have been threatened with disaster. This danger was averted by the splendid gallantry of the Canadians, and by the prompt despatch of reserves from other divisions in the vicinity.

The necessity for rapidly pushing troops forward to check the enemy's advance, and to close the gap between our left and the French right, inevitably led to the mixing of units ; this in its turn made the exercise of efficient command impossible ; and although large reinforcements were moved up and various other measures taken to meet eventualities, the situation was critical during the next few days. The ground gained by the enemy placed our troops in the salient in a very awkward position, and as there seemed little prospect of recapturing the original line the

Commander-in-Chief decided on the 1st of May to withdraw them to a safer line in rear which had already been fixed upon.

To withdraw a force at grips with a winning enemy must always be a difficult and delicate task, and in this particular case the conditions were specially unfavourable. The enemy had all the advantages of ground, he made violent attacks on the nights of the 2nd and 3rd of May while the rearward movement was going on, some of his front line trenches were less than 100 yards distant from ours, the surface of the sodden fields had been so broken by artillery fire as to be nearly impassable, the maintenance of reliable communication was impossible, and our troops were absolutely worn out so far as British troops ever can be. In spite of all this, and of much more, the retirement was effected by the morning of the 4th of May with scarcely any loss, and during that day the enemy shelled the trenches we had abandoned, being quite unaware that our men were no longer in them. General Plumer succeeded General Smith-Dorrien in the command of the Second Army while the above events were taking place, and it is doubtful if any commander was ever before suddenly called upon to handle so difficult a situation.

While the Second Army was still engaged in the battle of Ypres, the First Army made an attack on the enemy's trenches opposite the southern part of our line, this operation, usually spoken of as the battle of Festubert, being part of a joint attack made by the French and British armies on the front extending from near Armentieres to Arras. The rôle of the British was to hold the enemy on their front, and draw towards themselves hostile reinforcements which might otherwise be sent to oppose the main attack made by the French troops under General Foch, the chief objective of the latter being the Vimy Ridge. The battle commenced on the 9th of May and was continued on the 10th, it was resumed on the 16th, and terminated, so far as we were concerned, on the 25th. The French continued fighting in their attempts to take the Vimy Ridge until the 13th of July. We experienced the usual trouble with the enemy's machine-gun posts, with which we did not yet know how to deal, and we again felt the want of more artillery and ammunition. In fact, our co-operation ceased on the date mentioned because of the want of ammunition. The results of the battle were somewhat disappointing, the losses of both British and French being considerable and no immediate material advantage was gained. In consequence of the French losses, which were some of the heaviest in the war, Foch became rather unpopular in certain circles in France, by whom he was regarded, quite unjustly, as a leader who was careless of the lives of his men.

The battle of Loos, the first occasion on which we used gas, began on the 25th of September and continued until the 15th of October. It, also, was carried out in combination with an attack by the French armies under General Foch on our right, a third and more powerful attack being simultaneously made by the French armies under General Joffre in Champagne. The enemy's position at Loos was of exceptional strength and, as was the case everywhere else, there were few or no weak spots in the formidable defences upon which he had spent the greater part of a year in constructing ; the ground in front of the position was very open to view, and in other ways unfavourable to us as regards both the preparation and execution of the attack ; while we were further handicapped by bad weather interfering with observation of fire and aerial reconnaissance. Very satisfactory progress was made at the beginning of the battle but it could not be exploited, one reason for this being, amongst others, that the French on our right were unable to make any substantial headway in their efforts to gain complete possession of the Vimy Ridge. We were afterwards subjected to a series of severe counter-attacks, the battle swaying to and fro for several days, particularly in the neighbourhood of the renowned Hohenzollern Redoubt.

The French attack in Champagne also, though successful at first, did not fulfil expectations, but taking the results of these autumn operations as a whole there is no doubt that they caused the enemy genuine anxiety, and I sometimes think that he might have suffered a real set-back had the large number of men and guns then in the Dardanelles been on the West Front. Speaking of this period, Falkenhayn admits that " a serious crisis arose, which almost led to the withdrawal of the whole 3rd German Army on the Champagne Front"; while Ludendorff, in referring to the "powerful offensive near Loos and in Champagne," says that "the troops which had been transferred from the East (*i.e.* the Russian Front) arrived just in time to support the defenders of the West Front, who were holding out so gallantly, and avert a serious defeat."

Our captures at Loos included over 3000 prisoners and 26 field-guns, and many thousands of the enemy's dead were seen lying on the ground in front of our lines. We also lost heavily, including three Divisional Commanders, Capper of the 7th Division, Wing of the 12th Division, and Thesiger of the 9th Division. No troops in the world could have fought with greater gallantry than ours did, but gallantry is not of itself enough to cope with the destructive effect of modern armament; and the lack of adequate training and military experience in general from which the new divisions suffered, and the need for increased artillery support, very quickly made themselves felt. More troops, more training, more aeroplanes, more guns, more ammunition, were required before decisive results could be achieved.

With the exception of France, our Allies were no better off than ourselves, and some of them were worse. Before the war they were supposed to have, thanks to their system of universal service, large numbers of men available for mobilisation and on paper they had them, but when put to the test it was found that insufficient provision had been made for rifles, clothing, heavy artillery, ammunition, vehicles, and all the other things required. Russia had millions of men on her books, but could only put a comparatively small proportion of them in the field, and she was not always sure as to what amount of equipment she had. Some which she thought she had proved to be not forthcoming when wanted, while in one instance at least stores were "found" of whose existence no one seems to have been previously aware. Italy, also, had more men of military age than she could equip, and, like Russia, lacked both aeroplanes and heavy artillery. Belgium had naturally lost much of what she had at the beginning of the war, and Serbia had lost practically all. The two countries with the greatest surplus of men, Russia and Italy, were badly situated for making good their deficiencies by new production, as the former was difficult of access, the latter wanted coal, and both needed raw material.

In December 1915 Joffre assembled representatives of all the Allied armies at his headquarters at Chantilly, so as to ascertain the men and material they then had and hoped to have by the spring of 1916, and to try to arrive at some conclusions with respect to mutual assistance. The meeting, like those which followed it, was handicapped by the absence of a suitable representative from Russia. In all other cases the Allies were represented either by their Commander-in-Chief or his Chief of the Staff, but owing to distance and other causes Russia was always represented either by an officer permanently attached to Joffre's headquarters, or by another officer not then filling a high position in the Russian army, and neither of these could speak with the requisite knowledge or authority. The meeting had some good results, but each representative not unnaturally argued that his own front was the most important and had perhaps been authoritatively instructed to say so, and as everybody was short of nearly everything promises of assistance were rather reluctantly given and were usually conditional.

Joffre's task at this period was difficult, for the war had not yet proceeded far enough to admit of his being acknowledged as supreme commander of all the Allied armies. Even the smallest countries were quick to resent outside interference with their status as independent nations. This can be understood if we remember that the question was not merely one of directing the armies in the field but also of organising and equipping them, and this affected the commercial, industrial, and financial interests of the whole nation. Any suggestion at this time of introducing the same system of centralised command as that which the prospect of stark defeat compelled the Allies to adopt in 1918 would have been peremptorily turned down as too impossible for any self-respecting country to entertain. Joffre had therefore to make the best of a bad job, and I am inclined to think that he did all that he or any one else could then have done to unify the efforts of the different armies.

G.H.Q. in France were of course concerned only with matters on that front, and had nothing to do with the conduct of the war in general, either strategical or administrative. That was the business of the authorities in London, but it was the subject of a good deal of conversation with ministers and other officials who from time to time visited G.H.Q. The views of the General Staff were unanimous and simple. They were that the West Front was the main front, whether we liked it or not ; that the main decision must consequently be sought on that front ; and that every man, gun, and round of ammunition should be sent to it, except such as were absolutely required elsewhere for the defence of interests vital to the Empire. All our visitors did not agree, and perhaps suspected us of undue partiality to the front on which we were employed, but at least two of them, Mr. Asquith and Lord Kitchener, were as convinced as we were that so long as we won in the west temporary set-backs in other parts of the world would right themselves. Lord Kitchener once told me in connection with the enemy's activities in Persia and Afghanistan, that he did not care what happened there or in India if only we beat the German armies in Europe.

For one reason or another, however, we had become committed before the end of 1915 to operations in no less than three secondary theatres, Mesopotamia, Gallipoli, and Macedonia ; a fourth campaign was about to begin in East Africa ; a fifth had to be contemplated against the Turks east of the Suez Canal, and the western border of Egypt was also unsettled. In the aggregate these liabilities seemed likely, before finished with, to make such demands upon men, material, and shipping as might seriously jeopardise success in the main theatre, and this was the more probable because Russia had just been so crippled as to render her future assistance a very doubtful quantity. As far as an outsider like myself could judge, these secondary operations formed no part of any general Entente plan embracing the war as a whole ; the importance of making proper preparations to carry them out, and of carefully considering the extent to which they might develop, had been obscured by the desire to present the public with an easy and dramatic success ; and it was forgotten that any success of real advantage to us must equally be to the disadvantage of the enemy, who therefore might be expected to try his hardest to prevent it from being gained.

The whole situation being so full of peril, I felt it to be my duty to do what I could to bring about somewhat more efficient methods in the supreme direction of the war. Strictly speaking I had no right to interfere, but departure from official etiquette was a small matter in comparison with the danger in which the country seemed to stand, and therefore I decided to embody my views in a memorandum and send them unofficially to Murray, then Chief of the Imperial General Staff, to be disposed of as he thought fit. The memorandum, which strongly advocated better co-ordination of the Entente plans, was eventually circulated to the Cabinet, and to that extent it served its purpose.

A short time afterwards, when I happened to be at home, Lord Kitchener told me that I was wanted to take up the duties of Chief of the Imperial General Staff. For some weeks past I had suspected that this suggestion would be made, as I had received hints from influential quarters that I would be more useful in London than in France, and I had always opposed the change. It was distasteful to me to supersede Murray, who was an old friend and had taken up the appointment as recently as the 26th of September. Moreover, he was rapidly making the necessary improvements in the General Staff machinery, and I was not vain enough to suppose that I could do any better than he was doing, if as well. A minor reason for wishing to remain in France was that the open-air life and spirit of comradeship and cheerfulness which always prevailed at the front, no matter how bad the weather or how aggressive the enemy, were far more attractive than the gloomy despondency of London and the thankless work of Whitehall. Still another reason was that I could not help being influenced by the prevailing gossip that Lord Kitchener centralised all authority in his own hands, and would not allow the General Staff at the War Office to take that part in the strategical direction of operations which it ought to take. My acquaintance with him at the time was very slight, for although we had served together in South Africa I was then only a junior officer and we saw practically nothing of each other.

I therefore asked him to leave me in France, but to this he would not listen, and from the long conversation we had the same evening at York House it became evident that I ought to comply with his wishes. In the course of our talk he referred quite frankly to the unenviable reputation he had acquired, and asked me not to believe it for it was not true, and he assured me that I might rest satisfied that no action of his would endanger our working smoothly together. I was much impressed by his outspoken manner, and felt that I was in the presence of a man whose character was totally different from what I had been led to suppose ; but I still thought it would be best for both of us, and for the country, if before finally deciding we came to a definite understanding, in writing, on the particular points regarding which I was in doubt.

To this he agreed, and as soon as I returned to France I sent him a memorandum containing my proposals, one of them being that all operation orders issued to Commanders-in-Chief to give effect to the military policy of the Government should be sent by me, the Chief of the Imperial General Staff, and not, as hitherto, be issued in the name of the Army Council and over the signature of the Secretary of the Council—a civilian. This and certain other proposals did not meet with his approval, and in the letter which he wrote me by return of post he said that it would be impossible for him to retain the responsibility of Secretary of State for War without full executive power, and with his functions curtailed to the feeding and clothing of the army (the Ministry of Munitions having recently taken over the other services of maintenance) ; but that although he could not remain Secretary of State for War if my suggestions were accepted by the Government—as he thought they would be—he might still continue to be a member of the War Council, and " in that case you may rely on me to always do my best to support you in carrying out the difficult task you will have before you."

This example of patriotism and subordination of self was the more striking as coming from a man of his standing in the Empire and with his record of service, and I had not a moment's hesitation as to the right thing to do. His letter reached me at St. Omer about seven o'clock in the evening, and as I knew that he was passing through Calais at eleven o'clock the same night on his way to Paris, I got into my motor after dinner and went to Calais to meet him. He greeted me very cordially, albeit a little sadly, I thought, and with an air of disappointment. I came at once to the point and said that whatever happened I could not hear of his leaving the War Office, since there was no one who could fill the position which he held in the country, and I begged him to discuss with me the paragraphs in the memorandum to which he objected. As his train was due to start almost immediately for Paris he asked me to go with him. I jumped in, and we sat up talking till two o'clock next morning, the conversation being resumed after we had breakfasted in Paris.

I had two special reasons for wishing to abolish the existing system of issuing operation orders, and to vest this duty, unhampered, in the hands of the Chief of the Imperial General Staff. At the time the Army Council consisted of four military and four civil members (later increased by three additional military members, or eleven in all), besides the Secretary of State for War, and all these members had the right, if they chose to exercise it, to be consulted before any important orders were issued in the name of the Council. This would have entailed interminable delay, and as all the members had more than enough to do in their own departments without becoming entangled in the work of the General Staff, they were, in practice, not consulted, except in so far as their respective departments were concerned— a custom which must necessarily prevail under any system. Therefore while they shared the responsibility for the operation orders issued, they knew, in fact, little or nothing about them, and this was neither fair to them nor to the General Staff.

My second objection to this sham system was that it prevented the General Staff at the War Office from being recognised as the Great General Staff of our armies at the front, and in my opinion this recognition was essential. At the front the issue of operation orders was, as in all armies of the world, the business of the General Staff and of no one else, and my proposal brought the procedure at the War Office into conformity with this practice, and caused the pretended control of operations by the Army Council to disappear. It did not, as some people imagined, involve any diminution in the authority of the Secretary of State for War. It merely assigned a particular duty to the head of one department of the War Office instead of assigning it to the Army Council as a whole, made the position of the General Staff clear, and brought that Staff into more direct relations with the Cabinet.

When I had explained the proposal in this way to Lord Kitchener, and cleared up the other points with which he was not at first in agreement, the offending paragraphs of the memorandum—written in a hurry and not very happily worded in all respects—were amended in a manner satisfactory to both of us, and I returned to G.H.Q. at St. Omer. A few days later I left for England, and on the 23rd of December took up the new post.

The memorandum, as amended, was as follows :

GENERAL HEADQUARTERS,
BRITISH ARMY IN THE FIELD IN FRANCE,
5th December 1915.

DEAR LORD KITCHENER—You were kind enough yesterday to express your willingness to receive some observations of mine regarding the conduct of the war, with special reference to the status and duties of the Chief of the Imperial General Staff.

For a long time past I have given careful and anxious consideration to this question. Both the history of past wars and our experience in the present war show that certain conditions are normally essential to the successful conduct of military operations, though there have, it is true, been isolated instances of commanders of genius who have triumphed in the absence of these conditions.

These conditions are :

(I.) There should be a supreme directing authority whose function is to formulate policy, decide on the theatres in which military operations are to be conducted, and determine the relative importance of these theatres. This authority must also exercise a general supervision over the conduct of the war, and must select the men who are to execute the policy on which it has decided. Its constitution must be such that it is able to come to quick decisions, and therefore as regards the conduct of the war it must be absolute.

The War Council[1] should be capable of performing the functions of this supreme authority, provided it is relieved of responsibility to the Cabinet as a whole as regards the conduct of military operations, and that it has real executive power and is not merely an advisory committee.

The War Council will frequently find itself in a position similar to that of a commander in the field—that is, it will have to come to a decision when the situation is obscure, when information is deficient, and when the wishes and the powers of our Allies are uncertain. Whatever these difficulties may be, if and when a decision is required it must be made. If it is deferred success cannot be expected; the commander concerned will have a grossly unfair burden placed upon him ; and in fact the absence of a decision may be little less than criminal because of the loss of life which may be entailed.

(II.) In order that the War Council may be able to come to timely decisions on the questions with which it has to deal, it is essential that it should receive *all* advice on matters concerning military operations through one authoritative channel only. With us that channel must be the Chief of the Imperial General Staff. It is his function, so far as regards military operations, to present to the War Council his reasoned opinion as to the military effect of the policy which they propose, and as to the means of putting this approved policy into execution. The War Council are then free to accept or reject the reasoned advice so offered.

Advice regarding military operations emanating from members of the Cabinet, or of the War Council in their individual capacity, or from any other individual, should be sifted, examined, and presented, if necessary with reasoned conclusions, to the War Council by the Chief of the Imperial General Staff before it is accepted by the War Council.

(III.) All orders for the military operations required to put into execution the policy approved by the War Council should be issued and signed by the Chief of the Imperial General Staff, under the authority of the Secretary of State for War, *not* under that of the Army Council. Similarly, all communications from General Officers Commanding regarding military operations should be addressed to the Chief of the Imperial General Staff. In fact, the same procedure is required in London as obtains in the field—the War Council being in the position of the Commander-in-Chief of the

---

[1] The constitution of this War Council, or War Committee, is described on p. 253.

whole of the Imperial Land Forces, and, with the War Office Staff, constituting the Great General Headquarters of the Empire.

(IV.) The adoption of this system by which communications regarding military operations are issued and received by the Chief of the Imperial General Staff will greatly expedite the despatch of business, and will help to preserve greater secrecy than now prevails.

Instances have occurred in the war of the contents of the most important documents becoming public property within a few days. Than this nothing could be more harmful to the conduct of the war. It would be for the Chief of the Imperial General Staff to give orders as to the reproduction and distribution of these communications, and he would of course be responsible for seeing that the Secretary of State for War and the War Council receive at all times full information of all that they should know.

(V.) The Chief of the Imperial General Staff must be free to devote his entire time to the duties above indicated, and have sufficient leisure to think quietly out the many difficult problems which are continually arising, and also to keep himself thoroughly fit in mind and body. He must therefore be relieved as far as possible of War Office routine duties. To do this the Assistant Chief of the Imperial General Staff should become a Deputy Chief of the Imperial General Staff with authority to represent, as and when necessary, the Chief of the Imperial General Staff in all Army Council business.

(VI.) The number of General Officers Commanding with which the Chief of the Imperial General Staff should deal should not exceed the number which experience shows to be possible—about half-a-dozen.

For this it is necessary that a General Officer Commanding-in-Chief should be appointed to the Command of the Home Forces or those in Great Britain, as may be deemed best, his position being exactly similar to, say, that of the General Officer Commanding-in-Chief in France, except that the present system of administration need not be disturbed. He would also be responsible for Home Defence, the troops for this purpose being allocated, of course, under instructions issued by the Chief of the Imperial General Staff as in all other cases—*vide* para (III.).

I need not go more fully into my reasons for the above proposals, as I am sure they will be obvious to you. It is of paramount importance in war that there should be a definite plan of operations, and that that plan should be carried out with prompt-

R

ness and decision. It is impossible that this should be so if the War Council is itself compelled to listen to conflicting advice, and to decide between the merits of rival experts. It is equally impossible that this should be so if the War Council has to submit its plan for the conduct of the war to the approval of the whole Cabinet. The War Council is now conducting military operations in a number of separate theatres of war, and has control of large reserves which may be thrown into one theatre or another. France has no reserves left, therefore the decision as to the future conduct of the war by the Western Allies rests in great measure with the War Council. It is vital then that it should possess the machinery both to come to timely decisions and to have its decisions executed.

My proposals seem to necessitate some modifications of the Orders in Council which lay down the constitution of the Army Council and the duties of the Chief of the Imperial General Staff. If that is so those Orders should be amended for the period of the war. They were never intended, I suppose, to meet a situation such as now exists, and they certainly do not meet it.

I hope you will not think that I have any desire to make a bargain for myself, but I feel strongly that I cannot serve the War Council and my King and country as Chief of the Imperial General Staff unless the above conditions are fulfilled. It is my conviction that the system by which the war has been conducted hitherto has been such as to make victory very difficult indeed, if not impossible. Having no faith in it I could not do justice to it, and therefore if my proposals cannot be accepted you would be better advised to select an officer who sees in the existing system a possible means of bringing this war to a successful conclusion.

I hope, however, that the proposals may not be considered unacceptable, and that they will be adopted whoever may fill the post of Chief of the Imperial Staff. If the appointment were offered to me, I should have to make a few alterations in the General Staff organisation at the War Office, and would wish to replace two or three officers by officers from this country.

I need not trouble you with these alterations except to say that :

The Directorate of Home Defence and part of the Training Directorate would be handed over to the staff of the General Officer Commanding-in-Chief, Home Forces, as his staff. The remaining part of the Training Directorate would be placed in the Staff Duties Directorate.

One of these two Directors could be abolished.

The D.M.O. Branch would be divided into the two Directorates of " Operations " and " Intelligence."

The Chief of the Imperial General Staff would then have to deal with Deputy Chief of the Imperial General Staff, Director of Operations, and Director of Intelligence. The Director of Staff Duties would be under the Deputy Chief of the Imperial General Staff.

I enclose a duplicate copy of this letter, which I hope you will send to the Prime Minister should it ever be contemplated to offer me the appointment of Chief of the Imperial General Staff.—Believe me, yours sincerely,

W. R. ROBERTSON.

On the 27th of January 1916 the new method of issuing operation orders was authorised in the following Order in Council :

The Chief of the Imperial General Staff shall, in addition to performing such other duties as may from time to time be assigned to him under the Order in Council, dated the 10th August 1914, be responsible for issuing the orders of the Government in regard to Military Operations.

During the time we worked together Lord Kitchener would sometimes refer to the memorandum as " our bargain," and would ask his personal staff whether he was carrying his part of it out, thus showing a genuine desire to make everything go smoothly. For myself I never had occasion to give it another thought, and I shall always regret that the unfounded gossip to which I have alluded caused me to misjudge him, even though temporarily, and so add to the cares and anxieties he was then carrying, alone and unaided save by those loyal friends who really knew and appreciated him. I shall say more on this point in the next chapter.

To assist me in forming a proper general headquarters in London I took home Whigham as my deputy and Maurice as Director of Operations. The faithful Lucas accompanied me as a matter of course. I was sorry to have to move these officers from France, for besides condemning them to uncongenial work in London it meant placing them, in comparison with their contemporaries at the front, at a distinct disadvantage with regard to their prospects of advancement. But like the good fellows they are they made no wry faces, and expressed their willingness to go wherever

I thought they could best help me and be of most use to the State.

My eldest son Brian, who had come to France as my second aide-de-camp in May, six months after passing into the Royal Engineers from the Royal Military Academy, I left behind with his corps. He was afterwards employed as aide-de-camp to Sir Douglas Haig, and then on the General Staff of the XI. Corps, where he won the good opinion of his corps commander, Haking. He then served to the end of hostilities as an infantry brigade-major under Brigadier-General James. I am proud to feel that his services in the war were considered sufficiently meritorious to justify the award first of the Military Cross and later of the Distinguished Service Order, a decoration which I myself had been awarded some twenty-five years before.

I also left my chauffeur, Reginald Settle, in France. Educated at a public school previous to joining his father's business, he volunteered early in the war and had driven my Rolls Royce since the autumn of 1914. He was devoted to his car—which he would allow no one else to touch— and also to myself ; and he wished to accompany me home so as to continue driving me to the end of the war. This duty, as it would be in London, was not however quite suitable to a young man of his attainments and upbringing, and therefore I decided to leave him behind. He was a clean-living, attractive boy, and his death at the front a few weeks later, after receiving a commission, was a heavy blow to his parents. His only brother died in a French hospital at Mayence shortly after the armistice.

Settle was succeeded by Corporal Carthews, another good driver and loyal servant, who remained with me until his death from a sudden attack of influenza in 1918.

Whilst at G.H.Q. in France I always found the French General Staff most friendly and helpful, and think that the relations between the two staffs could hardly have been better. This was largely due to the French Chief of the General Staff, General Pellé, with whom it was always easy and pleasant to work. On the day of my departure from France I received the following letter from General Joffre :

MARSHAL JOFFRE CONVERSING WITH SOME FRENCH OFFICERS AT COLOGNE, 1919.

22 *déc.* 1915.

Mon cher Général—Je suis très touché des sentiments que vous m'exprimez au moment où vous quittez la France pour prendre les fonctions de Chef d'État-Major Impérial au War Office.

J'ai été très heureux de votre nomination à ce poste, parce que je suis certain que vous y emploierez au bénéfice de la cause commune les hautes qualités dont vous avez fait preuve comme Chef d'État-Major des Troupes Britanniques en France.

La cordialité de nos relations antérieures m'est un sûr garant que l'accord sera toujours de plus en plus intime entre nos armées alliées et nul mieux que vous n'était qualifié pour assurer en Angleterre la coordination de nos efforts.

Agréez, mon cher Général, l'assurance de mes sentiments les plus dévoués.

J. Joffre.

[*Translation.*

I highly appreciate the sentiments that you have been good enough to convey to me at the time when you are leaving France to take up the duties of Chief of the Imperial General Staff at the War Office.

Your nomination to this post gives me great pleasure, for I feel sure that you will display in it to the benefit of the common cause the same high qualities as those of which you have given proof while Chief of the General Staff with the British Army in France.

The cordiality of our relations in the past is a safe guarantee that the mutual understanding between our two armies will become still closer, and no one is better qualified than yourself to ensure in England the co-ordination of our efforts.

Pray accept, my dear General, the assurance of my sincere respect.

J. Joffre.]

CHAPTER XV

CHIEF OF THE IMPERIAL GENERAL STAFF, 1916

General situation in all theatres—Reorganisation of the General Staff—
Position of C.I.G.S.—Relations with Joffre, Cadorna, and Alexeieff
—War Council and War Cabinet—Relations between Ministers and
their professional advisers—Proposed war policy approved by
Cabinet — Send instructions to Commanders-in-Chief — Steps to
improve training and organisation of troops at home and abroad—
Home Defence—India and India Office responsible for Mesopotamia
—Need for comprehensive plan for utilising man-power—Cabinet
Committee set up to deal with the question—Lord Kitchener and
Compulsory Service—Many people objected to it—Problem of pro-
viding officers—Production of tanks—Evacuation of Gallipoli—
Operations in Mesopotamia—Campaign is handed over to the War
Office—Fall of Kut-el-Amara—Appointment of Maude as Com-
mander-in-Chief—His successes—Operations in Egypt and Mace-
donia—Disadvantages of employing armies of mixed nationalities—
East Africa—Smuts and Van Dewenter—Operations on the West
Front—Situation at the end of the year—Ministers' dissatisfaction
—Tendency to try new methods and plans—Joffre superseded by
Nivelle as Commander-in-Chief of French armies—His plan for
1917 rejected by Governments in favour of Nivelle's plan—My
relations with Joffre—Change of Government—My relations with
Lord Kitchener—The part he played in the war.

I TOOK up the post of C.I.G.S. (Chief of the Imperial General
Staff) with a profound sense of anxiety, as I realised that
the amount of work to be done was enormous and without
precedent, and that many things would be expected of me
with which I had had no previous dealings, for I had not
only to organise the armies and superintend their strategical employment in accordance with the policy of the Government, but also to make myself acquainted with numerous
matters, great and small, which affected almost every
branch of the life of the nation.   Moreover, it was impressed
upon me by several public men and others, especially after
the death of Lord Kitchener, that the country looked to
me to show the way to victory, and the feeling of this

responsibility never left me for an instant. A heavier burden could hardly have rested on the shoulders of any man, and I could only hope that I might be given the strength and wisdom to carry it fearlessly and efficiently. I am thankful to remember that, notwithstanding many disappointments, I never once felt or expressed, privately or officially, any doubt as to our ability to win, *provided* the Government, supported by the people, put into the war what war has always required—adequate men, material, and moral resolution,—and put them in at the right time and in the right place.

Though not so immediately critical as in the spring of 1918, the general military situation at the end of 1915 was darker and more complicated than at any period of the war. Russia had suffered crushing defeats at the hand of Mackensen, losing heavily in men, territory, and morale, and whether she would be able to recover from them sufficiently to be of effective assistance to the Allies in the future was at least doubtful. The Italian armies seemed unable to make material progress in expelling the Austrians from their positions beyond the Isonzo. On the West Front no tangible results could as yet be shown in return for the great expenditure of life incurred. Servia had been overrun, the remnants of her army driven out of the country, and the Anglo-French forces sent out too late to help her were now opposed by strong hostile forces in front, had an uncertain neutral on their flanks, and were left with no better objective than the passive defence of Salonika. The Dardanelles operations had been partially abandoned as a failure, Anzac and Suvla having already been evacuated, and the remaining troops were clinging to Cape Helles pending a decision as to whether they were to remain there or come away. On the western frontier of Egypt the Senussi tribesmen had established themselves within striking distance of the Nile valley; in the Sudan there were signs of trouble with the Sultan of Darfur, who had been approached by Turkish agents; and on the east the Turks were in possession of the Sinai Peninsula, and were being promised German support in an attack on Egypt from that side, thus endangering the most vital of our

Imperial communications—the Suez Canal. In Mesopotamia an Anglo-Indian force under Major-General Townshend, inadequate in strength and imperfectly organised, had retreated from Ctesiphon after the abortive attempt to capture Baghdad, and since the beginning of December had been besieged by a considerable Turkish army at Kut-el-Amara. Thus the " one bright spot on the military horizon," as Baghdad was thought to be by certain people only a few weeks before, had receded so far into space as to be wholly invisible. In East Africa we were unable to defend our territory, and British prestige was at its lowest ebb.

As regards our own share in bringing about this state of affairs it is no exaggeration to say that every mistake we had made in our wars with France more than a hundred years before had been repeated. We had committed ourselves to expeditions, on a vast scale and in remote theatres, which were strategically unsound, had never been properly thought out, and in the Dardanelles alone had already cost us considerably over 100,000 casualties. The false direction thus given to our strategy imperilled the chances of ultimate success, and at the best was bound to hang like a millstone round our necks for the remainder of the war—as it did.

It is one of the first principles of war that all available resources should be concentrated at the " decisive " point —that is, at the place where the main decision of the war is to be fought out. There may be a difference of opinion as to where that point should be, but there should never be more than one such point at a time, and once the selection is made, no departure from the principle just mentioned is admissible except (a) when it becomes necessary to detach troops for the protection of interests vital to oneself, for example the Suez Canal ; or (b) when by detaching them the enemy will be compelled as a counter-measure to send a still larger detachment in order to protect interests which are vital to him. This principle, as old as the hills, had been inexcusably violated in 1914–15, and however much we might afterwards try to mitigate the evils resulting therefrom they could never be entirely removed.

But there was another side to the picture. In spite

of losses and unfulfilled expectations the people of the Empire remained solid in their determination to see the war through to a successful conclusion, cost what it might, and so long as this spirit continued there was no reason for despair in the minds of their leaders and servants. That it would continue no one had the right to doubt, and whenever the outlook was black and the prospects of victory seemed remote, or even threatened to disappear altogether, renewed hope and strength could always be derived from a justifiable belief in the steadfastness of the British race. This belief was many times confirmed in 1916 and 1917 by letters which I received from private persons and public bodies expressing confidence in the General Staff and showing a firm resolution to win. Much encouragement was also given by individual public men who promised to support the General Staff to the full extent of their power in the measures recommended for prosecuting the war.

The first thing required of me was to give the General Staff at the War Office an organisation similar to that at G.H.Q. in France, though on a more extensive scale, and then hope that, as a result of its increased usefulness, the Government would accord to it that position in the direction of the war which a General Staff at Great Headquarters is intended to fill.

The reforms commenced with the room assigned for my own use in the War Office, the first and only day spent in it being quite the most exasperating day of my life. The telephone, which I have always detested, rang incessantly, and a constant stream of people of both sexes and all grades —girl typists, wives of officers, members of parliament, boy-scout messengers, general officers—entered the room, one after another, unannounced, either to see me on some trivial matter or some one else whose room they thought it was. To attempt to work under such maddening conditions was worse than useless. Lucas realised the position as well as I did, and by nine o'clock next morning he had taken possession of another room for me, from which all telephone apparatus was expelled, and access to which could only be gained through an anteroom where he or my private secretary kept constant guard so that I might be left in peace.

I have described in the preceding chapter the new system sanctioned by which the C.I.G.S., instead of the Army Council as a whole, became responsible for the issue of operation orders, and, as bearing upon this, I may now explain the change made in his status *vis-à-vis* the other military members of the Council. When the Council was first formed in 1904 the military members were given precedence amongst themselves according to their *appointments*, the C.I.G.S. being First Military Member, the Adjutant-General second, and so on. This system had been altered during the war, precedence being taken according to seniority of *rank*, and on arrival at the War Office I occupied the third place. I represented to Lord Kitchener that while I did not care two straws personally what place was allotted to me, I was in fact chief military adviser to the Government, and that in other respects the system was illogical and ought to be replaced by the original one. He did not agree, taking the view that one member was as necessary to the constitution of the Council as another, and therefore that each was entitled, subject to seniority of rank, to be recognised as the First Member. I objected that this could not work in practice, since, for example, it was for the C.I.G.S. to lay down, in conformity with the policy of the Government, where troops were to be sent, and it then became the duty of the Quartermaster-General to send their food there. It was not for the Quartermaster-General to lay down the place where food would be sent, and then for the C.I.G.S. to send troops there to eat it. This rough and exaggerated illustration of conducting the Council's business had effect, and as he disliked going back on the system but recently set up, he naïvely settled the matter by promoting me " temporary " General. As this was a higher rank than that held by any other Councillor it automatically made me First Member.

With respect to the distribution of duties as between the different members of the General Staff I separated the Operations and Intelligence Directorate into two, as I had done in France, Maurice taking charge of the Operations, and Callwell retaining the Intelligence. I was lucky to find Callwell in the department, as he was most helpful in making me acquainted with the situation in the various theatres of war, and with numerous other current questions about which I naturally knew little or nothing. He had joined the General Staff from the retired list at the beginning of the war, having previously had many years' experience in it, and I shudder to think what I would have done during the first few harassing weeks of my time as C.I.G.S. had I not had the benefit of his assistance. Later on he was succeeded by Macdonogh, whom I thought it best to bring back from G.H.Q. in France so as to utilise the knowledge he had acquired of that all-important front as chief of the Intelligence since 1914. Whigham, my deputy, had charge of all General Staff work not included in Operations and Intelligence, and acted for me at Army Council meetings, as on all other occasions, when I could not be present. Brigadier-General Bird was Director of Staff Duties and Brigadier-General Cockerill Deputy Director of Intelligence, and amongst the numerous other officers employed were Kirke, Bartholomew, Ellington, Earl Percy (now Duke of Northumberland), and Butler (a New Army officer and son of the late Master of Trinity College, Cambridge) in the Operations branch, and Buckley, French, Kell, and Cox in the Intelligence.

The method of dealing with the receipt and despatch of official letters and telegrams connected with the employment of the field armies was next taken in hand. According to the existing procedure—the old peace procedure and quite unsuitable for war—all communications arriving at the War Office were received and distributed, some of them first being printed, by the civil staff of the Secretary's department. They poured in by hundreds daily and referred to every imaginable subject, from a demand for more socks to the dispositions of whole armies. The department did its work manfully, and so far as concerned the socks and the multitude of other things required by the troops the system was probably a good one, but for the direction of military operations in face of the enemy it was impossible. Communications on this subject must reach the General Staff without a moment's delay, pass through as few hands as possible, and be distributed to such persons as the trained officers of the General Staff can alone decide. With the concurrence of the Secretary, Sir Reginald Brade, the system was so modified as to secure these results, and I formed a small section within the General Staff itself for dealing with the receipt and disposal of all telegrams and other important communications of a General Staff nature.

These and other measures made the General Staff a live organisation, caused it to be recognised as the Great General Staff of the armies in the field, and enabled it to furnish the Government with considered advice on important military questions, so that whether the advice were accepted or not ministers would be made aware of the probable military effect of their decisions.

For the purpose of keeping each other informed on matters with which we were mutually concerned, I had officers at the headquarters of Joffre, Cadorna, and Alexeieff respectively, and they had their representatives with me in London. Brigadier-Generals Yarde-Buller, Clive and Delmé-Radcliffe, and other officers were employed on this duty in France and Italy. Mainly as a result of their good work and friendly relations with the French and Italian staffs, there was always a complete understanding with those two countries. With Russia it was not equally satisfactory, although the representatives at both ends did their best to make it so. There were several reasons for this. Alexeieff and I were strangers to each other and so were our staffs; I could not meet him, as I frequently could Joffre and Cadorna, and discuss matters personally; he was inclined to press for more British divisions being sent to the eastern theatres, including co-operation with his forces in Armenia, which was at variance with my views; and he never seemed able to appreciate the tax imposed by long-distance operations on our already overstrained naval and shipping resources. Twice during 1916 I sent Callwell to explain these and similar questions to him, and to some extent he was successful in clearing up points of difference, while my permanent representatives also achieved something in the same direction, but the understanding was never as complete and stable as with France and Italy. It could not possibly be so, for although Alexeieff sincerely desired to work in close accord with the British General Staff, and to the best of my knowledge with all the Entente armies, he had, over and above the disadvantages just indicated, to contend with a very difficult situation in his own country, which daily became worse until it ended in the revolution of 1917.

The machinery employed by the Government for the supreme conduct of naval and military operations consisted, at the commencement of the war, of the Cabinet of some twenty odd members, aided by the Committee of Imperial Defence, and with the Admiralty and War Office acting as its executive agents. Later, the Committee of Imperial Defence gave place to a War Council composed of certain selected ministers, with the Prime Minister as Chairman ; this, in its turn, afterwards became known as the Dardanelles Committee ; and, finally, the latter was replaced by a War Committee. The last-named was in existence when I became C.I.G.S., and, as I had said to Lord Kitchener in my letter of the 5th December (reproduced in the preceding chapter), it was not well adapted to ensure decisions being promptly reached, for, notwithstanding some delegation of its powers to the War Committee, the Cabinet still seemed to be regarded as the supreme authority to whom the more important questions should be referred before action was taken.

When Mr. Lloyd George became Prime Minister in December 1916 the old-time Cabinet and its War Committee both disappeared, and, following much the same principles as I had suggested in my letter to Lord Kitchener, a War Cabinet of six or seven members assumed unrestricted control over the war-business of the nation. From a military standpoint—and leaving out of account the constitutional aspect of the question, about which I express no opinion—the change was welcome, if only for the reason that six men could be trusted to give a decision in less time than a score would ; but my experience leads me to add that the War Cabinet did not by any means provide a complete remedy for the evils from which its predecessor had suffered. Most of its members were ministers without portfolios, and having little if any first-hand knowledge of the questions with which they had to deal they were necessarily dependent upon those ministers who had it. Consequently the Secretary of State for War, the First Lord of the Admiralty, and the Foreign Secretary, none of whom were members of the War Cabinet, usually had to attend once a day when meetings were held, while other ministers, such as the Secretary of State for India, the Shipping Controller, the Minister of Labour, the Minister of the Air, and the Minister of Munitions, had also frequently to be summoned. The result was that the total number present was often not much less, and was sometimes more, than under the old system, and it is difficult to see how this could have been prevented, for whether the heads of the various State departments do or do not permanently belong to the body charged with the supreme direction of a war, they must be called in when important questions concerning their departments are being considered. The fact is that in a great war such as that of 1914–18 the ramifications of the numerous problems which arise are so widespread that the rapid despatch of business must always be exceedingly difficult to achieve.

In 1916, and throughout 1914–18 for that matter, there was much public criticism of the way in which the Government was conducting the war, and it was difficult to keep clear of the political controversies which arose, though I persistently strove to give them a wide berth. To me it was of no interest how the Government was composed so long as the army got what it wanted, and was not asked to undertake unsound and impracticable operations. This seemed the proper attitude for a soldier to take up, though perhaps it was unwise of me to disclose it as openly as I did. Since the end of the last century the professional careers of senior officers of the army have passed by degrees entirely into the hands of ministers, and, however necessary this system may be, the consequence of it is that, if an officer holding a high position shows that he has no political leanings one way or the other, he may find himself without friends in any political party and be suspected by all.

It goes without saying that professional advisers should

try their hardest to meet the wishes of ministers, but the doctrine is easier stated than practised. In war, especially in a long war, things do not proceed on simple and smooth lines, but bristle with knots and thorns to an extent quite unknown to those who have not experienced them. Professional advisers are the servants of the Government, and there would be an end of parliamentary government if they were able to override Government policy. On the other hand, the time may come when a policy is proposed which they feel convinced will, if pursued, have disastrous results, and they then have to choose between acquiescing in it, thereby jeopardising the interests of the nation, and saying in unmistakable terms that they can be no party to it. More than once when confronted with this dilemma I felt it my duty to adopt the second alternative.

In peace time differences of opinion may be allowed to go by the board without great harm being done, as it may be possible to adjust them at a more convenient season. In war the case is different—chickens remorselessly and rapidly come home to roost, errors can seldom be rectified (the enemy will see to that), and men's lives are at stake.

A minister once tried in the course of conversation to persuade me that the duty of a professional adviser begins and ends with giving his advice, and that after it has been given and ministers have considered it the orders of the Government should be carried out without further question or remonstrance. I was unable to agree with him as to the *chief* professional adviser, holding that he had a duty to the country as well as to ministers, and I said so, though I admitted that only special circumstances would justify the conclusion that duty to ministers conflicted with duty to country and must accordingly take second place.

It was upon such principles as these that I endeavoured to regulate my attitude. Whether they were right or wrong the reader must judge for himself, but I have no doubt whatever in my own mind that to their cumulative effect may be attributed my removal from the post of C.I.G.S. in February 1918, and therefore from the standpoint of personal advantage they were obviously wrong.

Having now cleared the ground by this short account

of the military situation at the end of 1915, the reorganisation of the General Staff, the arrangements for keeping connected up with the Great General Staffs of the Allies, the methods by which the Government conducted its war-business, and the relations as between the Government and its professional advisers, I will proceed to describe the nature of the work with which the General Staff had to deal.

Sundays excepted, I attended the meeting of the War Committee—later the War Cabinet—almost every day, in order to elucidate or justify our written recommendations as to the military policy to be followed, give an account of and explain the events of the last twenty-four hours in the different theatres of war, and do what I could to prophesy the events of the next twenty-four. It was not easy to do any of these things, because the reasons which prompted a given recommendation or expression of opinion might be of a technical nature or be the result of a lifelong study of the art of war, and it was not always possible to substantiate them off-hand in the course of a discussion in which a dozen or more ingenious debaters were taking part. I sometimes envied my naval colleague, who, although he had similar duties to perform, escaped much of the examination and criticism which fell to my lot. Amateurs who do not hesitate to lay down the law on questions of military strategy and tactics proceed more warily with respect to naval operations. They have many opportunities for picking up a smattering of military knowledge, whereas their acquaintance with naval matters may be limited to an occasional trip to the seaside or a bad attack of sea-sickness when crossing the Channel. The sailors do not, as a rule, give them much assistance to become more proficient, the phraseology they use being so strange and technical that the amateur, finding himself to be out of his depth, is only too glad to pass on to the discussion of other subjects in which his ignorance may not be so apparent.

The first question to which I had to ask for a clear and stable answer from the Government on becoming C.I.G.S. was what policy they wished to pursue in each and all of the theatres of war where British troops were employed, as upon this depended the action to be taken not only by the

General Staff but by all other branches of the War Office. Murray had shortly before submitted a memorandum on the subject, but for some reason unknown to me no decision had been reached. His views being in general agreement with my own, I summed up his main recommendations and sent them to the Cabinet for approval on the same day as I took up office. I at once received as complete an answer as circumstances permitted, and the hearts of the General Staff were particularly gladdened by the acceptance of the recommendation that, from the British point of view, France and Flanders should be regarded as the main theatre of operations. So long as this policy was *adhered to in practice* all would be well.

The next step was to ensure that the Commanders-in-Chief understood what they were expected to do, and having obtained an authoritative pronouncement as to policy I was able to tell them. I could not discover that they had any precise and up-to-date directions of the kind required. They had received various telegrams and other communications from time to time, and may have been given verbal directions, but something more was needed to enable them to look ahead, make their plans, and give effect to the wishes of the Government in the manner intended. They required to be furnished with concrete " Instructions " (" Directives " in French) explaining in concise and definite language, over the signature of the Secretary of State for War on behalf of the Government, the exact nature of their mission, and then leaving them to decide as to the method of its execution.

It may be mentioned, too, that besides their obvious use to Commanders-in-Chief, these instructions have another value. The mere act of putting them into writing for future guidance and record tends to lay bare any defects and inconsistencies there may be in the policy which they represent, and had they been drafted, as they should have been, in all cases in 1914–15 some of the projects then undertaken might have been consigned to oblivion before they became really dangerous. Even if they were not abandoned, there would at any rate be no question as to where responsibility rested. for once a commander receives his instructions it is his own

s

fault if, without remonstrance, he attempts to carry them out when of opinion that they are impracticable.

I next gave attention to the training and organisation of the troops, both at home and abroad. Egypt, the base for all operations in the Mediterranean, was in a state of chaos, and the British and Colonial divisions transferred there from the Gallipoli Peninsula, together with large reinforcements of partially-trained personnel from Australia and New Zealand, and other partially-trained drafts for Gallipoli and Salonika, constituted an unwieldy accumulation of some 300,000 men. These had either never yet been organised as fighting forces, or their organisation, such as it was, required drastic overhauling before proper value could be derived from them in the field. The sorting out of this medley of troops and the vast jumble of stores, transport, and equipment collected for their use, was a herculean task for the local military authorities, and will be further referred to later.

At home, again, there were hundreds of thousands of men who, for the most part, were without proper organisation either for the field or for purposes of training, and in addition there was a large number of divisions which as yet were only half-trained and half-equipped. Moreover, the number, composition, and distribution of the home defence troops bore little relation to the actual situation; the general plan of defence was fundamentally faulty; and with some commendable exceptions the defences themselves were insufficient and often of unsuitable types.

For all this no one in particular was to blame. On the contrary the War Office, commanders, and troops had worked their hardest and best under most adverse conditions. It was the natural outcome of having to create large armies at short notice, without the assistance of a previously-prepared plan, and of being frequently obliged to send troops abroad in small packets and on no method save that of meeting an urgent need in one of the many theatres in which we were fighting. It fell to Lord French, Commander-in-Chief in the United Kingdom, to straighten out the tangle at home. As I have stated elsewhere, there were previous to his appointment on the 19th December 1915, seven

Commanders-in-Chief at home, each of whom was directly under the War Office, thus making with the Commanders-in-Chief in France, Salonika, Egypt and Gallipoli, a total of eleven commanders with whom the C.I.G.S. had to deal. No man could possibly deal with such a number, and I was glad that the Government approved of my recommendation to unite all troops at home under one commander.

The organisation of the troops in Mesopotamia and the arrangements for the maintenance of the long and precarious line of communication in that country were notoriously bad, but with this theatre the General Staff was not directly concerned as the operations were conducted by the Government of India under instructions issued by the India Office. As I wish to avoid saying anything which might revive the controversial question of responsibility for the mismanagement of the early part of this campaign, I will merely remark that a sound system of command is a requisite condition of success, and that no worse system could have been devised than that of dividing the control of the military forces of the Empire between two separate departments (India Office and War Office) and two separate army head-quarters (Simla and London). British officers can do most things, but no human being could have made this vicious system work efficiently, and it is no reflection on either the India authorities or the India Office to say that it was bound to lead to serious trouble, if not to disaster, as unfortunately it did.

For some time I hesitated to put my finger into the Mesopotamian pie, but as matters seemed to be going from bad to worse I was at last compelled to point out to the War Committee the impossibility of continuing the existing arrangement, and I recommended, with Lord Kitchener's concurrence, that both operative and administrative control should be taken over by the War Office and be dealt with by it as in the case of all other campaigns. After some discussion the recommendation was accepted and the change took effect in the month of February 1916. As an illustration of the disadvantages incurred by different campaigns being conducted by different State departments, I may say that, previous to this change, neither the Imperial General

Staff nor the Army Council were entitled to communicate direct with the military authorities in India. All correspondence of importance had to pass through the India Office—the department responsible to the Home Government.

Another, and perhaps the most complicated, problem awaiting solution was that of man-power. In July 1915 the National Registration Act had been passed, and in accordance with it every person in Great Britain—Ireland being excluded—between the ages of 16 and 65 years had been registered. This was a useful and necessary preliminary to any legislation for universal service, but it was no more than that. Later, the " Derby Scheme " had been introduced so as to give the voluntary system of recruiting its last chance, its distinctive features being that men " attested " their willingness to join the army when wanted, and they then entered a so-called reserve where they remained undisturbed in their civil employment until called up. This produced good results at first but soon began to dwindle away, and by the end of 1915 it was quite clear, notwithstanding the wonders hitherto achieved under Lord Kitchener's inspiration, that the voluntary system was fast breaking down and must be replaced by compulsory measures. To the procuring of these I forthwith directed my energies.

No plan for substituting such measures had as yet been thoroughly considered, and the hard fact that the entire manhood of the nation would have to be utilised in the prosecution of the war, either in the fighting services or on other work of an essential kind, and utilised in an appropriate way, was, so far as my knowledge goes, still insufficiently recognised by any one in the Government with the possible exception of Lord Kitchener. I shall show presently that, for practical purposes, it never was recognised until the enemy made his last throw for victory in March 1918, and then the recognition was perilously near to being too late.

It was, perhaps, not surprising that, as late as December 1915, the important question of man-power had not yet been dealt with in a comprehensive manner. For several months after the outbreak of hostilities the belief had prevailed that the war would soon be over, and in the meantime shoals of men had come forward, voluntarily, as quickly as they could be handled. Even when this belief began to weaken, it was supposed that the only problem was the provision of an additional number of men for the army alone. " Business as usual " was still far from being dead, and when it was suggested that certain trades unconnected with the war might be discontinued, the reply was that an " awful outcry " would be raised. Moreover, ministers had, as a result of our general unpreparedness, been overwhelmed with other work, and some of them did not even know how many divisions had already been formed, let alone how many we might eventually want. I had several informal conversations with ministers, including Mr. Asquith and Mr. McKenna, the Chancellor of the Exchequer, during my first few days in London, and their common complaint against the soldiers was that they could get from them no definite and reliable opinion. It was evident to me that, whatever had been the case before, they were now more than anxious to have the advice of the General Staff as to what was to be done, and I made up my mind that on this score they should have no further ground for dissatisfaction.

Besides three cavalry divisions we had on the army books a total of seventy British infantry divisions, thirty-five being in France, others in Egypt, Mesopotamia, and Macedonia, and the remainder in different stages of formation at home. It was essential that the latter, except such as were required for home defence, should be completed with personnel and sent to the front as soon as possible, and that men should also be provided to meet the great expansion contemplated in heavy artillery, machine-guns, aeroplanes, mechanical transport, railways, tunnelling companies, and numerous other units outside the divisions. In addition, there must be sufficient reserves to make good the wastage caused by sickness and battle, and finally, after making provision to meet all these demands, it would be necessary to consider whether any further divisions should be raised, and if so, how many.

It was the business of the General Staff to advise on these matters from the standpoint of military policy, and it then rested with the Adjutant-General, after a decision

had been reached, to obtain the number of men authorised.
How many men could be spared for the army was of course
for the Government and not for the War Office to say, as
men were also needed for the navy, shipbuilding, food-
production, munitions, industries, and many other services
connected with the war. On the 27th December, four days
after I became C.I.G.S., the General Staff views on man-
power were laid before the Cabinet, and shortly afterwards the whole question was investigated by a " Cabinet
Committee on the co-ordination of military and financial
effort." At the back of my mind I had the intention of
obtaining at least two million men in addition to the two
and a half millions recruited since August 1914. How many
more might be required later could not yet be foreseen.

The investigation was particularly exhaustive respecting
the actual needs of the army, and the effect which these
needs, if met, might have on trade and consequently on
finance. If trade were crippled then money would become
short, in which case we might be unable either to maintain
the existing divisions or to continue giving subsidies to our
Allies, and there were those who feared that bankruptcy
was already in sight.

Trade and finance lay outside the War Office sphere and
were dealt with in the evidence supplied by the Board of
Trade and Treasury, but I cannot help remarking that the
views held by experts on the relation of finance to war seem
to call for revision. Before 1914 it was frequently said,
and on high authority sometimes, that future wars would
be of short duration, if not entirely prevented, because of
the financial strain and the general dislocation of commerce which they would entail. This prophecy was not
borne out by the Great War, though I would hesitate to
guess what may yet be the outcome of the colossal expenditure incurred in it. I am so profoundly ignorant of financial
strategy and tactics—never having had the wherewithal to
indulge in them—that I cannot even understand why public
servants like myself should pay income tax on their salaries
months before the same tax is collected from the business
community.

It would have assisted the other departments, as some

of them said, if a specific estimate of the number of divisions required to win the war could have been made by the War Office, but no such calculation was feasible, and the position I took up before the committee was that, owing to the world-wide character of the war, it was impossible to say how many men would eventually be required. In other words, I argued that we could not hope to win through on any basis of limited liability, and that the only limit we were justified in accepting was the last available man. From this position I never budged, and perhaps was sometimes thought to be obstinate and unreasonable, but the situation was much too grave to permit of watering down considered opinions in the vain endeavour to make things easier. To have shown any such weakness would have been tantamount to a betrayal of the trust reposed in me by virtue of the office I held. The committee gave me a very patient hearing, as they did all other War Office representatives, but the first results, the passing of the " Military Service Act " on the 27th of January 1916, were disappointing, as the Act rendered liable to military service only those men who were unmarried or widowers having no dependent children.

The inadequate scope of this half-baked measure, and the ease with which its provisions enabled military obligations to be evaded, were apparent from the first, and after further investigation by the committee the Bill was extended, in May 1916, to include married men and widowers with dependent children. The amended Bill still excluded Ireland, and in other respects was not as comprehensive and as free from hampering conditions as could have been desired, but it was a great step in advance, for it ensured a more reliable flow of recruits from Great Britain ; it established the principle, if it did not wholly enforce it, of national service until the end of the war ; and, thanks to it, close upon 1,200,000 men were obtained during 1916 out of the two millions I had set out to get.

When at the commencement of the enquiry I tried to convince Lord Kitchener that we must resort to all-round compulsory service he was not inclined to agree with me. This was only natural, as he had been marvellously successful in obtaining volunteers for the New Armies he had formed, and he hoped to finish the war without applying compulsion, especially as regards married men. Moreover, in his dealings with the representatives of Labour he had apparently promised, either by word or implication, not to apply it until it became absolutely necessary, if they would co-operate with him, as I believe they invariably did, in obtaining men under the Derby Scheme, and he was anxious not to appear guilty of a breach of faith.

But the chief reason which induced him to hold back was, I believe, the desire to conserve sufficient reserves to deal the finishing blow in the war when the psychological moment arrived. " Don't try to hurry things so," he would say when I was urging my view of the case. " What we should aim at is to have the largest army in Europe when the terms of peace are being discussed, and that will not be in 1916 but in 1917." Eventually he agreed with me that, owing to the increased demands by new services (tanks, aeroplanes, heavy guns, etc.), to the gradual decline of the voluntary system, and to the time it would take to start a new system and train the men produced by it, the introduction of compulsory measures could no longer be delayed, and thenceforward he whole-heartedly supported them.

He has been blamed for not introducing them in 1914, and no doubt if this had been done our man-power resources could have been tapped by scientific and equitable methods, and much discontent and disturbance of industry would have been avoided. We would not, for instance, have depleted the country of skilled engineers by placing them in the trenches, from which they had later to be withdrawn for employment in ship - building yards and munition-shops. But these were matters for the Government and not merely for the Secretary of State for War, who was concerned only with the army. Moreover, the necessary registration and legislation would have taken a considerable time to carry out and there was not an hour to lose, and much opposition might have been encountered had an attempt been made to introduce compulsion before the voluntary system was seen to be inadequate.

In confirmation of this I may say that when the Cabinet

enquiry was being held there were, to my personal knowledge—and quite irrespective of the opinions that may or
may not have been held by members of the Cabinet, regarding which I shall say nothing—far more prominent public
men outside the Cabinet who doubted the wisdom of introducing compulsion than is generally supposed. Some of
these maintained, amongst other objections, that the additional men procurable would not be worth the public discontent the change would create, and would be more than
outweighed by the additional troops required for the pre-
servation of internal order; while as to Ireland, it was
said that the attempt to apply compulsion would inevitably
produce a rebellion. As we now know these forebodings
proved to be without foundation, though it should be added
that as the Bill was not made applicable to Ireland the
fancied danger of rebellion there was not incurred.

Personally, I doubt if any such danger really existed, and
as is well known the rebellion, so-called, which occurred in
Easter week did not represent any considerable element in
Irish life as a whole, and was condemned by the greater
part of Ireland as indignantly as by England. As there was
at the time no Commander-in-Chief of the usual status in the
country, the task of restoring order was confided by the
Government to Lieutenant-General Sir John Maxwell, who
had recently returned from Egypt, and I sent Lieutenant-
Colonel Hutchison with him as his Chief of the General
Staff. Maxwell had a difficult and distasteful duty to
perform, as all soldiers have when called upon to use force
against their fellow-subjects, and I am sure that he honestly
tried to carry it out in accordance with the letter and spirit
of his instructions. In Dublin, where the rebellion started,
severe street fighting lasted for several days, about 100
soldiers and 180 civilians being killed. There were also
outbreaks in Galway, Wexford, and Drogheda, but these
were less serious, and the National Volunteers, composed
of Irishmen, helped to suppress them.

To revert to the question of man-power. It was frequently suggested to me during 1916 that the country was
still imperfectly informed of the dimensions of the struggle
in which we were engaged, and that it longed to have the

facts of the case plainly put before it. To speak in public, however, did not properly lie within my province, and I never spoke without obtaining the consent of the Secretary of State for War, and until convinced that it was my duty to speak. On those occasions when I felt it necessary to speak I was, with one exception, listened to with earnest attention, and no will deny that the country invariably showed the greatest readiness to comply with the ever-increasing demands made upon it.

The exception was at a meeting held at Woolwich Arsenal, which I had been requested to attend by the Ministry of Munitions. I had no sooner entered the room than I found that I was not wanted. I told the men that I had come at some inconvenience to myself and purely as a matter of duty, and that if they did not wish to hear me I would go away. Their leaders appealed to them to keep order, and as it had no effect I walked off the platform and returned to London. I discovered afterwards, to my astonishment, that some labour question was in dispute at the time between the men and the Ministry of Munitions, and that they had gone to the meeting to hear what the minister who accompanied me had to say, and for that purpose alone. Naturally, therefore, they did not wish to waste time in listening to me.

Connected with man-power was the question of providing a sufficient number of officers to keep pace with the expansion of the army and to make good wastage. The casualties amongst officers had amounted in 1914 to about 5700, and in 1915 to about 23,260, and it was expected that the number would be much larger in 1916, as several more divisions were to be put in the field. As early as the winter of 1914–15 G.H.Q. in France received complaints from regimental commanders that many of the officers sent from England were quite untrained, and instead of being a help were an actual danger to the men they had to lead. This was due to the fact that they had received their commissions straight from civil life before undergoing any military training. At the time a considerable number of men from the ranks were being recommended for commissions, and in order to give them some little instruction in the duties

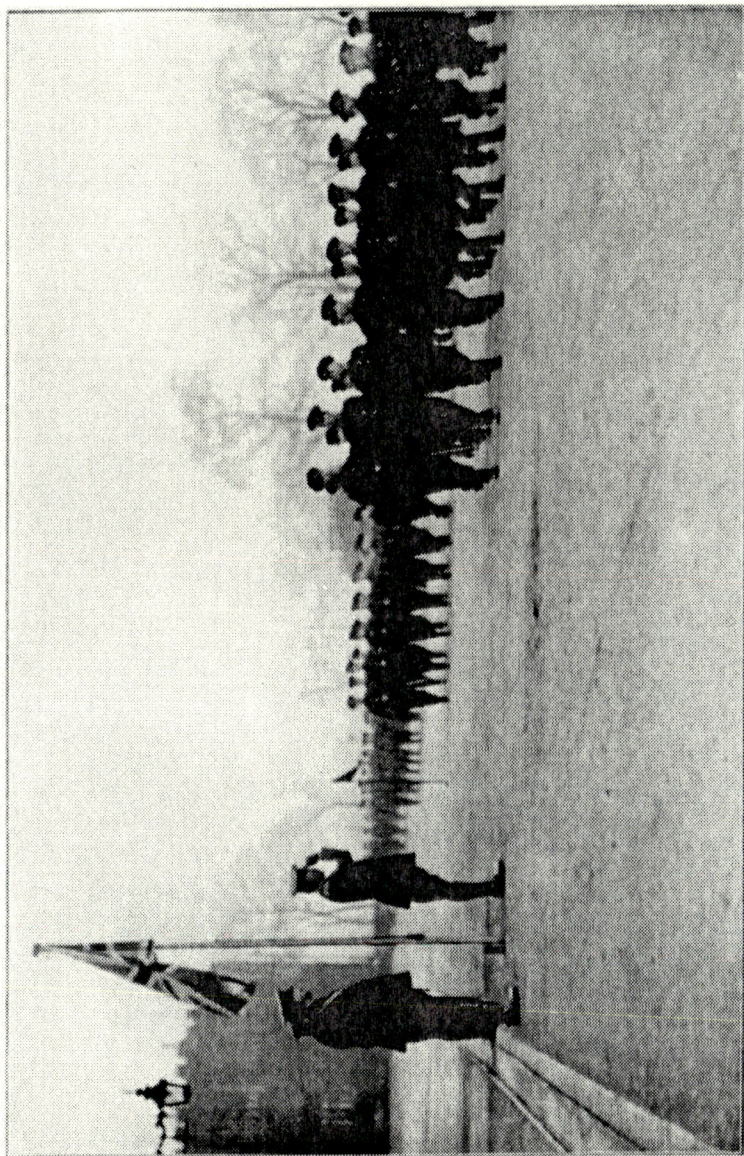

INSPECTING GENTLEMEN CADETS AT ROYAL MILITARY ACADEMY, JANUARY, 1916.

of an officer before appointing them to commissions the Commander-in-Chief ordered a Cadet School to be formed at Bailleul, the Artists Rifles—which had belonged to the Officers' Training Corps in peace time—being used for the purpose. The results were satisfactory, and in the spring of 1915 the school was transferred to near St. Omer and enlarged to deal with about 100 cadets at a time. The demand for officers was at first so heavy that only six weeks could be allotted to each class, but this was later extended to a course of three months, and it included experience in the fighting line. Instruction was given in all branches of training required by a platoon commander.

When I became C.I.G.S. the only sources, apart from the Cadet School in France, from which officers with some previous training were obtainable, were Sandhurst, Woolwich, the Honourable Artillery Company, the Inns of Court and Artists Rifles contingents of the Officers' Training Corps, and the Officers' Training Corps of the universities. The staffs of these Training Corps had not the necessary knowledge to train officers up to the required standard, and, moreover, as the demand had quite outstripped the supply, commissions were still being given to men coming direct from civil life. I therefore obtained Lord Kitchener's consent to organise at home a number of cadet battalions similar to the one which had given such good results in France, and in the month of February I brought Lieutenant-Colonel Hutchison to the War Office to superintend their organisation and training, he having been charged with the same duty when I was in France. Twelve cadet battalions were formed, each consisting of about 500 cadets; the course was one of three months, and the cadets had to pass an examination before receiving their commissions. Each battalion had a permanent training establishment of about 30 officers and from 80 to 100 other ranks, most of whom had had experience in the field.

The casualties amongst officers in all theatres rose from 23,260 in 1915 to 41,610 in 1916, and to 51,960 in 1917. (It will be understood that these are gross, not nett, figures, and include the wounded and sick who returned to duty after recovery.) To meet this increased wastage the number of cadet battalions had to be enlarged, and included cavalry, artillery, engineers, and army service corps, as well as infantry. The battalions were commanded by some of our best officers, full of energy and enthusiasm, and they answered their purpose so well that not only were the losses at the front made good but at the beginning of 1918 there was a reserve of about 10,000 officers at home. It was fortunate that we had this reserve to fall back upon in the critical months of April and May of that year. In all, more than 84,000 officers were supplied by the battalions during the war.

The General Staff had also to deal with the shortage of junior officers fit for employment on the staff. To meet this need in France we had started a staff school at St. Omer in 1915, and early in 1916 I formed one at Cambridge university under Lieutenant-Colonel R. Hare. The school was expanded in 1917, and a side to teach more senior staff officers was added to it.

Another new organisation introduced in 1916 was the Tank Corps, which in the earlier stages of its existence was recruited from selected officers and men transferred from other units, and was designated the " Heavy Branch Machine Gun Corps."

The official trial of the first tank, known as " Mother," took place in Hatfield Park early in February, Mr. Balfour (First Lord of the Admiralty), Mr. M'Kenna, Lord Kitchener, myself, and several other officials being present. Opinion was by no means unanimous that the machine would prove suitable for employment in battle, and it was in fact much inferior to the type evolved later ; but before we left the ground Lord Kitchener agreed to my proposal that a hundred should be ordered at once. In the following September about fifty tanks took part in the battle of the Somme. As in the case of all new inventions, the best value was not derived from the tank until the troops learnt how to use it, the chief difficulty being to obtain effective co-operation between the three arms—tanks, artillery, and infantry, and for this time and experience were required.

The War Office has been accused of obstructing the provision of tanks, and perhaps those who made the accusation did not quite realise all the difficulties which attend the starting of a new service and a new means of making war, and that these were accentuated in the case of the Tank Corps because of the shortage of men and steel. To divert men from the other arms and services—who were incessantly clamouring for personnel either to make good wastage or for purposes of expansion—so as to provide men to make and man tanks, of whose utility many officers, at the front as at home, were still unconvinced, was not a decision to be lightly taken : while as regards steel it was laid down, not by the War Office but by the authorities responsible for assessing the order of " priority," that the building of tanks should not be permitted to interfere with the output of guns, ammunition, aeroplanes, mechanical transport, and locomotives. Having made this explanation I should add that the great reputation eventually won, and deserved, by the tank as a formidable and indispensable fighting machine, is the more creditable to those who, in the face of adverse circumstances, were concerned in its production.

On a previous page I have said that the evacuation of Helles in the Gallipoli Peninsula was still under consideration at the end of 1915. Since September the Government had been undecided what course to pursue in regard to the Dardanelles, and early in October I had been summoned from France to advise. I recommended cutting our losses, and said that although evacuation must necessarily be attended with difficulty and risk it ought nevertheless to be a feasible operation provided that careful arrangements were made, especially with respect to secrecy. Later, General Sir Charles Monro was sent out to command and to advise, and he was followed by Lord Kitchener, who was to give a final decision. Eventually, in the third week of December, Anzac and Suvla were evacuated, but the question as to whether Helles, at the toe of the peninsula, should or should not be retained still remained to be settled.

The open confession of failure involved by complete evacuation was unpalatable to ministers, and some of them thought that we should lose prestige in the eyes of the eastern world, and so make further trouble for ourselves there ; some of the soldiers thought that Egypt would be seriously threatened by the liberation of the Turkish troops hitherto contained in the peninsula ; the sailors, for reasons not very convincing, were mainly in favour of continued occupation; while the withdrawal and re-embarkation of a force of 40,000 men, 150 guns, 4500 horses, and a vast quantity of stores was undoubtedly beset with enormous risks. Much more so than the withdrawal from Anzac and Suvla, for the hostile forces would be relatively stronger, surprise would be improbable, and bad weather would be more likely. It was impossible to say what our losses might not be, for apart from the uncertainty of what the enemy might do or omit to do, much depended upon the extent to which weather interfered with the operation. Some of the officers on the spot thought we might lose as much as thirty per cent of the force.

But, after all, the main question was what useful purpose would be served by keeping a detachment at Helles, now that the troops had been withdrawn from Anzac and Suvla ? Clearly there was none, and to continue hanging on to the place merely because we were afraid to leave it, was not only a waste of men but would be a constant source of anxiety.

On the 28th of December, five days after becoming C.I.G.S., I placed before the War Committee a memorandum drafted for me by Callwell, who was acquainted with my views, advocating the immediate and total evacuation of the peninsula. Lord Kitchener supported the recommendation, evacuation was approved, the necessary orders were despatched the same day, and by the 8th of January the operation had been completed, the only casualties being one man hit by a spent bullet and three men accidentally injured while embarking. Nearly all the guns were brought away, but some 500 animals had to be left behind. To extricate about 40,000 men in face of greatly superior forces, almost without a single mishap, was a performance which redounds to the credit of all soldiers and sailors who took part in it. Maude, with the headquarters of his division, the 13th, was one of the last to leave. This division had previously taken part in the withdrawal from Suvla and was afterwards sent to relieve a tired division at

Helles. Much of the credit for the retirement therefore belongs to it and its fine commander.

Having got rid of this commitment, my next desire was to send as many divisions as could be spared from Egypt, where the Gallipoli troops had been disembarked, to join the armies on the West Front, and to send back to the same front certain reinforcements which had been directed to proceed thence to Egypt just before I became C.I.G.S. Orders to this effect were issued, and within a short time the divisions were on their way to France.

Kut-el-Amara, in Mesopotamia, was a more difficult problem than Helles, for in this case we could not withdraw. We must first fight, and fight hard, and the administrative arrangements in this theatre were so defective that it was almost impossible to make a satisfactory plan for the fighting and at the same time be reasonably certain of relieving the garrison before it was starved into surrender. Exactly what could be done depended almost entirely upon the output of the line of communication, and this was doubtful in the extreme. The line was of great length—some 500 miles along the river—imperfectly organised in itself and at the base, and the amount of river transport was not nearly sufficient to convey the available troops to the front, supply them when there with food and ammunition, and maintain them in reasonable comfort and health. This lamentable shortage of river-craft hampered, in fact, the whole operation, and at the best must take a considerable time to remedy.

It has been said with much truth that a line of communication is the main artery along which flows the life-blood of the army in front, and that if any congestion or rupture occurs the whole military body becomes sick and may even die. Before any attempt had been made to advance as far as Baghdad every precaution should have been taken to establish a line of communication which would be not only good but very good. Our own history had furnished dozens of examples in proof of this—one being Lord Kitchener's advance to Khartoum—but they do not seem to have been remembered.

Three attempts were made to relieve Kut-el-Amara,

respectively beginning on the 4th of January, the 8th of March, and the 6th of April, and all failed, although one at least might perhaps have succeeded had everything gone smoothly and as expected. This seldom happens in war, and it did not happen at Kut-el-Amara, and in the last week of April the garrison of 2970 British and 6000 native troops, including followers, was compelled to surrender, after gallantly holding out under the most trying conditions for nearly five months. Thus was exacted the inevitable penalty for allowing operations to develop without any settled policy; without making proper preparations and providing sufficient means to attain the object in view; and without taking sufficiently into account what the enemy might do in order to frustrate that object.

The original purpose of the campaign had been the seizure of the Persian Gulf water-way up to the point where navigation for ocean-going vessels ceases, and the protection of the Karun oil-fields. Incidentally, the operation would exercise a useful effect on the tribes around the Gulf, and as no large force was required and the troops themselves were to some extent not suitable for employment in Europe, the campaign as at first intended may be regarded as justifiable. But to enlarge its scope by attempting to capture and permanently occupy Baghdad was, at the time the attempt was made, not within the limits of our means, and I happen to know that Lord Kitchener dissented from it, laying special emphasis on the disadvantages of the long and imperfect line of communication. (As previously mentioned, the campaign was being conducted at this period under the auspices of the India Office and not of the War Office, and therefore Lord Kitchener may have thought that he could do no more than express his disapproval of the decision.)

As in the case of the final evacuation of the Gallipoli Peninsula, it was thought that the fall of Kut-el-Amara would create serious disquiet, if nothing worse, in the Muhammadan countries adjacent to India; but happily, as with Gallipoli, it did nothing of the kind, and the prophecy I heard made that our eastern empire would be shaken to its foundations remained unfulfilled. I think we need to correct our ideas a little on the matter of prestige, as we call it. Prestige, no doubt, carries much weight in eastern countries, but in war it is apt to become a bogy, and to scare away the timid from doing what is clearly the right thing to do, or, what may prove to be worse, frighten them into a dissipation of strength in the vain endeavour to be safe everywhere at the same time. Years ago, when means of communication were few and slow, and education had not spread to its present dimensions, the eastern people knew little about the might of the British Empire and unimpaired prestige may then have been a necessity, but at the present day they are fairly shrewd judges of a situation, and may be trusted to appreciate a temporary set-back at something like its proper value.

This does not mean that the question can be entirely neglected. Orientals are as susceptible as other nations to the enemy's wiles and propaganda. In the early part of 1916 enemy agents were overrunning Persia and Trans-Caspia, and were also to be found in Afghanistan and at other places on the borders of India, spreading abroad the most ludicrous stories concerning the war and the imminent downfall of the British Empire, and backing up their statements with a plentiful distribution of promises and hard cash. To counteract these mischievous proceedings no effective steps had been taken, and the enemy was having things entirely his own way. The remedy did not lie, as was sometimes suggested, in sending packets of troops, varying from battalions to brigades, to " show the flag " or to support some professedly loyal chief, and without thinking of what it might ultimately cost to keep the same flag flying.

The General Staff had to resist more than one suggestion of this kind whilst I was C.I.G.S., and it was not an easy task, for they usually emanated from the " man on the spot," who is too frequently thought to be the most competent judge, whereas his outlook is often narrow and his advice by no means always the best to follow. What was needed was to despatch to the centres of intrigue and disaffection a few Englishmen of the right type to give our version of the state of affairs, furnish them with money

T

to pay handsomely for intelligence and other services rendered, and provide them with just sufficient escort to ensure their personal safety. On the advice of the General Staff measures of this kind were initiated, and in a short time matters assumed a different aspect. Of course, the best way of thwarting the enemy's designs and of making our position permanently secure was to give the Turks in Mesopotamia a sound beating, and arrangements for this were put in train.

Lieutenant-General Sir Percy Lake commanded in this theatre between January and August 1916, and was then succeeded by Maude, who had gone to Mesopotamia with his division from Egypt early in the year and had subsequently been in command of an army corps. When the question of a successor to Sir Percy was being considered by the Government, I had no hesitation in recommending that Maude should be given the appointment, and although no exception was taken to him no particular desire was shown to select him, one reason for this probably being that the officers whose names were mentioned as alternatives were much better known to the ministers with whom the decision rested. Maude was, in fact, almost entirely unknown to them at the time, and therefore it was the more gratifying to me that in the end Mr. Asquith accepted my recommendation.

I was quite ready to accept responsibility for it. I knew that Maude possessed a high standard of honour, a qualification without which, and historical exceptions notwithstanding, no man is fit to hold an important command. I also knew that he was careful of the interests of his men, held sound views on tactical and strategical questions, recognised the value of good organisation, and in every way seemed to be the ideal man to clear up the Mesopotamian muddle and give the Turks a thrashing into the bargain. How well he justified his selection is one of the most brilliant chapters in the history of the Great War. Wisely devoting his energies first to the improvement of the abominable line of communication and the training and organisation of his troops, he patiently laboured and waited until his preparations were sufficiently good to justify an advance, and when all was ready he struck with such skill and vigour that in less than three months the enemy was completely defeated. Kut-el-Amara was recaptured in February 1917 with more than 2000 prisoners, and on the 11th of March Maude entered Baghdad at the heels of the flying Turks and chased them north along the line of the German railway.

Some months later we received many reports indicating the concentration of large hostile forces about Mosul, but they were probably circulated for the express purpose of inducing us to send reinforcements from other theatres, and whatever truth there may have been in them (there was little or none) they did not seriously disturb the minds of the General Staff. Having at last established a reasonably good line of communication, and enjoying the assistance of Monro (Commander-in-Chief in India since October 1916) and the Indian authorities in general, we felt that we could safely leave the rest to Maude. His death from cholera on the 18th of November 1917 was a great loss to the Empire and to all those many comrades by whom he was both admired and beloved. Before the Great War he had served with distinction in Egypt, South Africa, Canada, and at home, and he left behind him a name for devotion to duty and uprightness of character that will endure for all time in the annals of the British army.

Murray in Egypt, like Maude in Mesopotamia, had much spade work to do in connection with the organisation, equipment, and training of his troops before he could dispose of the Turks lying east of the Suez Canal. One wonders why these essential matters had been permitted to get into such an unsatisfactory state, and in all theatres except France, for every soldier possessing a rudimentary knowledge of his profession is aware of their importance. The reason was that whereas our pre-war preparations for offensive action had been based on a scale not exceeding the employment of some half-dozen divisions, we had, in addition to sharing on the West Front in the greatest conflict the world has ever known, become engaged in five other campaigns, all of which were of considerable magnitude. These commitments would have taxed the resources and ingenuity of the most perfectly prepared nation, and in our case they were bound to lead to confusion, and, if nothing worse, be unproductive of useful results for a long time to come.

Murray's task was the harder because the normal organisation of the divisions which had returned from Gallipoli had been dislocated when they were sent there. A variety of personnel, animals, vehicles, etc., not required in Gallipoli were then left behind in Egypt and these had of necessity been meanwhile sent to the western frontier of the country or elsewhere, and were still absent, hundreds of miles away, when the divisions returned to Egypt. They had to be collected or replaced before the divisions could be reconstructed.

A further disadvantage was that at first Murray was not sole master in Egypt. When he was sent there at the end of 1915, on being succeeded by me as C.I.G.S., it was decided that he should command only the troops operating in the vicinity of the Suez Canal, and that the remainder should continue under the orders of Maxwell, who had previously commanded the whole. On hearing of this decision when I went to the War Office I represented to Lord Kitchener that it was impracticable, but he was anxious to retain Maxwell because of his unique experience in Egyptian matters, and as he would agree neither to put Murray under Maxwell nor Maxwell under Murray two kings of Brentford were set up. Both Generals tried their hardest to make the system work, but within a few weeks both were forced to say that it was an impossible one and ought to be discontinued. In March, Maxwell returned to England and Murray assumed command of all the troops.

The operations in Egypt, as in other theatres, were also hampered by the lack of war material, and Murray was usually worse off in this respect than other Commanders-in-Chief, for as the output was still much below the sum of our requirements he frequently had to go short in order that the more pressing needs of other fronts might be satisfied. In spite of these adverse conditions, and of having to build a broad-gauge railway as he advanced, and lay down a great pipe-line, with pumping stations, to bring fresh water from Egypt for his troops, he drove the Turks out of the

Sinai Peninsula before the end of the year and thus put a stop to further hostile designs in this quarter. He also effectually cleared the Senussi out of the oases of the western deserts of Egypt.

Of the campaign in Macedonia there is little to be said, except that for about three years it absorbed a large Entente force which contributed nothing material to the winning of the war, beyond detaining two or three German divisions of inferior quality, and a number of Bulgarian divisions who would probably have objected to serve outside the Balkan Peninsula. This is a hard statement to make, remembering the privations and sickness our troops experienced and the fine work they performed in the offensive of September 1918, but the fact remains that the Bulgars were defeated on the West Front and not in Macedonia. They had been at war since 1912, were exhausted, and realised that their side was beaten before the offensive began. Practically the only good point about the campaign was that it enabled the Entente to use Serb and Greek troops whom it might have been difficult to employ elsewhere. The total Entente force in Macedonia was usually much stronger than the enemy, numbering at one time about 650,000 men as against some 450,000 Germans and Bulgars, and the bad strategy which caused this situation had the result of creating frequent discussions as to what could be done to improve matters.

Scarcely a month passed in which some fresh plan was not proposed by one or other of the countries interested —Russia, France, Serbia, Greece, Italy, and ourselves. At one time it would be a question of increasing the force either for offensive or defensive purposes ; at another of reducing it so as to discontinue the waste of troops who were doing nothing and could do nothing, and were badly needed elsewhere ; at another of coming away altogether. No one policy held the field for more than a few weeks, and this is not to be wondered at, seeing there was no hope of achieving anything decisive by such offensive operations as were feasible, while on the other hand there were reasons why the force could neither be withdrawn nor reduced.

As might be expected, the enemy exploited the position

to his own advantage, and frequently spread false reports of his intention to make a preponderating attack and drive the Allies into the sea. What was worse, the reports sometimes had the desired effect of inducing the Allied Governments to reinforce this front at the expense of the West Front, and so use up shipping which could have been more profitably employed in other ways, and at the same time that shipping became an additional target for submarine attack. Nothing pleased the enemy more than to see the Allies add to the number of their troops in this theatre, which he facetiously described as the "entente internment camp." I remember that considerable excitement once prevailed because Falkenhayn, who had recently ceased to be the Chief of the German General Staff, was reported to have arrived in Macedonia, and although the British General Staff discredited the rumour some of the Allies insisted that it was true. Later, the Falkenhayn turned out to be a major having a somewhat similar name who was the German military attaché in Greece.

The Macedonian campaign was the more difficult to conduct because of the mixture of nationalities in the Allied forces, for although General Sarrail was theoretically in supreme command of the whole, no important measure could be taken without reference to the Governments concerned. The entire campaign, in fact, was complicated and tiresome, and more conferences were held, either at London or in France, in regard to it than to any other military question. Even when it did not figure in the agenda it invariably obtruded itself before the conference dispersed, and it is no exaggeration to say that at one period it made more demands on the time and temper of ministers and their naval and military advisers than all the other campaigns put together. Fortunately for the General Staff we had a very level-headed General, Milne, in command of the British contingent, upon whom we could always rely to give a sound opinion and make the best use of the troops he had. Milne was an old comrade of mine, having served with me on Lord Roberts' staff in South Africa, and under me in the Intelligence Division at the War Office when in charge of the Balkans section.

Throughout the war, ministers never seemed able to understand, what educated soldiers well know, that the employment of troops of different armies in the same operation is attended with many difficulties and complications, and that the aggregate fighting value of the force is thereby reduced to a corresponding degree. Military salads of this kind are sometimes justifiable and may be unavoidable, but it must be remembered that the mere counting of heads may give quite a wrong impression of the capabilities of the force, and that the appointment of an Allied Commander-in-Chief does not entirely remove the disadvantages incurred, though in some respects it may perhaps mitigate them.

The enemy acted more wisely than we did, either from choice or necessity, and kept his different nationalities on separate fronts where they could most conveniently be placed and maintained. Thus, there were Germans on the West Front, Austrians on the Italian Front, Germans and Austrians on different sections of the Russian Front, Bulgars in Macedonia, and Turks in Asia. From this principle he seldom departed, except for the purpose of temporarily stiffening a wobbling ally, or of providing for a special operation the requisite reinforcements which could not be found in any other manner.

In East Africa the campaign had commenced with the despatch of an expeditionary force from India to Mombasa in August 1914, and at the end of 1915 the position was such that the Government decided, just before I became C.I.G.S., to send out reinforcements, the bulk of which were to be provided by South Africa. Sir Horace Smith-Dorrien was appointed to the chief command, but in consequence of temporary ill-health he was unable to proceed beyond Cape Town, and his place was taken by General Smuts. The latter was succeeded at the end of 1916 by General Van Dewenter.

The campaign, though comparatively a minor one, was attended by great hardships, owing to the nature and climate of the country, the absence of roads, and the distances to be covered, while on the other hand the German commander, Von Lettow, displayed commendable skill in the way he employed his troops—mainly native levies—and sustained their morale under what must have seemed to them rather disheartening conditions.   Although the enemy was given no rest, first by Smuts and then by Van Dewenter, the operations dragged on for a long time, and in the circumstances this could not be avoided.   It was a matter of patience and perseverance both on the part of commanders and troops, and in the end they had their reward.   The enemy's elusive tactics were gradually worn threadbare, his troops were broken up into detachments without cohesion, and the last of them were driven from East Africa into Portuguese territory in December 1917.

In an earlier chapter I have mentioned that a Staff College training is a great help in war to officers employed on the staff or in command of troops, in that it enables them to understand each other's methods and generally to work together easily and efficiently.   This advantage is the more valuable when intercommunication is limited to the telegraph, and, again, if the officers concerned are not personally known to each other.   Before the Great War Generals Smuts and Van Dewenter were known to me only by name, and as they were not only not Staff College graduates but did not belong to the British army, I wish to say that from first to last I found no difficulty whatever in working with them. Their telegrams were models of lucidity and conveyed just the information and advice that the General Staff required to have, and I trust that the two Generals felt equally satisfied at their end of the wire.   If they did not I owe them a further debt of gratitude, for they invariably interpreted the instructions it was my duty to send them in the way in which they were intended to be understood.

On the West Front the most conspicuous events during 1916 were the battles of Verdun and the Somme.   The attack on Verdun was a desperate bid to cripple the French armies beyond hope of recovery, and lasted from the 21st of February to the 1st of July, the opening day of the battle of the Somme, which in its turn did not end till the 17th of November.   The Somme was the first occasion on which our resources in men, guns, and ammunition enabled us to start an offensive with a reasonable chance of success.   They were not entirely as good as could have been desired, but they were infinitely superior to anything we had enjoyed before.

Coupled with the heavy punishment meted out by the French at Verdun, who firmly and patiently fought on while we completed our preparations, the Somme battle marked a definite stage on the road to victory. The final overthrow of the enemy was henceforward no longer in doubt, provided the Allies resolutely kept up the pressure at the decisive point and resisted the temptation to embark on side issues. In support of this opinion I shall quote Ludendorff's account of the condition of the German armies at the time. He says, " The strain during this year (1916) had proved too great. The endurance of the troops had been weakened by long spells of defence under the powerful enemy artillery fire and their own losses. *We were completely exhausted on the Western Front. . . . We now urgently needed a rest. The army had been fought to a standstill and was utterly worn out.*" (The italics are mine.)

But the far-reaching effects of the year's fighting on this front were not in all cases appreciated by ministers, some of whom asserted that the battle of the Somme had been a ghastly failure, and persisted in measuring the amount of our success by the kilometres of ground gained, with little or no regard to the moral ascendancy our troops had established. Moreover, although there was plenty of evidence that the enemy had suffered heavily, both in men and morale, the Allies had themselves sustained great losses, and millions of German troops were yet in the field. On the Eastern Front Brusiloff's celebrated advance had resulted in the capture of half a million prisoners and an enormous amount of war material, but the Russians had also lost heavily, and throughout their ranks the sinister influence of German propaganda continued to spread with demoralising effect. The Rumanians, who had joined the Allies on 28th August, had been thrown back from Transylvania and through Wallachia, and three whole Russian armies had been sent south to save the situation. Finally, the enemy was careful to play on the fears and nerves of those who, unacquainted with the practical side of war in general and with the conditions of the Great War in particular, were apt to give more attention to his cunningly-devised communiqués than to the importance of strict adherence to sound strategical principles.

In face of these circumstances it was uphill work trying to convince some of those with whom I was brought into contact that, given perseverance in the right direction, victory was assured. Such a statement would be received with an impatient shrug of the shoulders as if to say, " We have heard the same story scores of times before, and are still as far from winning the war as ever we were." As might be expected, this dissatisfaction, or disappointment, was the most pronounced when the fighting was severe, and it would be argued that, as the attacker was more exposed to loss in crossing the open than the defender was in his dug-out, the right policy for us was to assume a defensive rôle and leave the enemy to do the attacking. The whole problem appeared to be, so it was said, purely one of mathematics. To this I would demur, pointing out that although the attacker might at first be the heavier loser he might hope to make a good bag later, and that there were other things to be taken into account besides figures. Armies like boxers, I would observe, could not possibly win battles, and certainly not wars, if they restricted their efforts to self-defence and never led off to damage their opponents ; the preliminary step to victory was, as always, the wearing-down of the enemy's power of resistance, and this was not to be achieved without loss.

Fresh ground would then be taken up by my questioners, who would suggest that as Russia had many millions of men at her disposal while we were short of them, she and not we ought to undertake the wearing-down business. We could provide her with the armament she needed, of which we would require less, and incidentally the plan would solve our man-power difficulties, leaving a greater number of men available for employment in those industries which it was essential for financial and other reasons to maintain. To this I replied that perhaps Russia might not make such good use of the armament as would our own troops, and that in any case it would be wise to equip the latter with what they still wanted before giving too much away. To some extent this advice prevailed, but not so far as could have been wished, and much of the armament as well as other war material sent to Russia was put to indifferent use, or not used at all, while some of it, falling into the enemy's hands, was eventually used against us on the West Front.

Discussions of this nature were bound to arise, for we had suffered unprecedented losses, and it was the duty of ministers to consider every means of reducing them in future. The case was much more serious when, from the end of 1916 onwards, a desire was evinced to adopt not only new tactics but new strategy — strategy that would find a " way round " to victory in place of courting heavy losses in trying to achieve what was held to be impossible, the defeat of the enemy on the West Front. There, it was said, the existing stalemate would continue, and we ought to show greater " imagination " in our plans. We were too wooden in our ideas and too heavy-footed in our movements. " Why go on battering our heads against a brick wall ? Why not follow the example of Germany which has been so successful in Servia, Russia, and Rumania, and give first a punch here and then a punch there ? " I was once asked, while the speaker, suiting the action to the word, struck out right and left with his clenched fists against the imaginary foe. I could only reply that the conditions were not the same, and that although war was certainly not an exact science, and had no fixed code of rules, there was in it one good working principle—the concentration of superior force at the decisive point—which could never be disregarded without great risk, and which, if whole-heartedly applied, would generally bring success.

The persistence with which views such as the above were pressed forward caused me much anxiety, but consolation could always be had from the knowledge that the same thing had happened in past wars and that in spite of it we had won in the end. That valuable book *Ordeal by Battle* contains some pertinent remarks on this subject, which I extracted, kept on my table, and frequently read. I hope that the author, Mr. F. S. Oliver, will not object to my reproducing them here. They are as follows :

As we read and re-read British history we cannot but be impressed with the fact that our leading statesmen, misled by the very brilliancy of their intellectual endowments, have always been prone to two errors of policy which the simpler mind of the soldier instinctively avoids. They have ever been too ready to conclude prematurely that a certain line of obstacles is so formidable that it cannot be forced ; and they have also ever been too ready to accept the notion that there must surely be some ingenious far way round, by which they may succeed in circumventing the infinite.

The defect of brilliant brains is not necessarily a want of courage—daring there has usually been in plenty—but they are apt to lack fortitude. They are apt to abandon the assault upon positions which are not really invulnerable, and to go off, chasing after attractive butterflies, until they fall into quagmires. Dispersion of effort has always been the besetting sin of British statesmen and the curse of British policy. There is no clearer example of this than the case of William Pitt the Younger, who went on picking up sugar islands all over the world when he ought to have been giving his whole strength to beating Napoleon.

Very few obstacles are really insurmountable, and it is usually the shortest and the safest course to stick to what has been already begun. Especially is this the case when your resources in trained soldiers and munitions of war are painfully restricted. At the one point, where you have decided to attack, the motto is *push hard* ; and at all others, where you may be compelled to defend yourselves, the motto is *hold fast*.

The peril of British war councils in the past has always been (and may be still is) the tendency of ingenious argument to get the better of sound judgement. In the very opposite of this lies safety. We find the true type of high policy, as well as of successful campaigning, in the cool and patient inflexibility of Wellington, holding fast by one main idea, forcing his way over one obstacle after another which had been pronounced invincible —through walled cities, into the deep valleys of the Pyrenees, across the Bidassoa—till from the crests of the Great Rhune and the Little his soldiers looked down at last upon the plains of France.

Further reference to the different plans proposed for 1917 will be made in the next chapter, but mention should be made here of the plan for the West Front drawn up in November 1916 at a conference of the Allied Commanders-in-Chief held at Chantilly under the presidency of General Joffre, and at which I was present. The exhausted condition of the German armies was not then as well known to us as it has since become, but we knew sufficient about it to realise the wisdom of taking full advantage of the successes gained in the Verdun and Somme campaigns, first by continuing to exert pressure on the Somme front, so far as the winter season would permit, and secondly by preparing to attack the enemy early in 1917, with all the resources that could be made available, before he had had time to recover from his difficulties. The conference decided upon a plan of this nature, but it was not carried out, as General Nivelle, who shortly afterwards replaced General Joffre in the command of the French armies, substituted another plan, and, as will be explained in the next chapter, this change had the effect of postponing the date of the opening of the combined offensive.

Whilst at the War Office, as well as before that time, I had been on the most friendly terms with General Joffre, and happening to be in Paris shortly after he vacated his command I called one evening at his house. What passed between us I shall not repeat, but it will be no breach of confidence to say that such references as were made to his replacement showed him to be a great patriot, actuated by the sole desire to serve his country faithfully, though he naturally felt disappointed in being deprived of the opportunity of leading to victory the armies he loved so well, and with whom he had stood up against the onslaught of 1914 and afterwards held the enemy at bay for two years while our armies were being prepared to come to his aid. One end of his room was packed with floral tributes sent by his admiring countrymen, and he told me of many other testimonies of affection and confidence which he had received from those who appreciated the value of his services. I have never seen a more pathetic picture than this fine old soldier, who had hitherto been the most prominent figure in the Allied armies and was now prevented from reaping the success which his stout heart and indomitable will had made possible. France produced many capable Generals in the Great War, but it would be hard to think of one better qualified than General Joffre, if as well, to be at the head of her troops during the early stages of it, especially in August 1914 when a repetition of the failure of 1870 was deemed sufficiently imminent to justify the removal of the seat of government from Paris to Bordeaux.

I can speak with some personal knowledge on this point, for I saw Joffre on two or three critical occasions in August and September of 1914, one of them being at two o'clock in the morning after he had made a long motor drive. This is an hour when a man's courage and judgment are not at their best, and for myself I have always regarded with suspicion pessimistic telegrams sent from the front after 11 P.M. But although the situation was as bad as it could be—hence Joffre's journey—he was as calm and imperturbable as ever, and one felt him to be a real tower of strength against which weaker natures might confidently lean for support. When his original plan for meeting the enemy in 1914 had collapsed he carried on his shoulders a burden which would have broken down an ordinary man, but he never wavered in his determination to return to the attack. The opportunity for this came at the Marne in the first week of September, and he seized it with such promptitude and success as will always place him in the front rank of great commanders.

When making one of my periodical visits to Paris in 1917 I invited Joffre, then a Maréchal, to dine with me at the Hotel Crillon and meet a few British officers with whom he was acquainted. We had a most enjoyable evening, the Maréchal evidently being very gratified at the attention shown him, and he told me a good deal about his anxieties and intentions during the early part of the war. Whilst we were at dinner it became known outside that Père Joffre was at the hotel, and on leaving he received a tremendous ovation from the crowd which had assembled in the Place de la Concorde.

Like most other senior French generals Joffre absolutely refused to converse in any language except his own, but he was quick to grasp the sense of what was said to him, no matter how quaint the words or vile the pronunciation. Once when having *déjeuner* together at his headquarters we were discussing a new plan which had been suggested for winning the war, and for the moment I could think of no more apt remark to make about it than that if it were attempted we would find ourselves in the soup. Not knowing how to render the phrase in idiomatic French, I gave it to him literally as, " nous nous trouverons dans le consommé." He immediately tumbled to the meaning, and immensely enjoyed my lion-hearted effort not to be defeated.

In December 1916 Mr. Lloyd George became Prime Minister in place of Mr. Asquith, Lord Derby succeeding the former as Secretary of State for War. All public men are liable to be either over-praised or over-blamed, and whether Mr. Asquith was or was not an exception to the rule is no business of mine. I may say, however, that my experience of him as Prime Minister—which extended over more than half the duration of the war, and the most difficult part of it—was that he showed a much more sympathetic recognition of the difficulties with which our commanders and troops in the field were faced than did some of his colleagues ; and he was always ready to give an impartial hearing to the views of the General Staff, whether able to accept them or not.

Lord Kitchener's tragic death in June 1916 was an irreparable loss to the Empire and to the Entente. He was easily the most outstanding personality at the Allied conferences, and was listened to with more deference than was vouchsafed to any one else during the two and a half years that I attended these meetings. At the War Office and in Downing Street I found him to be a staunch supporter of the General Staff, and his aptitude for detecting essentials enabled him to give us much constructive assistance. I did not realise how valuable his help was until deprived of it, when, in addition to carrying my own load, I had to shoulder as best I could part of the load which he had hitherto borne. Without quite knowing why sometimes, he had a wonderful knack in being right in the things that really mattered.

For some months before his death it was common talk that his relations with certain members of the Government were the reverse of happy, and that intrigues were afoot to get him removed from the Cabinet. What amount of truth there was in this gossip I do not pretend to know, but I had not been a week in the War Office before I was warned by a friend that " they " hoped I would " down K." He did not say who " they " were, and my reply was that I was not concerned with " downing " anybody, and certainly not Lord Kitchener.

Like some other great men Lord Kitchener was exacting, and had no use whatever for those who raised petty difficulties at a time when prompt action was required ; while as to his alleged habit of over-centralisation all I can say is that it was never displayed during the six months I had the privilege of working with him, and that he was as ready to listen to the advice of his departmental heads as were any of the other seven Secretaries of State under whom I have worked.   Nor did he disclose any sign of that ruthless and domineering disposition attributed to him by those who wished to injure his good name.   On the contrary, he was a kind and delightful chief to serve, once his ways were understood ; and I know that he many times stood up against opposition in high quarters so as to protect officers who were threatened with unfair treatment.   As an instance of this, his last words to me were, when I said good-bye to him on the eve of his departure to Russia : " Remember what I have told you about —— and mind you look after him."   The officer in question was then being subjected to a persecution which Lord Kitchener thought to be undeserved.

Of all ministers and soldiers, so far as my knowledge goes, Lord Kitchener alone was convinced from the first that the war would be one of prolonged attrition.   Ever looking further forward than his contemporaries, he always maintained in his talks with me that 1917 would be the decisive year, and this conception might have proved remarkably correct had not the clock been put back twelve months by the Russian revolution, which he, no more than all others at the time, could foresee would occur.   Indeed, it might have proved accurate notwithstanding the revolution had not the Chantilly plan for the West Front in 1917 been rejected.

There were officers who, holding high posts in London

Lord Kitchener arriving at the Royal Military Academy on the 25th May, 1916, when he held his last parade.

Brig-Gen. Cleeve (Commandant).   Lord Kitchener.

before 1914, enjoyed all the advantages to be derived from a constant study of the problem of war with Germany, and who yet utterly failed, not only at first but for months afterwards, to grasp the character and magnitude of the struggle. Lord Kitchener, having none of these privileges, and without any War Office or other home experience to guide him, and suddenly summoned to assume supreme military charge, at once perceived, with a marvellous instinct, the stupendous effort the Empire must make. He developed our military forces with a rapidity previously unknown to the world, and to an extent undreamt of by his predecessors in Whitehall, and not only did he not fail—as his detractors have said—to realise the importance of increasing the output of munitions, but he achieved much in this respect for which the credit has been assigned to or filched by others. The unexpected enormous demand for munitions, foreseen by nobody, not even by the systematically-prepared Germany, could not be met by a stroke of the pen. There were no Krupp's works in England. It must be a matter of many months, and if blame is to be cast upon any one for the shortage in 1914–15, it should be attributed to those ministers and their military advisers who held office in the years before the war.

Lord Kitchener was as fully alive to the necessity for increasing the output of munitions as for increasing the number of divisions, and when proposals of this kind were submitted to him he usually doubled the amount recommended, thus earning for himself the nickname of the " doubler." As to the progress actually made, it may be mentioned that between the autumn of 1915 and midsummer of 1916—i.e. just before the battle of the Somme —the supply of heavy guns, howitzers, machine - guns, and ammunition to the field armies was very largely increased, and this was mainly the work of the War Office and not of the Munitions Ministry, which, doing valuable work later, had not yet had time to make itself felt at the front.

On the whole I would say that the achievements and foresight of Lord Kitchener place him in a class entirely by himself ; and they justify the conclusion that no man in

U

any of the Entente countries accomplished more, if as much, to bring about the final defeat of the enemy.

A few days before he left for Russia I was due to inspect the cadets at the Royal Military Academy, Woolwich, and thinking that he would enjoy a brief respite from his War Office duties I asked him to go in my place. At first he demurred, but in the end he went, and in this way it came about that he held his last parade on the same ground where, as a cadet, he had begun his military life some forty-seven years before.

In order to fill in the details of my own career, and at the risk of being accused of partiality in the above appreciation of Lord Kitchener, I must add that, quite unknown to me, one of his last acts at the War Office was to recommend to the King that I should be promoted General. This promotion was announced in the *London Gazette* of the 3rd June 1916, or about twenty-eight years after the date of my first commission.

CHAPTER XVI

CHIEF OF THE IMPERIAL GENERAL STAFF, 1917–18

IN the first week of January 1917 I went with certain
ministers of the newly-formed War Cabinet to Rome, where
an Allied Conference was to be held to consider future plans.
We travelled from Paris in company with M. Briand, M.
Thomas, General (now Marshal) Lyautey, and other French
representatives. M. Briand, who had been Prime Minister
since October 1915, was a delightful fellow-traveller, and the
life and soul of the party. General Lyautey had just been
appointed War Minister from the position of Governor-
General of Morocco. He also was an interesting personality,
and, being of a type more suited for business in the field
than in parliament, he apparently did not expect to hold

office for more than a short time. He ceased to be War Minister, and returned to Morocco, two months later, when M. Ribot replaced M. Briand, M. Painlevé, a famous mathematician and scientist, then becoming War Minister. Generals Sarrail and Milne from Macedonia also attended the conference, and the principal Italian representatives were M. Boselli and Baron Sonnino, Prime Minister and Foreign Minister respectively. Many Allied conferences had been held in 1916, either at London, Paris, or Calais, but this was the first to take place in Italy, and the Italians gave us a most hospitable reception.

The number of persons present at these conferences was seldom less than a score, and when the whole of the Allies were represented the number would approximate to a hundred or more. Besides the delegates of the various small countries, each of the principal Powers would, as a rule, be represented by its Prime Minister, the ministers for foreign affairs, the army, navy, and munitions, these being accompanied by their professional advisers, commanders-in-chief, secretaries, and other assistants.

The extent to which the conferences were productive of decisions largely depended, as at all conferences, on the personality of the president, who was invariably the Prime Minister of the country in which the meeting was being held. M. Clemenceau stood out by himself in this respect. He had a tactful, but nevertheless masterful, way of getting through the business on hand, and I can recollect many instances when he succeeded in extracting a decision and bringing to an end the discussion of thorny questions which threatened to be both abortive and interminable.

The proceedings were the more prolonged, not to say tedious, because they usually had to be conducted in two languages, French and English. Some of the English representatives could neither speak nor understand French; whilst most of the French and the other foreign representatives had little or no knowledge of English. Consequently not only had the greater part of the discussion to be duplicated, but while it was being interpreted for the benefit of those who had not understood the original, those who had understood it were apt to engage in whispered conversation amongst

An Allied Conference at the Quai d'Orsay.

MR. ASQUITH.   MR. LLOYD GEORGE.   INTERPRETER.   LORD KITCHENER.   THE AUTHOR.

BARON SONINO.

M. SALANDRA.

themselves and so distract the attention of those who were trying to listen to the translation. The translation, too, as is usually the case, did not always convey the intended meaning, the result being that further explanations had to be made in order to clear away possible misunderstandings. There is no doubt that ministers and others were at a great disadvantage if they did not possess a fair working knowledge of French—the language used by practically all the Allied representatives except ourselves and the Americans.

My duties frequently took me across the Channel either to attend conferences, or to see Sir Douglas Haig, or for some other purpose. In 1917 alone I crossed from England no fewer than thirty-two times, the arrangements for the voyage being made by Admiral Bacon, in naval command at Dover, who could always be depended upon to produce, at any hour of the day or night, and practically in any weather, one of his destroyers for my use, no matter how hard they might be working. The South-Eastern and Chatham Railway Company was equally obliging in providing railway facilities, and I was thus able to leave the War Office about 1 P.M., after attending War Cabinet meetings, and be at G.H.Q. in France, one or one and a half hour's drive from the French port, in time for tea.

Admiral Bacon struck me as being a man of great energy, who was always busy devising new schemes and inventions for outwitting the enemy, of whose activities he was constantly well informed, and he was an enthusiastic supporter of the British army on the West Front. I first made his acquaintance early in 1915 when, as a " Colonel," he came to France with the battery of the 15-inch howitzers which, as a director of an English firm, he had been instrumental in making. Wishing to see what they were like I visited their first halting-place between Boulogne and the front, and found that on entering the grounds of the château which had been allocated as their billet for the night, one of the howitzers had collided with the gate, bringing down the greater part of a masonry pillar, and had then gone to rest several feet below the surface of a large flower-bed. The howitzers were of considerable weight and size, as were also the tractors which drew them, and required rather skilful driving. They did good work for us, and at a time when we had practically no modern heavy artillery except a few 9·2-inch howitzers.

The Admiral, who joined us from the retired list of the navy, was not the only person in the war who held both naval and military rank. The record example was that of a civilian, who, from Deputy General Manager of a railway, became both Major-General and Vice-Admiral in less than two years.

Admiral Bacon was in command of the Dover Patrol from the summer of 1915 to the end of 1917, and had a fine body of officers under his orders. Some of the destroyer commanders I met on my voyages across the Channel were boys not long out of their teens, and all were pronounced optimists, full of high spirits, and animated by the single desire to " have a go " at the enemy. Twice I crossed under the care of Commander Evans, who had been with Captain Scott's last expedition to the South Pole. On one of these voyages Evans had some £4,000,000 or £5,000,000 of bullion on board, packed in small bags which were lying on the floor of his cabin and the ward room !

I may say here that throughout my time as C.I.G.S. the relations between the General Staff and Admiralty were without exception extremely cordial and helpful. This was an improvement upon what I had seen at the War Office years before, when each department was inclined to go its own way in disregard of the other. The navy was, I always thought, the chief offender—which was excusable perhaps, for it was then commonly thought to be sufficient in itself for all war purposes, and the army to be hardly worth considering, except for garrison duties abroad. This better understanding between the two services was, as I have said elsewhere, partly due to the establishment of the Naval War College, but mainly to the genuine goodwill shown by the three officers who in turn held the post of First Sea Lord—Sir Henry Jackson, Sir John (now Lord) Jellicoe, and Sir Rosslyn (now Lord) Wemyss, who were always most anxious to work in close accord with the army in every possible way.

It is to be hoped that we shall hear no more about one

fighting service being of supreme importance to the country, and the others of little or none. Having an Empire scattered all over the globe, connected together not by roads and railways but by the sea, it is a platitude to say that we must maintain a navy second to none in the world. But it is equally true that ships cannot fight on land, that land fighting occurs in all great wars, and therefore that land forces are necessary. Again, neither the navy nor the army can fight effectively without the assistance of the Air Force Each service is in fact the complement of the other two, and this view is now accepted, I think, by the officers of all three.

During 1917 the War Cabinet came to the conclusion that the organisation of the Admiralty was not satisfactory, one of the alleged faults being that the First Sea Lord had such a multitude of duties to carry out that he could not give his attention to the really vital questions connected with the employment of the fleets. Some thirteen years before, as described in a previous chapter, the Admiralty system had been taken as the pattern for the War Office : it was now decided that the War Office system, as modified and developed by further experience, should be taken as the pattern for the Admiralty, and I was requested to assist the sailors in making the necessary alterations. I therefore placed Whigham at their disposal for a few days, so that he might explain our methods to them, more especially in regard to General Staff duties.

Lord Fisher was not a member of the Board of Admiralty whilst I was C.I.G.S., and I had no official dealings with him in connection with the Great War. We had, however, several private conversations about it, and although I did not always agree with him—more especially with his idea of landing a force in Schleswig-Holstein, of which I had heard years before—I could not help admiring the incisive manner in which he expressed his views. On one occasion I was invited by Lord Rosebery to meet him at dinner, and the three of us, no one else being present, had a very interesting talk. Lord Fisher had much to say about submarines and the submarine menace, then at its height, and he repeatedly punctuated his arguments by driving the prongs of his

dinner fork into our host's tablecloth. At last Lord Rosebery quietly drew his attention to the destruction he was
causing, for which he at once apologised, but he immediately
forgot the admonition and down came the fork again. Like
other mortals Lord Fisher had his defects, but I should
imagine that few people would deny that to him is due
a good share of the credit for the rapidity and efficiency
with which the navy began its heavy task in August 1914.

In response to an invitation I received from General
Cadorna whilst at Rome, I spent a fortnight the following
March in visiting the Italian front. I first went to his
headquarters at Udine, and afterwards to different parts
of the line on the Isonzo and Trentino fronts. Lucas
and my son Brian went with me, as did also General
Weygand and another French officer, the French government having decided to send them when they heard of my
projected visit. I was met in Italy by Brigadier-General
Delmé-Radcliffe, who was head of the British mission at
Cadorna's headquarters, and Colonel Boriani of the Italian
army. The Colonel was an entertaining travelling companion as well as a fine fighting soldier. He had been
wounded seven times in the war, and as far as I could
make out he was never so happy as when in the thick of a
fight at the head of his beloved Sicilians. He could converse in English quite fluently, and had once written a
military book in the language, but like most people who have
to cope with a foreign tongue he occasionally erred in being
somewhat too literal. I remember one instance of this
which caused us some amusement, though I am glad to say
that we were sufficiently well-behaved not to show it. He
was translating the menu for us, which was written in
Italian, the joint being " hind quarter of veal." This he
rendered as " the posterior of a young beast " !

I was much impressed with the administrative efficiency
of the troops. They were well housed, clothed, and fed ; the
transport was in good condition ; and the road communications through the steep and lofty hills were most skilfully
constructed. No German divisions had as yet been employed on this front, and although the season was not
suitable for active operations one could not help noticing

VISIT TO THE ITALIAN FRONT, MARCH, 1917.

THE AUTHOR. GENERAL WEYGAND. CAPTAIN ROBERTSON.

the absolute quiet which everywhere prevailed — a very different state of affairs from what we were accustomed to on the West Front. It was seldom that firing of any kind was heard beyond an occasional rifle shot, and I do not remember once seeing an aeroplane in the air.

A special train was placed at my disposal and everywhere I was accorded great hospitality, for which I had to thank the Italian Foreign and War Ministers, and the Italian ambassador in London, the Marquis Imperiali, as well as General Cadorna and the other officers whom I met.

During my visit I presented, in accordance with His Majesty's commands, the G.C.M.G. to His Royal Highness the Duke of Aosta, commanding the 3rd Army, and other decorations to Lieutenant-Generals Pecori-Giraldi, Piacentini, Di Robilant, and Mambretti, respectively commanding the 1st, 2nd, 4th, and 6th Armies.

On the eve of my departure for England I received the following telegram from His Majesty the King of Italy :

Au retour à Rome de ma visite aux navires de guerre je tiens à vous exprimer mon vif régret de ne pas vous rencontrer au front. J'espère de vous voir à une occasion que je souhaite prochaine. En attendant je vous confère comme marque de ma considération la Grande Croix de l'ordre des Saints Maurice et Lazare. Cette décoration vous sera remise par mon Ambassadeur à Londres. VITTORIO EMANUELE.

I may add here that at the end of the war His Majesty conferred upon me the further honour of the " Order of the Crown of Italy, Grand Cross."

Throughout 1917 the question of obtaining a sufficient number of recruits to meet the requirements of new services and to supply drafts was a constant source of anxiety, and it will serve to explain the views of the General Staff regarding man-power and the military situation in general if I quote from a speech I made, by request of the Government, at a conference on the " trade-card " system held on the 4th April 1917 at the Ministry of Munitions. Representatives of the various trades unions were present, Mr. Arthur Henderson being in the chair. Admiral Jellicoe was also deputed to speak. I said :

The War Office has often been blamed for doing wrong things, but the War Office has a duty to perform. It has to win this war, and to do that it must have men. But it is not a leech. The War Office takes the men which the Government give it, and can take no more. The War Office has never attempted to lay down how many men it can have, or where they are to come from. It has told the Government what men it ought to have, but it has always left the Government to devise the means of providing them and to specify the number.

It has also been said that the War Office does not make the best use of the men it gets. The War Office makes mistakes. Who does not ? No doubt there have been cases of injustice to individuals and many anomalies, and men have been taken who should not have been taken, square pegs have been put into round holes, and so on. I admit all this, but look at the situation with which we were faced at the beginning of the war. We were unprepared for this war, as were all other nations in Europe except Germany and France. We had no organisation such as continental nations have for calling up the population and sorting out men according to their qualifications for military service, for industries, for munitions, agriculture, and so forth. We had no system of universal service, but had to call on volunteers—we had to improvise as we went along, and we have been living from hand to mouth throughout the war. The consequence of improvising is confusion, waste of effort, friction, and injustice. With the best will in the world these things could not be avoided. But there is no use in crying over spilt milk, or in laying blame on individuals, ministers, or the Government. It is not their fault. It is the fault of the system or rather the want of it, and that is due to want of foresight and preparation before the war on the part of the nation as a whole.

Another point I wish to refer to is the criticism of military operations which has sometimes been made. Here, again, mistakes have occurred, but marvellously few considering we had to form large new armies. The critics are chiefly disgruntled and otherwise undesirable members of the community who, having failed in their own professions, think they know all about the professions of every one else, and instead of loyally putting their shoulders to the wheel employ most of their time in sowing discontent and distrust of those in authority. Let us treat them with the contempt they deserve, as do the soldiers at the front. I am gratified to say that, more than in any campaign in which I have taken part, criticisms within the army itself have been practically non-existent, and this I regard as a great tribute to the loyalty and discipline of the nation which has produced the men of whom our New Armies are composed.

Our progress with the war is bound to be slow because of the colossal numbers engaged, and because Germany enjoyed a great advantage at the start. It is a difficult and long business in war to make up for a bad start.

She (Germany) has been preparing for war and nothing else for years past, and has recently made extraordinary efforts. She now has many more divisions in the field than last year, and has increased the number of her soldiers by about a million. She has been able to do this by her domineering autocratic government, acting in total disregard of the most elementary principles of humanity and international law. After over-running Poland she compelled thousands of men to emigrate to Germany and to work in German mines and munition factories, thus releasing large numbers of Germans for military service. Her next method of obtaining men was to pass last November what is called the auxiliary service law, by which all persons, both male and female, in Germany, between the ages of 17 and 60, were placed at the disposal of the Government. This measure alone has probably set free for military service considerably over one million men. She has adopted a system of slave-raiding in Belgium and northern France, whereby thousands of Belgian and French civilians have been forcibly removed from their homes and compelled to work as slaves for their enemies in Germany, thus releasing still more Germans for military service. We must meet this desperate effort the enemy has made, and to meet it we must have men.

You ask how many men do we want ? My answer is the same as I made to the Government a few days after taking up my present post. It is that we ought not to expect to win a war such as this unless and until every man and woman in the country does a full day's work of an essential nature. Many times during the last sixteen months the question of man-power has been considered, and I have never varied my statement to the Government. I have always said that it is impossible to put a limit to the number of men needed for the army, because the task is so enormous that we must have *all* the men who can be spared from the navy, the various industries, agriculture, and other employments essential to the prosecution of the war. It is not for me to say how many men can be got, or from where they are to come, but surely it should be possible, seeing the great reserve of men still in the country and with a proper adjustment of man-power, to give the army the men needed, and our immediate needs are half a million men between now and July next. The failure to get these men will undoubtedly involve a prolongation of the war and consequent prolongation of hardship and misery.

We have done much. Our troops at the front are the wonder

of the world.   No one has ever approached the colossal task that
we have so successfully accomplished.   Individuals throughout
the Empire have behaved magnificently in the way of absolute
selflessness, and have given up everything—their money, their
time, their position, their prospects, their friends, their lives—
to the State.   But the question is, have we done all that we can
do—for Germany is not yet beaten ?   Do not think I am
despondent.   I am perfectly confident of success provided we
remain determined to win, but although fully persuaded of the
righteousness of our cause and therefore fully confident of victory,
I think the way to victory may be long and certainly will be hard.
We have been saved by our navy from the horrors of war being
brought into our own homes, with the result that many people in
the land are still ignorant of the urgency of our position.   I for
my part feel that an enormous responsibility rests upon me, as
I am asked to win the war and it is impossible to do that unless
sufficient men are forthcoming.

In order to obtain the men needed it seems to me that, for
the duration of the war, we must one and all be willing to subordinate our personal liberty and will to that of the State.   It is
only in this way that the State officials—the Government—can
have the free hand necessary to enable them to organise the
resources of the Empire to the best advantage.   We must practise self-denial and self-sacrifice, and, after all, what is demanded
of us at home in comparison with what is demanded of our men
at the front, many of whom are every day making the supreme
sacrifice ?   Or what are our privations as compared with those
of the countries which have been invaded and devastated for
generations to come, homes broken up, industries ruined, men
deported as slaves, and old people and children left without food
or shelter ?   It is upon methods of outrage such as these that
the Germans are relying to induce the Belgian and French people
to submit to their terms.

As I have said, it is difficult for us at this distance to realise
what these things mean, but we may realise them one day if we
do not, before it is too late, take every means in our power to
crush that overbearing spirit which has degraded a great nation,
has brought all this misery upon the world, and has defied every
law of God and man.   We must in fact win.   The point is, what
do we mean by winning ?   I doubt if this is properly understood.
I take it there is no desire on the part of any one of us to crush
the German nation, and the sooner the German people know that
the better.   Our aim is, as I understand it, to deal German
despotism such a blow as will for generations to come prevent a
recurrence of the horrors of the last two and a half years.   In
short we are fighting in the cause of freedom, and before we can

get freedom Germany must be taught to realise that might is *not* right. Until that is done there can be no true freedom either for individuals, or families, or societies, or for the Empire.

We are a law-abiding race, and as far as I know my country-men all they need in a situation like this is to be told the truth, and what it is they are required to do. I have told you all that it is possible to tell you with regard to the number of men we need, and although a great strain has already been put upon us, I must also tell you that we must be prepared for a still greater strain before we finish the war. I know you are ready to face that strain, and if we all face it, resolutely set our teeth, and are true to ourselves, we shall, with God's help, secure that freedom for which we have been compelled to fight.

I did not obtain the half-million men for the army which I said were required by July, but it should not be assumed that those present at the meeting were responsible for the failure. There were other reasons for it, as I shall show later.

The difficulty of providing drafts in 1917 can be under-stood when I say that while we then had on the West Front a greater number of divisions than before, the fighting being prolonged and severe, we took into the army only about 820,000 men as against 1,200,000 in the previous year. This reduced number of recruits was accentuated by the fact that the 'proportion of wounded men who recovered sufficiently to admit of being sent back to the front became less as time went on. In the early part of the war we could rely upon some sixty per cent of the wounded becoming available for redrafting, but by the end of 1917 we had to modify this estimate in order to make allowances for those men—an ever-increasing number—who had been wounded more than once. Obviously men wounded for the third, fourth, or fifth time were not likely to recover so quickly, if at all, as men wounded for the first time, and medical and other officers concerned were reluctant to send them back to the trenches. Many hard cases of this kind came to my notice during the war, and it was not pleasant to see men, perhaps fathers of families, being repeatedly sent back to the front, while there were others in the country who could be spared and were not called upon to perform any military service.

I may also observe that the necessity for keeping fighting

units up to "establishment," or authorised strength, is much more important than is usually supposed by the layman, and sometimes even by the professional if he is not employed at the front. The fallacy prevails that a battalion of, say, five hundred men is only fifty per cent inferior in fighting power to one having its authorised strength of about a thousand men. This is far from being the case, because in war there are in every battalion some hundred and fifty to two hundred men who are necessarily employed on duties which take them away from their platoons, and this number remains more or less constant no matter what the total strength of the battalion may be. Hence if a battalion loses five hundred men in action its fighting strength is reduced not to five hundred but to between three hundred and four hundred men, and its whole fighting organisation thereby becomes dislocated and imperfect.

Weakness in numbers may also affect morale. Battalions usually take a very local view of matters, and judge the progress of events largely by what happens immediately around them, and if they know that they are weak and may continue to be so for an indefinite period they cannot be expected to fight with the same confidence as they would if supported by the knowledge that their ranks were full. Nothing, in short, is more discouraging to a battalion than to see its ranks depleted without observing signs of their being replenished.

To meet the situation as above described, and bearing in mind that the Russian revolution was certain to react to our disadvantage on the West Front, it was clear that the Military Service Act of 1916, as well as the method of its application, called for drastic amendment. This Act was perhaps as good as we could hope to get at the time it became law, but it was hampered by many conditions which tended to nullify its value, it was in itself too limited in scope, and it was unaccompanied by proper machinery for co-ordinating the man-power activities of the various departments concerned — *e.g.* War Office, Admiralty, Munitions, Board of Trade. In September 1916 a Man-Power Distribution Board was set up, and in the following

December a National Service Department was established, but neither of them exercised really effective control over the competing interests of the different departments, which continued to tug with added vigour, each in its own direction, in proportion as the shrinkage of man - power resources became more pronounced.

Subject to the orders of the Government and to the instructions of the Secretary of State for War, recruiting was, as I have explained in an earlier chapter, primarily the business of the Adjutant-General, but as C.I.G.S. it was my duty to take a hand also, and at the end of November 1916 I recommended that the military age should be raised to fifty-five years, and that *all* men up to that age should be utilised for such national work as the Government deemed essential to the prosecution of the war.   This meant, of course, all-round liability to national service.   A few days later events occurred which led to a reconstruction of the Government, Mr. Lloyd George becoming Prime Minister, and for the moment consideration of the recommendation was unavoidably postponed.

From time to time in 1917 various questions connected with man-power were referred to committees and individuals appointed by the War Cabinet to enquire into them, and certain improvements of a minor nature were made, but they were far from being adequate.   They remained so when the duty of dealing with man-power was subsequently vested in a Minister of National Service.   Then, as before, a smaller share of the men available was allotted to the army than a judicial review of the circumstances showed to be necessary, and eventually some twenty-five per cent of the battalions on the West Front were disbanded in order to help to fill up the remainder.

The problem with which ministers were faced was difficult, as most problems in war are, since many conflicting demands for men for the three fighting forces, for ship-building, food-production, munitions, and other national services had to be reconciled.   Still, the outstanding factor was that if, for lack of men, the armies on the West Front were beaten the war would certainly be prolonged, if nothing worse than that, and therefore their maintenance at full strength unquestionably ranked second in importance to no other requirement.

Unfortunately, arguments of this nature failed to carry sufficient weight in adjusting the different claims until, in the spring of 1918, the truth of them was driven home by the enemy in such a manner that it could no longer be disputed. Measures to provide more men were then taken, and the Act of 1916 was amended by the Military Service Act (No. 2), which raised the military age from forty-one to fifty-one years and, by Order in Council, this age could be increased to fifty-six years and the operation of the Bill be extended to Ireland. If these measures had been taken in 1917 the heavy losses we suffered in 1918 might have been fewer, the ultimate drain upon our man - power might therefore have been less than that which actually took place, and the necessity for sending boys to the front under nineteen years of age would have been minimised if not entirely obviated. Exactly why they were not taken at an earlier date is a question that I shall not attempt to answer, since, as already observed, it was for the Government, who had all the facts before them, and not for the General Staff, to determine the man-power effort, both as to time and amount, that the nation could properly be called upon to make. I will merely say that there seemed to be no justifiable grounds for supposing, either in 1917 or before or after that time, that the people would flinch at any demand that might be made upon them, and it will be agreed that of all the Entente countries not one was more eager to do its duty or was more easy to lead than our own.

While on the subject of men I may mention that in the winter of 1916–17 a very desirable change was made in the composition of the infantry training battalions at home, which had heretofore received recruits irrespective of their age, the ages varying between boys of eighteen and men of forty-one years. It was clearly objectionable, both from a training and social point of view, to mix up boys with men old enough to be their fathers, and, moreover, after the spring of 1917 the training battalions comprised the only infantry of the home army, and as they were almost daily deprived of men for drafts for the armies abroad there was and could be no stability in the arrangements for home defence.

The Adjutant-General and I therefore arranged to place all recruits of about the age of eighteen in "Young Soldier Battalions," where they remained for four months whilst undergoing their recruits' course of training. They were then passed on by complete companies of 250 strong to "Graduated Battalions," where they stayed for eight months and so reached the age of nineteen years, at which they were eligible to be sent abroad. The companies were transferred to the Graduated Battalions at intervals of two months, and as these battalions had five companies each they were able to send abroad one company every two months and still have four companies left, the personnel of which had been under training for periods varying between four and twelve months. This was an advantage that greatly simplified home defence duties.

We secured, in course of time, excellent commanding and company officers who took a keen interest in their young charges, and the latter, living in a kind of public school atmosphere, derived far greater benefit, civil as well as military, from their twelve months' training than had been possible under the old system. All officers spoke in the highest terms of the good behaviour of their boys, and I always regard this innovation in the composition of training battalions as one of the best things in which I had a hand during the war. When these lads, many being under nineteen, were sent out to help to stem the disaster on the West Front in the spring of 1918, they more than upheld the reputation they had deservedly earned while in England.

Of the operations in 1917 sufficient reference has already been made to those in Macedonia, Mesopotamia, and East Africa.

On the East Front Germany had matters all her own way. It had been decided in the autumn of 1916 to send to Russia an inter-allied mission in substitution for the ill-fated visit of Lord Kitchener, and the Secretary of State for War proposed that I should accompany it. I explained to the Prime Minister, then Mr. Asquith, that I could not possibly leave my work at the War Office, and he was good enough not to take me away. Further, I had grave doubts whether the mission would, at that late hour, make any material improvement in what was evidently a bad situation, and they proved to be only too well founded. The mission started at the middle of January 1917, and on the 12th of March, shortly after it returned to England, the revolution broke out. On the 15th of March the Czar abdicated, and before the end of the year Russia had concluded an armistice with the enemy preparatory to the settlement of terms of peace.

To what extent Lord Kitchener might have been able to stave off the revolution and keep the Russian armies in the field, had he not been drowned when going to Russia, it would be futile for any one to attempt to say, but there can be no question that he was far more likely to succeed than was the mission which went in his place. He had the insight to appreciate the gravity of the situation ; the prestige and experience to ensure his advice receiving an attentive hearing ; and the Czar and Alexeieff were longing for his assistance. The mission was without most, if not all, of these advantages. Being a mission of many members, it lacked the valuable element of personality ; and it does not seem to have been afforded—whatever it may have sought— the best opportunities whilst in Russia for obtaining reliable information as to the real state of affairs, either at the front or at Petrograd. Alexeieff, who died in 1918, practically of a broken heart, always maintained that the death of Lord Kitchener was the greatest misfortune that ever befell Russia.

In the Egyptian theatre Murray attacked the Turkish main position near Gaza in March and again in April, but this was not destined to fall until a stronger force with a more powerful artillery could be brought against it. The offensive was resumed, with success, at the end of October under the direction of General Allenby, who had taken the place of Murray in June, and following the capture of Beersheba, Gaza, and Jaffa, Jerusalem fell into our hands on the 7th of December. The collapse of Russia having left the whole of the Turks in Asia on our hands, the advance into Palestine had for its main object the thwarting of hostile designs against Mesopotamia, and not the capture of Jerusalem or any other town.

Operations on the West Front were, as stated in the preceding chapter, based on the plan recommended by General Nivelle, which had been accepted by the French and British governments in lieu of the plan proposed at the Chantilly conference held under the presidency of General Joffre. According to it the British armies were to attack from the southern part of their line so as to draw the enemy's reserves in that direction, and then the French armies were to deliver the main attack from the Aisne front with the object of breaking through the trench barrier. A feature of the plan which seemed to have a special attraction for ministers was that, if the main attack did not produce material results within about forty-eight hours, the fighting was to be deliberately stopped so as to prevent a repetition in 1917 of what was regarded as the failure on the Somme in 1916.

The two governments further agreed, at a conference held at Calais on the 26th and 27th of February, to vest supreme control of the operations in General Nivelle, the British Commander-in-Chief to conform to such instructions as General Nivelle might see fit to issue. The proposal to make this innovation came as a complete surprise both to Sir Douglas Haig and myself, as neither of us had heard anything about it before it was put forward on the evening of the 26th. The conference was being held, so we had been given to understand, mainly in regard to another matter—transportation.

Not having been consulted, and having no idea that the nomination of General Nivelle as Allied Commander-in-Chief was contemplated, Sir Douglas and I had had no opportunity of considering what it involved, and our position was the more awkward because General Nivelle had, so he told me, been informed by his government beforehand of what was intended. We were not in favour of the proposal, but as the two governments had apparently made up their minds to adopt it, I concluded that, apart from suggesting certain amendments as to procedure, we could do no more than express our dissent and leave responsibility for the future to the War Cabinet. The bearing of the decision upon the whole question of what is called " unity of command " will be dealt with later.

One of my objections to the decision was that as the operations might have—as in fact they did have—far-reaching consequences, it was not wise to entrust them to a General who, although he had won high distinction at Verdun in 1916, had done so in a comparatively subordinate capacity, and therefore had yet to prove his fitness for so important a post as that of Commander-in-Chief of the combined Franco-British armies.

While the conference was in progress news was received that the Germans were withdrawing from their positions on the Ancre and Somme to the previously-prepared Hindenburg Line. This retreat radically interfered with the plan that Nivelle had designed, and the alterations which necessarily had to be made to it led to delay in its execution. Eventually the British armies attacked from the vicinity of Arras on the 9th of April, and the French armies attacked on the Aisne front a week later. The operations entailed much heavy fighting and did not terminate until the third week of May, and although we gained a great victory at Vimy, the results elsewhere fell far short of the expectations that had been formed by those who were in favour of the plan. Soon afterwards General Nivelle was succeeded in the command of the French armies by General (now Marshal) Pétain.

I do not propose to enter into the controversy which took place in France over what became known as the Nivelle affair, or to discuss the extent to which that General was responsible for the failure to win the decisive victory anticipated. I may say, however, that I had not the slightest faith in his theory that he could, if he desired, break off the battle at the end of forty-eight hours, for once a commander commits his troops he cannot hope to be able suddenly to stop fighting at the moment which best suits his own purpose. The enemy has something, often a great deal, to say in the matter, and, as just mentioned, the fight did in fact go on for weeks. The General Staff at the

War Office, like Haig and his staff, were convinced, as for months past, that before a break-through on the scale contemplated could be accomplished the enemy's resistance must be worn down by preparatory attacks made in great strength, and it was not possible for Nivelle or any one else to forecast how long such attacks would take to produce the required effect.

In fairness to the General it should be stated that, besides his inexperience as Commander-in-Chief, and the interference with his plan caused by the German retirement, he must have been sorely handicapped if, as was afterwards alleged, some of his senior commanders had little or no belief that the plan would succeed. M. Painlevé has told us that at a meeting of French generals held before the operations began, the President of the French Republic being present, General Nivelle asked to resign because of the want of confidence shown towards his plan. I have never been able to understand why he did not insist upon one of two things being done ; either that he should be allowed to resign, or that only those commanders who had absolute trust in his judgment should be allowed to assist him. A man does not require to be a soldier to know that no plan, however good, has much prospect of success if those charged with its execution think that it will end in failure. No one has so heavy a load of anxiety to bear in war as a Commander-in-Chief, who carries in his hands the lives of his men, and there is no greater addition to this load than the knowledge, or suspicion, that he does not possess the confidence both of his subordinates and superiors.

General Pétain accomplished valuable work in pulling together the French armies after their ill-success, and I doubt if any one could have done it better. I had not seen much of him before he took over his new command, but afterwards we frequently met. He was essentially practical, held sound ideas on tactics and strategy, and it was at all times a pleasure to work with him.

He was succeeded as Chief of the French General Staff— a post he had held for about a fortnight only—by General Foch. This General had been in semi-retirement for the previous five months, having been removed in December

1916 from the command of the " Groupe des Armées du Nord "—our next-door neighbours from the time we arrived in Flanders in 1914—and had afterwards held temporary command of the " Groupe des Armées de l'Est " whilst General de Castelnau was away with the inter-allied mission sent to Russia. Before his removal from the command in the north General Foch had been, next to General Joffre, one of the most prominent French leaders, and the omission to make greater use of his talents between December 1916 and May 1917 may seem incomprehensible when it is remembered that he was destined to become the Generalissimo of the allied armies, and to lead them to complete victory from a situation which threatened to involve them in complete defeat. The reader may find an explanation of the omission in my later remarks on the subject of unity of command.

I saw much of General Foch whilst serving in France in 1914–15, and had several conversations with him when visiting France in my capacity as C.I.G.S. In reply to a letter I sent him at the end of 1916 he wrote :

3.1.17.

Mon cher Général—Je vous remercie des sentiments que vous m'exprimez au moment où je quitte le contact immédiat de l'armée Britannique. J'ai pu apprécier toute sa valeur dans les jours difficiles du début de la guerre notamment, comme aussi la droiture et l'énergie qui ont toujours inspiré son commandement, vous en particulier. Si nous avons vaincu, si nous avons d'abord arrêté la formidable invasion, c'est bien à notre union sincère et étroite que nous le devons. L'histoire nous rendra cette justice que jamais Alliés ne travaillèrent ensemble d'un cœur si uni. Vous comprendrez facilement comme ces souvenirs me sont précieux quand ils me reviennent tracés par votre plume. Vous avez aujourd'hui une grande et magnifique armée. Les directions que vous lui donnez sont des plus heureuses. Nous pouvons en toute confiance envisager l'avenir. Je n'en reste pas moins par l'esprit près d'elle, dans le souvenir et dans l'espoir le plus absolu. C'est dans ces sentiments, mon cher général, que je me dis—Tout à vous,   F. Foch.

[Translation.

I thank you for the sentiments you express at the moment when I sever my connection with the British army. I have

THE AUTHOR SAYING GOOD-BYE TO MARSHAL FOCH AT COLOGNE STATION, MAY, 1919.

learned to appreciate its worth, especially in the difficult days at the beginning of the war, as well as the honesty and energy of its commanders and of yourself in particular. If we have succeeded, if we have at the first checked the enemy's formidable invasion, it is entirely due to the sincere and intimate relations that have existed between us. History will do us the justice to say that no allies ever worked together with greater single-mindedness of purpose. You will readily understand that I value these recollections the more, coming as they do from you. You now have a large and magnificent army. The directions you are giving it are perfectly sound. We may look forward to the future with full confidence. Having these thoughts in mind, and with implicit faith, I shall be with your army in spirit no less than before. It is with these feelings, my dear General, that I subscribe myself—Yours always, F. FOCH.]

When he became Chief of the French General Staff in 1917 our relations became still closer, and from first to last I do not remember any appreciable difference of opinion between us with regard to the general lines upon which the war should be prosecuted. He, like myself, held that the only sound policy for the Allies to pursue was to concentrate as far as possible all their strength against the principal enemy, and anything which, without good cause, entailed a departure from this principle he abhorred as much as I did.

He was exceedingly easy and pleasant to work with, this doubtless being due in a great measure to his ability to understand the English temperament. We Allied Generals always found it difficult to appreciate each other's point of view and methods, but I believe that Foch found less difficulty than others, and this advantage must have been very helpful to him when he became Generalissimo. Of his other qualifications for this position it would be unbecoming of me to speak as they are within the knowledge of everybody, and it is no disparagement of them to say that he was fortunate in being allowed, as a result of the gravity of the situation when he assumed command, to make and carry out his plans with a comparatively free hand.

On the 7th of June our 2nd Army won a brilliant victory by the capture of the Messines Ridge—a masterpiece of modern tactics—and this opened the way for the third battle of Ypres, which commenced on the 31st of July and did not terminate until the first week in November. This battle, better known as Passchendaele, was fought for the most part under atrocious conditions of weather ; impassable mud and unfordable craters covered the whole German front ; and no praise could do justice to the sufferings and achievements of the British soldier in this long and terrible struggle. Further to the south we attacked the enemy at Cambrai on the 20th of November, the fighting here being continued until the 7th of December. This action brought the operations on the West Front to a close for the year.

Meanwhile, in the last week of October, the 2nd Italian Army, demoralised by insidious propaganda, had been heavily defeated at Caporetto by the Austrians (reinforced for the first time by some German divisions), and this led to a general retreat to the line of the Piave. The battle commenced on Wednesday the 24th of October, and about two days later, when we first became aware of the extent of the disaster, General Foch and I agreed, with the approval of our Governments, to reinforce the Italians with five divisions each from the West Front. During my visit to Italy the previous March I had discussed with General Cadorna the question of sending troops to his assistance in case of need, and subsequently, working in conjunction with the French and Italian staffs, detailed arrangements were made by my staff for the transport of the reinforcing troops by rail and, as far as possible, for their dispositions and employment on arrival. Consequently no delay was incurred when the need for these troops arose.

The reports we received from Italy regarding the number of German divisions present were of an alarming kind, the number given varying between fifteen and thirty. Judging from our own sources of intelligence, and bearing in mind the strain imposed upon the enemy by our offensive in Flanders, it was impossible to believe that more than seven or eight divisions had been sent. This proved to be correct, and the only two divisions that had been taken from the West Front were at once replaced by two others from the Russian front.

THE AUTHOR, ACCOMPANIED BY AN ITALIAN ARMY COMMANDER, INSPECTING ITALIAN TROOPS.

On Sunday the 28th of October, the news received having
become still more serious, I motored over to Walton Heath
to see the Prime Minister, as soon as I had finished my
morning's work, to suggest to him that I should go to
Italy, ascertain the true state of affairs, and arrange to
give further assistance if it was really required. As our
divisions had been fighting almost continuously since the
previous April they needed time to rest and refit, and I was
averse from sending more than the five if it could be avoided.
The Prime Minister agreed to my going and I left London
early next morning, reaching General Cadorna's headquarters
on the Wednesday. I found him at Treviso, Udine, his
previous headquarters, having been occupied by the enemy
two days before. Having discussed matters with him, and
observed the condition of the retreating troops, I telegraphed
my report to the War Cabinet, and then proceeded to Rome
in order to see the Italian War Minister before returning to
London.

While at Rome I was the guest of Sir Rennell Rodd, the
British ambassador, to whom I am very grateful for the
hospitality Lady Rodd and he were good enough to show
me. On the Saturday evening, just as I was about to start
for the railway station, I received instructions from London
that certain members of the War Cabinet were leaving for
Italy to confer with the French and Italian ministers, and
to consider the question of forming a Supreme War Council.
I was requested to be present, and will deal with the formation of this Council and the whole question of so-called
" unity of command " after making a few observations on
certain plans suggested during 1917 as alternatives to full
concentration of effort on the West Front, and after discussing the general situation as it appeared to the General
Staff at the end of the year.

These alternative plans having been already described
by several public writers, their principal features are
generally well known. The first one put forward was that
proposed early in January for an offensive across the Italian
front, its object being to " knock out " Austria and so
bring down Germany, and British troops from the West
Front, to the extent required, were to be employed. As

far as I could understand, those in favour of this plan argued that our best policy in future would be to attack the enemy not where he was strongest, namely on the West Front, but where he was weakest. I doubt if they sufficiently bore in mind that if it would be to our advantage to " knock out " Austria, Germany would try to prevent her from being knocked out, and a glance at the map of Europe will show that she was far better placed than we were for transferring troops to the Italian front, and therefore could always hope to counter our offensive designs in that direction.

Put in another way, and leaving out of account the dubious conclusion that the defeat of the weak (Austria) would involve the downfall of the strong (Germany), the policy of attacking the weak could only be justified on the assumption that we could in the meantime pin the strong to his present positions, otherwise the attempt to fight the former might merely lead to fighting the latter in another place. As no such assumption could be entertained the proposal was fundamentally unsound.

General Cadorna was entrusted with the duty of working out the details preparatory to a final decision being given, but before he had completed his task the plan had been superseded by the acceptance meanwhile of Nivelle's plan, which entailed the employment of the full strength of our armies on the West Front, and was itself a substitute for the Chantilly plan.

Another plan was that suggested early in October for transferring divisions from the West Front to operate against the Turks from the vicinity of Alexandretta. A project for sending an expedition to this region had first been mooted in December 1914, and there was then something to be said in its favour, but the Dardanelles enterprise began to take shape soon afterwards and for the moment put an end to it. It was revived in the autumn of 1915 when the evacuation of the Dardanelles had to be considered, and as circumstances had meanwhile changed to our disadvantage it was then properly rejected by the General Staff, just before I became C.I.G.S., and was again dropped.

It was still more impracticable in October 1917, for the enemy's communications had been much improved; he was in a position seriously to oppose an attempted landing; and his submarines, of which there were none in the Mediterranean in 1914, were now particularly active. Further, at least six divisions must be sent, requiring for their transport about a million tons of shipping, and the Entente were already at their wits' end to know how to find ships for the thousands of American troops waiting to cross the Atlantic, for maintaining the large forces then employed in eastern theatres, and for meeting their own domestic requirements.

These were, however, but insignificant objections as compared with the very obvious one that the operation could not possibly be carried out in sufficient time to admit of the divisions being brought back by the spring, when a heavy attack on the West Front might have to be met. Instead of sending them on such an absurd errand it was important that they should be given opportunities for rest and training before being called upon to meet the attack with which we were threatened.

Being required to advise upon the project at short notice, I examined it one Sunday morning at a conference held in the War Office, the First Sea Lord, the Deputy First Sea Lord, and representatives of the railway and shipping authorities being present, and our conclusions were such that the proposal had once more to be laid aside. This proved to be fortunate when, a week or two later, it became necessary to assist the Italians by sending divisions from the West Front, and still more so when the German offensive on that front had to be met in March 1918.

Although the Alexandretta plan was abandoned, the theory that the principal enemy could be overthrown by the defeat of a minor one was not yet extinct; and following on Allenby's successes in Palestine at the end of the year it was suggested that he should continue and develop his operations with the object of putting the Turkish armies completely out of the war. The General Staff were unable to regard this plan with any more favour than that accorded to its predecessor, but it found supporters at Versailles, and at the conference held there at the end of January and beginning of February 1918 its adoption was recommended, subject to the West Front being made secure.

A recommendation of this sort was not of much value, since it left unanswered the vital question as to the means required to make and keep the West Front secure, and whether, after providing them, there would remain over sufficient troops for Allenby. To submit for approval a plan depending upon conditions of a purely military character was to throw upon the Supreme War Council—that is, upon civilian ministers—a task which did not come within either its province or its competency to perform. The advocates of the plan were not entitled to have it both ways, and to place themselves in the happy position of the man who can say, " heads I win, tails you lose." It was for them, before submitting their recommendation, definitely to make up their minds as to whether there were sufficient troops for the double purpose of an absolutely reliable defensive in France and a really effective offensive against the Turks, remembering at the same time that the transfer of divisions backwards and forwards between Picardy and Palestine could not be accomplished by a stroke of the pen, but would be a matter of many weeks and much shipping. If the answer was in the affirmative the plan would, to that extent, be justified ; if in the negative, the plan ought to be pronounced impracticable, and in unequivocal terms.

With a large part of their country in German hands, and with the constant arrival of German divisions from the Russian front, it was not to be expected, apart from what may be called mere strategy, that the French would look upon the plan with any marked approval, and after some discussion it was settled that no troops should be taken away from the West Front. Even this compromise was liable to react detrimentally in respect of drafts and other matters, and, what was still more important, it prevented the West Front, where we obviously could not be too strong, from being reinforced by troops that could safely be brought away from Palestine. I therefore strongly advised against it, but it was accepted, and accordingly no troops were withdrawn from Palestine until this was enforced by the enemy's attack in France some six or seven weeks later.

The aim of the General Staff had for long been to replace British infantry in eastern theatres by native infantry from India, and then entrust the Palestine operations to the latter and mounted men, both of whom could be spared from the decisive theatre. The question of raising more native battalions was first taken up in 1916, when Sir Charles Monro became Commander-in-Chief, and, thanks to his co-operation and administrative ability, about a hundred and fifty battalions as well as other units were added to the Indian army, being sent to Palestine or Mesopotamia as soon as ready. Indirectly, therefore, he had a notable share in the success of the Palestine campaign of 1918, for when, in September of that year, the offensive was carried out against Damascus and Aleppo nearly three-fourths of the infantry belonged to these same Indian battalions, the bulk of the British infantry having before that time been hurried off post-haste to the West Front.

As can be imagined, it was a most unpleasant duty to have to oppose plans of operations which ministers wished to see adopted, especially on those occasions—fortunately very rare—when it had to be performed before Allies. The Palestine plan, supported by the Prime Minister, was an instance of this, and immediately after the meeting at Versailles at which the project was discussed I expressed my regret that I had been obliged, in the presence of foreign delegates, to differ from him, and assured him that I had done so with the greatest reluctance, and only because of the risks involved with respect to the situation on the West Front. I represented to him that if I had remained silent the other delegates would naturally have thought that I agreed with the proposal, or at any rate had no particular objection to it ; that my name would appear in the conference proceedings and, in case of future reference, would imply agreement unless my objections were recorded ; and I re-minded him that naval and military officers had been publicly condemned in the past for neglecting to state their opinions on professional questions brought before conferences to which they had been summoned, and therefore that I was placed in the dilemma of having to choose between laying myself open to the same charge, and giving offence to ministers with whom it was essential, in the general interest, that I should work in harmony.

The Prime Minister did not agree with this way of looking at things, and was angry at the course I had taken. He said that as I had already informed him of my objections there was no necessity to repeat them at the conference, and that it was sufficient that he should know them. He then turned away, leaving me wondering why I had been instructed to attend the conference if not for the purpose of giving advice when important military questions were under discussion.

I may explain that I had especially in mind the remarks made regarding the duty of naval and military advisers by the Dardanelles Commission a few months before. For the convenience of the reader I will quote a portion of them :

We also think that the naval advisers should have expressed their views to the (War) Council, whether asked or not, if they considered that the project which the Council was about to adopt was impracticable from a naval point of view.

. . . .

We are unable to concur in the view set forth by Lord Fisher that it was his duty, if he differed from the Chief of his Department, to maintain silence at the Council or to resign. We think that the adoption of any such principle generally would impair the efficiency of the public service.

The following also appears in the report :

Mr. Lloyd George did not concur in the description given by Lord Fisher of the position he occupied in the War Council. On being asked the question, " If the experts present did not express dissent, did you assume that they assented to what was done ? " he replied, " Certainly."

Several other ministers gave similar evidence on this point, the conclusion drawn from it by the Commissioners being that :

The Chairman and ministerial members of the War Council looked to the naval and military experts to express their opinions if they dissented from the views put forward by the heads of their respective departments.

To revert to the recurring desire to start new plans or change old ones, it has to be remembered that the same thing has happened in other wars, particularly in those of long duration. It was the more likely to be a feature of the Great War because the latter was of such dimensions as to affect every part of the national life, and military operations thereby passed to an unprecedented extent under the control of ministers—that is, of men untrained in either the theory or practice of war. A further inducement to make changes of plan was the comparative ease with which, in appearance, they could be arranged owing to the greater facilities afforded by modern means of communication.

It is not my purpose to enlarge upon the evils which accompany the tendency to change from one plan to another —at bewilderingly short intervals and without sufficient military reason—beyond observing that it has an unsettling effect on the troops, and monopolises much of the time of commanders and their staffs which ought to be given to other matters. At a guess I would say that in 1917 at least twenty per cent of the time of the General Staff at the War Office was occupied in explaining, either verbally or in writing, that the alternative projects put forward were either strategically unsound or were wholly impracticable.

The General Staff must expect to have the same experience in future wars, and they must try neither to despair nor to become impatient, but they will not find these precepts easy to practise, and for myself I must confess to frequent failures. Much will depend on the personality of ministers and of their responsible professional advisers, and whether the former have sufficient confidence in the latter to accept their opinion without asking for it to be substantiated in every detail by lengthy memoranda and tabulated statements, or by the test of police court cross-examination and a bout in dialectics.

I say " responsible " advisers because advice given by others, although they may be professionals, is often without value and may be positively mischievous. Such advice poses as being expert, whereas the person who gives it can seldom possess the information on which to base a reliable opinion, and as he is not responsible for the execution of his proposals his outlook is quite different from that of the person who has the responsibility. I frequently told ministers that if I were not C.I.G.S. I could produce half-a-dozen different plans for winning the war, quickly and at small cost, but as it was I had but one plan, and that a hard one to carry out—the defeat of the German armies on the West Front.

The task of keeping the strategical direction of the war on right lines became harder as the end of 1917 approached. For more than three years we had endured terrible sacrifices without victory being either achieved or coming clearly within sight, the German barrier was still intact, Russia had made terms with the enemy, Italy had been severely defeated, and for these and other reasons misgivings arose in the minds of some people as to whether we could after all hope to win through.

I do not refer to those who were accused—sometimes quite unjustly—of being pacifists, but to those who, in 1917 as in 1916, could see only their own difficulties and losses, and apparently would never be prepared to admit that the enemy had suffered from either unless and until he wrote them a letter to that effect. This attitude of mind was not only stupid but grossly unfair to our men and their leaders. The British General Staff in France have since had the satisfaction of finding their views regarding the state of German morale in 1917 confirmed by Ludendorff, who has said that " The (German) troops had borne the continuous defensive with extreme difficulty. Skulkers were already numerous. They reappeared as soon as the battle was over, and it had become quite common for divisions which came out of action with desperately low effectives to be considerably stronger after only a few days. Against the weight of the enemy's material the troops no longer displayed their old stubbornness ; they thought with horror of fresh defensive battles and longed for the war of movement. . . . There had been incidents, too, which indicated that their cohesion was no longer the same."

Although there could at the time be no certainty as to the actual amount of progress made in wearing down the enemy's power of resistance, we knew enough to feel satisfied that there was no occasion for either gloom or despair provided we were prepared to face the music. It was with the object of preventing despondency from arising in the public mind that as early as the month of July I took advantage of a speech I had been asked to make to point out that " There comes a time in every war when each side has to put forward its greatest effort, when the strain becomes greater every day, and when a little extra effort may suffice to turn the scale. That time has come now, and in this war as in all wars victory will incline to that side which best retains its cohesion and confidence."

There were other people who, with more justification than the pessimists I have mentioned, doubted if we could decisively win as early as 1918, and argued that we ought not to make the attempt until 1919, by which time the output of tanks, aeroplanes, and other mechanical means of warfare would be enormously increased, and America would be able to exert her full strength.

Questions of the above nature had several times to be dealt with by the General Staff towards the end of 1917, and although we were able to dispose of those which threw doubt upon the ability of the Entente ultimately to emerge victorious—always provided that the armies were not starved for men—it was not so easy to advise on the best military policy to be followed in the year 1918—that is, as to whether a supreme effort to win should be made then or should be deferred till the following year.

Had we been engaged in a war in which the British army alone were fighting a single belligerent, and in which considerations other than these of a purely military character were of little or no account, a definite opinion could have been formed with comparative ease. But nothing resembled these conditions in a world war of some twenty or more nations, and there were many factors about which we could not possibly make a reliable forecast, such as the political, social, and economic situation and the general staying power of the different members of the Entente, the effect of submarine warfare, the naval and shipping position, and food production. I used to estimate that of the total effort of which the nation was capable only twenty-five per cent

Y

was purely military, the remaining seventy-five per cent being of a non-military nature; and when asked sometimes what our chances of winning were, I would reply: "Why ask me, with my twenty-five per cent? Ask those who manipulate the seventy-five."

But certain elements stood out quite clearly, one of the most comforting being the continued staunchness of the men and women of the Empire, who only asked of their leaders to tell them, without hesitation, what they were required to do in order to win, and this being so there was no insuperable difficulty in reaching a conclusion which would be sufficiently reliable for all practical purposes.

The total collapse of Russia, the defeat of the Italians, the depletion of the French reserves of man-power, the unsatisfactory position in regard to drafts for our own armies, and the probability that, owing to the alleged scarcity of sea-transport, America would not have a really large force in Europe before the autumn of 1918, all pointed to the necessity of adopting a defensive policy in that year, or at any rate for the greater part of it. This did not mean, as some seemed to think, that in the meantime we should not be called upon to fight, or that we could do just as much or as little fighting as we chose. On the contrary it meant that, as the initiative would rest with the enemy, he and not we would dictate the amount of fighting to be done. If a waiting policy on the West Front would be of advantage to us, obviously it would be to the disadvantage of the enemy, who might therefore be trusted to try and force a decision as quickly as possible, and the arrival of six divisions from the Russian front in November and nineteen in December was a sufficient indication that this was his intention.

Again, his economic conditions were known to be worse than those of the Entente, and his recent peace proposals showed that he felt compelled to bring the war to an end with the least delay. Further, the strain to which his troops had been subjected by our persistent attacks on the West Front would be aggravated by cold and want during the coming winter, and might well reach breaking point before the expiration of 1918 if those attacks were resumed and as relentlessly pushed home as in the previous year.

Assuming that it was to the enemy's interest to win such a success before we could further increase our resources, and before America could effectively intervene, as would bring the war to an end—at least for the time being—the next question was, where would he make his main attack ? He had three objectives, the Channel coast, Paris, and Italy, and of these the first and third could hardly be regarded as feasible before the month of May on account of climatic conditions. This delay would not suit the enemy's purpose. The second objective was feasible at almost any season, and the attack could be aimed at the point of junction between the British and French armies, which, as everybody knows, is the danger point.

Macedonia might perhaps be regarded as a fourth objective, but the Bulgarians had apparently no intention of doing any more fighting if they could help it ; the country was difficult and the communications bad ; and in any case a victory here could not be relied upon to cause the Entente to come to terms. Ludendorff had hitherto not seemed to agree with the views of Falkenhayn, who was always a " westerner " of the most pronounced type, and has declared that " No decision in the east, even though it were as thorough as it was possible to imagine, could spare us from fighting to a conclusion in the west." But by the end of 1917, with the experiences of 1916 and 1917 behind him, it was to be supposed that even Ludendorff, notwithstanding his eastern tendencies, would realise that he could never win until he had gained a complete victory in the west, and that the sooner he made the attempt the greater would be his chance of winning. As a matter of fact he did realise it, though at the time we could only guess that he might, for he has admitted that " The condition of our Allies and of our army all called for an offensive that would bring about an early decision. This was only possible on the western front. All that had gone before was only a means to the one end of creating a situation that would make it a feasible operation. . . . I set aside all idea of attacking in Macedonia or Italy. All that mattered was to get together enough troops for an attack in the west."

After a long and careful review of the whole situation

the conclusions I reached towards the end of 1917 were that the campaign of 1919 might never come ; that although there were strong reasons why we should defer offensive action on the West Front in 1918 until the Americans arrived in full strength, we might, quite apart from the question of whether we should or should not deliberately aim at obtaining a decision that year, be compelled by the enemy, in self-defence alone, to fight our hardest ; that he might commence his attack at any time from February onwards, according to the rate at which he could bring over his surplus divisions from Russia ; and, finally, that we must be prepared to endure in 1918 a greater strain than any we had yet undergone. The corollary of these conclusions was that we should at once send to the West Front every man, gun, and aeroplane we could lay hands on, and make available every ship we could for helping the Americans to bring over their divisions as quickly as possible. *If this were done* we might confidently hope to break up the enemy's offensive, while the gradually increasing strength of the American troops might enable us to seek and obtain a final decision before the year expired.

Shipping and men were, as for months past, the cardinal factors, and we used to calculate that, to maintain a given number of men in Egypt or Salonika, the amount of shipping required was some six times greater than that required to maintain the same number on the West Front. There were towards the end of 1917 probably no fewer than 1,200,000 men in distant theatres, who, be it noted, were mainly fighting Turks and Bulgars and not Germans, and although a large proportion of them were native troops and therefore not altogether suitable for employment in France, they contained a considerable number of British troops who could well be spared without incurring any risk, as our successes in Palestine and Mesopotamia had removed all danger to Egypt, Persia, and India. By reducing our forces in these theatres to a defensive minimum we would set free not only more troops for the West Front but also more shipping for the Americans. As already shown, this was not done.

Towards the end of 1916 the enemy had made a flashy

attempt to score points by overrunning Rumania, but in the west, according to Ludendorff, he had been " fought to a standstill." Fortunately for him, at this particular moment Joffre was superseded, Foch shelved, and Nivelle's plan adopted in place of that proposed at the Chantilly conference. The result of this change of plan was that when the enemy withdrew in February 1917 to the Hindenburg Line he got away without serious molestation, broke up Nivelle's plan to some extent, and, while it was being reconstructed, gained time for that rest and recuperation which his troops so sorely needed. Instead of enjoying this advantage he would have had to submit to further punishment if the Chantilly plan had held good, as the direction it gave to the projected offensive would not have been so greatly interfered with as was the case with the operations which Nivelle had designed. The Russian revolution brought the enemy further relief from his difficulties ; he derived some moral and material advantage from his unrestricted submarine warfare ; and in the month of October he repeated his Rumanian adventure in Italy with considerable success.

On the other hand his troops on the West Front had suffered very heavily, both in numbers and morale, from the determined attacks to which they were subjected throughout the year, and this, coupled with the powerful addition to the Entente strength afforded by the entry of America into the war, would undoubtedly have made his position little, if any, less serious at the end of 1917 than it was at the end of 1916 had not so many of our troops been locked up in secondary theatres, and had not our divisions been so reduced in strength owing to the lack of drafts.

The situation being what it was, the armies on the West Front were once again unable to reap the fruits of their efforts, and it was even conceivable that, in warding off the attack which threatened them, they might become so depleted and exhausted as to find it very difficult to hold on until sufficient American troops arrived to redress the balance, while at the best it was to be feared that they would lose heavily in men and guns. The year therefore closed with considerable anxiety as to the future, and this was increased in January by the arrival of more German divisions from Russia.

With regard to shipping, I may add that the Admiralty Staff, whose views on the question of strategy coincided with those of the General Staff, had for long wished to cut down the tonnage employed in distant waters, because of the difficulty of finding naval escorts to protect the transports against the enemy's submarines, especially after it became necessary to help in safeguarding the passage of American troops across the Atlantic.

It was obvious from the day that America declared war, the 6th April, that the rate at which she could make her assistance felt would be governed by sea-transport, and in the numerous consultations I had with General Pershing, General Bliss, and other American representatives between the summer of 1917 and February 1918, it was always found that the troops which could be made ready for despatch by a certain date were much in excess of the tonnage said to be procurable. These two generals displayed every desire to expedite the arrival of their troops, and were prepared to meet the British General Staff more than half-way in any suggestion put forward which might conduce to that end, but of course nothing substantial could be accomplished unless the requisite shipping was forthcoming.

The question was constantly discussed, but no satisfactory decision was reached. Everybody was short of shipping, and everybody wished to use for themselves what they had or could borrow from others. The General Staff, having no jurisdiction over the matter and no certain knowledge of it, could do no more than advise that the operations in the distant theatres should be so restricted as to ensure the greatest economy in shipping, and continue to emphasise the importance of getting the American troops into France. It rested with the Government to say, on the advice of the shipping and other departments, what amount of tonnage could be provided for the latter purpose. The problem was beset with many difficulties, but I cannot help thinking that all the countries concerned could have done more in 1917 to solve it than they did, seeing what was accomplished in the spring of 1918 under pressure of the German offensive. Exactly by what means transports were then found to convey the large number of troops brought over with such astonishing rapidity I do not know, as I had ceased to be C.I.G.S., but the tonnage provided was far in excess of the amount previously said to be procurable.

I now come to the question of "unity of command," and it is no exaggeration to say at once that the measures taken under its name at the well-known Rapallo and Versailles conferences resulted not in unifying the command of the armies but in dividing it, thus making it more complicated than before.

As early as the autumn of 1915 various proposals were put forward, both by ministers and soldiers, for setting up some form of Allied body charged with ensuring more unified action and whole-hearted co-operation, but for reasons unknown to me they failed to materialise. Some progress was made, however, in the required direction in that conferences between the Allied ministers and Allied military authorities took place much more frequently during 1916 than they had previously done.

In February 1917, as already told, Nivelle was given command of the Franco-British armies engaged in the operations designed by him in lieu of those recommended at the Chantilly conference in November 1916, but this merely placed the commander of one army in temporary command of another for a particular purpose, and did nothing to ensure permanent co-ordination and direction of the Entente operations in general.

Nivelle's failure to provide the expected victory checked for the time any further desire on the part of ministers to try new systems of command, and nothing more was heard of the matter for some months so far as they were concerned. The Allied military authorities, however, discussed it in the summer of 1917, when considering the effect of the Russian collapse and the consequent probability that a defensive rôle would be imposed upon us pending the arrival of the Americans, and their deliberations favoured the establishment of an inter-allied staff, to be located at Paris, but again nothing came of the idea.

The question next came up at the Rapallo conference in November, after the Italian reverse, and it was then decided to form a " Supreme War Council " consisting of the Prime Minister and one other minister of each of the Great Powers. Each of these Powers was to delegate a permanent military representative as " technical adviser " to the Council. These officers were to have no executive power, but to act only in an advisory capacity. It was arranged that the Council should have its permanent head-quarters at Versailles, though its meetings would not necessarily always be held there.

The establishment of the Council filled a much-felt want, for it enabled ministers to meet regularly, helped to secure co-ordination of national policies, the proceedings could be properly recorded by the permanent secretariat, and in many ways it furthered the methodical despatch of business. But it should be noted that, although the object of setting up the Council was to ensure the better co-ordination of *military* action, the members of the Council were ministers, and therefore it was a political and not a military body. Consequently, it did nothing to improve the system of *military* command, while in one respect it struck deeply at the root principle of all military organisation, in that the " technical advisers " were empowered to advise the Council, *i.e.* their ministers, independently of their General Staffs.

It is the right of a government to select its own professional advisers and to change them as often as it pleases, but it ought not to appoint independent advisers in addition, for such a proceeding must produce divided responsibility, delay, friction, and confusion. No business, military or other, could be smoothly and efficiently conducted if the board of directors employed two separate managers to advise them on the work of one and the same department, more especially if one of the managers were responsible for carrying out the instructions of the board, while the other had no such responsibility.

In order to avoid all risks in this respect the French nominated as their representative General Weygand, the deputy of their Chief of the General Staff ; the Italians were represented by an officer deputed by General Cadorna, their

Chief of the General Staff ; and the Americans nominated their Chief of the Staff, General Bliss. The British representative, appointed by the War Cabinet, was alone given a position not under the Chief of the General Staff of the army to which he belonged.

It seems clear that, in setting up the Council, the real object of ministers was not so much to provide effective unity of military command as to acquire for themselves a greater control over the military chiefs. That there was no intention of unifying the command by the appointment of an Allied Commander-in-Chief seems equally evident, not only from the constitution of the Council itself, but also from the fact that a few days later the Prime Minister stated in the House of Commons that he was " utterly opposed " to the appointment of a Generalissimo, as it " would produce real friction and might create prejudice not merely between the armies but between the nations and governments."

Irrespective of what the Prime Minister may or may not have had in his mind when using these words, I may point out that, before agreeing to the appointment of a Generalissimo, it was essential that the Allied ministers should be agreed amongst themselves as to the policy they wished to see carried out, since without " unity " of policy the establishment of so-called " unity " of command might lead to the operations being conducted in the interests of one ally rather than of the others, and so defeat its own ends. Whether these considerations had any influence on the Rapallo decision I do not know, nor shall I discuss the extent to which unity of policy existed.

The creation of a properly constituted High Command became a matter of increased importance in January 1918, as it was imperative that strong strategical reserves should be available for use when and where required to deal with the expected German attack, and to ensure this the intervention of some authority superior to the French and British Commanders-in-Chief was necessary. For example, the British and French fronts might be attacked simultaneously, in which case it might be advisable to give ground on one front in order to furnish additional troops for a counter-stroke on the other. Or one front alone might at first be attacked and be in need of help, while the Commander-in-Chief of the other might be expecting an equally heavy attack to be made upon himself later, and therefore not feel justified in sending assistance to his colleague. In circumstances such as these, it would only be natural that the two Commanders-in-Chief should consider themselves bound both by their duty to their governments and their troops to take a local rather than a general view of the situation. Other cases might be quoted—such as the despatch of further reinforcements to Italy—in which some superior authority ought to step in and, having assessed the relative importance of the different fronts, issue such instructions to the Commanders-in-Chief as would best further the success of the operations in general.

In my opinion it was ridiculous to think that control over the strategical reserves could be separated from control over the operations as a whole, and therefore, failing the appointment of a Generalissimo—to which the Prime Minister had told parliament he was opposed—the duty must be performed jointly by the Chiefs of the General Staff, the responsible executive officers of the Governments. I communicated these views in a memorandum I sent to the Prime Minister on the 30th of January while attending the Versailles conference previously mentioned. They were concurred in by Sir Douglas Haig and Generals Foch and Pétain at a meeting we held next day, and arrangements for putting them into practice, including the formation of an Allied Staff, were discussed by General Foch and myself.

On the 1st of February the subject was considered by the Supreme War Council, and it was then suggested that the duty in question should be vested in the " technical advisers " of the Council. No decision was reached, and as it was important that the matter should be put on a sound footing, I sent to the Prime Minister a second memorandum in which I again advocated the principle of assigning the duty to the Chiefs of the General Staff. When the Council met on the following day, however, it was decided to adopt the alternative system, and the technical advisers thus became an " Executive Committee," with General Foch as president. The committee was empowered to determine the strength, dispositions, and employment of the strategical reserves, and to issue orders thereon to the Commanders-in-Chief. In short, it was made to constitute the High Command of the Allied armies.

I took little or no part in the discussion at this second meeting, as it did not seem either appropriate or desirable for me to intervene. The proposal to utilise the technical advisers in the manner indicated had emanated from ministers themselves ; my impression was that they had made up their minds to adopt it ; I had already recommended a system of a totally different nature ; and, moreover, the selection of officers to exercise the powers of High Command rested with the Council and not with the Generals. I also knew that the Prime Minister was strongly in favour of the proposal, and I remembered that, as stated earlier in the chapter when referring to the Palestine operations, he had only the day before resented my expressing opinions in front of the Council that were at variance with his own when, as in this case, I had already made them known to him.

I record these few explanatory details of my share in the proceedings so as to amplify the statement made by the Prime Minister in the House of Commons on the 19th of February 1918 when he was describing what had passed at the conference. The statement, which I read with some surprise, was :

Everybody was free to express his opinion, not merely ministers but generals. The generals were just as free to express their opinions as the ministers, and as a matter of fact Sir Douglas Haig did call attention to what we admitted was a weak point in the proposal. I think he called attention to two points, and we promised to put them right, and some of the time we occupied was time occupied in adjusting the arrangements arrived at at Versailles to the criticisms of Sir Douglas Haig. They were points in regard to the army and the Army Council, and constitutional points, not points that went to the root of the proposal itself. I want the House again, at the expense of repeating myself, to recollect that this passed the Versailles Council without a single dissentient voice as far as all those who were present are concerned, and as far as I know it was completely accepted by every military representative present.

The decision to set up the Executive Committee was a proof that ministers were as strongly opposed to having an Allied Commander-in-Chief as they had been at Rapallo; and it must be remembered that, although from a military standpoint there was much to be said for a Generalissimo, there was, besides the question of unity of policy, a further important matter that required attention—namely, the placing of troops under a foreign officer having no responsibility to the parliament of the nation to which they belonged. Had there been any outstanding General who would satisfy all the countries concerned this objection would have counted for much less, but no such General was forthcoming.

There is no reason to suppose, however, that these considerations had any bearing upon the decision, which may more correctly be attributed to a desire on the part of ministers to increase their control over military affairs. This desire had been manifest for months past, and the new arrangement promised to provide the means for achieving it, since ministers may have thought that a committee of their own Council would be more amenable to their influence than would either a Generalissimo or the Chiefs of the General Staff.

In short, no minister, with the possible exception of M. Clemenceau, seemed at this period to have the slightest wish to appoint a Generalissimo; so far as I know the appointment was never discussed by them; and if it had been proposed it would probably have been rejected on the plea that there was no General fit to hold the post. Sir John French, Generals Joffre and Nivelle, and General Cadorna, had all been superseded in the chief command of their respective armies; Sir Douglas Haig had been made subordinate to General Nivelle; and even General Foch had been removed from the command of the French armies of the north and afterwards employed on less important duty. Throughout my time as C.I.G.S., not one of the principal military leaders, as far as I could see, was regarded by ministers as a sufficiently capable commander to whom the supreme command of the Allied armies might confidently be entrusted, while on the other hand I can recall more than one instance of their being considered mediocre and incompetent. I may add here that, throughout the war, there was an undue tendency to assess the capacity of senior commanders by results alone, in disregard of the fact that in no sphere is accident so active as in war ; that Generals, even good ones, are as liable as other people to make mistakes ; and that the extent of their success is largely governed by the ability and nerves of their subordinates.

The system of forming committees and councils for the purpose of commanding armies in the field is historically notorious for giving miserable and mischievous results. The Executive Committee was unlikely to prove any less harmful, for it had in it two flaws that were particularly dangerous. First, the proper handling of the strategical reserves called for quick decisions and complete knowledge of the situation, and this could not possibly be expected from a body which would first have to adjust the conflicting views of the Commanders-in-Chief as to the strength and intentions of the enemy, the liability of the different fronts to attack, and their relative importance.   Secondly, the Commanders-in-Chief would receive orders from two independent sources, their respective Chiefs of the General Staff and the committee, and this must obviously lead to confusion.   The only remedy, and that but a partial one, for these defects was that the members of the committee should be either the Chiefs of the General Staff themselves, or the deputies of those officers, and this was realised by Italy, France, and America.

The Italian army being commanded by the King in person, the Italian representative was automatically in the position of a deputy.   America was represented by her Chief of Staff ; while, as just mentioned, General Foch, the French Chief of the General Staff, was appointed president of the committee.   Hence these three countries were secured against the dangers attaching to duality of advice and executive command.

I advised the Secretary of State for War, Lord Derby, on my return from Versailles to London, that we ought to follow the example of France and America and make the C.I.G.S. our representative on the committee ; and that as he could not always be at Versailles he should be permanently represented by a deputy to act for him in case of urgency. Only by this means could confusion and complication in the direction of the operations be prevented. The other military members of the Army Council shared this opinion, and during the first week of February frequent communications on the subject passed between the Council and the War Cabinet.

The matter remained in this position on the 7th of February, when I went to Eastbourne for a few days in order to shake off the effects of a bad cold. Three days later, having heard unofficially that there had been further developments, I returned to London and, on the 11th, was informed by Lord Derby that, during my absence, an arrangement as to the procedure to be followed had been come to by him and the Prime Minister, to which Sir Douglas Haig, called to London, had assented. In a conversation I subsequently had with the latter I did not gather that he had given an unqualified assent, but in any case it was not a matter to which his assent need necessarily have been sought.

The arrangement made was, that while the C.I.G.S. should continue to be the supreme military adviser of the Government, the military representative at Versailles should " be absolutely free and unfettered " in the advice he gave as a member of the Executive Committee ; that he should be an Army Councillor (thus enabling him to issue orders to the Commander-in-Chief) ; and that I should be succeeded as C.I.G.S. by Sir Henry Wilson, whose place I would take on the Executive Committee. (This General had, I learnt, been recalled from Versailles to London the day after I went to Eastbourne.)

I was not surprised, nor will the reader be, at the decision to remove me from the War Office, for, as already shown, I had been unable to agree with some of the strategical plans the Prime Minister wished to see adopted, and my opposition to the Palestine plan a few days before was the culminating point of previous refusals to lend my authority and name to acts which, I was convinced, were unsound and a danger to the Empire. This incident, coupled with my warnings as to the consequences likely to ensue from the armies on the West Front not being kept up to strength, doubtless decided the Prime Minister to try another C.I.G.S. whose strategical views might be more in conformity with his own, and who could devise a way of winning the war without the additional men for whom I had asked. Further, Lord Derby had already told me in the course of conversation that the Prime Minister could not " get on " with me. After that there was nothing more to be said, and I said nothing except to ask when it was desired that I should hand over my duties to my successor.

The question of taking up the new post at Versailles was on a different plane. On the principle that a soldier should obey orders, put personal considerations aside, and do the best for his country wherever he may be sent, my first impulse was to accept the post, but after careful reflection I resolved that I could be no party to a system which established a dual authority for the military direction of the war. Having made up my mind, I told Lord Derby that, whilst anxious to do everything in my power to serve His Majesty's Government and to help to retrieve the situation in which the country was placed, I felt that to undertake a duty on the pretence of giving assistance when convinced that I could not possibly give it would be of no benefit to ministers and would bring disgrace upon myself.

In the conversations which took place during the next two days Lord Derby stated that he was most desirous and always had been that I should remain C.I.G.S., and he suggested a procedure which would allow me to remain, and at the same time would satisfactorily adjust the relations between myself and our representative on the Executive Committee. This procedure I was able to accept as it stood, but when he referred it to the War Cabinet for approval the only result was that, whilst my continuance as C.I.G.S. was not disapproved, the original arrangement as to the status of our representative at Versailles remained unaltered. This being the only point in dispute, the proposed *modus operandi* came to nothing.

The following day, the 14th, I personally stated the whole case afresh to the War Cabinet. This also came to nothing, and the post of C.I.G.S. was then offered to Sir

Herbert Plumer, notwithstanding that Sir Henry Wilson had been nominated a week earlier. On the 16th, Sir Herbert Plumer having the day before declined the offer (a fact of which I had not been informed), the Prime Minister personally asked me to acquiesce in the original arrangement. I took an hour to think the matter over once again, and then sent him a written reply to the effect that I could not go back on what I had already said.

The same evening the Press Bureau issued a notice that the Government had accepted my resignation as C.I.G.S. Strictly speaking, this was not correct. I had not resigned for I was not in a position to do so, having been told on the 11th that I was to leave the War Office.

I must apologise to the reader for describing in such detail this particular phase of my military life, for it can be of little interest to any one except myself. My excuse is that the circumstances were not fully represented to the general public at the time, and I wish to prove to those whose good opinion I value that there was no ground for the report circulated that I was opposed to making a change in the system of command. On the contrary, I submitted proposals for such a change, while, as already explained, the appointment of a Generalissimo—made later under stress of the German attack—was not yet in the picture as a practical proposition, either in the person of General Foch or of any other General. My opposition referred solely to the manner in which the system adopted by the Supreme War Council was to be carried out, and the procedure I suggested was the same as that put into practice by France and America.

I certainly had no faith in the system, as I was convinced that effective military command could not be exercised by a body working as a " committee " of a " council," but, wishing to make the best of it, I was anxious that its dangers should not be aggravated by our having, unlike the other Powers, a representative who would be independent of his General Staff. This was the only point at issue, and is a sufficient answer to the statement that I had adopted an intolerable attitude in refusing either to go to Versailles or to remain in London as C.I.G.S. Whether

I stayed in London or went to Versailles could make no difference to the pernicious arrangement which created two separate military advisers and executive officers. Moreover, it was plain from what had recently passed that, wherever I might be, my advice would not be accepted unless it happened to be of the desired kind, and if that were so the period of my usefulness had evidently come to an end.

Had I seen a practicable and honourable way of filling either post I should certainly have taken it, for I naturally did not wish to forfeit the opportunity of finishing the war as C.I.G.S., or in some other responsible position, while by declining both posts I might find myself out of active employment altogether, and would thereby inflict hardship upon my family by the financial loss incurred. Seeing no such way I determined to do what any average Britisher in my place would have done—act according to my convictions be the consequences what they might.

Elsewhere I have stated that, as a result of the enemy's last bid for supremacy in the spring of 1918, British reinforcements were hurriedly despatched to the West Front from the eastern theatres, divisions and brigades thus turning up of whose existence the troops in France had never before heard ; that the scope of the Military Service Act of 1916 was enlarged so as to produce more recruits ; and that much more shipping was provided for the transport of the American armies. In order to complete the story, and in justice to the British armies on the West Front, I should add that while these belated measures were being carried out, the critical situation created by the omission to take them earlier was saved, as often before in our history, only by the courage and tenacity of the regimental officers and men, who, fighting steadfastly on till help arrived, helped to convert into complete victory the greatest defeat the British army has ever suffered.

As to the " Executive Committee," it broke down, as an organ of command, within a few weeks of its constitution. Early in March Sir Douglas Haig reported that he was unable to furnish the troops which the committee desired to have under its orders as part of the strategical reserve,

z

and thereupon its functions of command ended, though it nominally remained in existence till the month of May.

On the 18th of February I left the War Office for the fourth and last time, having first telegraphed my thanks to Monro and the other Commanders - in - Chief for the readiness with which they had always met my wishes and helped to make the military machine run easily.

My dealings with the Prime Ministers and other ministers of the Overseas Dominions who visited England from time to time, and with the High Commissioners and General Officers of the Overseas Forces, were equally happy, and I was greatly indebted to these gentlemen for the whole-hearted manner in which they co-operated with the Imperial General Staff, so far as the conditions of their respective countries would permit. It had been thought before 1914 that the Dominions ought specifically to state what number of troops they would contribute in the event of a great war, and within what period of time these troops would be forthcoming, so that definite plans could be prepared. To the best of my recollection no such statement was made, and we could not expect that it would be, for so long as there is no Imperial body charged with the control of Imperial policy there can be no complete co-ordination of the Imperial Forces.

I think I may say that the relations between the General Staff and the administrative staffs and services of the War Office were also mutually helpful, including the oft-abused Finance Branch, of which the head was Mr. (now Lord) Forster, his principal assistant being Sir Charles Harris. I would wish it to be understood that the reason I have omitted to mention more fully the work of the administrative officers is only because they were not under my orders, and not because I do not recognise that all General Staff plans must ultimately depend for success upon the assistance of these officers. I relied in a special measure upon the advice of Sir Sam Fay and Sir Guy Granet, of the Great Central and Midland Railways respectively, who placed their services at the disposal of the War Office during the war. They were in charge of the arrangements for the conveyance by rail, river, and sea of all men, supplies, stores, etc., for all theatres, and to them is due a share of the credit for the improvement of the Tigris line of communication from Basra to Baghdad, and for the provision of an efficient railway service from Egypt through the Sinai Peninsula to Palestine.

As regards the officers of the General Staff itself, all I need say is that, without exception, they had given me loyal and able assistance during the arduous times of the two preceding years. Lucas had been, as always, a devoted comrade, displaying ability and initiative much above the ordinary, and having but one object in life—to serve me to the utmost of his power. I can never adequately repay him. He and my civilian private secretary, Brooke, another faithful helper, had often kept me straight on matters of a personal nature—or had tried to do so—and saved me from numerous worries about which I was sometimes never even allowed to hear.

I must also acknowledge the generosity shown by many people outside the War Office, who, in their desire to lighten my cares, invited me to spend Sunday at their country houses. I always had far more of these invitations than I could possibly accept, often from people whom I had not before known, but occasionally I was able to take advantage of them, coming back to work on the Sunday evening greatly refreshed in mind and body. This form of hospitality was many times accorded to me at Witley Park, the country residence of Lord and Lady Pirrie, and thirty-five miles from London.

When I first made the acquaintance of Lord Pirrie, in 1916, he flattered me by saying that a few years before he had been interested in reading a farewell address I gave to a party of officers when they were leaving the Staff College. My remarks referred, amongst other things, to the relations which ought to exist between superiors and subordinates and *vice versa*, the importance of sound administration, and other matters of a like nature. Apparently he felt that the principles which I had impressed upon my officers were equally applicable to his own army of workers, and he accordingly brought them to the notice of his staff.

Lord Pirrie's achievements in the shipbuilding industry are a striking example of what can be accomplished by a man who takes the long view, has the courage to act upon it, and realises the value of good organisation. It is a matter of regret, I have always thought, that his unique experience was not utilised and his advice sought at a much earlier period of the war than they were. If they had been, many matters connected with the building and repairing of ships might not have got into the unsatisfactory condition they were in when, in 1918, he was asked to remedy them as Controller-General of Merchant Shipbuilding.

I was also fortunate while at the War Office in regard to a residence in London. Early in the summer of 1916 Sir George and Lady Fowke gave me the use of their house in South Street, and in November of that year the King graciously placed York House, St. James's Palace, at my disposal for the duration of the war, a privilege which added greatly to my personal convenience. Although I ceased to be C.I.G.S. nine months before the war ended, His Majesty allowed me to remain at York House until February 1919, when it was put into the hands of the decorators preparatory to becoming the residence of the Prince of Wales.

I enjoyed, too, the hospitality of the Naval and Military, Cavalry, Bath, Savage, and Ranelagh clubs in London, and the New Club at Brighton, of which I was made an honorary member in each case, and I was admitted, *honoris causa*, into the " Worshipful Guild and Fraternity " of the Cloth-workers Company of the City of London.

In a multitude of different ways I discovered whilst C.I.G.S. that there were far more generous-minded and appreciative people in the world than I had supposed, and I had further proofs of this when it was announced that I had left the War Office. A member of the House of Lords, then unknown to me except by name, sent a pencilled note from his sick-bed in London asking me to take my family to his house in the country and stay there as long as I wished. Another and highly valued friend, who must also be nameless, offered a cheque with which to provide myself with a home in place of York House, which he thought

I would at once be required to vacate. Letters arrived daily by the score from persons of all classes, and although they referred to my past services in much too flattering terms, the sincerity of motive which had prompted them was unquestionable, and I was gratified as well as surprised to find that I had won the esteem of so many of my fellow-countrymen.

These observations should perhaps be qualified in the case of one of the letters, which afforded me so much amusement as to deserve special mention. The writer, a man I had not met for nearly thirty years, after deploring the loss my departure from the War Office would be to the State, went on to ask for the temporary loan of four pounds! Why he did not ask for the round sum of five pounds I have never been able to understand, for his chances of receiving the loan could hardly be affected by so small a matter as an extra sovereign.

CHAPTER XVII

COMMANDER-IN-CHIEF, GREAT BRITAIN

Appointed Commander-in-Chief of Eastern Command—Excessive number
of men retained in United Kingdom—Reorganisation of the Eastern
Command Staff—Become Commander-in-Chief, Great Britain—
Reorganisation of Headquarters Staff—Organisation of commands
Inspections—Good work of hospitals—Defence schemes—Anti-
aircraft defences—Air warfare of the future—Science should be
given a more prominent place in our war preparations—Visits to
the Grand Fleet—Co-operation of American Navy—Admiral Sims—
Discontent on demobilisation—Industrial unrest—Chairman of Com-
mittee on Officers' Pay—King reviews young soldier battalions in
Hyde Park—Appointed to command the British Army of the
Rhine.

ON ceasing to be C.I.G.S. I was offered and accepted the
Eastern Command, which includes that part of England
lying roughly between the south-east coast and a line
drawn from the Wash to Chichester, but is exclusive of
Aldershot and London, both of which constitute separate
commands. I took up my new post, which was much
inferior in status to the one I had previously held, on the
19th of February.

About ten days later I went to Lincoln as the guest of
Sir William Tritton, one of the pioneers in the production
of the tank. During my two days' stay I visited the works
of Messrs. Foster & Company, of which my host was the
executive head ; opened a club which had been established
for the employees at Bracebridge, just outside the town ;
and was shown round the works of Messrs. Ruston &
Proctor. The programme also included a civic welcome,
the Mayor and Corporation meeting me on the boundary of
the city, whence I was conducted to the famous old Guildhall
to receive an address.

There were at the beginning of 1918 nearly a million

and a half of men in the United Kingdom borne on the strength of the army, of whom about half a million were in the Eastern Command, and it was frequently asked why the number should be so great. It certainly was much greater than it ought to have been, and as C.I.G.S. I had many times endeavoured, though without much success, to get it reduced. The responsibility for reducing it rested with the Army Council as a whole and not with the General Staff, as each department of the War Office retained men at home on services connected with its own special duties, and the General Staff could do nothing except try to bring about a reduction so as to set free more men for the battle-fronts.

Of the million and a half men some 80,000 were in the Flying Corps, which was supervised by an Army Councillor and had not yet become a separate service ; close upon 50,000 belonged to the army medical corps, under the Adjutant-General ; some 90,000 belonged to the army service corps, under the Quartermaster-General ; others to the army ordnance corps and army pay corps ; others again to the labour corps, of whom there were nearly 200,000 ; some 46,000 were borne on the strength of the army who were not employed on army work but under the Ministry of Munitions, in agriculture, or in dock and transport work ; and finally, the number of sick and wounded at home usually amounted to some 300,000 or 400,000 men. After making these and many other deductions, less than one-third of the million and a half remained over as potential drafts for the armies abroad, and the majority of these were not sufficiently trained, or were not old enough, to go to the front.

I mention these facts because it was commonly supposed that the enormous numbers retained at home were for home defence, whereas the men earmarked for that purpose were sometimes only about one-tenth of the whole, and these, as explained in the previous chapter, were largely composed of youths under nineteen years of age and therefore were not eligible to be sent abroad. In consequence of the situation created by the German offensive in March the long-delayed reduction in the strength of the troops at home was made, though unfortunately it was largely effected at the expense of sending out boys under nineteen years of age.

As priority of treatment had to be given to the armies abroad, it followed that the troops at home were in a constant state of change, and that the majority of the officers and non-commissioned officers were unfit for active service either on account of health, age, or professional capacity. Some of the officers had been sent home on grounds of inefficiency, and others had not been allowed to go to the front because they had had no experience there—a defect for which they obviously were not answerable. Officers such as these could not well avoid a sense of disappointment, but they loyally stuck to their monotonous work of preparing men for the front, where they themselves were considered to have failed or were not permitted to go.

I had a large staff at my headquarters in Pall Mall, which, according to peace custom, was divided into two branches—General Staff and Administrative Staff. This system, set up on the recommendation of the Esher Committee in 1904, works fairly well in peace time, but in time of war it is not the one used in the field, and it did not work well at home as regards the administrative side. The amount of work to be done was far too great for any one officer to supervise, and it was also much mixed up with questions connected with home defence, and therefore instead of retaining a " Major-General in Charge of Administration," it would have been better to follow the method which obtained at the front and divide the duties between two branches.

With the approval of the War Office I introduced this system, the two branches being respectively placed under a Deputy Adjutant-General and a Deputy Quartermaster-General, who relieved the Major-General in Charge of Administration of the mass of detail with which he had previously tried to cope. Major-General Sir F. Robb held this appointment, and as he had exceptional knowledge of all administrative duties I could safely leave them in his hands. I was thus enabled to give, as I did, most of my time to visiting the troops, observing the conditions under which they were trained, and investigating the arrangements

THE AUTHOR AND SOME CANADIAN OFFICERS AT THE CANADIAN CAMP AT SEAFORD, 1918.

for home defence, more especially those at the three important ports of Harwich, London, and Dover. By the end of May I had visited at least once every station and camp in the command.

On the 3rd of June, Lord French having been appointed Viceroy of Ireland, I was given command of the whole of the forces in Great Britain, with headquarters at the Horse Guards. Lord French had commanded the troops in Ireland as well as those in Great Britain, but it was decided that in future the Irish Command should be directly under the War Office.

The Chief of my General Staff was Major-General Romer, who had served under me at the War Office before the war. Adjutant-General and Quartermaster-General duties were under one officer, Major-General Sir H. Tagart. In this case again I felt it necessary to divide the duties into two branches under a Deputy Adjutant-General and Deputy Quartermaster-General, these posts eventually being held by Brigadier-General Lucas (my old aide-de-camp) and Brigadier-General Jones of the army service corps.

Besides the officers of these three branches, I had a number of Inspectors of the different arms and services whose duty it was to visit the troops at training, and to keep me informed of the progress made and the difficulties encountered.

My personal staff consisted of Lieutenant-Colonel Eddowes, private secretary, and Captains Peek, Bovey, and De Burgh, as aides-de-camp. Peek and Bovey had both been with me in the same capacity in the Eastern Command. Colonel Stanley Barry was military secretary.

The Generals in charge of the various commands were : Fielding, London ; Murray, Aldershot ; Woollcombe, Eastern ; Sclater, Southern ; Maxwell, Northern ; Snow, Western ; McCracken, Scotland ; Pulteney, the XXIst Army Corps—an independent formation of three divisions composed almost entirely of youths under nineteen years of age ; and Dallas, the Kent Force—largely composed of cyclists. These Generals gave me excellent assistance and made my task quite easy.

Being well informed as to the Eastern Command, I

commenced a series of inspections of the other five commands, and during the next six months visited in turn nearly every military station in them from Cromarty in the north to Plymouth in the south.

For long journeys the railway companies usually provided a special saloon for myself and staff, which was a great convenience as it enabled us to do a certain amount of work *en route*. On going to Aberdeen on one occasion we discovered on arrival that the doors of the saloon on the platform side had been locked before we left London so as to prevent people at the stopping stations from entering during the night, and by some mistake the key, a special one, had not been given to the guard. It was at first proposed that we should get out by the window, and then it occurred to us to try the doors on the other side. These were found to be unlocked, and having descended on that side I climbed on to the platform at the dead end of the line, thus presenting myself in a very undignified manner to the Lord Provost and other high officials who had come to the station to receive me.

When making these tours of inspection I endeavoured to visit as many of the military hospitals as my other duties would permit, and it is a pleasure to record that the officers and men whom I questioned spoke in the highest terms of the way in which they were treated.

This is not the place to refer to the services rendered, at home as in the field, by the regular officers and nursing service of the army medical corps, nor is it necessary to do so, but in regard to the V.A.D. establishments it may be said that of all the good work done during the war by the women of Great Britain none surpassed the devoted service of those engaged in the care of the sick and wounded. The greater credit is due to them because in not a few cases the value and amount of their work were not known to, or appreciated by, the public in general. Hospitals and convalescent homes sprang up all over the country, and as some of them were in rather out-of-the-way places they were seldom if ever visited by any one except the inspecting medical authorities. One could but feel unbounded admiration for the way in which the staff silently worked on, month after month and year after year, content with the knowledge that they were doing their best to alleviate the sufferings of those under their charge.

I remember in the South African war stories being current that some of the non-professional nurses who found their way out to that country were held in absolute terror, either because they were ignorant of their duties, or because they thought that these duties consisted in talking to their patients or otherwise forcing their attention upon them at a time when what they most needed was to be left alone in peace. " Too ill to be nursed," was said to have been written on a card and placed on his bed by one man who suffered from these amateurs. In the Great War the amateur element was absent, so far as my experience goes. The hospitals were models of cleanliness, comfort, and efficiency, and it was recognised in a way unknown before that the healing of the body is best expedited by keeping the mind cheerful and contented. All honour to the women who came forward to do this important work, and, what is more, stuck to it regularly and systematically.

The country is also indebted to those civil practitioners, surgical and medical, who gave their services free and to whose unremitting care and attention it was due that many a poor fellow was restored to health whose condition at first seemed hopeless. Amongst those so employed was my friend Sir Peter Freyer. He was Consulting Surgeon in the Eastern Command throughout the war, and travelled hundreds of miles every week in visiting the hospitals within his area. In 1918, when food was strictly rationed, I suggested that as he was doing army work he should apply to be issued with army rations, which were on a more liberal scale than the amount allowed by the regulations of the Food Controller. He applied, and the answer he received was that as he was not in receipt of army pay for the army work he was doing he could not be supplied with army rations !

The arrangements for home defence, on land, had been greatly improved under the direction of Lord French. There was, for reasons that need not be described, little probability that they would ever be put into execution, but as there could be no certainty about what the enemy might try to do, it was only a reasonable precaution to ensure that the troops should be capable of turning out quickly, and that every officer and man should be acquainted with his duties in case of emergency. With this object in view I occasionally issued instructions, without previous warning of my intention, which put the coast defence schemes into force. The tests brought to light many defects, and caused all ranks to take a greater interest in this part of their work.

It can be understood that the practical execution of the schemes involved considerable interference with the telegraph, telephone, and railway systems ; entailed, in some cases, in accordance with arrangements made with the civil authorities, the evacuation of the inhabitants, cattle, transport, etc., from the locality threatened ; and in many ways disturbed the everyday life of the country. Rather elaborate measures had therefore to be taken when testing the schemes so as not to lead the whole community to believe that a hostile landing was, in fact, taking place. Otherwise there would have been unnecessary dislocation of business, to say nothing of the alarm that might have occurred.

I usually issued the order for the tests late at night or early in the morning, according to the conditions affecting the scheme, and I discovered after the first few tests that garrisons were very much on the *qui vive* if I was known or suspected to be in the neighbourhood. It was difficult to prevent my presence becoming known, as certain preliminary arrangements had to be made, and I had to be accompanied by several staff officers. Consequently I was not always able to bring off my intended surprise—without which the test naturally lost something of its value—but on one occasion at least I may claim to have scored, though in a somewhat different manner.

I was visiting a large garrison on the east coast, and so determined were the staff and commanding officers not to be caught napping that they remained at their posts for two consecutive nights, waiting for the arrival of the appointed code-word which put their scheme into force. But it never came, and while these officers carried out their weary vigil my staff and I slept peacefully in our beds !

Even when I left on the evening of the third day they seemed to doubt, from what they said to my staff, whether I was really going away or intended to double back on my tracks at a later hour. The incident provided us with much mutual amusement, and it may have taught the officers something more about the details of their defence scheme than they had hitherto known.

The anti-aircraft defences were, when I took over the command in Great Britain, probably the best of their kind in the world so far as London was concerned, and I imagine that the Germans realised how perfect they were, for no further attacks were made during the war. Owing to the initial lack of means this result had taken nearly four years to achieve, and in the meantime London had been subjected to many raids. The loss of life and damage to property were, however resolutely accepted, and instead of causing panic and despair they made the people more determined than ever to see the war through to a finish. Thus, again, had the enemy mistaken the psychology of his opponent.

As C.I.G.S. I had for long endeavoured to supply Lord French with the resources he needed, but as the output of aeroplanes was never equal to requirements until 1918, if then, it was impossible to give him what he wanted without starving the armies on the West Front. That they should be so starved was what the enemy most desired—hence the raids—for without a proper complement of aeroplanes to assist them the armies would have been at a hopeless disadvantage. The same remarks apply, though to a less extent, to the other fronts on which we were fighting, and from all of them requests to be supplied with more aircraft were constantly being received.

Again, anti-aircraft guns, of the really useful type, were required in large numbers by the navy and for arming merchant vessels against submarine attacks, while search-lights and other equipment for the defences were also deficient. In these circumstances it was not feasible to satisfy every need, and home defence had, as a rule, necessarily to take second place.

For reasons that can be understood, I shall not describe the air defences in detail. They were under the command of Major-General Ashmore, assisted by a very capable and hard-working body of officers and men, a due proportion of whom were always on duty throughout the twenty-four hours. The first requisite was to ensure that immediate notice of an impending raid should be received by all concerned, as the time taken by the hostile machines to reach London from, say, the mouth of the Thames, was only just sufficient to allow of our own machines climbing up from the ground to an altitude equal to that at which the enemy was probably flying. A sharp look-out on the coast and rapid methods of transmitting information were therefore of the first importance. In both cases the arrangements were about as perfect as they could be made.

It was supposed by most people that the one and only object of the anti-aircraft guns was to bring down the enemy's machines, but this was only one of two. The other, almost equally important, was that the guns should compel the enemy to fly at a great elevation in order to be safe against their fire. In this way they reduced his chances of bombing his objectives, and restricted him to a smaller aerial space in which our own aeroplanes, assisted by search-lights at night, would have to look for him. Aprons, formed of long strands of wire and suspended between captive balloons, helped to serve the same purpose of keeping the enemy well up in the air and to limit his available lines of approach. Once a balloon unfortunately broke loose when two men were working on it. One poor fellow dropped when at a great height ; the other was never seen again, or the balloon.

On the fighting fronts the aeroplane has proved itself to be indispensable in collecting information, directing artillery fire, bombing the enemy's depots, railways, camps, etc., but perhaps its most important feature, and the one with the greatest future, is that it permits of the war being carried into the enemy's country, irrespective of the situation on land and sea. The ostensible object of raids of this kind may be to inflict damage upon naval bases, supply depots, and other military establishments, but non-military places will also suffer, for although raids upon them may theoretically be classed as unjustifiable, the limits of what is permissible and what is not are very elastic in these days.

Modern war being largely a matter of war against economic life, it has turned more and more towards the enemy's home country, and the old principle of making war only against armies and navies has been consigned to the background. Raids on non-military places and people may be regarded as barbaric, and they may, by exasperating the inhabitants, have the opposite effect to that intended —the breaking down of the country's morale—but they are bound to play a prominent part in the next contest, and on a far more extensive scale than in the Great War. A new weapon, such as the aeroplane or submarine, will always open up new paths for itself, and in the case of the aeroplane the path can be followed within a few minutes of the declaration of war—if not before.

I make these observations about future aerial warfare because in the Great War we had no good defences against air-attack with the exception of London and its immediate vicinity. In the next war the enemy's radius of action will doubtless be much increased, as well as the number and destructive power of his aeroplanes, and, in the air as on land and sea, our best form of defence will lie in the ability to attack.

In this respect as in some others we need to take greater advantage of the assistance that can be afforded by science than we have hitherto done. In the Great War valuable methods of submarine warfare were quickly discovered ; sound-rangers were invented by means of which a particular sound, such as the discharge of a gun, could be located at great distances and even in the din of battle, and upon it our own guns could be laid ; the tank was produced in large numbers and proved itself to be an indispensable weapon in trench warfare ; means of defence against gas were provided in a few weeks, and of offence in a few months ; while the surgical and medical arrangements for the sick and wounded surpassed anything before seen. All this was mainly due to science, which, conspicuously absent in our pre-war preparations, had hurriedly to be called in at a time of stress. It is to be hoped that not only in the fighting services but in every State department, in peace and in war, science will in future be definitely given a place consistent with its great importance to the national welfare.

In 1917 and again in 1918 I was invited by Admiral Beatty to visit the Grand Fleet in the Firth of Forth, and the spectacle it presented, strengthened by the fine business-like looking ships of our American Allies, caused me to understand why the enemy refrained from repeating his Jutland effort.

From conversations I had with the Admiral the arrangements for home defence as between the navy and army did not appear to be as good as they ought to have been, and for this I myself was not blameless. With regard to purely naval operations, I found that control over the naval forces employed off the coasts of Great Britain was much more centralised at the Admiralty than was the control over the land forces exercised by the War Office. At first it seemed to me to be overdone, notwithstanding that the sea is all one, but as the sailors may be presumed to know their own business best I shall not dare to criticise them. There is of course much difference in the characteristics of the two services, their field of operations, and the means of acquiring and distributing intelligence of the enemy's movements, and the same system of command may not therefore be practicable for both.

In visiting other Scottish ports I saw something more of the work being done in the North Sea by the Americans in combination with our own sailors, and, as is well known, they also co-operated effectively with us in the Atlantic. One of the most pleasing features of the war was the excellent relations which existed between the soldiers and sailors of the two great English-speaking nations, and in securing this result Admiral Sims took a place second to none. He is a typical naval officer, downright in the expression of his opinions, and was actuated only by the desire to do his best for the common good. We frequently met when I was C.I.G.S., and in our journeys together between London and Paris when attending Allied conferences he would sometimes show that besides being a fine sailor he was also an accomplished raconteur, his racy stories helping to while away many a tedious hour, and to give a more cheery aspect to what, at the moment, might be rather a dreary outlook.

At the beginning of 1919 there was much discontent amongst the troops at the manner in which demobilisation was being carried out. Regulations on the subject had been carefully prepared by the War Office before the Armistice, and presumably in consultation with the other State departments concerned ; but when put into force they were subjected to many modifications, while it was impossible in some cases to decide into which category men fell for demobilisation owing to the vague and complicated conditions under which they had entered the army. Moreover, the men had been led to believe at the general election in the previous December that demobilisation would be immediate and rapid ; they knew that employment was being snapped up by others who had already been demobilised or who had escaped military service altogether ; and for many reasons they were more anxious to return to civil life than to continue military training at home.

To make matters worse, demobilisation was not dealt with solely by one department in the War Office, for although the Adjutant-General was responsible for the greater part of it a considerable amount of personnel was demobilised under the instructions of the Quartermaster-General, with the result sometimes that men who had joined the army under similar conditions found that they were not treated similarly in regard to demobilisation. Of two such men one would be demobilised under instructions issued by the Adjutant-General, while the other, employed in the administrative services under the Quartermaster-General, might find himself retained.

The state of affairs was becoming extremely unsatisfactory, both as to the feeling of the troops and the maintenance of sufficient forces to meet our liabilities, when Mr. Churchill became Secretary of State for War in February 1919. Within a few days of taking office he issued instructions which put matters on a proper footing. Demobilisation regulations were made clearer, the men were definitely informed as to when they were likely to be demobilised, and those who had to be retained were given the increase of pay and other privileges to which they were in the circumstances entitled.

There was about this period also much industrial unrest. This was only to be expected, seeing the wholesale dislocation caused by the war, and at the departmental meetings which I attended in Whitehall, when actual or threatened strikes were being discussed, it was evident that there was something to be said on the side of the men as well as on that of the employers. Troops were frequently held in readiness to assist the civil authorities, but only at one place—Glasgow—was any considerable number used, and fortunately order was quickly restored.

Whilst at the Horse Guards I was inundated with requests to take part in various public ceremonies, but besides my distaste for making speeches in public—especially when there is nothing useful to be said—I had more than enough to do to get through my military duties. My rule was, therefore, to decline all such requests except when it seemed really necessary to comply with them. One of these exceptions was when I went to Worcester in January 1919 to lay the foundation stone of the first block of buildings to be erected in " Gheluvelt " park as Homes for the sailors and soldiers of the county who had become disabled in the Great War. (The park was given the name of " Gheluvelt " because of the distinction gained at that place by the Worcestershire Regiment in 1914.) Curiously enough I remembered only the day before the ceremony, while the guest of Lord Beauchamp at Madresfield Court, that it was at Worcester that I had enlisted some forty-two years earlier, and the announcement of this fact in a speech I made at a public luncheon at the Guildhall came as a great surprise to all present, and lent an added interest to the address of welcome with which the Corporation had presented me in the morning.

As a preliminary to the revision of the rates of officers' pay the Army Council appointed a committee at the end of 1918, of which I was nominated chairman, to report on the necessary expenses of life in the army. We went carefully into the matter, obtaining much evidence from officers well qualified to give it, and had no difficulty in showing that, while most officers were receiving, with the exception of certain temporary increases, much the same pay as fifty or more years ago, the cost of living had gone up a hundred per cent. In order to effect a reasonable adjustment we recommended amongst other things that married officers of the age of thirty and over should be treated as such by the State, and be given corresponding privileges in respect of rations, quarters, and travelling ; that all officers, married or not, should be treated more liberally, in money or in kind, in the way of " allowances " for fuel, light, and quarters, the system to be made sufficiently elastic to ensure fair compensation being given for the cost incurred, no matter where the officer might be stationed ; that the amount of uniform should be reduced to the minimum, steps taken to cheapen the cost, and the initial outfit to be paid for by the State ; and that all questions of officers' emoluments should be decided on the basic principle that the more senior regimental officers should have secured to them such remuneration as would be an adequate return for their length of service and the responsible duties they have to perform, and as would enable them to maintain and educate their families in a manner consistent with their station of life. The committee had the satisfaction—not the usual experience of committees—of seeing many of their recommendations adopted in the revised scale of pay and allowances issued the following July, though there were some not unimportant omissions.

On the 1st March the King held a review in Hyde Park of several Young Soldier Battalions, brought in from stations outside London, which had been ordered to join the Army of the Rhine in replacement of the battalions sent there from the West Front when the Rhine territories were first occupied by the Allies in the previous December. Unfortunately greatcoats had to be worn as the weather was not very fine, and this rather spoilt the effect of the parade, but the battalions nevertheless presented a good appearance, considering that practically all the personnel were under nineteen years of age. After the parade the King was good enough to express his appreciation in the following letter :

It gave me much pleasure to inspect in Hyde Park to-day the battalions about to proceed overseas to join the Army of the Rhine.

The steadiness on parade and general soldierly appearance of all ranks was most satisfactory, and reflects great credit alike upon the men themselves and upon those responsible for their instruction.

Since 1916, when separate battalions were first formed at home for the reception and training of recruits of 18 years of age, many thousands of young men have passed through them, and have earned high praise from their officers and non-commissioned officers for their keenness to learn and their consistent good behaviour.

Commanders at the front have also told me of their intelligence, courage, and devotion to duty in the field.

I am confident that this high reputation will be jealously guarded and maintained by the 14 battalions inspected to-day, also by those other battalions which are proceeding to the Rhine, and which I much regret to be unable to see before their departure.

GEORGE R.I.

1st *March* 1919.

A few days after this parade Mr. Churchill offered me the command of the British army of the Rhine, adding that in view of the services I had rendered in winning the war it was appropriate that I should command the troops employed in enforcing compliance with the terms of peace. I did not suppose that the appointment would be of long duration, but I was nevertheless glad to accept the offer. On the 14th April I handed over command of the forces in Great Britain to Sir Douglas Haig and left the Horse Guards, where, for about eleven months, I had occupied the same room and sat at the same table as used by many previous Commanders-in-Chief, including the Duke of Wellington.

CHAPTER XVIII

COMMANDER-IN-CHIEF, BRITISH ARMY OF THE RHINE

I LEFT London for the Rhine on the 18th April (Good Friday), being received by Lieutenant-General Sir J. Asser (commanding the British troops in France) and his staff at Boulogne, and reaching Cologne the following day. I took with me the same aides-de-camp as I had at the Horse Guards, my private secretary at first being Lieutenant-Colonel Seymour of the Scots Greys, and afterwards Lieutenant-Colonel Dillon of the Munster Fusiliers, who had been one of my students at the Staff College. Dillon's knowledge of French and the French army was very useful, and in every way he was an ideal staff officer. In November 1919 he took over the command of one of the Rhine battalions, being succeeded by Lieutenant-Colonel Newman. The latter was followed by another gunner, Lieutenant-Colonel Gore-Browne, and both gave me great assistance. The same may be said of Peek, whom I was sorry to lose when, having been with me for nearly two years in all, he went home to rejoin his regiment, the 9th Lancers. He had been badly wounded at the beginning of the Great War, afterwards being repatriated. To the regret of his many friends he was killed in March 1921 while serving in Ireland. Lieutenant Phillips, who came to me as A.D.C. in July and remained till I returned to England for good, was a first-class manager of our mess, and made all arrangements for the entertainment of my numerous guests.

The principal members of the headquarters staff whom I found at Cologne were Major-General Sir A. Montgomery, Chief of the General Staff, Major-General Sir A. F. Sillem, Deputy Adjutant-General, and Major-General Sir E. Chichester, Deputy Quartermaster-General. Montgomery returned to England in August, and some time afterwards his appointment was reduced in status and filled by Brigadier-General Fuller. Sillem was replaced in June by my friend Hutchison from the War Office, who, in November, took charge of both Adjutant-General and Quartermaster-General's duties, Chichester returning to England. A great deal of work devolved upon the staff throughout the year, first in giving the army a settled organisation and preparing it to resume active operations—a matter to which I will refer later —and afterwards in connection with the repeated reorganisations which had to be made consequent on demobilisation.

I took over command from Sir Herbert Plumer on the 21st April. The army then occupied the territory extending north-west from the Belgian frontier to the left bank of the Rhine, from Dusseldorf on the left to about ten miles above Bonn on the right, as well as the Cologne bridgehead (with a radius of 30 kilometres) on the right bank. On our right was the American army of occupation, with headquarters at Coblence, and on the left the Belgian army, with headquarters at Aix-la-Chapelle. French armies held the country between the Americans and Switzerland, their principal headquarters being at Mayence, Metz, Kaiserslautern, and Strasburg. The whole were under the command of Marshal Foch, who remained with his staff at Paris.

At Cologne there was a British naval flotilla of twelve motor launches under Commander the Hon. P. Acheson. It was a useful addition to the army of occupation and did good work in patrolling the Rhine, on which there was a considerable amount of traffic that required watching.

GENERAL ALLEN, COMMANDER OF THE AMERICAN ARMY OF THE RHINE,
WITH THE AUTHOR AND COLONEL GORE-BROWNE.

Not being allowed to go through Dutch waters, the flotilla came to the Rhine by way of the French rivers and canals, entering at Havre and reaching Cologne after a journey extending over several weeks.

The British zone of occupation measured something over 2000 square miles and had a population of nearly two and a half million souls. It was divided both for military and civil purposes into five army corps areas, these areas, as well as their sub-divisions, being made to coincide as far as possible with the German civil boundaries. My instructions were that each area should be regarded in the same way as a " command " at home, and that all troops in it, whether forming part of the army corps or not, should be under the orders of the corps commander for administration, discipline, and defence duties.

Similarly, each corps commander was responsible for the civil administration of his area, which he carried out through the medium of the local civil authorities. The only exception to this arrangement was Cologne and its suburbs, which were placed under a separate " civil administrator " attached to the staff of the Military Governor. The back areas of Malmedy, Montjoie, and Schlieden, being unoccupied by troops, were administered by specially appointed officers reporting direct to general headquarters.

The so-called " Military Governor " was merely the senior staff officer at general headquarters for civil administrative measures : he commanded no troops, and therefore could issue no orders to corps commanders except with my authority. The real " Military Governor " was in fact none other than myself, the Commander-in-Chief. The title must have often puzzled the Germans, and it certainly tended to create confusion in the minds of the corps commanders, but as it had been in existence since we entered the country I decided not to change it so as to avoid causing further confusion. I did, however, issue instructions to corps commanders to make it clear that they were responsible to me for their respective areas, and that the Military Governor was not a commander, but the staff officer through whom my instructions regarding civil administration were conveyed to them.

The occupied territory was, of course, under martial law, and as this term is rather imperfectly understood by the general public I may explain what it means as applied to a conquered country. In the first place it is not, as so often supposed, the same thing as " military law." Military law is the law governing the soldier in peace and in war, at home and abroad. It is contained in the Army Act, supplemented by other Acts, Rules, and Regulations, and the Act is brought into operation annually by a separate statute, generally known as the Army Annual Act. It is part of the statute law of England, and, with the important difference that it is administered by military courts and not by civil judges, is construed in the same manner and carried out under the same conditions as the ordinary civil law of England.

Martial law is something entirely different, and it differs according as to whether it is applied to our own country or to a conquered country. In the former case it means that exceptional powers are assumed by the Crown, acting through its military forces, for the restoration and maintenance of good order. In other words, the ordinary law is suspended and government by military tribunals is substituted. In a sense, it is not legal, for as the English law does not presuppose the possibility of civil war it makes no express provision for such a contingency. The fact that martial law is " proclaimed " makes no difference from the purely legal standpoint. The proclamation merely means that as the ordinary civil administration is inadequate to deal with the situation, the Government, in the rightful exercise of its duties, has decided to replace it temporarily by military administration.

As there is no " law " to govern their actions, the military authorities charged with the application of this kind of martial law have necessarily to act according to their own judgment, in conformity with the instructions they receive from the Government, and in order to obviate any question as to the legality of the measures taken by them, it is usual to pass an " act of indemnity." If these measures are honestly taken, and in accordance with official instructions, an officer may rely on the act of indemnity for meeting any legal question that may be raised.

As applied to a conquered country martial law is simply the will of the conqueror. The commander of the troops stands temporarily in the position of Governor of the country he occupies, and imposes such laws on the inhabitants as he thinks expedient for securing the safety of his army and the good government of the district which, by reason of his occupation, is for the time being deprived of its ordinary rulers. The legality of the laws he imposes cannot be called in question because there is no human means of doing so, but it is his duty to conform to what is known as the " laws and usages of war " in the administration of the occupied territory.

This brief explanation will suffice to show the principles upon which the civil administration of the Rhine districts occupied by British troops was based. As already stated, the Military Governor's branch of the headquarters staff was charged with carrying it out, working in connection with the German administrative officials at Cologne. Lieutenant-General Sir Charles Fergusson was Military Governor from the commencement of the occupation to July 1919, and was succeeded in turn by Brigadier-General Clive and Major-General Kennedy. Exclusive of deciding questions of general policy, I was relieved by these officers of practically all civil administrative work, and was thus free to devote my time and attention to the troops.

Justice was administered by "summary" and "military" courts, the former being either permanent courts or courts composed of regimental officers, while the military court, or court-martial, was assembled as and when necessary by the area commandant concerned. As a rule prisoners served their sentences in German civil prisons, a check being kept on this by a British " Inspector of Prisons." The German civil authorities were as desirous of maintaining the peace and ensuring good administration as we were, and although it is not to be supposed that they accepted our rule with any special pleasure, they quite realised the position, recognised that they were much better off than their compatriots in the unoccupied parts of Germany, were formal but correct in their attitude, and promptly carried out the orders they received.

At different times there was, as in other parts of the world, England included, disagreement between employers and workmen, but considering the shortage of food and coal, and the fact that the country was passing through a form of revolution, there was far less trouble than might have been expected. My policy was to keep clear of all labour disputes except when they threatened to interfere with the interests of the troops—such as the stoppage of electric light, water supply, or railway transport—or to cause disturbances for the suppression of which troops might have to be employed. The procedure I laid down was that all disputes likely to lead to a strike must in the first instance be submitted to a German " court of conciliation," in which both sides were represented ; if no agreement was reached the case was submitted to a British court of arbitration, whose decision was final and binding.

The officers of the Military Governor's staff rendered excellent service in settling many strikes which threatened to become serious, and throughout the thirteen months of British military administration no great or prolonged strike occurred. It should be added, perhaps, that when a strike did occur no picketing was allowed ; protection was always afforded to those men who wished to work ; every consideration was given to the point of view of the workmen, who, by our intervention, frequently obtained the terms they demanded ; and any one who did not abide by our decision, whether employer or employee, was liable to be dealt with as an offender, and was so dealt with when the occasion required.

For reasons that can be understood, no one in the Rhine Army was allowed to " fraternise " with the inhabitants, and to meet this unusual condition of military life additional facilities were afforded to officers and men for taking part in games, theatricals, concerts, day-trips on the Rhine, and other forms of recreation and amusement. The Y.M.C.A., Church Army, Men's Leave Club, and similar societies gave invaluable help in this respect, and I am sure that thousands of the young men who served in the command will remember with gratitude for the rest of their lives the many happy hours which these institutions provided for them.

One of the theatres in Cologne was appropriated for the use of British performers, and a suitable proportion of seats at the opera were, by my orders, permanently reserved for the troops, the prices paid varying, in English money, from a few pence to about two shillings. The opera was said to be one of the best in Germany and certainly was very good, completely putting in the shade the operatic efforts usually heard in England.

When I arrived on the Rhine the British army there consisted of five army corps, each of two divisions, with a cavalry division and various other troops, making a total strength of about 220,000 men. To meet the requirements of demobilisation the army was still in process of reconstruction, divisions, brigades, and battalions of the old field armies from France being broken up, recast, and renamed, and amalgamated with some sixty Graduated and Young Soldier battalions from home. Of the latter some battalions were retained intact, and others were broken up and distributed amongst the old battalions from France.

One result of all this dislocation was that the regimental traditions and reputations which had been established during the fighting disappeared to a great extent, and to make matters more difficult the army was for some time deficient in two important classes of men—cooks and commanding officers—without which it is impossible to have efficiency and contentment. Only a few of the young battalions had been supplied with trained cooks before leaving England, while many of the old units had lost theirs by demobilisation ; and of the ninety battalions in the army thirty had not yet received their permanent commanding officers, and in most of the remaining sixty these officers had but just been posted and knew little or nothing about their men or their men about them.

The same may be said of the junior regimental officers, many of whom had recently been brought in from disbanded battalions ; they were mainly " temporary " officers, the regular officers having been sent home to join the regular units then in process of re-creation ; and as their military experience had been confined almost entirely to trench-warfare they were but indifferently qualified, as a rule, to deal with the new duties of administration and training which now devolved upon them.

Further, commanders of all grades found themselves, consequent on the reduction of the field armies, tumbling down the ladder, and Generals who had commanded divisions for months and years in the fighting were placed in command of brigades ; brigadiers in the war dropped down to the command of a battalion or even a company ; battalion commanders fell to a company or a platoon.

Most of the regular non-commissioned officers had also been sent home to join the regular units, the battalions on the Rhine thus being left chiefly with non-regulars who, as a rule, were young both in age and service and incapable of exercising proper authority over the men. These and practically all the men were entitled to be demobilised at varying dates according to the conditions under which they had entered the army, and, for the same reasons as those which had led to dissatisfaction at home, to which reference has been made in the preceding chapter, there was some discontent amongst the men with respect to the manner in which demobilisation was being carried out. To allay disturbing elements of this kind it was essential to have good regimental officers, personally known to and trusted by the men, and as just explained these were seldom forthcoming.

Practically every post brought me appeals from employers or relatives in England to release men who were held to be entitled, either legally or on compassionate grounds, to be set free. Some hard cases came to my notice, and hard or otherwise all were sympathetically dealt with by my staff as far as the regulations would permit. Some of my correspondents were very grateful for the help we were able to give them. Here is a letter I received from the wife of a man whose release was expedited :

DEAR SIR—Just a line thanking you very much for seeing into Mr. ——'s case for me. For you have done a great lot for me in sending him home, and I hope that the best of luck follows you for ever. Once again thank you very much.—Yours truly greatfull,

The unsatisfactory state of affairs above described could not have been wholly prevented, but there it was, and it was not calculated to make the general atmosphere either contented or exhilarating, or to render easy the preparations which had to be made for an advance into unoccupied Germany if that became necessary in order to compel her to sign the treaty of peace—when ready for signature.

My first step was to assemble the corps commanders, Morland, Godley, Jacob, Haldane, and ·Braithwaite, discuss the situation with them, and inform them of my intentions. This I did immediately after assuming command, and I also began a tour of inspections so as to make myself personally acquainted with the officers and men, and with the state of readiness of the army for resuming active operations. During the first two months I was engaged in carrying out these inspections every day in the week except Sunday (when I visited the hospitals), and having regard to the conditions under which the army had been thrown together it was not surprising that many shortcomings were evident.

Besides the disadvantages to which reference has been made, I had to contend against the assumption—fostered by what had been said during the general election—that the war was " over," from which it was argued that training was no longer necessary. Further, many of the young infantry soldiers from home had not been instructed in the use of the rifle ; the young artillery soldiers could neither drive nor shoot ; and some of the cavalry regiments were so weak in numbers that they could not move from one station to another without borrowing men from other regiments to lead their spare horses. Sometimes I almost despaired of ever straightening out the tangle and reaching a reasonable standard of efficiency, but British officers and men are made of good material, and once a matter is properly explained and they understand what is expected of them, they may be depended upon to respond. They did so on this occasion. Everybody put his shoulder to the wheel, and by the middle of June, when a further advance into Germany was contemplated, reorganisation had been fairly well completed ; the troops, elated at the prospect of going forward, presented a cheerful and workmanlike appearance ;

and I felt satisfied that they were capable of carrying out the mission assigned to them.

I had been summoned to Paris to confer with Marshal Foch and the Commanders-in-Chief of the Allied armies as far back as the end of April, as it was thought that we might have to advance about the middle of May, but owing to the slow progress made in completing the peace negotiations no movement of troops became necessary until the 17th of June. On that day the divisions began to concentrate east of the Rhine, and by the evening of the 19th were in readiness to cross the line separating occupied from unoccupied territory. Five days later Germany undertook to sign the treaty ; her delegates for that purpose passed through Cologne from Berlin *en route* to Versailles on the 27th, and on the 28th the treaty was signed.

During the spring and summer of 1919 I received several distinguished visitors at my headquarters, the first to come being the King and Queen of the Belgians. Their Majesties arrived by aeroplane on the 26th of April and returned to Brussels in the same manner, despite very unsettled weather, on the 28th of April. The same evening the King sent me the following telegram :

The Queen and myself express to you our most sincere thanks for the kindness you have shown to us in Cologne. It was a great pleasure to see you and to visit a part of the British sector of occupation on the Rhine.

ALBERT.

The Duke of Connaught, accompanied by Lieutenant-Colonel Sir Malcolm Murray, arrived on the 6th of May and spent three days with the army. Amongst other events His Royal Highness inspected three battalions of the Rifle Brigade, of which he is Colonel-in-Chief, and held a review of the Northern Division, about 10,000 men, on the German parade ground just outside the town. This review was of interest as being the only one of its kind held by a member of the Royal Family during the occupation.

General Liggett, commanding the American army of occupation, paid me a visit at the same time as the Duke of Connaught ; General Pershing came to present me with the

General Michel, Commander-in Chief of the Belgian Army of the Rhine, inspecting a Guard of Honour at Cologne.

American distinguished service medal on the 12th of May ; and General Bliss came two days later. General Liggett was succeeded by General Allen, with whom, as well as with General Michel, commanding the Belgian army of occupation, I frequently exchanged visits. Italian, Japanese, and Chinese Generals were also amongst my visitors.

Marshal Foch, with General Weygand and others of his staff, came on the 16th of May and left the following day. He had begun a tour down the Rhine at Strasburg a few days earlier, the first since the Armistice, halting at Mayence and Coblence *en route* to Cologne. He travelled on board one of the Rhine steamers, the *Prince Bismarck*, and on entering the British zone was received with a salute from our naval flotilla ; a squadron of aeroplanes followed his course down the river, the banks of which were lined with troops at Bonn and other places ; and at Cologne he was greeted with rousing cheers from the troops assembled on the Hohenzollern bridge and from others who clustered round his motor-car as it proceeded from the quay to my house outside the town. Thousands of Germans came to see the man of whose name they had heard so much, and although they did not contribute to the cheering their demeanour was, as always, strictly " correct."

As the car slowly forced its way through the troops, who, with the exception of the guard of honour, were not " formed up " but had been allowed to line the road in their own way, the Marshal was much moved at the welcome accorded him, and compared the anxious times we had experienced together between 1914 and 1918 with the drive we were then making on the banks of the Rhine, saluted by German policemen and acclaimed by British soldiers— a termination to the Great War which in those far-off and critical days would sometimes have seemed, had we thought of it at all, to be impossible of realisation in May 1919, if ever.

After we had discussed the operations which might have to be undertaken, he motored round part of the bridgehead east of the Rhine, being greatly impressed, as all my visitors were, with the tidiness and general prosperity of the country, the multitude of children to be seen, and the orderly behaviour of the inhabitants.

Marshal Joffre made a tour of the Rhine Provinces similar to that of Marshal Foch, and arrived at Cologne by rail, accompanied by la Maréchale, on the 24th of September, leaving the same night for Aix-la-Chapelle after dining at my house. He was received by a guard of honour, composed of cavalry, infantry, and tanks, on the Dom Platz, where large numbers of Germans congregated to see him. He evidently felt gratified at the opportunity of renewing his acquaintance with British troops, and it was equally a pleasure to us to receive him.

Other French officers who came to Cologne were Marshal Pétain, Commander-in-Chief of the French armies ; General Mangin, commanding part of the French armies of occupation, an interesting personality who had seen much service in the French colonies and was with Colonel Marchand at the time of the Fashoda incident ; General Fayolle, commanding another part of the French armies of occupation, with headquarters at Kaiserslautern ; General Gouraud, commanding the Strasburg area, who had served with the French contingent sent to Gallipoli, where he was severely wounded ; and General Degoutte, who later succeeded General Mangin at Mayence and eventually became Commander-in-Chief of all the Allied forces of occupation. These Generals spoke in high terms of the appearance of the troops shown for their inspection, and of the soldier-like manner in which they moved on parade. A typical example of this appreciation was provided in a letter I received from General Gouraud, who wrote :

Croyez que je n'oublierai jamais votre cordial accueil et l'émouvante revue où j'ai l'honneur de voir défiler devant moi de magnifiques détachements de troupes britanniques sur la place de la cathédrale de Cologne.

I should add that the relations between the British troops and the French, Belgian, and American armies were throughout of the most cordial nature as regards work, while as to play there was much friendly rivalry in racing, horse-shows, and football, and some mutual benefit was, no doubt, also derived from the other forms of amusement and recreation for which reciprocal invitations were given.

DRIVING THROUGH MAINZ WITH GENERAL MANGIN, COMMANDER OF ONE OF THE FRENCH ARMIES OF THE RHINE, AND ACCOMPANIED BY AN ESCORT OF ARAB CAVALRY.

The Army Council, represented by the Secretary of State for War (Mr. Winston Churchill), the Chief of the Imperial General Staff, and the Adjutant-General, arrived at Cologne on the 17th of August and left on the 20th of that month. They were shown as many of the troops as time would permit them to see, including a review of the 6th Army Corps, the women-workers, clubs, and regimental institutes, and on the last day they descended the Rhine from Remagen, 15 miles above Bonn, to Cologne, accompanied by the naval flotilla and two squadrons of the air force. The reverberations of the naval salute in the defiles of the Rhine when the party went on board, the sheets of white foam thrown up by the rapidly-moving motor launches, the humming of the aeroplanes in the cloudless sky, and the wonderful colouring of the surrounding country characteristic of the Rhine valley, constituted an impressive spectacle not easily to be forgotten.

After their return to England the Council sent me the following telegram :

Please convey to all ranks Rhine army the thanks of the Army Council for their message of August 21. The Council have greatly valued the opportunities of personal touch with the troops afforded them by their visit, of which they retain the pleasantest memories. The Council were deeply impressed with the soldierly bearing and the fine spirit shown by the troops under your Command, who worthily uphold the best traditions of the British army.

In returning the visits of the Allied Generals I was always shown great courtesy and hospitality, the guards of honour with which I was received usually being drawn up in the principal square of the town and consisting of at least a battalion of infantry, cavalry also being included if available. The general arrangements and the turn-out of the troops were a proof that the ceremony was not merely a matter of form, but that pains had been taken to make it a genuine mark of respect to the representative of the British army.

One of the first of these visits was paid to General Mangin at Mayence on the 2nd of June, when, by the King's command, I presented him with the K.C.B. The General lived in the palace of the Duke of Hesse, which was frequently occupied by Napoleon during his campaigns beyond the Rhine, and the room in which he slept is still retained in much the same order as when he used it. I was told that when Marshal Foch was staying here with General Mangin he was invited to sleep in the bed. His reply was, " Thank you, but I am too small."

The following morning I reached Metz, where, after visiting the battlefield of Verdun during the day, I dined with the garrison commander, General Maud'huy, who occupied the same house as that in which the German commandant had lived, and to which I used to go to report my arrival when at Metz before the war. General Maud'huy is a native of Metz, and as a boy of about ten years of age was living in the town at the time of the 1870 war. He told me that some years later, when he had become an officer of the French army, the German authorities at Metz refused to give him permission to go there to attend his mother's funeral.

On the 20th of July I paid another visit to General Mangin, who met me at Bingen and accompanied me in the train to Mayence, where the arrival platform and waiting-room were profusely decorated with flags and flowers. Outside the station a fine-looking French battalion formed the guard of honour, a squadron of African cavalry escorted us through the town to the palace, and there we were received by a battalion of African infantry. In the evening there was a dinner-party, a dance, and a torchlight tattoo, which, as seen from the palace windows overlooking the Rhine, presented a remarkably brilliant spectacle.

The following day I went to Strasburg as the guest of General Gouraud, who, after *déjeuner*, made a very complimentary speech about the British army, for which I was quite unprepared and therefore experienced some difficulty in giving, in French, a suitable reply to it. I spent the evening at the house of M. Millerand, then Governor of Alsace and now President of the French Republic, who had invited about thirty people to dinner. In the course of our conversation, which was very interesting to me, he recalled the fact that we had first met on the West Front in 1915 when he was Minister of War.

VISIT OF GENERAL GOURAUD TO COLOGNE, 1919.

THE AUTHOR.   GENERAL GOURAUD.   LIEUT.-GENERAL SIR A. GODLEY.

On the 23rd I arrived at Kaiserslautern, and after *déjeuner* went with General Fayolle for a four hours' motor drive through the beautiful country of the Vosges. He was a charming host and, like the other French generals, did all in his power to render the visit agreeable.

On the 31st of July I went to Aix-la-Chapelle to present about thirty decorations to certain Belgian officers and men. A battalion of Belgian infantry and a squadron of cavalry, as well as a detachment of French troops, were formed up in the square in front of the Rathaus, and after the presentation was over I met a number of Belgian and French officers at the General's house.

By the invitation of M. Clemenceau I attended the peace celebration held at Paris on the 14th of July, the British contingent consisting of 1000 men from the Rhine and about half that number from England. Paris was seen at its best, which is saying a good deal, for there is no city in the world so well adapted for a public display or that so well understands how to make it attractive, and all classes seemed to combine to give the proceedings an air of genuine rejoicing. In the evening a dinner was given by M. Poincaré at the Élysée to about 120 officers, to which I had the honour of being invited. Madame Poincaré was the only lady present.

I was also invited to attend the Belgian peace celebration at Brussels on the 22nd of July, but was prevented by duty from going.

At the British peace celebration in London on the 19th of July I was not present, as I was not asked to attend.

In September I took a few days' leave for deer-stalking at Langwell, the Scottish home of the Duke and Duchess of Portland, where I had received some lessons in the art of stalking from the Duke himself during two brief visits in 1918.

Admiral Sir Michael Culme-Seymour and Lord Charles Beresford were of the party, as they had been the year before and on many previous occasions. Sir Michael, I believe, had not once missed for over twenty years. These two fine old sailors were splendid company, and amused us greatly by the downright way in which they expressed their opinions about things naval and otherwise. I remember that Lord Fisher had just written one of his characteristic letters to *The Times*—its subject has escaped my memory —and the editor telegraphed to Lord Charles asking for his views upon it. On the Thursday evening Lord Charles told us that he would devote Sunday to the preparation of his reply, and would write something pretty hot. " Don't make a fool of yourself, Charlie," advised Sir Michael in his characteristically blunt manner. But man proposes and God disposes. When I left Langwell on the following morning Lord Charles seemed to be in his usual health and was certainly in excellent spirits, much good-humoured chaff taking place between him and Sir Michael during breakfast about a new suit of clothes he was wearing. On the Saturday evening, having retired early to his room, he was seized with a sudden illness and within a few minutes was dead. The contribution to *The Times* was therefore never written.

Sir Michael, over 80 years of age, was a marvel of vitality and energy. He would walk all day over the moors killing his one or two stags, sometimes three, and when not out stalking would take his place on the tennis-court or the golf links little inferior to men years younger than himself. Some months later his health broke down, and when I was next at Langwell, in October 1920, we received the news of his death.

Langwell is situated on the east coast of Scotland, 43 miles south of John o' Groat's house. It stands on high ground flanked north and south by the deep and wooded gorges of the Berriedale and Langwell rivers respectively. These streams unite in the little village of Berriedale at the foot of the hill, the combined stream then flowing for some two hundred yards through a defile, the sides of which are nearly 300 feet high, before discharging its waters into the North Sea. Amid this grand highland scenery, and at the point of confluence of the two streams, is the memorial recently erected by the Duke in honour of the officers and men of his Caithness estates who served in the Great War. It is one of the most impressive and best-designed war memorials I have seen.

The Duke is not only an excellent all-round sportsman himself, but does everything he can to ensure that his

guests have good sport and plenty of it   Whenever I go
to Langwell, or think of the pleasant days I have spent
there, I find it difficult not to break the tenth command-
ment.

In November I went to Cambridge to receive the honorary
degree of LL.D., which that university was kind enough to
confer upon me and other officers of the fighting services in
recognition of our work during the war. The ceremony of
giving the degrees was presided over by Mr. Balfour, and
was of a rather more elaborate kind than usual as he was
installed Chancellor of the university on the same day.
The undergraduates, of whom a large number were present,
surprised me by the mildness of their behaviour during and
after the proceedings, as I had always understood that it
was their custom on these occasions to behave in anything
but a mild manner.   They rode on the roofs and bonnets of
the motor-cars conveying the new " Doctors " to the college
where the official luncheon was to take place ; the heels of
some of them found their way through the glass of the car
windows ; and they insisted, with rare good humour, on
carrying us on their shoulders into the college grounds when
we left the cars. This, however, was the sum of their
attentions, and it gave us as much amusement as it seemed
to give them.

I had been informed earlier in the year that the university
of Oxford was desirous of showing me a similar kindness by
the granting of an honorary degree as D.C.L., but I could
not leave my command at the time the ceremony took place.
The invitation was renewed in 1920, and I was then able to
be present. M. Paderewski and M. Venizelos were amongst
those who received degrees on this occasion.

Soon after the peace treaty had been signed instructions
were received from the War Office to proceed with the
reduction of the Rhine army. At first it was the intention
to retain six divisions, and two of the ten divisions then
on the Rhine were ordered to England on 31st July. Many
different instructions were subsequently received, and in the
end it was decided to retain only about 15,000 men as the
permanent garrison, with an independent division of about
the same strength for temporary service in East Prussia and

Silesia pending the taking of the plebiscite after the peace treaty had been ratified. Demobilisation, and consequent reorganisation, accordingly continued for the greater part of 1919, and as the treaty was not ratified until the 10th of January 1920 it was then found that the independent division could not after all be employed in the manner intended, as the majority of the men were due for demobilisation before the end of March and some of them at a much earlier date. The division was therefore ordered to be demobilised forthwith, and the battalions for the plebiscite area were sent out from home. By the end of February demobilisation had been completed and the Rhine garrison had been nearly reduced to its assigned strength.

The ratification of peace caused another modification of our arrangements, as by the terms of the treaty the civil administration of the occupied territory passed out of the hands of the military authorities and was vested in a civilian body styled the " Rhineland High Commission," composed of representatives of France, Belgium, America, and Great Britain. I believe that this system of setting up a civilian body as the supreme authority during the military occupation of a conquered country is without precedent, and there was a chance that it might lead to difficulty in application.

For example, the civil administration, which had hitherto been supervised by the Allied Commanders-in-Chief, reverted to the German authorities, subject to certain saving clauses with respect to the Allied troops and to the " ordinances " that might be issued by the Rhineland High Commission. The German authorities were thus left responsible for the maintenance of order, but not being allowed to retain any troops in the occupied territory they had only the police to rely upon, and they were of indifferent quality. If and when the police required assistance the German authorities had to apply to the Commission, and the latter had then to instruct the Commander-in-Chief of the Allied forces to direct the Allied Commander-in-Chief concerned to furnish the requisite troops, or, if the Commission deemed it desirable, they could declare a " state of siege," or martial law as we would call it, upon which the military authorities would resume complete control. In either case, therefore, these authorities would suddenly be required to deal with a situation with which they might have previously had no connection, and about which they might know little or nothing.

The use of military forces to assist the civil power is a difficult task in one's own country ; the use of Allied troops to assist German police, in the circumstances just described, was likely to be even more complicated. The necessity for giving this assistance did not, I am glad to say, arise during my period of command, but had it arisen I have no doubt that a way out of the difficulties would have been found, as they were fully recognised by the Commission. My relations with the Commission were particularly cordial, a result which I feel was mainly due to the good offices of the British representative, Sir Harold Stuart.

America, I may add, had as yet no legal status on the Commission, for not having ratified the peace treaty she did not come under its terms, and therefore while the French, British, and Belgian areas were administered under the new system, in the American area the old system was continued, the American General remaining the supreme authority. Like the practical man he was, the General solved the difficulty by issuing to the inhabitants of his area the same orders as were issued by the Commission to the other areas. Another rather quaint feature was that the Commission, called into being by the ratification of peace, had its headquarters at Coblence in the area of the Americans who were still at war !

Consequent on the reduction of the army and the change in the system of civil administration I was ordered to hand over my command to a more junior officer, Lieutenant-General Morland, on the 3rd of March.

Previous to leaving, my wife and I had the honour of being invited to stay with the King and Queen of the Belgians at their palace at Laeken. Thanks to the kind reception accorded to us by Their Majesties, the visit was most enjoyable and interesting.

General Degoutte came from Mayence to Cologne to bid me good-bye, and General Michel and his wife came over from Aix-la-Chapelle for the same purpose. Colonel Biddle, the popular American liaison officer attached to my headquarters, with Mrs. Biddle, General and Mrs. Allen, and other Americans, entertained us at dinner at Cologne on the 25th of February, and on the 27th we were similarly entertained at Coblence by the Rhineland High Commission, M. Tirard, the French representative on the Commission, being the chief host. The dinner was followed by a ball, at which General Degoutte and other French Generals from Mayence and General Allen and many American officers and their wives were present.

Next day Sir Harold Stuart took me for a motor drive through the American area on the right bank of the Rhine, and in the course of it Gore-Browne made an excellent snapshot of us while standing near the stone at Ems which marks the spot of the historic meeting between Benedetti and King William of Prussia just previous to the Franco-German War of 1870. On return to Coblence I was received, for the last time, by an American guard of honour, and after luncheon parted company with General Allen and my other American friends.

There were more farewell gatherings at Cologne during my few remaining days on the Rhine. They included a dinner with some forty-five members of the headquarters staff, with whom I spent one of the most gratifying evenings of my life, notwithstanding the thought that I was separating from some of the best fellows in the world. The series was brought to an end on the night of the 3rd of March, when, having previously attended the opera with the Hutchisons, I left for Calais at 11 P.M. by the special train which I had used throughout my period of command.

Although I had caused it to be known that I did not wish for any one to see me off from the station, a number of officers and their wives assembled on the platform, which was covered with the red carpet used by the ex-Kaiser on his visits to Cologne, the Inniskilling Dragoons sent their band, and the 10th Middlesex formed a guard of honour, the commanding officer—Dillon, my old private secretary —irregularly, but affectionately, taking command of it. It was a bad wrench parting with so many good friends, and

AT LAEKEN PALACE.

H.M. THE QUEEN OF THE BELGIANS, LADY ROBERTSON, H.R.H. PRINCESS MARIE-JOSÉ, AND THE AUTHOR.

the train carried me away with a sharp pain in my heart and the tune of " Auld Lang Syne " ringing in my ears.

Hutchison and Gore-Brown accompanied me to Calais, and there I was received by General Gibb, commanding the British troops in France, his staff, and a guard of honour formed by the Labour Battalion of the King's Liverpool Regiment—a fine body of old soldiers wearing, for the most part, several medal ribbons. I felt that this was probably my last parade in an active capacity, which now extended over a period of more than forty-two years, and, as can be imagined, each hand-shake, each good-bye, became harder than its predecessor. I was glad when the boat cast off, and the sound of " Auld Lang Syne " had died away.

The two people I last recognised were the faithful " Hutch," who had walked on alone to the end of the quay so as to give me a final salute as I stood on the bridge, and my German attendant on the special train, who waved a table napkin from the saloon window, his regrets at my departure—though probably quite sincere in themselves —possibly being mixed with fears that the future might have in store for him a less pleasant life than when his only duty was to see to the creature comforts of the English General commanding at Cologne.

The anti-climax of these events was experienced when, on a dark and dismal night, I arrived at Victoria Station. Here there was no guard of honour, no official greeting of any kind, and having secured a broken-down taxi I drove off to my residence in Eccleston Square, and thereupon joined the long list of unemployed officers on half-pay.

Dobson, my soldier-groom and a typical artillery driver, accompanied me home, having been almost continuously with me for thirteen years. I owe a great deal to him for the way in which he looked after my horses and saddlery during that period. Robinson, my soldier-valet in the war and belonging to the K.R.R.C., had been demobilised shortly after the Armistice. He also rendered me much good service, and, besides seeing to my personal affairs when serving on the West Front, was very helpful in the frequent journeys I made between England and the continent when C.I.G.S. I was fortunate to have had two such good men with me.

Before leaving Cologne I sent a short letter of adieu to
Marshal Foch, to which he replied thus :

26.3.20.

MON CHER GÉNÉRAL—Vous avez été très aimable de penser à
moi en quittant Cologne et moi j'ai été très malheureux de ne
pas vous y trouver quand je m'y suis rendu. Les circonstances
dans lesquelles nous nous sommes connus et pratiqués, depuis le
début de la grande guerre, nous avaient permis une mesure
exacte et complète de nous-mêmes. Nous avions souvent
travaillé ensemble dans des journées critiques, nous avions joints
tous nos efforts pour sortir des crises. Et de cette union aussi
franche et aussi droite que possible nous avions bien tiré des
solutions heureuses pour nos armées. Nous n'avions pas perdu
tout notre temps. De ces souvenirs, dont je suis fier, je vous
reste particulièrement attaché, soyez-en bien convaincu. J'ai
toujours présents à l'esprit, votre conscience, votre expérience,
votre activité, avec une parfaite droiture dans les relations.
Aujourd'hui le commandement de Cologne ne pouvait tant
exiger, et c'est pour cela que j'espère bientôt vous voir dans un
de vos grands commandements devenu plus important. En tout
cas, mon cher Général, je souhaite que les circonstances de la
carrière me permettent de vous retrouver souvent, ce sera là
toujours, pour moi, une grande satisfaction. Récevez une fois de
plus l'assurance de mes bien attachés sentiments.

F. FOCH.

[Translation.

It was most kind of you to think of me when leaving Cologne,
and I was very disappointed not to find you there at the time of
my visit. The conditions under which we became acquainted
and have worked together since the commencement of the Great
War have enabled us to get to know each other very intimately.
We have worked together in critical times, and have combined
our efforts in overcoming the crises as they arose. From this
concord, as frank as it was straightforward, we have been able
to reach decisions of the best advantage to our armies. We have
made good use of our time, and you may rest assured that these
memories, of which I am proud, make me particularly attached to
you. I always have in mind the perception, experience, activity
and perfect honesty which you showed during our relationship.
The Cologne command does not now call for the same qualifications as before, and for that reason I hope you may soon be given
a command of greater importance. In any case, my dear
General, I trust that circumstances will permit of my frequently

meeting you, which will always be a great pleasure. Pray
receive once more the assurance of my closest regard.

F. Foch.]

I had reason to believe when I left the Rhine that
I should be appointed to command the forces in Ireland,
but the Government decided otherwise.   Ireland was not
altogether a bed of roses, viewed from the standpoint of
the Commander-in-Chief, and such disappointment as I felt
at remaining unemployed was further mitigated on the
29th of March, when, on the recommendation of Mr. Churchill,
the Secretary of State for War, His Majesty promoted me
Field-Marshal.

CHAPTER XIX

SOME FINAL REFLECTIONS

Characteristics of British soldier—Unpopularity of the army as compared with the navy—Study of military history by statesmen—Results of its neglect.

HAVING now brought to an end the story of my military career, it is with a feeling of regret that I take leave of the British soldier, with whom I served for so many years, in all grades, in different countries, in peace and in war. He may not possess to the same extent the élan and logical mind of his French comrade in arms ; he may not be such an adept at expedients or at first fight with such vehemence as his American kinsman ; he is apt to be rather a slow starter and casual in things military ; but once he realises that he is up against a tough proposition and decides to take off his coat, there is no limit to his staying power as there is none to the initiative and daring of which he is capable, and the tougher the proposition the firmer becomes his resolution to overcome it. His world-wide reputation for stubborn resistance is well deserved, for in ill fortune as in good it is seldom that a British regiment has failed to hold together. This indestructible cohesion, the most valuable quality that an armed body of men can possess, is not to be attributed merely to hereditary causes. It is largely based on reciprocal confidence and respect, and can only be secured when the men in the ranks have implicit faith in the ability and justice of their officers, and when the officers have the same belief in the valour and discipline of their men. It is gratifying to know that, notwithstanding the levelling tendencies of the age in which we live, and the fact that our armies were mainly composed of personnel taken straight from civil life, these mutually good relations were as readily and spontaneously forthcoming in the Great War as when they proved their worth in the days of Marlborough and Wellington.

As I have remarked in an earlier chapter, the British soldier has no use for those who, showing no personal interest in him, would push him about as a pawn on a chessboard, and, like other sane mortals, he is not prepared to be killed " by order." But win his esteem, make him proud of himself and his regiment, remind him of his home, and he will flinch at nothing. " Why on earth do you want bands ? " once demanded a staff officer of a General who was then serving on the West Front and had suggested that the regimental bands—left behind in England—should be sent out. " Why on earth do you ask such a d——d silly question ? " inquired the General in reply. " But since you ask I will tell you. I want my men occasionally to hear ' It's a long, long way to Tipperary ' and their other favourite music-hall songs, and on Sundays to hear the church hymns they were accustomed to hear when they were boys at home." The bands were sent out, eventually.

There is an old proverb that one volunteer is worth three pressed men, but without being in any way unmindful of the hundreds of thousands of our race who joined the fighting forces of their own free will, many of whom were living in remote parts of far distant continents, it may still be said that the truth of the proverb received little, if any, support from the evidence to be derived from the Great War. The conscripts, so called, were not less ready to accept the sacrifice by which victory is achieved than were those who entered the armies as volunteers, just as those who were soldiers only for the war were no less resolved to conquer than were the men who belonged to the regular forces.

It was sometimes alleged during the Great War, and after it, that appropriate use was not made of the officers of non-regular units, and that regular officers not endowed with half their intellectual ability were given appointments in preference to them. Not improbably this statement was born of the opinion, rather commonly held, that the best brains of the nation gravitate more generally to the learned professions or to commerce than to the fighting services. I question if this opinion is substantiated by the history of our Empire, and as regards the early period of the war it should be remembered that an officer who has served in the army for only a few weeks is not likely to be so competent, or to command the same confidence from those above and below him, as one whose service may run into several years. In the army as in civil life efficiency and success depend upon systematic training.

Later in the war, when the non-regular officers had acquired much the same experience at the front as many of their regular comrades, there was, perhaps, more justification for the complaint, but here again it should be remembered that, as in all cases of improvisation, waste of valuable material is bound to occur when large armies have to be created at short notice, and cannot be entirely prevented. One can only hope that, in the nation's interest, every effort will be made to minimise it. Subject to these remarks, I cannot think that any responsible General would make the slightest difference in the treatment of either officers or men, whether belonging to the new army or to the old, and I am sure that all regular officers admired the keenness with which the non-regulars shouldered their new duties, and rapidly learnt to appreciate the importance of discipline.

Unfortunately for the British soldier, whether regular or non-regular, the army is not popular in the sense that the navy is. The latter usually enjoys full public support, the army seldom does except in war, and consequently it labours under considerable disadvantages in its efforts to prepare for war, and from this it has followed that our wars have so often been a case of " muddling through." In the Great War nearly every household in the country had at least one of its members in the army ; every one having a shred of justification, or even none at all, hurried to put on khaki ; and one hoped that at last the army had made good in the eyes of the people. In fact the height of success seemed to have been attained, for the people and the army had become one and the same thing, and the brick wall that used to separate them seemed to have been effectively broken down. But no sooner was the war over than the dislike to military uniform reasserted itself, every one who could promptly discarded it, the officers at the War Office setting the example, and the army quickly drifted back to the position it had held before the war. This disappointing result was perhaps not surprising, and it need not be a cause of anxiety, since it was only natural that there should be a reaction after the long years of war through which we had passed. The resolution shown by all classes at home during these years, and the deeds of the men who fought at Ypres, on the Somme, at Passchendaele and Gallipoli, more than prove that, if correctly informed by its parliamentary representatives, the country may safely be trusted to answer the call of duty, in the future as in the past. To think otherwise would be a libel on the living and an insult to the dead.

A matter of more immediate importance is that the nation should realise the necessity for having educated leaders—trained statesmen—to conduct its war business, if and when war should again come along. This is a direction in which much-needed preparation can be made without the expenditure of cash, and it may be the means of saving tens of thousands of lives and hundreds of millions of money. In all trades and professions the man who aims at taking the lead knows that he must first learn the business he purposes to follow : that he must be systematically trained in it. Only in the business of war—the most difficult of all—is no special training or study demanded from those charged with, and paid for, its management. This is the more to be regretted because, as the Empire is scattered all over the globe, occupies about a quarter of the world's surface, and exceeds in population one-quarter of the human race, the problems which confront British statesmen are far more numerous and intricate than those which have to be dealt with by the statesmen of other countries. Long after August 1914 ministers could be seen groping uncertainly forward in the discharge of their duties, having no good knowledge of the principles or methods which should guide them ; the numerous questions which daily arose came too frequently as a surprise, whereas they ought to have been foreseen ; and the ability to deal with them on sound lines had too often to be acquired by experience—the most costly of all schools.

Years before the close of the last century thinking men urged that those intending to follow a political career should prepare themselves for it by a careful study of military history—that is, of the defence of empires—but although some of the universities took steps to provide facilities for this study, it continued to be shunned in favour of more popular subjects, such as social reform, which were, and still are, deemed to have greater value for the Cabinet aspirant.

Far be it from me to suggest that embryo statesmen should study military history with a view to becoming generals and admirals. As a great military writer has truly said : " War is, above all, a practical art, and the application of theory to practice is not to be taught at any university, or to be learned by those who have never rubbed shoulders with the men in the ranks." This being so, the statesman should never attempt to frame a plan of campaign for himself—that way lies disaster, as was proved in the Great War ; he should never try unduly to influence the professional, whose function it is to frame the plan, to go back on his considered judgment ; once he has approved of a plan he should not interfere with its execution, or limit the number of troops to be employed ; and, in general, he should recognise the line beyond which his interference in the domain of the naval and military leader becomes an impediment rather than an aid to success.

But although the statesman is not required to handle fleets and armies, and, from lack of practical experience and acquaintance with details, should never attempt to handle them, he ought to have a correct knowledge of the way in which the use or misuse of those instruments may affect the welfare of the State, and he is required to have the same kind of knowledge with respect to finance, shipping, industry, food, and all the many other component parts of the nation's strength. Here, again, he should not attempt to become either a bank manager, a ship-builder, a cotton-spinner, or even a farmer, but he ought to be able to appreciate the values, relative and collective, of the resources with which these experts deal, and to recognise the point where, in the nation's interests, his control should intervene and where it should be withheld.

It is much too commonly supposed that war is a matter solely for armies and navies, and that a statesman's duties are concerned almost entirely with those services. This is as wide apart as the poles from being the truth. War draws into its vortex every element of the national life, nothing escapes it, and upon the statesman devolves the responsibility, once war is declared, for combining the whole diplomatic, political, financial, industrial, naval, and military powers of the nation for the defeat of the enemy.

It seems impossible that he can properly carry out this task unless previously fortified with a good knowledge of the business of war, and there is little doubt that if political and military history had been more carefully studied by British statesmen in the years before the Great War, the evils attending constant changes from one military plan to another would have been better understood by them ; there would have been less repetition of the mistakes made in the Napoleonic wars of dissipating our forces in secondary and unsound enterprises ; our commercial, industrial, and man-power resources would have been more intelligently co-ordinated and brought into requisition at an earlier date ; income-tax would probably now be at a lower rate than six shillings in the pound ; and, most important of all, fewer wooden crosses might be seen on the battlefields of France and elsewhere.

Again, a knowledge of military history is as indispensable to the statesman in peace as it is in war. At the present moment, for example, there is an outcry for greater economy, and the fighting services, being of an unproductive character, are rightly regarded as being amongst the first where reduction of expenditure should begin. An essential preliminary, however, to this step is the adoption of a sound and stable policy based on established principles of war, and on a comprehensive survey of the whole question of Imperial Defence. If our military edifice is built on this foundation, it will be both safe and economical ; if it is erected on the shifting sands of opportunism and political expediency, it will be neither economical nor able to weather the storms to which it may be exposed.

These observations on the duties of the statesman may

seem to imply that he alone made mistakes in the Great War, and that the soldier and sailor were convicted of none. I can assure the reader that this is far from being my opinion, so far as the soldier is concerned. He frequently omitted to practise the things that he had been so careful to learn before the war ; he was taught a great deal that he had not before known ; and he was compelled to realise that the principles he had been at such pains to lay down required much amendment in their application. My desire is not to draw an unfavourable comparison as between the statesman and the fighting man, but to emphasise the increased importance of the statesman's duties, and the necessity of their being undertaken only by men who have been educated to carry them out. I have seen the Government machine at work at close quarters for many years during peace, and for a longer period than any other British General during war, and the conclusion to which I have come is that the conduct of modern war is so complex that, in the Cabinet as elsewhere, the days of the amateur are over.

It is for this reason, and at the risk of appearing to trespass beyond my legitimate sphere, that I venture to suggest that all those who aspire to exercise ministerial control over the future destinies of the Empire should make military history the subject of much more systematic study than has hitherto been the custom. By this means only, so it seems to me, can they hope efficiently to discharge the duties devolving upon them in peace, and usefully to assist in guiding their country through the ordeal of war.

DATES OF PROMOTION

Enlisted . . . . November 1877
Lance-Corporal . . . . February 1879.
Corporal . . . . April 1879.
Lance-Sergeant . . . . May 1881.
Sergeant . . . . January 1882.
Troop Sergeant-Major . . . March 1885.
Second-Lieutenant . . . June 1888.
Lieutenant . . . . March 1891.
Captain . . . . . April 1895.
Major . . . . . March 1900.
Lieutenant-Colonel . . . November 1900
Colonel . . . . . November 1903
Major-General . . . . December 1910.
Lieutenant-General . . . October 1915.
General . . . . . June 1916.
Field-Marshal . . . . March 1920.

FOREIGN HONOURS RECEIVED DURING THE GREAT WAR

American—Distinguished Service Medal.

Belgian—L'Ordre de la Couronne (Grand Cordon), and Croix de Guerre.

Chinese—Order of Chia Ho (Excellent Crop) 1st Class.

French—Légion d'Honneur (Grand Officier), and Croix de Guerre avec Palme.

Italian—Order of St. Maurice and St. Lazarus (Grand Cross), and Order of the Crown of Italy (Grand Cross).

Japanese—Order of the Rising Sun (Grand Cordon).

Russian—Order of St. Alexander Nevsky, with Swords.

Servian—Order of the White Eagle, 1st Class, with Swords.

The Russian Order was one of the last of its class bestowed on a foreign officer by the late Czar.

The American medal was presented by General Pershing, and the Legion of Honour was received from the hands of General Joffre.

The French Army Order, or *citation*, regarding the award of the Croix de Guerre was as follows :

" Officier Général du plus grand mérite et des plus distingués. Après avoir rempli en France, sous les ordres du Maréchal French, différents postes de haute confiance dans lesquels il a déployé les qualités de bravoure, d'énergie et d'endurance, qui l'ont rendu légendaire dans les Armées Brittaniques, s'est vu confier par son Gouvernement le poste de Chef d'État Major Impérial qu'il a rempli pendant la plus grande partie de la Guerre et où il s'est particulièrement distingué."

INDEX

THE END

Printed in the United States
47097LVS00003B/42